AF893170

SHOCKWAVE POWER SOLUTIONS

Noel Rabinowitz
Sasha Magee

New Riders

New Riders Publishing, Indianapolis, Indiana

Shockwave Power Solutions

By Noel Rabinowitz and Sasha Magee

Published by:
New Riders Publishing
201 West 103rd Street
Indianapolis, IN 46290 USA

Printed in the United States of America
1 2 3 4 5 6 7 8 9 0

CIP data available upon request

Warning and Disclaimer

This book is designed to provide information about the Shockwave computer program. Every effort has been made to make this book as complete and as accurate as possible, but no warranty or fitness is implied.

The information is provided on an "as is" basis. The authors and New Riders Publishing shall have neither liability nor responsibility to any person or entity with respect to any loss or damages arising from the information contained in this book or from the use of the disks or programs that may accompany it.

Publisher Don Fowley
Publishing Manager David Dwyer

Marketing Manager
Mary Foote
Managing Editor
Carla Hall
Development Editor
John Kane
Project Editors
Jennifer Eberhardt, Charles Gose
Copy Editors
Charles Gose, Howard Jones
Technical Editors
Andy Hock, Kirk Keller, Joe Rowe
Associate Marketing Manager
Tamara Apple
Acquisitions Coordinator
Stacey Beheler
Administrative Coordinator
Karen Opal
Cover Designer
Karen Ruggles
Cover Production
Aren Howell
Book Designer
Anne Jones
Production Manager
Kelly Dobbs
Production Team Supervisor
Laurie Casey
Graphics Image Specialists
Steve Adams, Debra Bolhuis, Dan Harris, Clint Lahnen, Laura Robbins
Production Analysts
Jason Hand
Production Team
Angela Calvert, Daniel Caparo, Kim Cofer, Beth Rago, Scott Tullis, Christine Tyner, Pamela Volk
Indexer
Jennifer Eberhardt

Dedications

This book is dedicated to our brothers, without whom we would be only children: Jason Rabinowitz and Amos Magee.

Acknowledgments

First, our families, without whom this book would have been much shorter: Bobbie, Alfred, Rachel, Jesse, Ashley, Zachary, and Eva Rabinowitz, Janice Caspar, Estelle Schneider, Pete and Bebe Magee, Marie, Lisa, Ralph, and Rob Stone, Nettie, Max, David, Judith, Gloria, John, Matthew, Colin, Aubrey, and Simon Buten, Iris and Gerald Newman; Joe Rowe for fixing our screwups; Rachel Schindler for getting us into this; Ken, Harry, Bruce, Sarah, Chris, Lisa, John, and the rest of the Shockwave team for the tools and the parameters; the crew at E-Line for the server space; John Kane, Stacey Beheler, Jennifer Eberhardt, Tami Apple, David Dwyer, Don Fowley, and all the other folks at New Riders for being nuts enough to do this a second time; Lalit, Greggy, Dave(s), Dan, Doug, Tracy, Sally, Pam(s), Mark, JT, and the rest of the Director team; Randy, Mike, and the rest of the Authorware team.

Clients and colleagues who contributed material or experience: Josh Koppelman, Infonautics Corporation; Lee Swearingen and Kathy Clarke, DXM; George Williams, Andersen Consulting; Rodrigo Flores, Action Technologies; Tom Wang, Organic Online; Rocky Mullin, Organic Online; Carl De Cordova, Apple Computer; William Hurley, Apple Computer; Tim and Dana Morgan, Digital Dreams; Josue Guillen, Institute for Global Communciations; Marti Atkinson, Ph.D., Instructor, Electronic Publishing, University of California at Santa Cruz; Cassie Ferguson, Brandt Herrett, Eddo Stern, Dylan Thede, and Mike Ziemba, students of Advanced Web Topics, University of California at Santa Cruz; Mark Westlund, Rainforest Action Network; John Hammer and Mr. Weiss, New York Hall of Science; Wayne Neale, Ph.D., Eastman Kodak Company; G. Donald Bain, Director, Geography Computing Facility, University of California; Chris Manners, Miller Freeman.

Shoutouts: Fred Sharples, John Newlin, Christian Hunt, Carrie Meyers, Buzz Kettles, John Dowdell, Victoria Dawson, Lee Allis, Karl Miller, Sarah Allen, Rix Kramlich, Karen Silvey, John Ware, Alex Zavatone, Kevin Ellis, David Mendels, Miles Walsh, David Lasner, Andrea Coffey, Matt Connors, and all the other folks at Macromedia we forgot. Libero Della Piana, Cobie Howard, Liam Skilling, Krista Hiser, Josh Schwartz, Shane Zarintash, Jane, Julie and Nora Heafey, Liane Shayer, Eric Hellis, Erich Strom, Sari Gilman, Ada Shen, Jenny Perlin, Chris Daly, Theo Rodriguez, Mimi Ho, Danny Hosang, Lakisha, Dawn, Liane, John Tran, Robin Templeton, Ronetta Walker, Charles Washington, Malkia Cyril, Sarah Rivera,

Raquel Jones, Scott Kildall, Astrid Javier, Astrid Wessels, Anne Pallotta, Rick Nagin, Lewis Lubka, Arnold Bechetti and Marilyn Bachtell, Juan Lopez, Richard Fallenbaum, Danny P., Bonnie Weiss, Sharon Rose, Mike Napp, Aaron Cohen, Jane Hodes, Miguel Espinosa, Linda Bohlke, Lauren Garlovsky, Andreas Laras and Laura Petricola and munchkins, Jantje Boichel, Therese Bruno, Roger Rohrbach, Jeremy Yun, Melongem, Lina Hoshino, Blake Dawgert, Ray Chen, Abie and Tracy, Eric Hellis, Liane Shayer, Erich Strom, Laura Cheu, Jason McKinney, Mike Jonath, Jim Balderston, Amie Fishman, Gretchen Schuessler, Richard Taylor, Carlos Barrera, Karen Talbot, John Anderson, and Dan Messe. A very special thanks to you, if by any chance your name was omitted in error. You have all been supportive and we appreciate it.

Trademark Acknowledgments

Contents at a Glance

Table of Contents

INTRODUCTION

Introduction

Welcome to Shockwave Power Solutions. This introduction strives to answer several preliminary questions you might have about this book, such as the following:

- *What's going on here?*
- *What's this book about?*
- *Why should I listen to you guys?*
- *Who should read this book?*
- *What's in this book?*

What's Going On Here?

In June 1995, the Web changed. Of all the changes that have taken place on the World Wide Web over the last year and a half, none have shaken it like the introduction of Shockwave. Suddenly, the static, silent browser window, where the closest thing to animation was the bar graph showing the progress of the latest download, began to move and shake!

While the Web before Shockwave had its strengths—reasonably legible presentation of huge volumes of text, access to widely distributed information, simple creation, strong standardization, and bandwidth conservation—it resembled old-time mainframes more than the graphical, animated, and interactive applications that are the hallmark of contemporary computing.

The release of Netscape 2.0 and its plug-in architecture have changed the playing field. Plug-ins provide software developers with a way to extend Netscape's functionality by adding new capabilities, which provide new kinds of content.

Macromedia was one of the first companies to take advantage of this new capability and immediately pushed it to the limit. Shockwave proved that plug-ins were going to change the Web—possibly beyond recognition.

Note

> Although Java is not a plug-in, it falls under this category. Java, which was not generally available until the release of Netscape 2.0, provides the content provider with a way to add richer information to sites.

This exciting technical advance merges the engaging and creative power of interactive multimedia with the dynamic, far-reaching, and rapidly expanding delivery channel of the Internet.

The Internet, particularly the Web, has become a significant mass medium in its own right. Shockwave is a key enabling technology in the maturation of the Web medium. With Shockwave, you can pack an astonishing set of services and tools into a rich media interface and fully integrate them into the Web for narrowband delivery.

Going far beyond the mere addition of a new file type to the HTML standard, Shockwave represents a fundamental shift in the way the medium of the Web can be used. As soon as they appeared on the Web, Shockwave movies changed the landscape drastically. It is no accident that the product is called Shockwave—the aftershocks are still being felt today.

What's This Book About?

Shockwave Power Solutions is *solution-oriented*, meaning that we'll present Shockwave techniques in a real-world setting. Many of the examples featured in this book are actual jobs that we or others have done. When we do present techniques in isolation, they are techniques that we know are important for Shockwave developers, based not only on our experience providing Shockwave solutions for clients, but also on our discussions with other Shockwave developers and on our experiences presenting Shockwave workshops at conferences.

We explore all three of Macromedia's Shockwave technologies: Shockwave for Authorware, Shockwave for FreeHand, and Shockwave for Director. We also deal with Backstage, Macromedia's recently acquired Web development tool, which is an excellent complement to Shockwave.

We deal with Shockwave for Director in the most depth, because we have more experience with Shockwave for Director than with the other technologies and because it is the most flexible of the products. We have included many advanced techniques, such as linking media and external text, using frames, and passing parameters.

Why Should I Listen to You Guys?

InfraRed Communications, of which we are the founders, is a recognized Shockwave leader. On that L.A. day in June 1995, when Macromedia and Netscape announced Shockwave, the movies they used were created by InfraRed Communications.

FIGURE I.1
This movie, announcing Netscape and Macromedia's collaboration, was called "the best 100 K I have ever seen" by one participant at MacWorld '96.

Our first book, the *Macromedia Shockwave for Director User's Guide*, was the first Shockwave book on the market. We have spoken on Shockwave at the Macromedia Users Conference, MacWorld, Web Development, and Internet World, and have been profiled in *Web Week*, *MacWorld*, and the *San Francisco Bay Guardian*.

Clients whose sites we have shocked include Apple Computer, the Electronic Library, Action Technologies, Colgate, and many others.

Who Should Read This Book?

Shockwave Power Solutions is valuable for anyone interested in learning what Shockwave is, how to use it, and what it can do. It will be useful for Shockwave experts, as well as those of you just starting out. It is also valuable in determining what variety of Shockwave to use on your site.

Shockwave Power Solutions is for people involved in every stage of the Web development process. Site planners, production staff, artists, writers, and even managers will find this book a valuable guide to getting the most out of

Shockwave. The book is oriented toward helping you find ways to utilize the technology to serve your purpose—whether it be attracting people to your site, internal corporate training, interactive Web applications, or just plain fun.

This book also is intended for multimedia developers and graphic artists who use Macromedia's Authorware, FreeHand, and/or Director. There are many ways you can turn your skills toward the Internet, and we aim to help you do just that. *Shockwave Power Solutions* does not require that you be an expert in any of these products, but a basic familiarity with at least one of them is assumed. We also assume familiarity with the Macintosh or Windows platforms and general Web knowledge.

Familiarity with any of the following will be helpful, but not necessary:

- Adobe Photoshop
- Adobe Premiere
- Equilibrium DeBabelizer
- Macromedia SoundEdit 16
- HTML
- JavaScript

What's In This Book?

Shockwave Power Solutions is divided into six sections. We recommend reading Chapter 1, "What Will Shockwave Do for Your Website?," first, but the other sections can be attacked in any order you choose.

Part I: Overview

We start with the hows and whys of Shockwave. Chapter 1, "What Will Shockwave Do for Your Website?," is an overview of what Shockwave is and how it does what it does. This chapter also serves as an introduction to the techniques featured in this book. In Chapter 2, "Power on the Web," we discuss the challenges that Web content providers face. We will also touch briefly on how the real-world examples in Part V, "Shockwave Solutions," demonstrate the way Shockwave can be used to address these challenges. Chapter 3, "Comparing Authorware, Director, and FreeHand," features a brief overview of each of the Shockwave source products.

Part II: Second-Generation Shockwave

This section covers the features of each Shockwave technology. Chapter 4, "Understanding Shockwave for Director," addresses the basics of shocking your website with Director, including file size reduction and other concerns. Chapter 5, "Shockwave for Director 5," touches on the new features in Shockwave for Director 5; Chapter 6, "Shockwave for FreeHand," does the same for Shockwave for FreeHand. Chapter 7, "Understanding Shockwave for Authorware," provides the basics of how to design an Authorware piece for the Web. Chapter 8, "Developing Shocked Sites with Authorware," provides information on how to make the most of Shockwave for Authorware's network-enabled features.

Part III: Advanced Shockwave for Director

This section details the new features in Shockwave for Director 5.0, as well as some of the more esoteric features that are carried over from the original release. Chapter 9, "External Casts," describes ways to take advantage of the capability to share casts between movies. In Chapter 10, "Working with Frames," we show you how to deal with these pesky aspects of the Web. Chapter 11, "Linked Text," outlines ways to take advantage of this powerful feature carried over from Shockwave for Director 4.0. Chapter 12, "Talking with the Outside World: Parameters and JavaScript," shows how to use the new parameters feature and JavaScript to make your movies more effective.

Part IV: Industrial-Strength Shockwave

This section covers topics that are important for you as a Shockwave developer to know, regardless of which plug-in you are using. Chapter 13, "Detecting the Plug-In," demonstrates how to use JavaScript to avoid the dreaded broken plug-in icon. Chapter 14, "Advanced Compression Issues," goes into detail about how Shockwave's compression works and provides ways to analyze your movies with an eye to making them smaller.

Part V: Shockwave Solutions

In this section, we discuss in-depth some solutions to real-world challenges. Chapter 15, "Cosmetic Shockwave and Beyond: Infonautics," discusses using Shockwave in simple cosmetic ways—as exemplified by the Infonautics Corporation's Electric Library. Basic uses of Shockwave are also a stepping stone to more advanced immersive environments.

Chapter 16, "True Multimedia on the Web: DXM," examines some advanced uses of Shockwave. The examples, shocked by DXM, demonstrate successful design solutions for true multimedia on the Web. There is a discussion of how Shockwave can be used for online marketing of multimedia titles, and then there is a bit on sound for the Web and looking ahead to broadband solutions.

Chapter 17, "Immersive Retailing and Simplified Menu Metaphors: Andersen Consulting," examines interface issues for the corporate Web as investigated by Andersen Consulting. The chapter offers case studies of two very interesting design challenges: immersive retailing and simplified menu metaphors.

Chapter 18, " Advanced Applications: Action Technologies' Metro," discusses the integration of Shockwave solutions into a Web-based software application—Action Technologies' Metro. This chapter also examines how Shockwave solutions address basic communication challenges on the Web.

Chapter 19, "Creating Identity: Organic Online," covers the basic issues of how the Web is used to create identity. The content is taken from a discussion we had with Tom Wang, a Strategic Planner with Organic Online, Inc.

Chapter 20, "Creating Complex Applications: Apple Computer," addresses the possibilities of incorporating Shockwave as parts of compound applications on the Web. We also discuss the ways in which Apple Computer is using Shockwave publicly and internally.

Chapter 21, "Voice Recognition Interfaces: Digital Dreams," tackles an exciting use of Shockwave's open architecture—speech recognition. Taking advantage of Shockwave's extensibility and Apple's PlainTalk technology, Digital Dreams has made speech-aware Shockwave movies a reality. We examine the uses of speech on the Web and the Xtras in Shockwave.

Chapter 22, "Education and Non-Profit: Rainforest Action Network," discusses how Shockwave can be used by educational and non-profit organizations on the Web. The suspense-filled plotline is the story of how a non-profit organization, The Rainforest Action Network, came to have their website shocked and related implications for non-profit Shockwave.

Part VI: Wrapping It Up

We close with some final words. Chapter 23, "Future of Shockwave," discusses where Shockwave is going and where it will take us. Appendix A, "HTML Quick Reference," provides a guide to the HTML `<embed>` parameters for each plug-in. Appendix B, "Lingo for Shockwave Quick Reference," provides documentation on the Net-specific Lingo commands available in Shockwave for Director.

Online Chapter

We collected some of the more useful information available to Shockwave developers in a handy list format and formatted them as appendices. However, two of these appendices are not included in the book. Instead, they are provided online at the New Riders website at `http://www.mcp.com/newriders`.

Appendix C, "Setting Up Shockwave," provides documentation instructions for the Shockwave plug-ins, as well as how to configure your server to handle Shockwave files. Appendix D, "Shockwave for Authorware Function and Variable Reference," provides documentation of the Shockwave for Authorware additions to the available functions and variables.

Who the Heck Is Crazy Enough to Publish You Guys Anyway?

The staff of New Riders Publishing is committed to bringing you the very best in computer reference material. Each New Riders book is the result of months of work by authors and staff who research and refine the information contained within its covers.

As part of this commitment to you, the NRP reader, New Riders invites your input. Please let us know if you enjoy this book, if you have trouble with the information and examples presented, or if you have a suggestion for the next edition.

Please note, though: New Riders staff cannot serve as a technical resource for Shockwave or for questions about software- or hardware-related problems. Please refer to the documentation that accompanies Shockwave or to the applications' Help systems.

If you have a question or comment about any New Riders book, there are several ways to contact New Riders Publishing. We will respond to as many readers as we can. Your name, address, or phone number will never become part of a mailing list or be used for any purpose other than to help us continue to bring you the best books possible. You can write us at the following address:

New Riders Publishing
Attn: Publisher
201 W. 103rd Street
Indianapolis, IN 46290

If you prefer, you can fax New Riders Publishing at 317-581-4670.

You also can send electronic mail to New Riders at the following Internet address:

```
ddwyer@newriders.mcp.com
```

New Riders is an imprint of Macmillan Computer Publishing. To obtain a catalog or information, or to purchase any Macmillan Computer Publishing book, call 800-428-5331.

Thank you for selecting *Shockwave Power Solutions*!

PART I

OVERVIEW

CHAPTER 1

What Will Shockwave Do for Your Website?

This chapter is an examination of what Shockwave is and why it can be a useful and powerful addition to your website.

What Is This Shockwave Thing Anyway?

Shock wave *n* 1: a compressional wave of high amplitude caused by a shock to the medium through which the wave travels. 2: a violent, often pulsating disturbance or reaction.

Shockwave is Macromedia's catchall name for the Web-capable add-ons to their applications. Currently, three different, but parallel, Shockwave plug-ins exist: Shockwave for Director, Shockwave for Authorware, and Shockwave for FreeHand. Each technology consists of a plug-in, or user-oriented piece, and a separate author-oriented piece.

A *plug-in* is an additional piece of code that can be added to an application to make it perform additional functions. Programs such as Netscape Navigator or Adobe Photoshop allow you to extend their functionality simply by dropping a plug-in into the appropriate plug-ins folder. Although we describe the installation process in detail for all three Shockwave plug-ins in Appendix C, "Setting Up Shockwave," they work almost as soon as you drop them into the plug-ins folder. While Appendix C is not included with this book, you can find it at the New Riders website at `http://www.mcp.com/newriders`.

Table 1.1 summarizes Macromedia's Shockwave technologies as they currently exist. A more detailed discussion of each of these technologies and their underlying applications is available in Part II, "Second-Generation Shockwave."

TABLE 1.1

MACROMEDIA'S SHOCKWAVE TECHNOLOGIES

Product	*Summary*	*Benefits*
Shockwave for Director	Macromedia's technology that enables you to publish Director movies on the World World Wide Web. In essence, Shockwave for Director is the Director playback engine plugged into a World Wide Web browser application. Intended as a tool for all networked environments.	Director provides the capability to produce eye-catching and illuminating animations and responsive interactivity. It can perform a wide range of functions, from things as simple as buttons that actually go down when you click them to those as complex as arcade-style

Product	*Summary*	*Benefits*
		games. The application can make your website come alive with sounds and animation that react to the visitors to your site.
Shockwave for Authorware	Macromedia's technology for publishing Authorware courses on the Web. Also, essentially the Authorware runtime playback engine embedded in a Web browser application. Targeted mainly for intranet applications, but will work very well over the Internet as well.	Like Director, Authorware makes your website a dynamic place. It has less animation capability, but can be used to develop training and educational pieces quickly and easily. It provides many tools for evaluating students and trainees and can present complex information simply.
Shockwave for FreeHand	A plug-in to display FreeHand files, such as maps and logos within a browser. Intended for all network environments.	FreeHand provides the capability to display comlex vector-based graphics on the Web. Because FreeHand graphics are scaleable, you can present very detailed information, such as maps or technical drawings, in a small space.

For the purposes of this chapter, we will use the term "Shockwave" to refer to Macromedia's Web technologies collectively.

Authors' Note

Naming Shockwave

Because of a historical accident, the lamentable length and awkwardness of the official name, and because it was the first to appear, many people refer to *Shockwave for Director* as *Shockwave*.

The original code name for the Director-on-the-Internet technology was Shockwave. Because, like many WWW applications, the beta release of Shockwave was widely distributed, the name gained a large amount of recognition. This led to Macromedia's

decision to use the code name as the actual product name. When the success of Shockwave became apparent, Macromedia began exploring the possibilities of creating equivalent applications for Authorware and FreeHand. To get marketing and public relations leverage out of the recognition Shockwave had already achieved, Macromedia changed the name of the currently existing Shockwave to Shockwave for Director. That allowed room for the other products to capitalize on the Shockwave name.

Because the nearly universal law of software product names insists that any name longer than three syllables will be shortened, "Shockwave for Director" has not caught on. After several months of referring to Shockwave for Director as simply Shockwave, there was serious inertia. Furthermore, Macromedia did not see fit to choose names that could be shortened effectively. At press time, there has been no consensus among users or developers on names for the other Shockwave products. To give you an idea of the depth of the problem, the leading candidate for Shockwave for FreeHand is "ShockHand," a name which by no means rolls off the tongue.

Plug Me In!

Plug-ins are available for each technology and for various platforms: Macintosh 68 KB (Quadra series), PowerMac, Windows 3.1, and Win32 (Windows 95 and Windows NT). Currently, the plug-ins are available for Netscape Navigator 2.0x and Microsoft Internet Explorer. Versions for browsers on the Sun SPARC and SGI platforms are in the works.

In order for a visitor to your website to view the Shockwave items embedded in your page, he must have the appropriate plug-in installed. Each type of Shockwave file requires a separate plug-in. If the user does not have the appropriate plug-in, a broken plug-in icon will appear, as shown in figure 1.1.

One of the greatest challenges a Shockwave developer faces is how to handle visitors who do not have the appropriate plug-in. Unfortunately, Netscape Navigator 2.0x does not provide a way to handle this gracefully. Through an awkward oversight, Navigator cannot provide information about which plug-ins it can handle to JavaScript or Java. This problem will be remedied in the next version of Navigator. Ways to handle this as well as non-Netscape browsers are discussed in Chapter 13, "Detecting the Plug-In."

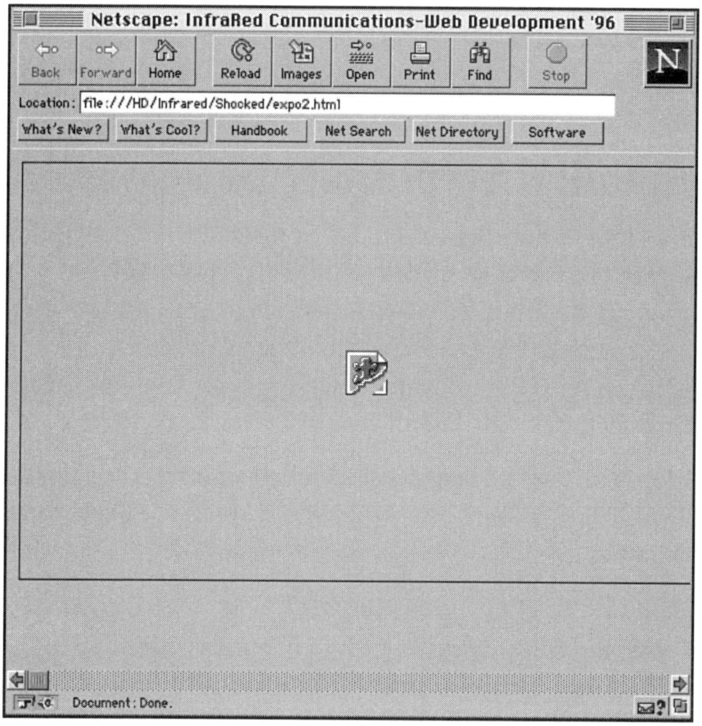

FIGURE 1.1

The broken plug-in icon appears if the user does not have the appropriate plug-in installed.

If your visitor does have the plug-in, he will get the full benefit of the best the Web has to offer. Each of these plug-ins is freely available and can be downloaded from the Macromedia website at `http://www.macromedia.com`. Unfortunately, the installation process differs from plug-in to plug-in, and there is no easy way to install all three. Appendix C, "Setting Up Shockwave," includes installation instructions for each plug-in. While Appendix C is not included with this book, you can find it at the New Riders website at `http://www.mcp.com/newriders`.

Putting Your Shockwave Movies on a Page: The <embed> Tag

Like other plug-in media types, Shockwave movies are put into an HTML page by adding an `<embed>` tag. Browser applications figure out how to deal with this tag by the extension of the file name. (See the section titled "How Afterburner Works" later in this chapter for an explanatory table.) The `<embed>` tag has different parameters, depending on which type of file is being embedded. We explain the parameters for each type of Shockwave in the appropriate chapter. A reference to the `<embed>` tag for Shockwave can be found online at the New Riders website at `http://www.mcp.com/newriders`.

Making It Small: Afterburner

The second component of the Shockwave technologies is the Afterburners. The Afterburners are utilities that enable you to compress FreeHand graphics, Director Movies, and Authorware pieces, as well as split Authorware courses into smaller chunks for easier downloading. Afterburner does one additional thing that is crucial for developers; it renders the files unreadable so that people browsing the Web cannot steal your work.

The Shockwave for FreeHand package also includes an Xtra called the URL Manager, which enables you to make objects in the FreeHand file clickable links to arbitrary pages.

The Afterburners for Director and FreeHand are implemented as Xtras, whereas the Authorware Afterburner is a separate application.

How Afterburner Works

Every form of compression has a CODEC (COmpressor/DECompressor) algorithm that enables computers to shrink or compress file sizes and then expand or decompress the files later. In Shockwave, Afterburner acts as the compressor and the Shockwave plug-in acts as the decompressor.

In Director, for example, Afterburner takes Director movies (DIR files), crunches them down in size, and spits them out as DCR files (Director CompRessed). These DCR files are zapped across the Net, then decompressed and played back by the Shockwave for Director plug-in. The process is often referred to as *burning a file*. The resulting compressed files are often called *burnt* files.

Afterburner for FreeHand works almost identically, except that it takes FreeHand files (FH5) and outputs FHC (FreeHand Compressed) files. And, of course, it requires the Shockwave for FreeHand plug-in. Afterburner for Authorware, however, adds some additional features and will, therefore, be dealt with separately in Chapter 7, "Understanding Shockwave for Authorware."

Note

Each Shockwave technology adds one or more new file types. Because file types on the Web are identified primarily by their extension, we included a table of the applications (see table 1.2), their original file types, and the "burnt" file types:

TABLE 1.2

SHOCKWAVE FILE TYPES

Application	*Original File Type*	*Burned File Type*
Authorware	APP (Windows), PKG (Mac)	AAM (map file) AAS (segment file) AAB (MacBinary file
Director	DIR, DXR	DCR
FreeHand	FH5	FHC

In Shockwave, Afterburned files play back just like the uncompressed original file. No loss of performance occurs. Current releases of Afterburner primarily compress graphics files. Future releases, however, will include configurable audio compression and more graphics compression options, probably implemented as Xtras.

Afterburner opens up a whole world of creative possibilities to Shockwave developers designing for the Web because it gives them approximately twice the bandwidth to play in. This will enable much more detailed images, more sound, and more involved interactivity.

Interestingly, Afterburner has proven in many cases to be a more compact technique for compressing static bitmaps than GIF or JPEG. One test, for example, revealed that a Director movie that contains just an 8-bit PICT image of 132 KB can be turned into a 44 KB DCR. Imagine that! The same image saved as a GIF is 77 KB.

How Good Is Compression with Afterburner?

In evaluating the usefulness of any compression scheme, you have to ask several questions. What is the compression ratio? Is it lossless or lossy? What are the processing requirements for both compression and decompression? The following sections answer these questions.

Compression Ratio

Comparing the size of the uncompressed source file with the compressed Afterburner file yields what is known as the *compression ratio* for Afterburner. Several factors determine how small a Director movie will "burn." For one thing, Afterburner does not compress the audio portion of the file as effectively as other elements. It is a real winner, however, in compressing the bitmapped cast members.

There is no way to know exactly what compression ratio you will get when you burn a file. Typical ratios for Authorware and Director are 2:1, with FreeHand files compressing slightly less, but this is only a rough guideline.

Compression Schemes: Lossy and Lossless

In general, compression schemes are either lossless or lossy (no better words have been invented, unfortunately). *Lossy compression* shrinks file sizes by permanently removing nonessential, irrelevant, or redundant information. The resulting file is forever degraded. This is an acceptable compromise for many kinds of media files for which quality is happily sacrificed for a commensurate reduction in file size. There are many sophisticated lossy compression schemes—such as MPEG, JPEG, and Cinepak—but we are not so concerned with them here.

The most direct method of lossy compression is to simply throw out information, a technique called *bit reduction*. Reducing the bit depth or the resolution of bitmapped images, for example, dramatically reduces file size, as does reducing the sampling frequency or bit depth of audio files. For images, dithering can be used to lessen the degradation that results, and lost color information can be restored or simulated later using other techniques. We use these methods frequently when authoring Shockwave movies.

Lossless compression reduces file sizes without degradation or change to the file. PKZIP and StuffIt are examples of tools used for lossless compression. (In fact, they use a very similar algorithm to Afterburner's.) Lossless compression is extremely important for compressing data that cannot afford to lose even one bit of information without becoming useless. Director files made for Shockwave contain precise information for animation, as well as

Lingo code for interactivity and so on. Therefore, lossy compression schemes cannot be used on Director movies.

The process that PKZIP, StuffIt, and Afterburner use to compress a file is too complicated to go into in any detail here, but a quick (and undoubtedly distorted) summary in the following Note will give you an idea of what compression ratios to expect.

Note

The compressor looks for repeated patterns of data and keeps what is essentially a glossary of each of those patterns. It then replaces each pattern with the index reference, which is—in general—much smaller. In addition to the compression of Afterburner, Director itself deals with a string of repeated values (such as in a solid-color portion of an image). An uncompressed series of four red pixels in an 8-bit image would require four 8-bit bytes of data because it would be represented as red, red, red, red. Compressed, however, that same series of pixels would take only two bytes of data, because it would be represented as four red. This compression process is called *run-length encoding*. As you work with Shockwave, you will discover that images with large areas of solid colors compress very well.

Processor Requirements

Compared to the horsepower required to move 256-color bitmaps around the screen, the processor load decompressing files puts on the Shockwave plug-ins is pretty much trivial. Effectively, any machine that can run the Shockwave plug-ins will have no trouble with the decompression part of the process. In addition, the download bottleneck is so tight—even on the fastest networks—that decompression seems to take no time at all.

What Is Shockwave Good For?

Because they provide the zillions of people who use Macromedia's flagship products the opportunity to apply their skills directly to the Web, Macromedia's Shockwave technologies achieve two major goals. The first (and certainly foremost on Macromedia's list of priorities), is to provide a new target for multimedia developers and a new way of distributing their work. The second is to add the dimensions of time, motion, audio, and interactivity to the Web.

The Internet Is Not Flat and Round and Shiny: Content-Based Shockwave Development

For the last several years, the primary target for multimedia creations has been CD-ROM. The CD-ROM platform, however, has several severe disadvantages, such as incompatibilities in various drives and other components of the system, extremely limited shelf space, awkward distribution channels, and slow speed.

Although it won't displace CD-ROM distribution immediately, Shockwave solves most of the problems of the earlier method of distribution. It does, however, raise one new issue, which is hardly insignificant: how to get the user to pay for it?

By bypassing the CD-ROM drive altogether, Shockwave clearly makes the incompatibilities that might lurk there irrelevant. Users also are able to immediately test compatibility with their system, doing away with the necessity for returns.

Clearly, shelf space is not an issue on the Internet (although it does raise an interesting how-many-angels-can-dance-on-the-head-of-a-pin type of philosophical question). The distribution channel, as well, is fairly obvious. The bypassing of the distribution bottleneck means that the success of a Shockwave creation is a struggle for the hearts and minds of the audience, not a struggle for 16 square inches of shelf space.

One problem with CD-ROMs that Shockwave clearly does not solve is the question of speed. Two years ago, it would have been difficult to find a multimedia developer who could imagine working with a method of distribution slower than CD-ROM. Now, however, through a combination of Macromedia's compression and compromises on the part of developers, thousands have made the move to Internet distribution. Still, there are still compromises that have to be made, and how to make the best of those compromises forms much of this book.

The new issue that Shockwave brings up is that of a new payment, or business, model. The CD-ROM business follows very closely the model of records or books. The customer buys the disc, takes it home, and it is his to keep.

How the Shockwave business will make money, however, like the profitability of Internet business in general, is still to be determined.

Because of the last two issues, content-based work is still the vast minority of all Shockwave for Director and FreeHand work on the Web. The exception here is intranets. Much of the Shockwave work for intranets is strongly content oriented, largely because the bandwidth limitations are much less stringent. Also, most of this kind of work is commissioned specifically for its application. Because most of the Authorware users are oriented toward corporate work, most of the Shockwave for Authorware productions are also of this type.

The Internet will not replace CD-ROM distribution next week (or even next year, most likely). But when the problems of payment and bandwidth are solved, the end of CD-ROM multimedia will be underway.

Making the Web Come Alive: Enhancing the Web with Shockwave

In many ways, this category is more immediately exciting for Shockwave developers and, therefore, constitutes the bulk of this book. It is a whole new opportunity for multimedia developers who don't want to or cannot make the investment to learn a programming language such as C++ or Java.

Shockwave can add graphic interest to your website by making your logo spin or your graphics move. It can make that detailed map of your store the gateway to different departments. It enables you to provide an interface that acts like a regular application or is as bizarre as you can imagine.

With Shockwave you can call attention to the latest addition to your website with fireworks, complete with explosions. Detailed drawings of a circuit board can be available to your field technicians 24 hours a day. And, of course, when your ship comes in, if your site is shocked, your ship will really come in, complete with lapping waves and your personal foghorn.

Each of these applications can be accomplished with Shockwave, and in every case, they will be more effective at grabbing and holding the interest of people wandering by your website or favorably comparing you to your competitor.

The examples in the next chapter and throughout the book outline many of the uses for this type of Shockwave development. This is a major new market opportunity for Director and FreeHand developers and a great chance for content providers to make their websites be as attractive and effective as possible.

For Web designers, Shockwave heralds a great leap forward in the possibilities, as well as the standards of their Web offerings. Shockwave raises the stakes for website design and opens a significant new mass market and demand for the services of Net-savvy, skilled Director developers.

Conclusion

After reading this chapter, you should have a good idea of what Shockwave is, and some idea of how it works and what its focuses are. In the next chapter, "Power on the Web," we explore some of the challenges facing Web developers and the ways Shockwave can help them meet and exceed these challenges.

Chapter 2

Power on the Web

This chapter presents a basic conceptual framework that you can use to think about Shockwave power solutions. This helps you understand how Shockwave is being used now and potential uses of Shockwave as part of an overall Web strategy. We have categorized Shockwave content in a way that helps you to understand and interpret the significance of the techniques and the real-world Shockwave examples found in Part V of this book.

This chapter is organized into the following sections:

- *Valued Web resources and services*
- *Seeing the Big Picture of the Web*
- *Entry-Level Shockwave*
- *Enhanced-Level Shockwave*
- *Advanced-Level Shockwave*

Valued Web Resources and Services

Power on the Web means that your audience is repeatedly visiting your site in the numbers that you want. Moreover, power on the Web means that your website is conducive to deep interactions with your audience. Capturing a sustained visitor base is a goal of such paramount importance to all organizations providing Web content to the public that their Web masters, managers, and designers often live and die by the traffic they produce.

More and more, organizational and business functions are embodied in Web resources and transacted on private internal networks, or intranets. Justifying the intranet Web depends on making these Web resources demonstrably superior to previous methods and processes. Just as crucial is showing that a vast majority of your organization is consistently utilizing the Web tools provided. The underlying goals of efficiency, cost savings, speedup, and standardization can be foiled if the user migration to the intranet Web services is too disruptive, slow, or incomplete.

Having a powerful vision for the Web, in both the Internet and intranets, means looking far beyond having top-notch graphic design and text content. Long-term Web power can be achieved by providing dynamic, interactive, and most important, useful content. Sites that offer valuable and unique resources that cannot be found elsewhere in the world or within the Web are more likely to enjoy user loyalty and sustained growth in the interactions with their target audience.

The types of Web offerings that could previously pass as valuable resources, such as "related links" or "Hot News," are not sufficiently powerful anymore. They are shallow Web resources. Many Web users, tired of chasing related links in a house of mirrors now want outstanding sites that offer added value, not added hype. They will spend time engaging your site and resources if they feel that their time is well spent there. Thus, deepening the power of the services and resources offered is an excellent way to achieve the goal of sustained growth in user traffic.

Providing distinctive and valuable Web services and resources is a problem for which Shockwave offers many solutions. In order to use Shockwave effectively in this unfolding contest for distinction and functionality, you need to know where Shockwave fits into the big picture of all Web services.

Seeing the Big Picture of the Web

Surrounded by the crowded and evolving milieu of the Web, it is sometimes hard to see the best ways to proceed and easy to get lost entirely. When developing Shockwave websites, we have found it strategically useful to be able to see where our shockwork fits into the "Big Picture" of the Web. Finding no ready-made model of the Web that is most relevant to Shockwave development, we offer this framework for your consideration.

The Big Picture of the Web, mapped out in in figure 2.1, categorizes Web resources into orders of increasing interactive power. *Interactive power* on the Web is the all-important power of attracting your audience and interacting with them. Interactivity also gives your audience members the power to relate to one another via your Web resources. Interactivity is the most basic and far-reaching vehicle for adding value and utility to the Web; therefore, interactive power has become the fundamental dimension of our big picture of the Web.

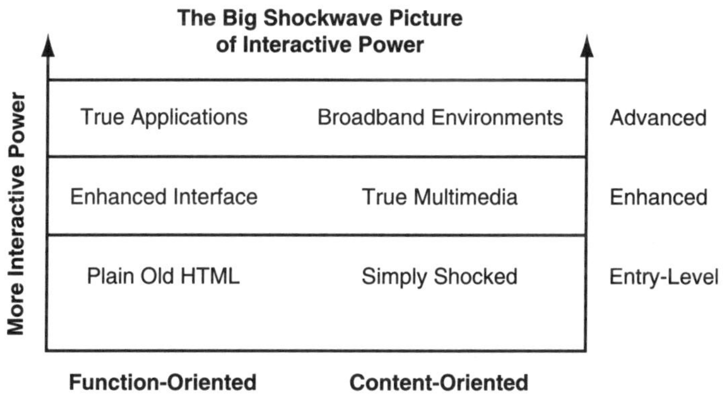

FIGURE 2.1

The big Shockwave picture is a conceptual framework for Shockwave solutions. Solutions are organized into levels of increasing interactive power, with distinctions made between function- and content-oriented solutions.

The Big Picture groups Web services and resources into three levels of progressively greater interactive power: 1) Plain Old HTML and Simply Shocked, 2) Enhanced Interface and True Multimedia, and 3) True Applications and Broadband Environments.

Within each of the three levels of interactivity, we distinguish between Shockwave solutions that emphasize the HTML functionality and those that emphasize the Shockwave content. Making this distinction, first touched on in Chapter 1, "What Will Shockwave Do for Your website?," helps you to identify the role of the Shockwave portion of the website and rate Shockwave's contribution to interactive power. In every application of Shockwave, a balance is struck between the static HTML content and the Shockwave content. Controlling this balance enables you to decide how much or how little attention to draw to the fact of being Shocked or to the Shockwave content itself.

In functional-oriented solutions, the HTML part is central to the value or interactivity of the site and Shockwave is peripheral. In content-oriented solutions, the rich media conveyed by Shockwave is a value unto itself, becoming the primary focus as the HTML, and ultimately the browser itself, grows ever more incidental—a mere delivery vehicle. Thinking about the balance of emphasis helps you clarify your goals and concentrate your resources into the appropriate Shockwave solutions.

Of course, the categories are not perfectly distinct. Evolution to a higher level of interactive power is not always linear. It is a cumulative process with the higher levels inheriting interactive collateral from the lower. Also, it should be noted that function and content are not mutually exclusive extremes, but overlap each other.

The taxonomy of Shockwave solutions is a tricky business because most individual sites have a wide range of interactivity and emphasis within the site. But we can see that a vast majority of shocked sites today fall within the first two levels of interactivity, the Simply Shocked and the Enhanced Interface/True Multimedia. The big picture indicates the direction in which more advanced Shockwave solutions will progress.

The big picture presented here has broad relevance. It can illustrate the position of existing or emerging multimedia resources or technologies on the Web. It is especially illustrative of Shockwave's potential. Because Shockwave combines ease of development, interactive power, multimedia prowess and open architecture, Shockwave enables winning solutions at all levels of the Web's interactivity. Shockwave is fast becoming the ubiquitous standard for true interactive Web multimedia. From what is today portrayed as "cutting edge" to the truly advanced applications of the future, Shockwave is adding a whole new layer to every part of the Web.

Simply Shocking: Entry-Level Interactivity

The point of entry into the big Shockwave picture of interactivity is Plain Old HTML, otherwise known as the "unshocked" Web. HTML in the raw is the functional-oriented side of this embryonic level of Shockwave. The maiden shocking of a site is very often an exercise in "shocking for shocking's sake."

In today's Web terrain, a large part of the power of a shocked site is the very fact of being a shocked site. Companies using Shockwave are sending a message of innovation or technology leadership. They also use Shockwave to project a certain hipness. Today's prevalent motivation for shocking is that many visitors will visit a shocked site just because it is simply shocked. Therefore the content-oriented category of entry-level Shockwave—Simply Shocked—contains animated logos, company theme songs, and other cute diversions.

In this sense, much of the current uses of Shockwave may appear gratuitous, or tangential to the purpose of many sites. In our view, what appears gratuitous is only bad if it is irrelevant, distracting, or annoying. There is a certain shock value that comes with putting multimedia on the Web today. It is this shock value that appeals to many users and commands their attention. Thus, Shockwave can be very powerful—even in gratuitous applications—simply because it is cool, new, or fun.

Note

> Recognizing the importance of simple Shockwave and purely cosmetic uses of multimedia on the Web, Macromedia has created as series of free-standing applications, called Power Applets, that grind out customizable primitive animations such as animated billboards or bullet charts in the form of Shockwave movies or JAVA Applets. This is intended to lower the cost of developing entry-level Shockwave, encouraging the acceptance of Shockwave and frees Shockwave developers to concentrate on the more interesting intermediate and advanced projects.

Discussions of Entry-Level Shockwave

In Part V, "Shockwave Solutions," there are several examples in the simply shocked category. There are no examples of Plain Old HTML—we all know what that looks like.

Guide to examples and discussion of Entry-Level Shockwave solutions:

Plain Old HTML	*Simply Shocked*
No examples	Chapter 15, "Cosmetic Shockwave and Beyond: Infonautics"
	Chapter 19, "Creating Identity: Organic Online"

Chapter 15, "Cosmetic Shockwave and Beyond: Infonautics," includes two examples of our animated billboards. The first billboard was created for the Electric Library (see fig. 2.2) and the second is our very own InfraRed Communications billboard. These examples illustrate the kind of branding and simple fun that Shockwave can add in the form of entry-level interactivity.

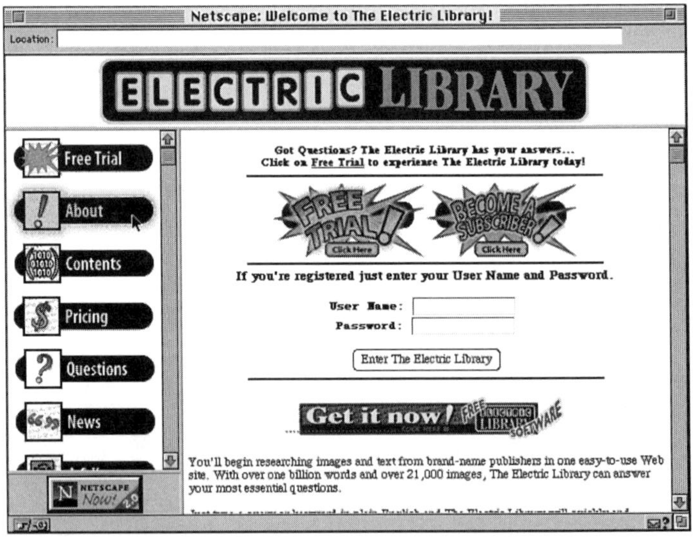

FIGURE 2.2

Animated billboards, such as the Infonautics logo shown here, are a popular and simple use of Shockwave.

Chapter 19, "Creating Identity: Organic Online," discusses how simple shocking helps identify organizations as technology leaders and enables you to reach a certain audience.

Deceptively Simple

The potential danger of adding simple fun with Shockwave is creating unwanted nuisances or confusion for your audience. Irrelevant movies, long downloads, system crashes, non-working frames, and the evil broken graphic icon are all basic problems that can muck up the simple joys you are trying to give your users. In providing even the simplest Shockwave solution, you need to consider a host of technology issues, which are detailed in the rest of the book.

The basic techniques and styles needed to understand and streamline Shockwave content are found in Part II of this book, "Second-Generation Shockwave." These techniques include basic design, bandwidth reduction, and using new features of Shockwave. There is also a key discussion on detecting whether the user has the Shockwave plug-in installed. This advanced technique, discussed in Part IV, "Industrial-Strength Shockwave," is very important, even for the simplest Shockwave solutions.

Enhanced-Level Shockwave

As Shockwave penetrates the mainstream, the novelty will begin to wear off. Proliferation of shocked sites will cause user expectations to rapidly increase, forever changing the standards of "cool." Even more powerful Shockwave solutions are needed to justify the use of Shockwave. This takes us to the second level of Shockwave power solutions. This higher level of interactivity, shown in figure 2.1 as enhanced-level solutions, significantly augments the interface and multimedia content of the website.

Discussions of Enhanced-Level Shockwave

In Part V, "Shockwave Solutions," there is a discussion and many examples of enhanced-level Shockwave solutions.

The function-oriented side of enhanced-level Shockwave solutions, enhanced interface, consists of features that add cosmetic depth, greater interactivity and friendliness to the user interface. The power of enhanced interface features is to provide the user with the same standards as found in the GUI of stand-alone apps. The use of standard navigation buttons, fast feedback, audio cues, rich images, and animated images attracts users by enabling them to interact in more effortless and intuitive ways with the website.

Enhanced interface Shockwave solutions do not focus the user on the multimedia itself, but rather acts as a gateway or a catalyst to the whole content of the page or site resources. Here Shockwave takes the place of some of the straight HTML parts and also adds complementary media. This could mean replacing HTML hyperlinks with rollover buttons and `goToNetPage` commands, adding ambient music, or replacing bitmaps with scaleable/scrollable graphics.

The content-oriented side of enhanced-level Shockwave solutions, True Multimedia, consists of resources that highlight the multimedia content. In this sense, Shockwave is already being used as a new method of multimedia content promotion and delivery.

With true multimedia Shockwave solutions, the HTML is peripheral and the shocked content is central. Useful, informative, and entertaining resources—such as little movies, presentations, basic training/demos and short infomercials, interactive kiosks and games—can be made available on the Web using true multimedia Shockwave solutions.

The following is a guide to examples and discussion of Enhanced-Level Shockwave solutions:

Enhanced Interfaces

Chapter 6, "Shockwave for FreeHand"

Chapter 15, "Cosmetic Shockwave and Beyond: Infonautics"

Chapter 19, "Creating Identity: Organic Online"

Chapter 20, "Creating Complex Applications: Apple Computer"

True Multimedia

Chapters 7 and 8, on Shockwave for Authorware

Chapter 16, "True Multimedia on the Web: DXM"

Chapter 17, "Immersive Retailing and Simplified Menu Metaphors: Andersen Consulting"

Chapter 19, "Creating Identity: Organic Online"

Chapter 20, "Creating Complex Applications: Apple Computer"

Chapter 21, "Voice Recognition Interfaces: Digital Dreams"

Chapter 22, "Education and Non-Profit: Rainforest Action Network"

Enhanced Interfaces

With Shockwave for FreeHand, you can provide rich images containing more information than static graphics. As discussed in Chapter 6, "Shockwave for FreeHand," scaleable vectored graphics can make great navigation interfaces, (see fig. 2.3) hierarchical text documents, maps, and much more.

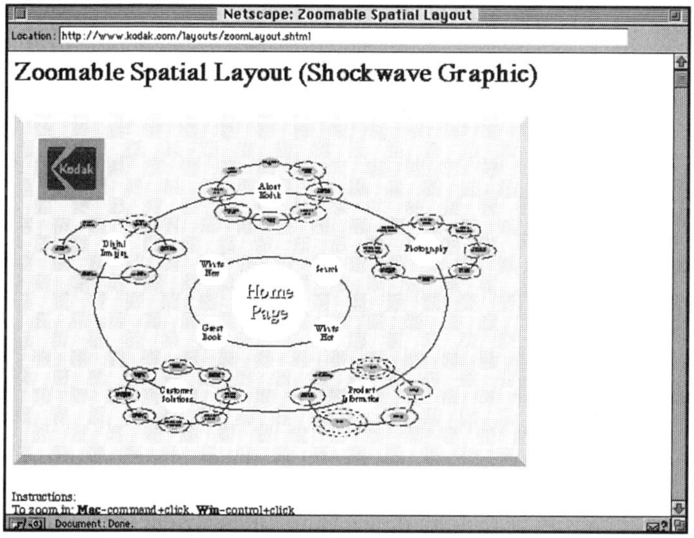

FIGURE 2.3

The Shockwave for FreeHand site map for Kodak enhances the navigation interface of the site by taking advantage of scaleable vector-based graphics.

Shockwave makes it easy to provide multimedia standard button menus for your Web pages. The Infonautics Electric Library, discussed in Chapter 15, "Cosmetic Shockwave and Beyond: Infonautics," is a good example of Shockwave interfaces. Apple's shockwave homepage menu, discussed in Chapter 20, "Creating Complex Applications: Apple Computer," is another example of Shockwave button menus.

Using True Multimedia to Market Titles Online

Th Shockwave movies shown in Chapter 16, "True Multimedia on the Web: DXM," are engaging and rich in media and interactivity. Three important varieties of True Multimedia—interactive advertisements, site tours, and games—are typified in the DXM example movies. The game "Fireboy on Ice" (see fig. 2.4) is not only a case study in Shockwave games, but it shows how well-suited Shockwave is to the task of marketing interactive titles online. Furthermore, DXM's sound effects CD, called Earshot, is a good source of audio for true multimedia titles on the Web.

FIGURE 2.4

"Fireboy on Ice," shocked by DXM, is an online game and an example of using multimedia previews for online marketing of CD titles.

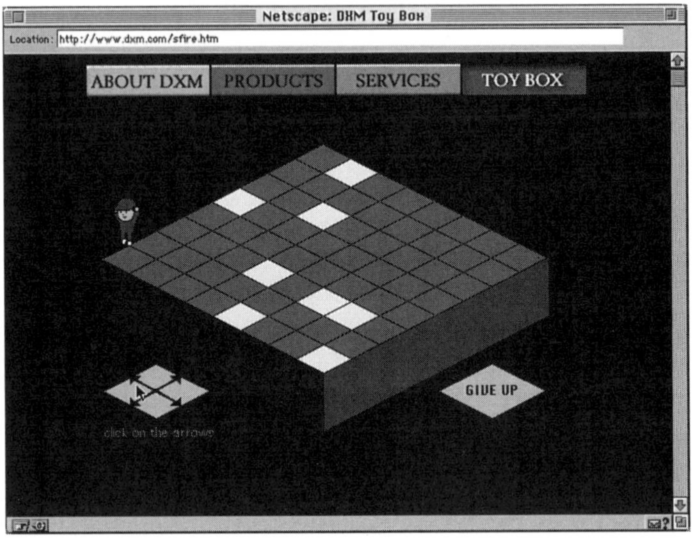

Training Pieces and Education

At 28.8 kbps modem speeds, advanced training applications are not very practical. However, excellent and fairly detailed introductory trainings or product demonstrations can be delivered even at these slow speeds. In Chapter 20, "Creating Complex Applications: Apple Computer," there is an example of a prototype online tutorial designed to be used on a regular basis to train tech support staff on Apple's QuickTime Conferencing product (see fig. 2.5).

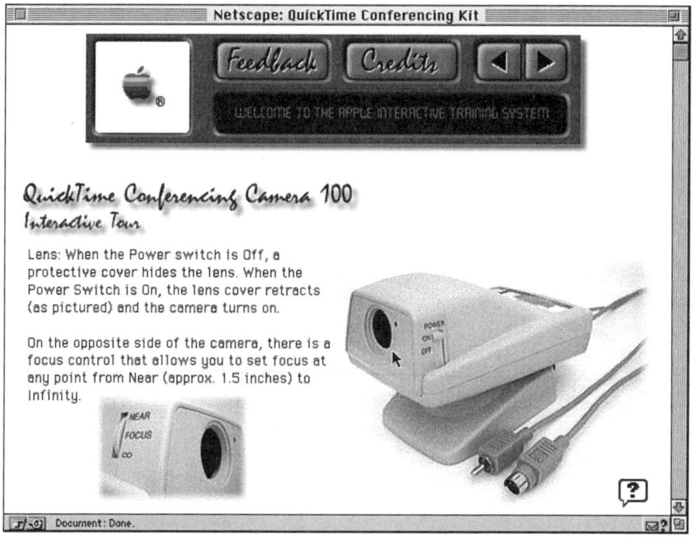

FIGURE 2.5

Apple's QuickTime Conferencing is a prototype online multimedia tutorial using Shockwave for Director.

On intranets, where network speeds are higher, using Shockwave for Authorware is a great way to provide training, education and demos. Chapters 7, "Understanding Shockwave for Authorware," and 8, "Developing Shocked Sites with Authorware," discuss design techniques in Shockwave for Authorware including how to use the built-in segmenting architecture to download media elements as they are needed. Segmenting is the best solution to today's lack of streaming. Shockwave for Authorware is the most content-oriented of all the Shockwave flavors as it can launch its own window to run in and push the browser to the background entirely.

Another example of using Shockwave for training is found in Chapter 17, "Immersive Retailing and Simplified Menu Metaphors: Andersen Consulting." The example is a movie used to train intranet users on the basics of the Internet—history, resources, terminology, and so on.

Online quizzes and training pieces made with Shockwave for Director can utilize speech recognition that adds another layer to the user interface as discussed in Chapter 21, "Voice Recognition Interfaces: Digital Dreams" (see fig. 2.6).

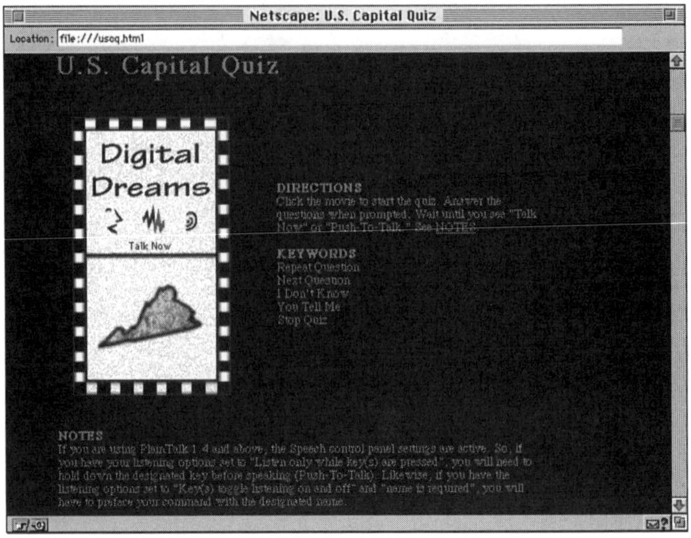

FIGURE 2.6

The U.S. Capital Quiz online multimedia questionnaire utilizes voice recognition for the input of answers and commands.

Finally, there is a discussion with Professor Marti Atkinson of the University of Califonia at Santa Cruz on how Shockwave can be used for educational purposes by students and teachers in universities and high schools in Chapter 22, "Education and Non-Profit: Rainforest Action Network."

Online Solicitation

Interactive multimedia with game-like characteristics can be used to great advantage for online sales and solitication. The Rainforest Action Network movie, discussed in Chapter 22, is an example of how interactive multimedia helps to interest potential subscribers in the mission of the Rainforest Action Network and, therefore, stimulate donations (see fig. 2.7).

FIGURE 2.7

Shockwave enables the Rainforest Action Network to present an interactive multimedia presentation for their "Join Online" page.

Advanced-Level Shockwave

The next step toward greater interactive power in the big Shockwave picture of the Web takes us to the advanced-level Shockwave. Here you can create full-blown software applications on the Web that take full advantage of Shockwave multimedia as a central part of the user interface. In this function-oriented side of full-power Shockwave, the multimedia, or shocked part, is full-blown, but it is still subordinate to the application as a whole and to the extensive HTML and back-end scripting. Broadband Immersive Applications comprise the content-oriented side of full-power Shockwave Solutions.

Discussions of Advanced-Level Shockwave

In Part V, "Shockwave Solutions," there are a lot of thought-provoking discussion and some examples of advanced-level Shockwave solutions.

The line differentiating Web resources from true software applications is beginning to blur. Web resources are rapidly maturing into Web applications as the result of higher-speed networks, more robust and friendly server software, ubiquitous open architecture Web browsers, powerful open architecture plug-ins such as Shockwave, and now component architecture systems like ActiveX, OpenDoc, LiveConnect, and so on.

This shift toward utility and true applications is the crux of the quantum leap into advanced-level Shockwave. Web-based applications replace and recombine other methods of working, or enable whole new classes of communication.

Web-based software applications are complex apps that depend almost entirely upon the Web for their front end. Web-based software applications have rich feature sets and, therefore, comprise a long-lasting addition to the user's desktop. Integrating Shockwave into Web-based applications enables you to create sophisticated multimedia front ends to these genuine software applications.

Web-based software applications with Shockwave may incorporate heavy back-end scripting and links to relational databases to enable the Shocked Web app to interact with various data. Shockwave enhances these Web-based software applications by allowing totally unique user interface metaphors and heavily integrated multimedia components.

On today's intranets, Shockwave can flex even greater power because of the higher connection speeds at which are typically available via ethernetted LANs and WANs. This gives us a glimpse into what content-oriented full-power solutions will look like when the promise of broadband networks is fulfilled. In addition, hybrid applications that combine networked content with content coming off a local CD or hard drives give an immediate glimpse into broadband applications of the future.

The following is a guide to examples and discussion of advanced-level Shockwave Solutions:

True Applications

Chapter 12, "Talking with the Outside World: Parameters and JavaScript"

Chapter 15, "Cosmetic Shockwave and Beyond: Infonautics"

Chapter 17, "Immersive Retailing and Simplified Menu Metaphors: Andersen Consulting"

Chapter 18, "Advanced Applications: Action Technologies' Metro"

Chapter 19, "Creating Identity: Organic Online"

Chapter 20, "Creating Complex Applications: Apple Computer"

Chapter 21, "Voice Recognition Interfaces: Digital Dreams"

Broadband Environments

Chapter 9, "External Casts"

Chapter 14, "Advanced Compression Issues"

Chapter 16, "True Multimedia on the Web: DXM"

Chapter 21, "Voice Recognition Interfaces: Digital Dreams"

Chapter 22, "Education and Non-Profit: Rainforest Action Network"

Smart Shockwave Movies

One difficulty of using Shockwave as a component in a true application on the Web is communicating information into the Shockwave movie. Chapter 18, "Advanced Applications: Action Technologies' Metro" details techniques for making Shockwave smarter. The example movie is taken from a Web-based software product called Metro. Metro is a very sophisticated workflow management development environment made by Action Technologies. This movie features a Shockwave user interface.

In Chapter 18, we discuss how passing parameters enables Shockwave to have state memory—a critical capability for true applications. We also take on some basic architectural and design issues that arise when shocking a true Web-based application.

Online Retailing and Immersive Advertising

Direct commerce over the Internet is greatly facilitated by Shockwave. Companies selling products of all types are using the Web as a broad sales venue. Shockwave provides great opportunities in Web marketing in the areas of branding and relationship marketing. Providing a cool virtual environment for shoppers to browse and shop online is a key Web application for Shockwave.

Andersen Consulting has prototyped an online shopping experience for a clothing company wishing to reposition itself as a leader on the Web. The "Basement One" movies are a good example of a multimedia sales environment. This example, discussed in Chapter 17, "Immersive Retailing and Simplified Menu Metaphors: Andersen Consulting," shows how true multimedia can be used to create a rich environment to explore products and personalities. This environment draws viewers into a world of characters and lifestyles to create a positive association with the products. We have categorized it as true application because of the extensiveness, functionality, and repeated use of the entire site it comprises.

Developing an ongoing relationship with customers and building an immersive world around a product is a powerful application for Shockwave. Chapter 19, "Creating Identity: Organic Online" has a discussion and tactics for Web marketing, sales, and customer support. Any company targeting a customer base on the Web can benefit from using Shockwave to help solve the problem of relating to the market over the Internet.

Speech Recognizing Applications

Shockwave for Director is an open-architecture environment. That is, it supports xObjects and Xtras. This open architecture allows the widest power imaginable in customizing Web applications to any desired purpose. An early and very intriguing example of this power is a plug-in Xtra to Shockwave for Director that enables speech recognition to be incorporated into your interactivity.

Chapter 21, "Voice Recognition Interfaces: Digital Dreams," discusses the speech recognition Xtra developed by Digital Dreams in the broader context of the implications brought on by Xtras in general. There is also discussion about ways that speech recognition can become a part of multiplayer games, workgroups, and playgroups using Shockwave.

Components of Powerful Apps

There are currently several obstacles to Shockwave becoming an ideal front-end for true Web-based applications. Most of the issues revolve around data manipulation and integration of programming structures. With seamless integrations into component integration systems such as OpenDoc (discussed in Chapter 20, "Creating Complex Applications: Apple Computer,") Shockwave will fast become a very powerful part of custom applications on the Web.

It is too early to see robust true applications that pass significant data through a Shockwave front end. Solutions like this are not yet practical, but in Chapter 23, "Future of Shockwave," we discuss some enabling technologies that may soon be available for such purposes.

Broadband Immersive Applications

HTML-based software applications are not yet widespread, and the integral use of Shockwave in true Web apps is just now emerging. The final category of broadband immersive applications is a speculative projection based on future merging of technologies that exist today in experimental or narrow-use forms. Broadband immersive applications are the content-oriented full-power solutions.

With the coming onslaught of broadband public networks like cable modems, ADSL, broadband ISDN and others, we can expect Shockwave to be a pervasive standard delivery platform for already existing multimedia. As delivery options proliferate for multimedia content vendors, the CD-ROM appears more like a necessary evil than an optimal solution. Broadband Shockwave sidesteps the CD-ROM rat race by shortening the sales cycle, eliminating resellers, and stocking nightmares. Stepping down the Internet road 12 to 24 months we see the emergence of a tremendous multimedia marketing advantage with Shockwave.

The intriguing possibile use of Shockwave is the creation of broadband immersive multimedia applications. These applications are not yet fully imagined, let alone implemented. But even at this stage of the game, it is possible to make some intelligent speculation based on a solid understanding of the dynamics of the Web's evolution and a keen eye on emerging experimental technologies.

In the short term, intranet-based titles and hybrid CD-ROM/Web titles may be the best way to appreciate the potential of the broadband future. There are technique chapters of relevance to broadband environments. Chapter 9, "External Casts," and Chapter 5, "Shockwave for Director 5," have techniques on linked media as would be used for a hybrid title. The advanced compression issues discussed in Chapter 14, "Advanced Compression Issues," will be important for some time to come. Even if bandwidth were increased ten-fold tomorrow, it would still not be enough. Compression techniques will be critical for Shockwave developers for some time to come.

Conclusion

Shockwave Power Solutions is not intended to carry you away in a wave of wishful hype, but rather we hope to provide concrete techniques and examples, sober appraisals and insights firmly grounded in the real advances of technologies, the actual goals of organizations vying for their niche on the Web, and the demands and affinities of the Web-seeking masses. We hope that the big Shockwave picture of interactive power, together with the many techniques and case studies, will provide you with the tools you need to create power solutions of your own.

Chapter 3

Comparing Authorware, Director, and FreeHand

It should come as no surprise that Shockwave for Authorware, Shockwave for Director, and Shockwave for FreeHand depend, respectively, on Authorware, Director, and FreeHand to create their source files.

Each of these programs is a legitimate contender for the title of best in its field, with Director claiming the title without much contention. Because there is rampant confusion about the respective roles of the three products, we have included table with the intended market segment for each product (see table 3.1).

TABLE 3.1

AUTHORWARE, DIRECTOR, AND FREEHAND: FAST FACTS

Product	*Current Version/Price*	*Target Uses*
Authorware	3.5/$4,995	Corporate training, interactive multimedia reference, Human Resources, kiosks, and simulations and prototypes
Director	5.0/$799	Games, animation, presentations, interactive advertising, and exploratory multimedia
FreeHand	5.5 (Mac)/$195 5.0 (Win)/$195	Graphics, design

The three products also differ in terms of their metaphors and the features they provide.

All three products work identically on Macintosh and Windows. FreeHand and Director files are *binary-compatible*, meaning that files created on one platform work on both platforms. Authorware files, however, need to be converted, which is a one-step process, assuming you have a version of the application for the appropriate platform. To create files that work on Windows, for example, you need a Windows version of Authorware and a Macintosh version for the Macintosh. This process is transparent to the user and is simply a matter of opening a Macintosh file on Windows or vice versa.

Currently, none of these plug-ins have Unix versions. Macromedia has announced, however, that versions of the Shockwave for Director plug-ins will be available for SGI and Sun-based Unix workstations. There is no word, currently, on the availability of Unix plug-ins for Authorware or FreeHand.

Now that you're armed with this general information, the rest of the chapter focuses on the specific features and capabilities of Authorware, Director, and FreeHand.

Working with Authorware

The most common request asked of the Macromedia marketing folks is to explain the difference between Director and Authorware. The most obvious, immediate difference is the price. Authorware's higher price reflects its orientation toward a corporate and institutional market. Authorware includes many features designed to facilitate use in a corporate setting, such as workgroup features and reusable content and structure. A sample Authorware production you will be working with in Chapter 8, "Developing Shocked Sites with Authorware," is shown in figure 3.1.

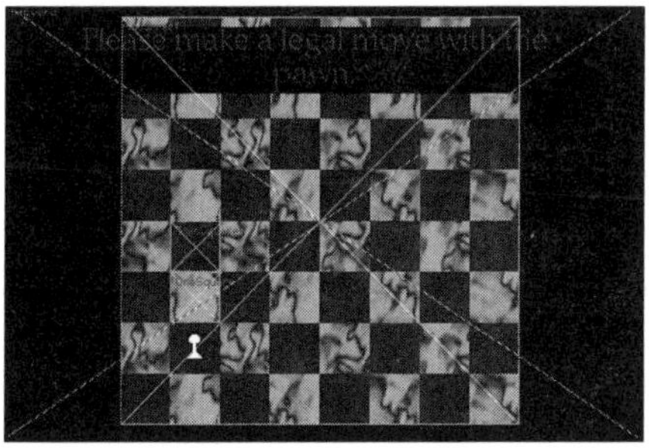

FIGURE 3.1

Authorware includes many features designed to facilitate use in an institutional setting.

> **Note:** An Authorware production is called a *course*. Additional files contain stores of icons and are called *libraries*.

Authorware's strengths are in its capability to reuse portions of a course. Assets such as images and sounds can be stored in library files, with links to those resources from the actual flowline of a course. This can be a major benefit for a Shockwave developer, because a library element only needs to be downloaded once, but used multiple times. Portions of logic also can be reused, enabling developers to test a template and make sure it performs as expected, then reuse the template without copying it. Because there is only one copy of the template:

- You don't have to worry about keeping track of multiple versions of essentially the same template.
- The resulting code will be smaller in size; hence, downloading will be much faster.
- It will be much easier to maintain the code. After all, code reuse is one of the cornerstones of object-oriented programming.
- Several developers can work on the same course without worrying that the foundation will disappear out from under them.

Authorware Metaphor: The Flowline

The primary Authorware metaphor is the flowline. Control passes down the flowline (see fig. 3.2), which branches depending upon the user's input (at interaction icons), calculations of test scores or survey answers (decision icons), or clicked hypertext.

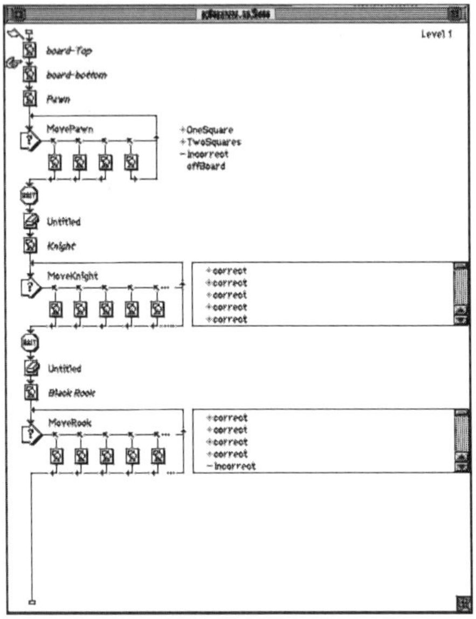

FIGURE 3.2
Authorware's primary metaphor is the flowline.

Who Uses Authorware and What Can It Do?

Authorware was designed to be a tool for educators, rather than programmers, and the flowline enables construction of a fairly robust application without requiring extensive programming. Like most multimedia programs, however, Authorware is mostly used by people who are full-time—or nearly full-time—multimedia developers. The price tag, of course, also discourages casual users.

Authorware is used primarily for reference, training, and education. One of its more common uses is as a personnel guide. Photographs or videos of personnel can be combined with personal information, phone numbers, maps, or just about anything else. This kind of application is often used in a kiosk setting. A visitor to an office can quickly determine how to find the person they are looking for or who the appropriate contact is. Shockwave for Authorware enables everyone in the office to access this same information without leaving their desks.

When to Use Shockwave for Authorware

Although Authorware is not for everyone, when it fits your needs it puts sliced bread to shame. You should use Authorware when one or more of the following is true:

- You have Authorware content you want to repurpose for the Web
- You want to create training applications that adjust to the levels and abilities of the user
- You want to create an intranet application that provides large amounts of media
- You have an application that combines large amounts of text and graphics or animations with interactivity

These last two points are explained in more detail in the following two sections.

Shockwave for Intranets

Authorware's pedigree as a tool for educators has led to its prominence in two areas: corporate training and educational institutions. Its position in the educational field is helped by Macromedia's aggressive educational pricing policy. Because these are two fields where intranets are most commonly found, Macromedia was able to concentrate more on maintaining as many of the features of Authorware as possible when creating Shockwave for Authorware, rather than keeping bandwidth and security concerns at the forefront.

AUTHORS' NOTE

What Is an Intranet?

Intranets are most commonly found in corporate or institutional settings, and are characterized by one or more of the following:

- **High bandwidth:** Often up to Ethernet (10 Mbps) speeds.
- **Security:** Access to the outside world (the Internet) is not available or is available only through a firewall machine, which provides limited access.
- **Highly controlled:** Particularly in corporate settings, information available within an intranet is often strictly controlled by the MIS department. The software available to access and present the information also is controlled.

These characteristics make intranets a friendly place for Shockwave developers. The high bandwidth availability means that developers can provide a richness of content that often is not possible when targeting modem users. Security means that developers can use Xtras and other tools that might not meet the Internet's strict security standards, but users will be willing to trust them in an intranet setting. Finally, MIS control enables developers to assume that their audience has the appropriate plug-ins and other software to be able to access a Shockwave for Authorware course. At the very least, developers can be confident that users have somewhere to go for help if they do not have a plug-in.

Nobody is quite sure how many intranet Web servers exist. Estimates range from one-tenth as many intranet servers as are on the Internet to twice as many. It is, however, safe to say that there are hundreds of thousands of intranet Web servers in the U.S. alone. Clearly, intranets are a tremendous business opportunity for Shockwave developers, especially when you consider that corporations with the financial wherewithal to assemble an intranet almost certainly have the resources to fund multimedia development as well.

Shockwave for Authorware Applications

Many large corporations use Authorware to train their staffs. A software company, for example, might produce a training course on its new application for its sales force, combining a demonstration of the product's usefulness with a simulation of it in action showing ease of use. Video or audio of user testimony could be added to emphasize key points. Currently, these courses are usually distributed on CD-ROM, an awkward and often expensive process, particularly in the case of a company whose sales force is distributed across the country or around the world. These difficulties can be exacerbated by frequent revisions of the software or the addition of new competitive analyses, which require distribution of new copies. Shockwave makes distribution of this information easy: simply put it on a server and send an e-mail to the appropriate individuals, letting them know the URL. Because relatively few actual copies of the course exist and they are (often) centrally accessible, frequent updates become a much simpler process.

But let's not forget that Authorware's initial purpose was education, and it still performs that task admirably. From physical simulations of basic tools to math education, it is uniquely suited to a lesson-quiz model of education. After reading lesson material, which can include animations, sound, and video of the material involved, the student can be given a quiz, and perhaps even remedial work on areas in which he is weak. In a university setting, Shockwave can be used to decentralize this process. A student could work from his dorm room or apartment, avoiding the necessity of waiting for a terminal in an always overcrowded computer lab.

Using Director

Director is probably the most popular multimedia authoring program today. It has been around in one form or another since 1985, and there are now more than 250,000 Director users, according to Macromedia. Director is tremendously flexible and can be used for almost any task associated with multimedia.

Director Metaphor: You Are in the Chair

Director's primary metaphor is a feature film. You arrange cast members on the stage and orchestrate their movement in the score. Finally, you make the cast members do things by writing scripts for them.

The Score

The primary engine for Director movies is the score (see fig. 3.3). This window resembles a spreadsheet, with a grid-like arrangement divided into *frames* (horizontal axis) and *channels* (the vertical axis). Control in a Director movie flows from left to right in the score, frame by frame. The score contains information for where each cast member instance (called a sprite) is placed on the stage, as well as what they do when the user interacts with them.

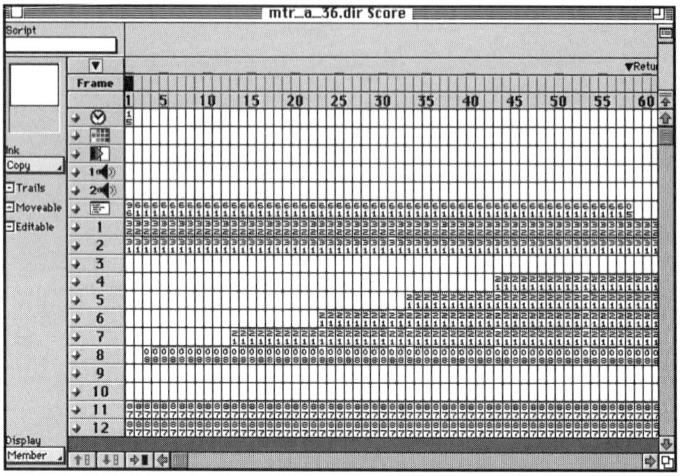

FIGURE 3.3
The score is the primary engine in Director.

Vertically, the score is divided into 48 sprite channels, two sound channels, and one channel each of script, palette, transition, and tempo. The sprite, or image, channels are ordered so that higher numbered channels are in front. Thus, an image in channel 48 overlaps any image in any other channel.

While working with Director, you'll find that you spend most of your time with the score. This is especially true when you're creating animation-heavy movies. Director 5 has added the capability to *script* the score—that is, generate score data on the fly using Lingo, Director's scripting language.

The Cast

The *cast* is a visual database of media objects (see fig. 3.4). These objects can be bitmaps, vector shapes, digital video movies, transitions, scripts, or sounds, among other items. Each cast member has a number and can have a name assigned to it as well. The cast contains visual representations of each element in the movie, and can be organized at the will of the user. A new feature in Director 5 adds multiple casts, so you can share cast elements between movies. This enables Shockwave movies that have been downloaded to share cast files.

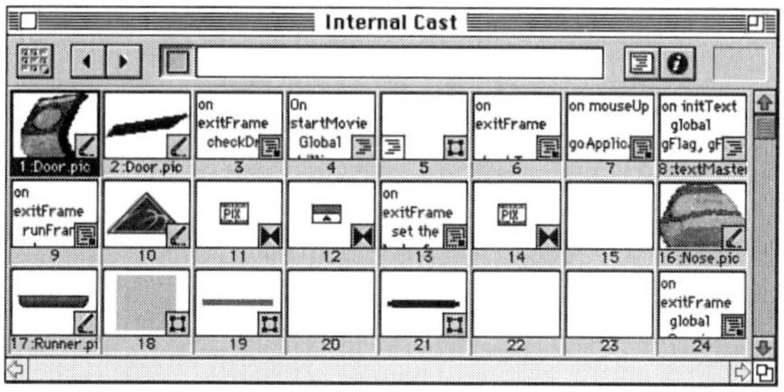

FIGURE 3.4

The cast contains a visual representation of the elements in a movie.

Of use to Shockwave developers is an additional feature of the cast window: the cast member info button, which enables you to determine the color depth and approximate size of the cast member. This can be extremely useful for shrinking your Shockwave movie as much as possible.

Scripts

Director ships with its own scripting language, called Lingo. Lingo evolved (back in the mists of the past) from Hypertalk, and like that language has an English-like syntax. Over the years of its evolution, Lingo has taken many of the powerful features of other languages, such as objects and inheritance, linked lists, case structures, and the like, without losing the ease of use that characterized its beginning.

Many new users are intimidated by Lingo, but the advantage of a scripting language, contained inside another program, is that you can get your feet wet one toe at a time. It is almost impossible to use Shockwave without using at least a little bit of Lingo, and Lingo is crucial for creating interactive movies.

Who Uses Director and What Does It Do?

Director is intended as a general-purpose multimedia tool and can be used for everything from simple animations to elaborate interactive worlds. The most common uses for Director include presentations, CD-ROM games, animation, and interactive titles.

Director Is Flexible and Scaleable

Director's greatest strengths are its flexibility and scalability. Almost any application you can think of that requires interactivity, animation, sound, or text is possible to create using Director. Director is not always the best choice for a given application, but it is nearly always a possible choice. With Director 5, Macromedia has finally provided a robust interface for extending Director, using the Macromedia Xtra architecture. This architecture enables the inclusion of new types of cast members, transitions, or custom code, which will allow tremendously powerful combinations of features.

Director has been used to create giant titles that span several CD-ROMs, for tiny movies that are less than 10 KB in size, and everything between. This scalability makes it an ideal choice for creating Web content. Imagine the results when the rich toolset that has been developed for creating CD-ROM titles and corporate presentations is focused on a small movie for the World Wide Web!

When to Use Director

Although Director is extremely flexible, it is not always the most appropriate tool for a Web application. You should use Shockwave for Director when one or more of the following conditions are true:

- You need animation and/or sound
- You need an interface that is more than one level deep
- You want to give the user more information about a potential link than a simple URL

- You want your interface to meet the same basic standards as desktop applications
- You want to show dynamic processes, such as planets revolving around a star, rather than showing planets with a circle representing their orbit.

Because Director is such a popular and flexible tool, it is already being used for many different purposes on the Web, from gratuitous animations to front ends to full-scale Web-based applications.

Working with FreeHand

FreeHand is arguably the top cross-platform drawing application available. Through many changes of ownership, it has managed to maintain its position at the top of its field, and the additions of Shockwave capabilities allow it to stand out even more.

The FreeHand Metaphor: The Page

FreeHand, like most drawing programs, is oriented around a simple paper metaphor (see fig. 3.5). With the provided drawing tools, the user draws objects on a page. Because it is a vector-based program, the drawn objects can be scaled and stretched with no loss of resolution. The view of the overall image also can be magnified or reduced with no distortion.

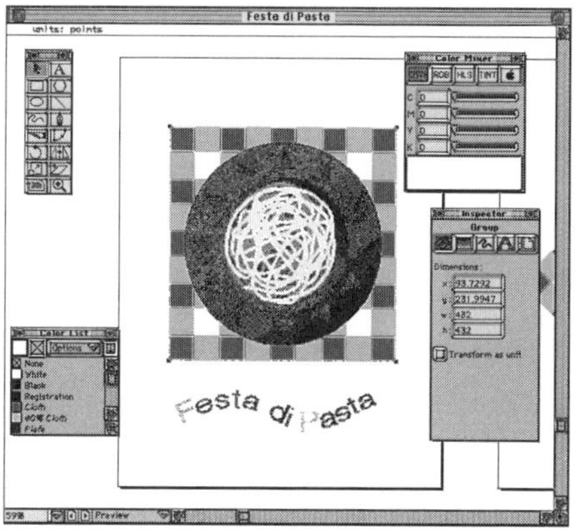

FIGURE 3.5

FreeHand is based on a paper metaphor.

Who Uses FreeHand?

Like most drawing applications, FreeHand is only now making the transition from a primarily print-oriented program to a tool in the arsenal of the multimedia developer. It has not yet made the transition satisfactorily, because things like clean export to Director are not yet available. But Macromedia's track record of successful product integration makes it likely that the transition will soon be seamless.

The primary users of FreeHand to date are graphic artists and designers. They use FreeHand for illustration, technical drawing, and maps, among other things. In many cases, artists even use FreeHand as a page layout tool. FreeHand's text-handling capabilities are also quite powerful, although using anything but common fonts in Shockwave is risky, because you can't depend on the user having the fonts you use.

One limitation of the Web is that images that are too large to fit in the size of one screen without sacrificing readability are impossible to display. Because Shockwave for FreeHand maintains the ability to zoom in and out on an image (see fig. 3.6), it is an excellent choice for displaying very dense images on the Web. The capability to attach URL links to objects in the FreeHand drawing means that maps and diagrams can be intuitive interfaces. FreeHand also can import images from Adobe Illustrator or CorelDraw! and serve as a way to present these image formats on the Web as well.

When You Should Use FreeHand

Although Shockwave for FreeHand does not have all the bells and whistles of Shockwave for Director or Authorware, Shockwave for FreeHand can be a quick way to add tremendous functionality to your website. You should use Shockwave for FreeHand when one or more of the following conditions are true:

- You have dense images, such as technical drawings, that cannot be presented in bitmap format and will benefit from zoom capability
- You have existing content in FreeHand, Illustrator, or CorelDraw! that needs to be displayed on the Web

- You want to make design work available for client review or for advertising purposes
- You have maps or other images that need to have arbitrarily shaped clickable areas

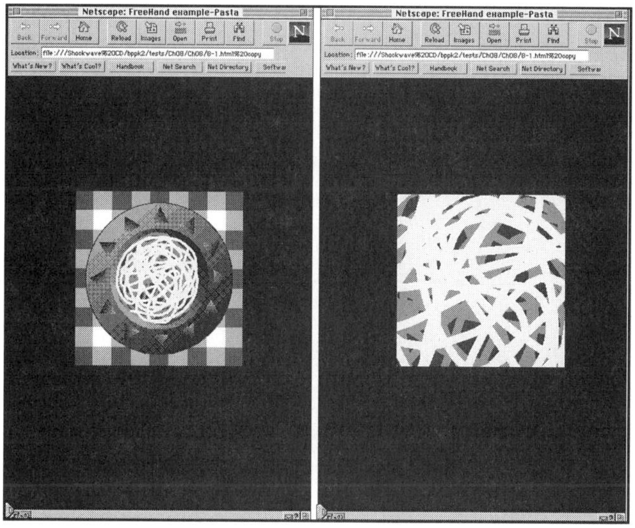

FIGURE 3.6

Shockwave for FreeHand's capability to zoom in and out makes it an excellent tool for displaying dense images on the Web.

Working with Nuthin'

No chapter comparing different types of Shockwave would be complete without a fourth category: Shockwave for Absolutely Nothing. So in the spirit of completeness, you should not use any Shockwave when any of the following conditions are true:

- You are targeting users with 9600 bps or slower modems
- You have not yet reconciled yourself to these fancy graphical systems that are the latest rage
- All of your users are among that 15 percent of Web users who are not using Netscape Navigator or Microsoft Internet Explorer
- You are trying to discourage repeat visits

Summary

This chapter has explored the relative strengths and weaknesses of Authorware, Director, and FreeHand. You should now have an idea about which technology suits your needs best. The next chapter, "Understanding Shockwave for Director," will explore in detail how to get started with Macromedia's first flavor of Shockwave.

Part II

Second-Generation Shockwave

CHAPTER 4

Understanding Shockwave for Director

Shockwave for Director 4 was Macromedia's first product for the Internet, and its success has made it clear that Web content providers and multimedia developers are both hungry for efficient multimedia on the Internet.

To take full advantage of Shockwave for Director 5, you must have a grasp of four topics: basic bandwidth-reduction techniques; features carried over from Shockwave for Director 4; an understanding of the <embed> tag and how it relates to Shockwave for Director; and features new to version 5. New features are covered in Chapter 5, "Shockwave for Director 5," but to take full advantage of them, it is necessary to understand the features carried over from Shockwave for Director 4.

Basics of Bandwidth Reduction

One of the major problems hindering broad acceptance of Shockwave on the Web is the perception that its movies are big. Many of the Shockwave movies you run across on the Net are, in fact, unpleasantly large. This does not have to be the case. Most large movies are too large because of three major reasons:

- **Sloppiness.** The creator simply throws a movie up on the Web without taking even basic steps to reduce the size of the movie.
- **Inexperience.** The creator simply is not aware of the techniques at his disposal.
- **Overkill.** Trying to do too much within the limitations of the Web delivery medium.

To help combat sloppiness, we urge you, the Shockwave developer, to run through the basic file size reduction techniques each time you prepare to upload a movie to your Web site. The problem of overkill is a tricky one, because it is essentially a judgment call. Are you attempting video quality animations? CD-quality or CD-length sound? If so, you might be better off using MPEG, QuickTime, or some other form of delivery specialized for that content. The second problem, inexperience, is one that we can definitely address.

The basics of bandwidth reduction for Director include the following:

- Small stage size
- Graphics bit-depth reduction
- Sound down-sampling
- Tiling

Each of these techniques is briefly addressed in the following sections. For more information, we recommend our previous book, *Macromedia Shockwave for Director User's Guide*. Note that these techniques are intended as guidelines rather than hard-and-fast rules. You might have reasons for violating one or all of these recommendations in a particular movie. We recommend, however, that if you do decide to ignore them, be sure that your reason is worth the additional file size.

> **Tip**
>
> If Shockwave for Director is the best choice for your material and you still are ending up with large files, you should definitely take some precautions to avoid alienating your audience. These precautions can include a warning that they are about to hit a large movie (perhaps including the file size), so they know what they're getting into. An alternative method is to load a smaller movie first, which will keep them interested while you download a larger one.

Small Stage Size

Small stage sizes are preferable in Shockwave for Director for several reasons. First, because of the screen space taken up by the browser interface, there is less screen real estate for the movie, and second, because a smaller stage will allow smaller graphics, which often means less download time. Finally, in most cases the movie will be integrated into a Web page, and you want to leave room for the other content on the page.

Netscape in its default configuration takes up 120 pixels vertically with its interface alone. This means that to be completely visible on a 640×480 screen, your movie cannot be taller than 340–360 pixels (depending on platform). This is a constraint that you will be wise to keep in mind when you design your movies. Unless you are targeting high-end users only, we recommend creating movies no bigger than 400×300. In Director 5, you can set the stage size using the Modify, Movie, Properties menu.

Bigger stage sizes require larger graphics. An 8-bit (256-color) graphic that takes up the whole stage on a 640×480 pixel movie is 300 KB in size, uncompressed. A full-stage graphic on a 400×300 stage is less than 120 KB before compression! Clearly, even the second graphic is too big, but this comparison should make it clear that only in very rare cases should you consider spending the extra bandwidth for a larger stage that will be outside the browser window for a large portion of the people viewing your site.

Many Shockwave for Director movies rely on context for instructions, explanation, or functionality. This context most often takes the form of text surrounding the movie. If your movie is in any way related to text on the same page, you should take that into account when you determine the ideal size for your movie. Again, the concern here is for users with smaller screens. With a 400×300 movie, you have room for only one line of text above or below the movie and maybe one sentence to one side of the movie on a 640×480 pixel screen. Including large amounts of text can mean a lot of frustrating scrolling for a user. We emphasize this point because 640×480 screens are a majority of the installed base of Macintosh and Windows computers.

Bit Depth Reduction

Bit depth (or color depth) reduction and sound down-sampling, are probably the most important techniques you can use to reduce the size of your Shockwave for Director movies. The process can be complex and takes some experimentation, but it can often save you 60 or 70 percent of a movie's size. To become proficient at bit depth reduction, it is first important to understand bit depth in general.

All bitmap graphics (which are the kind most often used in multimedia) have at least three parameters: height, width, and bit depth (or color depth). Height and width are measurements of the number of pixels in an image. Bit depth is the measurement of how many bits are used to represent each pixel. The file size of a graphic is a factor of the height×width×depth. A black-and-white graphic has a bit depth of 1, because each pixel is represented using 1 bit, which can be either 0 (white) or 1 (black). Remember that there are 8 bits in a byte. Therefore, a 400×300 black-and-white graphic is 400×300×1/8 bytes, or 15,000 bytes. A 24-bit graphic (which is the highest displayable on some computers) uses 8 bits to describe the amount of red, green, and blue in a pixel. The same-dimension graphic at 24 bit, then would be 400×300×3 bytes, or 360,000 bytes (roughly 350 KB). Images that are 16 bits work equivalently, although they use only five bits each for red, green, and blue. Table 4.1 shows the various color depths and corresponding sizes of an image.

Table 4.1

Bit Depths and File Sizes

Bit Depth	*Number of Colors That Can Be Displayed*	*File Size for a 400×300 Graphic*
1	2 (black and white)	15 KB
4	16	60 KB
8	256	120 KB
16	65,535	240 KB
24	16.7 million	350 KB

Graphics with a bit depth between 2 and 8 bits use a slightly different system to represent their colors. These color depths are often called *indexed color*, because each color is represented not by its red, green, and blue values, but by its index in a color table, or palette. Many, if not most, Macintosh and Windows computers can only display 256 colors at a time. They make the most of this limited set of colors by defining a palette of 256 colors, each with its own RGB value. A color in an image can then be described by a single byte, which refers to that color's position, or index, in the current palette. Two- and four-bit images follow a similar scheme, with correspondingly smaller palettes and image sizes.

Because anything more than 8 bits (or 256 colors) is wasted on a large portion of the market and also because images with lower color depths load faster and take less memory, most Director developers have traditionally used mostly 8-bit images in their work. This is certainly a good starting point for Shockwave movies, but due to size issues, it is usually best to reduce images to less than 8-bit if at all possible.

Exercise: Creating a Custom Palette

Both Macintosh and Windows computers have a *system palette*, which is the default palette for the machine. They are, of course, different, which can cause difficulties for the unprepared developer.

If you need to create a custom palette, you can do so, but again, we recommend maintaining the first ten and last ten colors from the Windows system palette. If you are on the Macintosh platform, the following steps show you one way to do this:

1. Dither the image(s) to a 236-color palette in Adobe Photoshop or an equivalent application. (In Photoshop, choose Mode, Indexed and select 236 colors.)
2. Import the file into Director (with the monitor set to 256 colors), and choose Import Palette Into Cast in the dialog that results.
3. Open the Custom Palette in the palette window by double-clicking on it in the cast window.
4. Select and copy all the colors. (Do not select the 20 or so black entries at the end.)
5. Open the Windows system palette. Select position 11 and paste. Name the palette appropriately in the resulting dialog box.
6. Select the cast member and choose Modify, Transform Bitmap. Select the new palette and click on the Remap Colors radio button.
7. Delete the original custom palette (the one with the black entries at the end).

Changing Color Depth

When you import a file that does not have the same color depth as your main monitor, you are given the option of changing the color depth of the image to match the color depth of the movie or maintaining the image's native color depth. Because you very rarely want to have a cast member that is more than 8 bits, you should set your monitor at 256 colors before creating a Shockwave movie, and remap or dither the image to 8 bits. If the image is an 8-bit image mapped to anything other than the current palette, you are given the option of importing the image's inherent palette or remapping to the current one, as shown in figure 4.1.

Figure 4.1

Importing a file that is not at the same color depth as your main monitor displays this Director dialog box, which enables you to change the color depth of the image to that of your monitor.

Tip

When remapping is selected without the Dither check box selected, Director matches each color in the image to the closest color in the current palette. When Dither is checked, Director attempts to match the original color as closely as possible by generating a pattern of similar colors.

Dithered images tend to compress less efficiently than remapped ones because the patterned areas are less regular. Although you need to judge each image separately, you should choose remap whenever possible.

Once you have imported or created all your images, you should examine them to determine whether any can be reduced to a lower color depth. Make a copy of the images you think have potential for color depth reduction (those with relatively few colors) and reduce them to 4, 2, or 1 bit(s).

Used judiciously, reducing color depth can be the deciding factor between an exceptionally compact movie and a sluggish, bloated annoyance to your users. To reduce color depth intelligently takes some work, however. It is often preferable to give up extra texture in your graphics for better compression or to be able to drop another 2 or 4 bits from your art. Remember that visitors to your website will probably not be spending anywhere near as much time looking at the graphics in your file as you have spent making them.

It also is important to know when to sacrifice download time. For a control panel, for instance, which is downloaded once but appears over and over again, an extra 10 KB or so is often worth it, especially if the user will be seeing the movie repeatedly.

Tip

Two techniques that will help you make maximum use of low-color-depth graphics are ink effects and colorized one-bit cast members.

Sprites on the stage can be assigned ink effects, which can combine to produce interesting results. Reverse Ink is particularly useful in this regard. We strongly suggest that for a movie that needs a little extra pizzazz, you experiment with some of the available ink effects.

A key technique is colorizing 1-bit cast members. When a 1-bit cast member is placed in the score, it can be assigned a foreground and background color with the tool palette. The black pixels of the image are displayed in the foreground color, and the white pixels are assigned the background color. The assigned colors can be different for each sprite. You can even have several copies of the same cast member on the stage, with different colors assigned to them. This is an excellent way of making maximum use of a single cast member, and of keeping bit depth to a minimum while still keeping your movie colorful.

Sound Downsampling

Afterburner does not compress sound. Because sound is a fairly weighty part of the multimedia mix, this can cause problems. Because of the lack of compression, sound can be very expensive in terms of download time, but it is too important to be ignored altogether. There are several things you can do to get the most mileage out of your bandwidth. The first, and most important, is to reduce the sample rate to 11.025 khz and the sample depth to 8 bits. You also should make sure the sound is mono. On the Macintosh, it is tempting to reduce the sample rate even further—to 5 or 8 khz. This is not recommended, however, because many Windows sound cards don't play any sound that is not a multiple of 11.025 khz. As far as music quality goes, 8 bits, 11.025 khz is somewhat sketchy, but even at that rate the sound still takes up 11 KB per second!

Note

Computer audio is typically sampled at 48 khz (DAT quality), 44.1 khz (CD-quality), or 22.050 khz, and at 16- or 8-bit. Because of the peculiarities of the digital sampling process, digital audio at a given sample rate has trouble reproducing sounds that have a frequency of more than half the sample rate. For example, a 48 khz digital file can't reproduce sounds of more than 24 khz accurately. Since the limit of human hearing is roughly 20–23 khz, this is rarely a problem. Reducing the sample rate below 44.1 khz, however, can cause an audible decrease in quality. Fortunately, even with music, most sounds are well below 11 khz. For instance, a typical range for a speaking human voice is 3-5 khz, and many bass and drum sounds are at the 50–250 khz range! When you downsample to 11 khz, however, you will lose most of the harmonics that are such a large part of the richness of music. Macromedia is in the process of introducing audio compression techniques that will make this tradeoff unnecessary in many cases, but currently you must decide if you can live with a thinner sound in exchange for reduced download times.

To use sound efficiently, you will want to loop sections of music. This is as easy as checking the loop check box in the Cast Member Info dialog box on the sound cast member. You should make sure, however, that your loop is seamless, and that the user has a way to turn it off, especially if your movie repeats or is long. One useful way to smooth out looped audio is to fade in and out, using the sound fadeIn and sound fadeOut Lingo commands. These commands smooth the audio transitions in your movie and give it a more finished quality overall.

Tiles

One of Director's built-in features that can save a lot of file size is the tiles feature. In conjunction with KPT Seamless Tiler or Xaos Tools' Terrazzo, you can have very attractive full-stage backgrounds for the price of a single 32×32 or 64×64 graphic. To create a tiled background, you should follow these steps:

1. Create the image that you want to use as a tile. The height and width should be 16, 32, 64, or 128 pixels, because the height and width of tiles in Director must be one of these values. If you created the image outside of Director, import it.
2. Open the paint window, select an empty cast member and click and hold on the pattern chip. You should see a Tile Settings entry at the bottom of the pop-up. Select it.
3. Click the cast member radio button and cycle through the cast members in your movie until you find the desired tile source image. Adjust the size of the source area so that it fits your tile.

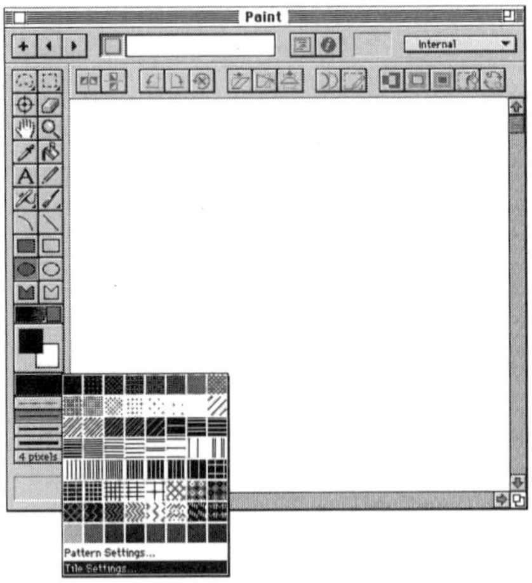

FIGURE 4.2

The Tile Settings dialog box is accessible through the pattern pop-up.

4. Using the QuickDraw filled rectangle tool, draw a rectangle big enough to cover the whole stage. Select the appropriate tile in the pattern pop-up menu in the tool palette.

These techniques should enable you to create a reasonably sized Shockwave movie that won't be a burden on your users.

Shockwave Features Carried Over from 4

The features added to Shockwave for Director in its first incarnation, version 4, consisted largely of Afterburner and some new Lingo commands designed to enable the Director developer to take advantage of the network. There also were some features of Director that were disabled, either for security reasons or because of the nature of the network. We discuss the Lingo commands and the features disabled in Director 4 in the following sections.

Lingo Featured in Shockwave for Director 4

In Shockwave for Director 4, Macromedia added several Lingo commands and functions to give Director developers the ability to access the network. When using these Lingo commands, it is important to understand the nature of the Internet.

Note

Because some of these commands are little-used and because some of them have been superseded or changed, we haven't included a full, dictionary reference of them here. Appendix B, "Lingo for Shockwave Quick Reference," contains a full reference to all the network Lingo available in Shockwave for Director 5.

The most important (and aggravating) dynamic of the Internet the Shockwave developer must deal with is speed. Speed is important not just because it takes time to download large files, but because even the smallest file takes several seconds to download. We call the former *bandwidth*, and the latter *latency*.

Bandwidth is the most obvious concern. Users who connect to the Net with modems can (and often will, given the opportunity) give you chapter and verse on the amount of bandwidth website developers waste. Most websites are designed to be browsed with a 28.8 kbps modem. Practically, this means about 2 KB per second of material gets downloaded. So if you begin a 100 KB download, you need to have enough going on to keep your user busy while that happens.

Bandwidth can vary drastically, however. A user on a T-1 line, for example, can theoretically get speeds of up to 50 times as fast as a 28.8 modem. So the 100 KB file that takes 50 seconds on a modem takes something on the order of a second or two on a T-1. Clearly, these are huge discrepancies that can be difficult to take into account.

Latency is a different matter. This factor—which is the time it takes for the user's browser to look up a server, initiate a connection, and begin a network operation—also is somewhat a function of connection speed, but is (or appears) mostly random. In fact, it depends largely on server machine speed and server load. It varies from a low of half a second or so to a high of five or ten seconds on a busy server. Compare this to a CD-ROM, where transfers typically begin within a fifth of a second, since even a second can throw a wrench into delicately timed operations, if it is not taken into account.

> **Note**
>
> Although it might be tempting (and, indeed, somewhat useful) to compare network latency to seek time on a hard drive or CD-ROM, these are two different issues. Remember that latency delays come in addition to seek time. They also are several orders of magnitude larger (a typical hard drive average access time is 10 milliseconds).

For example, it might seem safe to assume that a 2 KB text file (including settings or user information) will take at worst case, on a 14.4 modem, two seconds to successfully complete the download. On a busy server, however, that time can be as much as six or seven seconds, even on a T-1 connection. Even on a lightly-loaded server, that time might be three or four seconds.

The latency and bandwidth concerns have made it necessary for Macromedia to make the network Lingo additions operate *asynchronously*, meaning that Director can start these operations and go about its other business, checking back to see whether the operation is done.

GoToNetPage

The most commonly used network Lingo command is the `GoToNetPage` command. This command, when called from Lingo, instructs the browser to load the page called into the browser's current window. In Director 4, the only parameter allowed was the target page of the call. In Shockwave for Director 5, there is an additional optional parameter, which allows the targeted page to be loaded in an alternate window or frame. This is covered in detail in Chapter 10, "Working with Frames."

An example of the normal syntax for using the simple version of this command is

```
GoToNetPage "http://www.company.com/main.html"
```

> **Tip**
>
> The **`GoToNetPage`** command also takes relative URLs. The preceding example, for instance, could be **`GoToNetPage "main.html"`**. Note that relative URLs are relative to the *movie's* location, not the location of the HTML file in which it is embedded. Thus, the short version of the example would only work if the movie was in the same directory as the main.html file.

In many cases, you will be replacing a complicated image map with a Shockwave movie. `GoToNetPage` also can be used to call image maps. The syntax for this is to use the map as the target with a sample location for each button. Thus, the call would be

```
GoToNetPage "image.map?100,82"
```

This would be equivalent to clicking on the image at 100 pixels to the right of the image's left edge and 82 pixels from the top. You can find a sample point by clicking on each active part of the image map and recording the clicked pixel. Unfortunately, this method of finding sample points only works for server-side image maps. Client-side image maps are not accessible by this method.

Another handy feature of `GoToNetPage` is the capability to call CGI scripts. Because Shockwave only passes the target parameter to the browser, as long as it is one string (which was standard for HTML calls before the proliferation of frames), you can send anything you want as the target for this command. An example that sends the user name to the CGI script would be

```
GoToNetPage "script.cgi?user+name"
```

`GoToNetPage` begins to load the new page as soon as the browser application receives a response from the server. While the browser is waiting for the server to respond, your movie continues to play. Therefore, depending on the speed of your server, you should account for the several seconds that your movie will continue to play after the call is made.

Warning

Although it seems logical that you could use this command with a mailto: URL, this command currently appends a "/" to the beginning of the address. This is apparently an error in the Netscape Navigator 2.0x implementation of the call and should be fixed in 3.0. Until the 3.0 version becomes common, you should avoid mailto: URLs in Shockwave.

GoToNetMovie

The second main network Lingo command is `GoToNetMovie`. This operates just like a GoTo Movie command works in regular Director; it loads and goes to another movie. The difference here is that while the movie is loading, the current movie continues to play. Unlike `GoToNetPage`, the movie plays until all of the target movie is loaded. Any global variables are maintained across the two movies, as well. An example of this command would be

```
GoToNetMovie "movie2.dcr"
```

GetNetText

A powerful addition to the Shockwave Lingo toolbox is the `GetNetText` command. This command gets the contents of a text file, which can then be used in a Shockwave movie. This command can be used to add features such as daily messages or other contents that change to a Shockwave movie without the Web administrator having to go through the rigamarole of changing the Director movie, reburning it, and reuploading it. The `GetNetText` command also can be used to give people who don't know how to use Director the ability to customize Shockwave movies.

Note

For an example of using **GetNetText** for customization and daily messages, see Chapter 18, "Advanced Applications: Action Technologies' Metro."

At first glance, `GetNetText` seems simple. But to properly implement it takes a bit of work. The basic process is as follows:

1. Make the `GetNetText` call to the appropriate text file.
2. Display text for the user to read, or use animation or even a "loading" message.
3. Check periodically with a `NetDone()` function (described in the following section) to discern whether the file has finished loading.
4. When the file has finished loading, use the `NetTextResult()` function (described later in this chapter) to get the resulting text. Continue your animation or message while you process the text.
5. When the text has been processed, you can finally go about your business of using it.

`GetNetText` is definitely a case where you need to take into account network latency. Because the files tend to be relatively small (typically a couple of kilobytes at most), it is often easy to underestimate the time it will take to finish reading the file. It is most sensible in these cases to be prepared for the worst, so for safety's sake you should be prepared to keep the user occupied for 10 seconds in addition to the download time for the text file.

> For security reasons, `GetNetText` does not work on local files. This command only works on files located on the network (with an explicit or implied http:// preface).
>
> *Warning*

NetOperationID()

Because it is often desirable to have several asynchronous Lingo commands active at once, the `NetOperationID()` function provides a way to address each individual operation. This function returns an arbitrary but unique identifier for the last command started. This identifier can then be used to check the status of each command. The following example initiates requests for two text files and assigns them identifiers so they can be monitored separately:

```
on beginRequest
   global msgID, settingsID
   GetNetText "message.txt"
   put NetOperationID() into msgID
   GetNetText "settings.txt"
   put NetOperationID() into settingsID
end
```

NetDone()

The `NetDone()` function returns false until a network operation (usually `GetNetText`) is finished. If a parameter is included, it is assumed to be the identifier for a net operation. If there is no parameter, it refers to the last operation started. The following script checks to see whether either of the `GetNetText` commands initiated in the previous example have completed, and if so, calls the `NetTextResult()` function. This puts the resulting text into the appropriate variable:

```
on textLoaded
   global msgID, settingsID, message, settings
   if NetDone(msgID) then put NetTextResult(msgID) into message
```

```
  if NetDone(settingsID) then put NetTextResult(settingsID) into
settings
end
```

You probably will have to call this handler repeatedly. How often and by what method depends on what you are using to keep the user occupied while the text is being retrieved.

NetTextResult()

Once you know that a text request has been completed, you of course want to use the result. The `NetTextResult()` function returns the text read as a result of the specified `GetNetText` operation. Again, as with the `NetDone()` function, if you include a parameter it refers to the operation with that ID; otherwise, it refers to the last operation initiated. See the previous code example for this handler in action.

These are the most commonly used network Lingo extensions included in Shockwave for Director 4. There are others, which can be found online at the New Riders website, `http://www. mcp.com/newriders`, but with these simple tools you should be able to do the basics.

AUTHORS' NOTE

The `PreloadNetThing` Command

A feature of the network Lingo extensions that initially looks quite good is the `PreloadNetThing` command. In theory, this command downloads the specified object from the network into the user's local cache, making any further calls to that object relatively speedy. For reasons that are still unclear, however, this command has not been effective, which is to say it has not worked at all. Macromedia is addressing this problem.

Features Disabled in Shockwave for Director 4

Several features were disabled in Shockwave for Director 4. These fall into two categories: those disabled due to the nature of the network and those disabled for security. As you will see in the next chapter, "Shockwave for Director 5," Macromedia has come up with some compromises that might be acceptable in some cases, but otherwise, these limitations will be a fact of life in the foreseeable future.

Network Unfriendly Features

Basically, Macromedia has deemed all external files undependable in a networked environment. Because a connection that is good now will not necessarily be good 20 seconds from now, external files, such as QuickTime, and linked sounds and graphics are too risky for use. Director has no graceful way to handle missing files, and it is currently outside the scope of Shockwave to add that capability.

Does the movie wait until the file is available? Does it ignore it? Situations such as these make linked media a sketchy proposition at best.

Safety First

One thing guaranteed to halt Shockwave acceptance in its tracks would be any kind of security breach. As with any unproven technology (that isn't Java) on the Web, any hint of its being able to change or even read the files on the user's local drives would lead to its being banned in every corporation and university on the Internet. Because of these concerns, Macromedia chose to take the "better safe than sorry" route and disable any feature that could possibly cause a problem. These include—most prominently—XObjects as well as any Lingo command that gives the developer access to the user's file system (getNthFileNameInFolder, for example).

Many developers have complained that Macromedia went overboard with the functions they disabled, but any excesses are understandable, given the almost paranoid attitude toward security on the Net.

The <embed> Tag

The `<embed>` tag is the current way to add plug-in objects to an HTML page. Every instance of the `<embed>` tag has three basic parameters, the order of which is arbitrary:

Parameter Name	*Syntax*	*Notes*
the source file	src="*filename.ext*"	Browsers determine which plug-in to load based on the extension.
the width	width=*xdimension*	Dimension should not be in quotes.
the height	height=*ydimension*	Dimension should not be in quotes.

Shockwave for Director 4 added one more parameter, the `textfocus` parameter. This optional parameter has the following possible values:

Parameter Value	*Response*
onMouse	Shockwave begins responding to input from the keyboard after the user clicks anywhere on the movie. This is the default setting.
onStart	Shockwave begins responding to input from the keyboard as soon as the movie starts running.
never	Shockwave ignores all input from the keyboard.

To embed a movie called PANEL.DCR located in the same directory as the page your are embedding it in, sized 400×60, which never accepts text input, you would use the following:

```
<embed src="panel.dcr" width=400 height=60 textfocus=never>
```

The problem with the `<embed>` tag is that if the user does not have the appropriate plug-in installed, the broken plug-in icon will appear. Chapter 13, "Detecting the Plug-In" details this problem.

Summary

This chapter has covered the basics of Shockwave for Director 4. We have spent extensive time on the process of reducing file size, because this is crucial to being successful with Shockwave. The next chapter addresses features that are new in Shockwave for Director 5.

Chapter 5

Shockwave for Director 5

Shockwave for Director 5 is substantially the same as Shockwave for Director 4, only better. Some of the new 5 features reflect changes that were made in Director 5 itself. Some new features are Shockwave-specific and have nothing to do with the changes to Director 5. Then there are new features that simply remove earlier limitations. Any way you cut it, our friends at Macromedia have been keeping busy.

The chapter begins with a listing of the new features, followed by a discussion of their practical applications. Some old features are touched on as well. The chapter is split into the following sections:

- *Minor adjustments*
- *The Support Folder architecture*
- *Net Lingo features*
- *New Embed attributes*

The Minor adjustments section contains information about the new features and fixes. The new Support Folder architecture offers several important new possibilities for structuring Shockwave files. Net Lingo features help you expand control over the browser and net operations, and New Embed attributes provide additional power from within in the Embed tag.

Before we dive into the details of Shockwave for Director 5, here is a list of its new features:

- Director 4.0 compatibility
- Improved Lingo performance
- Afterburner is a Tool Xtra
- Support for rich-text formatting
- "Wait for..." commands are enabled
- Addition of Support Folder architecture
- Local preferences files
- Support for Xtras and XObjects
- Support for linked media
- Support for external casts
- Some Lingo commands re-enabled
- Support for HTML frames
- Writing to the Netscape status line
- Custom background color during download
- External parameter passing

The next section dispenses with the more straightforward of the new features in Shockwave for Director 5.

Minor Adjustments

Shockwave for Director 5 takes advantage of the improvements in Director 5, offering improved Lingo performance. Afterburner is now a tool Xtra, and rich-text formatting is supported. Finally, the "Wait for..." commands in the Tempo channel are no longer disabled.

4.0 Compatibility and Better Performance

Shockwave for Director 5 plays DIR, DXR, and DCR files created using Director 4. This backward compatibility smoothes the transition from 4 to 5 by enabling you to author for a single plug-in. Encouraging users to get the Shockwave for Director 5 plug-in lets them view your existing Shockwave for Director 4 content and new content created using Director 5.

Like the Director 5 application, Shockwave for Director 5 offers an improvement of up to 50 percent in the execution of Lingo scripts, which results in higher performance, more responsive playback, and interactivity.

Afterburner as Tool Xtra

Afterburner for Director 5 has been integrated into the Director 5 authoring environment as a tool Xtra, which simplifies the process of creating Shocked movies. In Shockwave for Director 4 it was necessary to open the DIR file in a free-standing Afterburner application to compress it into a DCR file. This is no longer necessary (or possible) with Shockwave for Director 5.

Compression is handled transparently for the Director author. The Shockwave author need not to do anything special to make use of compression beyond running the finished movie through Afterburner. The Afterburner Xtra must be located inside the Xtras Folder inside the Director 5 Folder. To use Afterburner from within Director 5, just select MacroTools:Afterburner from the Xtras menu.

Inside the Xtras dialog box, you simply select the path and filename. Just as in Afterburner for Director 4, the default filename extension is DCR and the default path is the same folder containing the DIR file.

Note

An interesting side-effect of the open architecture of Shockwave for Director 5 is the possibility for type-specific compression. In addition to the standard Afterburner compression in Shockwave for Director 5—which is a generic lossless compression like StuffIt or PKZip—Afterburner allows for type-specific CODECs to be installed in the form of Xtras. Type-specific compression can achieve much higher compression ratios because it can be tailored to the type of media being compressed.

Rich-Text Formatting (RTF Text)

Shockwave for Director 5 delivers the same support for rich-text formatting (kerning, tracking, line spacing, tabs, and indents) and anti-alias text featured in Director 5. This enables Shockwave authors to enhance the presentation of text elements in their shocked movies.

"Wait for..." Enabled

In Shockwave for Director 4, the "Wait for..." commands in the Tempo channel were disabled. The plug-in ignored any "Wait for..." commands in Shockwave 4, so it was necessary to use Lingo scripts to achieve the same effect. In Shockwave for Director 5, the "Wait for..." Tempo channel commands are enabled, allowing for convenient control of playback.

The Support Folder Architecture

The use of preferences files, Xtras and XObjects, linked media, and external casts is now supported in Shockwave for Director 5. These major enhancements to the Shockwave for Director 5 platform are made possible by the addition of the Support Folder architecture.

File Structure, Security, and Limitations

Linked assets (external casts, Xtras and XObjects, linked media) are still not available to a Shockwave movie from across the network, but now they are available when pre-loaded into the Shockwave Support Folder. Several commands that were completely disabled in Shockwave 4.0 are now available but work only with files pre-loaded into the Support Folder. Despite the Support Folder architecture, certain other limitations still apply in Shockwave for Director 5.

Tip

> Linked assets within the Shockwave Support Folder can be aliases (Macintosh), or shortcuts (Windows), enabling pointers to the actual asset residing in a different location—on a CD-ROM, for example.

The Support Folder Structure

The introduction of the Support Folder structure was conditioned by two major concerns: the problems of network-linked assets and potential security risks on the network. Linked media is still too problematic in a networked environment. It is possible to successfully retrieve the movie, but fail to retrieve the linked media. Until streaming is solved and reasonable ways are found to package together linked media with Shockwave files, linked assets will only be available if they are pre-loaded into the Shockwave Support Folder on the local drive.

The security concern that many corporate sites have about the use of the Internet and the World Wide Web is a more intractable problem. In many companies, there are few, if any, safeguards between their users' computers and the big, scary outside world. The potential for data piracy and/or corruption imposed by a connection to the Internet is a matter of great concern for many corporate systems managers. Much of the appeal of Java, for example, is that it is, in theory, a language with built-in security.

Because Xtras and multiple casts are such an integral part of Director 5, Macromedia was forced, with the release of Shockwave for Director 5, to figure out a way to enable the use of Xtras and multiple casts with a minimum amount of risk. The Support Folder solution, while not satisfactory to anyone, is a fairly reasonable compromise between ease-of-use and security.

On Macintosh, the Shockwave Support Folder is located within the Netscape plug-ins folder and has the same name as the Shockwave plug-in, plus the word "folder." In Windows, the Shockwave Support Folder is a subdirectory within the Netscape plug-ins directory. It has the same name as the plug-in, minus the extension (DLL).

When a Shockwave movie looks for a linked asset, it disregards all asset location information except the filename, and looks only within the plug-in support folder for the asset.

The downside of this structure is that the user must manually download all the linked assets into the Support Folder. The theory behind this mechanism seems to be that the user, by explicitly downloading the linked asset, rather than having it automatically download, is agreeing to trust the website.

Therefore, if any damage results, the user has only himself or the website to blame, and not Macromedia. It should be said that, though limiting file operations to the Support Folder is not an ultimate protection against unscrupulous Xtras, it does create a barrier seriously narrowing the range of possible mischief.

Security

A normal Director movie is capable of doing many things that could harm or infect the host machine. For example, it is unfortunately not very difficult to write an Xtra that would do real damage by deleting files or something of the like. The Shockwave for Director 4 plug-in simply disabled these features, such as file I/O commands, in order to protect the user. The following facilities were completely disabled in Shockwave for Director 4:

- XObject, XCMDs, and XFCNs in the movie itself
- The FileIO XObject
- The SerialIO XObject
- The OrthoPlay XObject
- The `MCI` command
- The `restart` and `shutdown` commands
- The `open`, `openDA`, and `closeDA` commands
- The `open window` and `close window` commands
- The `saveMovie` command
- The filename and path properties and functions `fileName of window`, `getNthFileNameInFolder`, `moviePath`, `pathName`, `searchCurrentFolder`, and `searchPaths`
- The `printFrom` command
- The `pasteClipboardInto member x of castLib y` command

In addition, the `quit` command stops the movie rather than quitting the application.

In Shockwave for Director 5, many of these features are re-enabled; however, their function is limited to operations within the Support Folder only. This is the compromise that Macromedia's designers struck to balance the need to support Director 5 features while maintaining network security.

Limitations

The Shockwave for Director 5 plug-in implements most of the functionality available in a Director projector. There are, however, some limitations:

- No linked media except when pre-loaded into the Shockwave Support Folder.
- No movie in a window. This was too difficult to implement under Windows, so it was disabled Shockwave on both platforms. This feature may be available in some future version.
- Custom menus are not available in Shockwave for Director.

Get and Save Preferences

One of the nagging limitations of Shockwave has been the lack of persistent state information. There are certain situations in which we would like the Shockwave movie to store information so that after the user leaves the movie and then returns, it remembers things about them. This could be information about the user, where they left off last, and so on. For example, a Shockwave game with persistent state capability could remember your high scores.

Shockwave for Director 5 offers two solutions to the state problem. External parameters is a solution discussed in detail later in this chapter. Using external parameters enables a server-side database to maintain state information for all registered users and pass that information into and out of the movie.

The second solution to the state problem is to store state information locally on the user's hard drive. Because file I/O was enabled within the Support Folder in Shockwave for Director 5, it became practical for Macromedia to provide a system for reading and writing a preferences file locally. This enables you to create titles with persistent state.

Using Preferences

Two new functions in Shockwave for Director 5 let you control preferences files: `setPref` and `getPref`.

The function `setPref prefName, prefValue` writes the `prefValue` string to a text file on the local hard drive. The `prefName` must be a valid filename, minus extension, for whatever system the title is designed to run on. To be safe, you should limit the name to 8 alphanumeric characters.

If no prefs filename matches the name specified, Shockwave for Director 5 creates a new text file inside the Preferences Folder within the Support Folder. If no Preferences Folder exists, Shockwave for Director 5 creates one.

The second function, `getPref(prefName)`, gets the `prefName` file from the local drive and returns the `prefValue` that was previously saved. If there is no file matching `prefName`, then `getPref` returns void. The `prefName` must be a valid filename, minus extension, for whatever system the title is designed run on.

EXAMPLE 5.1

Preferences in Practice

We have made a simple example movie that saves the user's name to the local hard drive. Using Netscape, open the file TESTPREF.HTM, located in the Chapter 5 folder in the accompanying CD. The movie has a text field in which you type your name (see fig. 5.1).

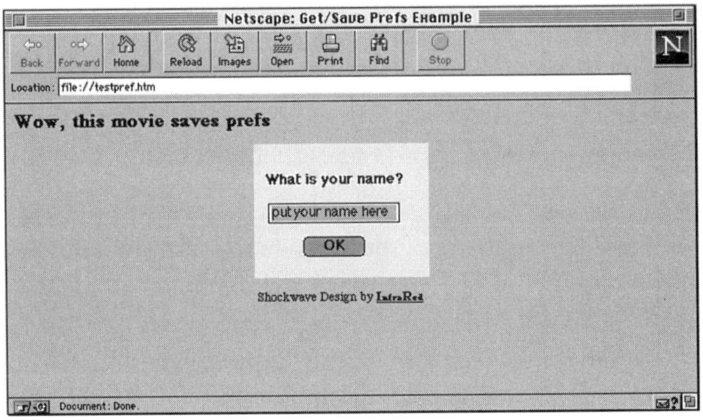

FIGURE 5.1

State information, such as the user's name, can be stored locally in a prefs file.

When you run TESTPREF.HTM, it looks for a prefs file. On the first go-around there is no user name yet saved in the prefs file. The movie has been scripted to ask you for your name. If you open the Director file TESTPREF.DIR in Director 5, you see the simple score script in frame 1, which uses the getPrefs command to read the prefs file:

```
on exitFrame
  set x to getPref("testpref")
  if voidp(x) then
    put "put your name here" into field "userName"
    go "changeName"
  else
    put x into field "userName"
    go "greeting"
  end if
end
```

The script reads the prefs file called TESTPREF.TXT from disk and passes the value into x. If the prefs file didn't exist, then it sends you to the "changeName" frame. Otherwise it passes your name into the text field and then goes to the "greeting" frame.

In Netscape, when you first type your name and click OK, the movie saves your name locally to the Support Folder (see fig. 5.2). You can confirm that a file called TESTPREF.TXT now exists in the Prefs Folder in the Support Folder on your hard drive.

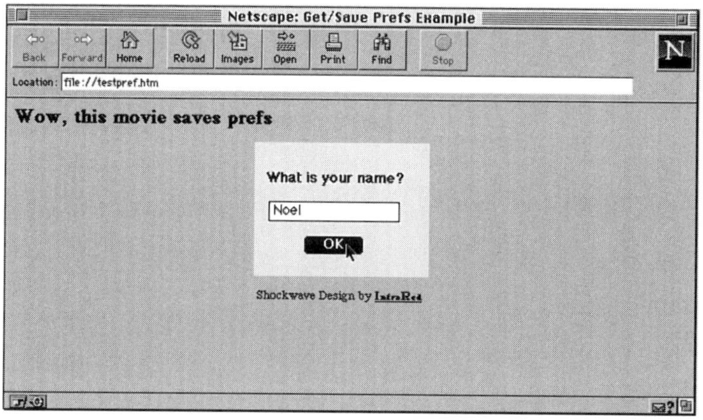

FIGURE 5.2

Type your name and click OK to save to the prefs file. Your name is now contained in the file TESTPREF.TXT on your hard drive.

In the movie, the cast script of the OK button is responsible for saving your name to the prefs file:

```
on mouseUp
  set x = the text of field "userName"
  setPref "testpref",x
  go "Cool"
end mouseUp
```

When you click on OK, the text you type is saved off to the TESTPREF.TXT file on your hard drive. Then the movie sends you to the "Cool" frame.

The next time you load the file TESTPREF.HTM in Netscape it remembers who you are (see fig. 5.3).

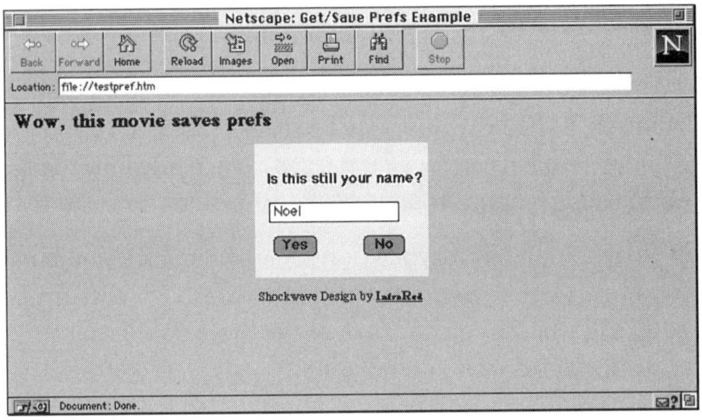

FIGURE 5.3

When you return to the page, the Shockwave movie remembers your name as stored in the prefs file.

Now you are asked if you want to change your name. Try changing your name and reloading the page. In the Netscape browser, hit the Reload button (or select Reload from the View Menu). When the movie reloads, your newest name appears.

This is only a bare-bones look at the possibilities of Get/Save Prefs in Shockwave for Director 5. A more in-depth discussion on designing with prefs can be found online from the "Shockwave Power Solutions" page at the New Riders website at `http://www.mcp.com/newriders`.

Xtras in Shockwave for Director 5

One of the major new features introduced to Director 5 is the Xtra technology. Xtras are the key to Director 5's open architecture. Xtras represent a major advance for Director 5, enabling developers to extend the functionality of Director.

Shockwave support for Xtras enables developers to take advantage of the broad range of Lingo, transition, and tool Xtras being created for Director 5 and the Macromedia Open Architecture. In the future, developers can look forward to the release of Xtras targeted at the needs of Shockwave developers—for example, Xtras that offer support for streaming audio and video.

The Four Types of Xtras

In Director 5, there are four types of Xtras.

- **Cast Member Xtras.** These are objects that can be inserted into a Director movie. In most cases, the Xtra must be present for the movie to properly interpret the cast member. An example of this type of Xtra would be one that lets the Director Developer insert a 3D object into the cast.
- **Transition Xtras.** These enable custom transitions that may be more interesting than the ones included in Director. If the transition Xtra is not present, Shockwave ignores the transition. An example of this Xtra is The Bytes, which is included on the Director 5 CD.
- **Lingo Xtras.** These allow the addition of custom functionality to Director. These Xtras can do almost anything a stand-alone program can do. If the Xtra is not present, Director or Shockwave returns a Lingo error. An example of this type is the FileFlex Xtra included with Director. These Xtras are analogous to the XObjects of Director 4 and earlier.
- **Tool Xtras.** These are used at authoring time to provide the developer with additional functionality. These Xtras are not needed at runtime. An example of this kind of Xtra is Afterburner.

XObjects also work if placed in the Support Folder and opened with the `openXLib` command. They work on both Macintosh and Windows.

Using Xtras with Shockwave

Because Xtras are essentially stand-alone chunks of code, they represent a potential security risk on the Internet. Macromedia Xtras are built in C or C++. These languages have no security, and because of the very nature of Xtras, Macromedia cannot limit their functionality in any way. These factors combine to make Xtras a potential agent of serious security problems. It would be reasonably easy, for example, for a programmer to create an Xtra that collected a list of every file on your hard drive and mailed it somewhere. For this reason, Macromedia has taken a very conservative attitude toward making sure that this risk is minimized. What that means is that for anyone to use a Shockwave for Director file that relies on an Xtra, they must already have the Xtra downloaded into the Support Folder.

One exciting example of using Xtras in Shockwave is the ShockTalk Xtra, a voice recognition Xtra made by Digital Dreams. ShockTalk makes it possible to post Shockwave movies that utilize a voice recognition interface—such as quiz games. The killer app for ShockTalk is a DCR movie that enables users to navigate hyperlinks by voice command. Currently, ShockTalk runs on the Mac only.

Using Linked Media and External Casts

This section discusses the use of linked media and external casts. For a more in-depth discussion of external casts, see Chapter 9, "External Casts."

Linked Media

In the world of unshocked Director, you can use linked media for a variety of purposes. For instance, QuickTime movies are only available as linked media—they cannot be contained within the Director file itself. Or, you might use linked bitmaps to facilitate the swapping in of finished artwork.

In the context of the Web, the primary reason to use linked media with Shockwave is to deliver prohibitively large media files such as digital video and audio by CD-ROM and deliver the small part of the movie over the Net. To use linked media in Shockwave for Director 5, just check the "Linked" box when you import. Save and burn as usual. All path information is discarded when you burn the movie. The Shockwave plug-in will only look in the Support Folder for any linked media in your movie.

The main hurdle for the user is to properly install the linked media into the Support Folder. They can either move the media to the support folder, or create pointers to the media with aliases (Macintosh) or shortcuts (Windows). Remember to warn users not to change the filenames of any linked media in the Support Folder. For commercial hybrid CD-ROM Web titles, you should provide a special installer to automate this potentially frustrating installation process.

Here is a brief example of a linked QuickTime movie. In Netscape, open the file LINKTST1.HTM from the accompanying CD. If you have not copied the QuickTime file PNEUMO.MOV or created a pointer from the CD to the Support folder, nothing will appear in the Shockwave window on the page. If you did copy or make a pointer, then you will see the link as pictured in figure 5.4.

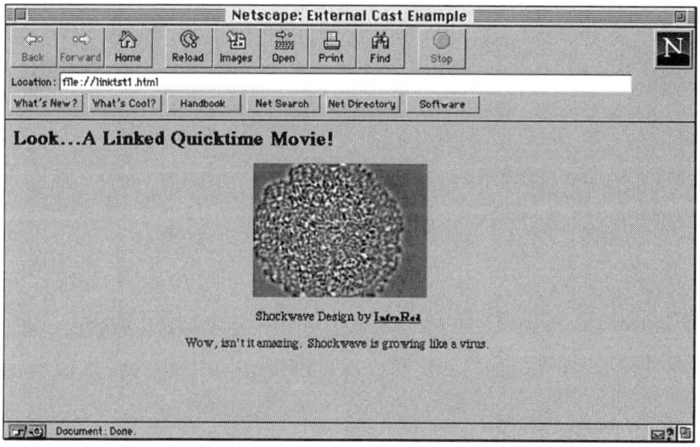

FIGURE 5.4

Linked media enables you to deliver hybrid CD-ROM/Web titles. Monster-sized media types like digital video and audio are delivered on the CD-ROM and other parts are delivered over the Web.

External Casts

Shockwave for Director 5 enables you to use multiple casts in your designs. In Shockwave for Director 5 these multiple casts can be downloaded separately and stored in the Shockwave Support Folder. Once installed, Shockwave movies can access different cast alternatives based on a user's selection while interacting with the movie. By taking advantage of multiple casts, authors can incorporate score templates into the design of their content, which enhances your users' interactivity and offers you improved development efficiency.

Here is a brief example of a movie that uses an external cast to store a bitmap animation. If you copy the external cast file EXTERN2.CST from the accompanying CD into your Shockwave Support Folder (or put a pointer to EXTERN2.CST) then you can open the file LINKTST2.HTM in Netscape and see the movie pictured in figure 5.5. To create an external cast in Director 5, just select File: New: Cast. Make sure the correct external cast window is active when you import the desired media.

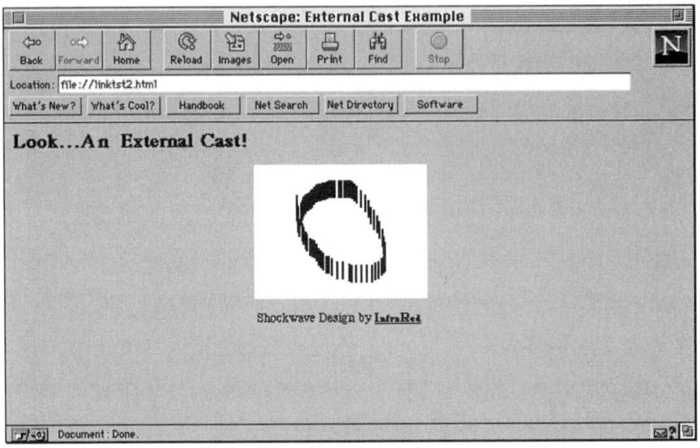

FIGURE 5.5

This movie uses an external cast to hold the animated bitmap. The external cast must be located in the Shockwave Support Folder to be accessed by Shockwave.

Finally, linked media can be referenced by an external cast as well. If you copy the external cast file extern3.cst and the QuickTime movie PENPOP.MOV from the accompanying CD into your Shockwave Support Folder (or put a pointer to EXTERN3.CST and PENPOP.MOV), then you can open the file LINKTST3.HTM in Netscape and see the movie pictured in figure 5.6. To use linked media in an external cast, you simply check the "Linked" box in the import dialog box when you import media into an external cast.

For a more in-depth discussion of external casts, see Chapter 9, "External Casts."

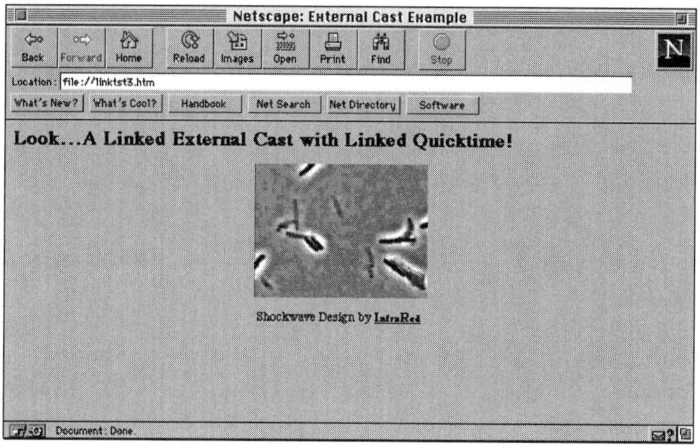

FIGURE 5.6

This movie has linked media in an external cast.

Net Lingo Features

Shockwave for Director 5 provides access to the variety of new Lingo extensions available with Director 5, with the exception of commands and expressions disabled to ensure "safe playback" over the network.

Several new commands are available for accessing the network from Director Lingo scripts. This section lists each of these new commands and functions and explains their use. Most of the commands listed here were also available in Shockwave for Director 4. We pay closer attention to the Net Lingo new in Shockwave for Director 5—namely, frame targeting and writing to the status line.

Summary of Net Lingo

Because the network is essentially an asynchronous place—that is, it takes time to get things from the Net, and in the meantime, Director can continue to interact with the user—most of the network commands involve starting an operation, checking to see whether it has completed, and then getting the results. This is different from most Lingo commands, which immediately return the result.

Four commands are available to start asynchronous operations:

- `GotoNetMovie uri`
- `GotoNetPage uri, target`
- `GetNetText uri`
- `PreloadNetThing uri`

`GotoNetMovie uri` retrieves and goes to a new Director movie from the network. The new movie occupies the same display area as the calling movie. The `uri` parameter is a universal resource identifier that specifies the HTTP item containing the movie. At present, only HTTP URLs are supported as valid `uri` parameters.

`GotoNetPage uri`, target opens an arbitrary URI. This opens a new page within the net browser. The target parameter is optional. If present, it specifies the target frame or window by name, or is one of the special values allowed by browsers for frame targeting (see the Netscape release notes on targeting windows for details).

Note

> If the "*target*" parameter is not an exact match for the name of a frame, it instead opens a new window with that name.

`GetNetText uri` starts the retrieval of an HTTP item, to be read by Lingo as text. The `uri` parameter is a universal resource identifier that specifies the HTTP item to be retrieved. At present, only HTTP URLs are supported as valid `uri` parameters. For a more in-depth discussion of `getNetText`, see Chapter 11, "Linked Text."

`PreloadNetThing uri` starts pre-loading an HTTP item into the local file cache. The `uri` parameter is a universal resource identifier that specifies the HTTP item to be referenced. This can be anything, including a director movie, an HTML page, a graphic image, and so forth. At present, only HTTP URLs are supported as valid `uri` parameters.

In general, an item that has been pre-loaded can be accessed immediately, because it is taken from the local disk cache rather than the network.

However, it is impossible to determine when an item may be removed from the local disk cache.

Two functions allow a Lingo script to determine the state of the asynchronous operation:

- **`NetDone()`.** This function returns true when the asynchronous network operation is finished. Until that point, it returns false.
- **`NetError()`.** This function returns the empty string until the asynchronous network operation is finished. Then it returns OK if the operation completed successfully, or a string describing the error if it failed to complete successfully.

Once an asynchronous operation has finished, three functions are available to retrieve the results:

- **`NetTextResult()`.** This function returns the text result of the operation. For a GetNetText operation, this is the text of the HTTP item.
- **`NetMIME()`.** This function returns the MIME type of the HTTP item.
- **`NetLastModDate()`.** This function returns the last modified date string from the HTTP header for the item.

One command can be used to abort a network operation in progress:

- **`NetAbort`.** This command aborts a network operation without waiting for a result.

Note, however, that the `NetTextResult()`, `NetMIME()`, `NetLastModDate()`, and `NetAbort` functions can only be called from the time `NetDone()` or `NetError()` reports that the operation is complete until the next operation is started. Once the next operation is started, we discard the results of the previous operation in order to preserve memory space.

It is possible to have more than one operation active at a time. When two operations are started, the Lingo script needs a way to identify them. After an operation is started, and until the next operation is begun, the function `GetLatestNetID()` can be called to retrieve a unique identifier for that operation.

`GetLatestNetID()` returns a unique identifier for the last asynchronous operation that was started. The unique identifier returned by `GetLatestNetID()` can be used by any of the following functions: `NetDone()`, `NetError()`, `NetTextResult()`, `NetMIME()`, `NetLastModDate()`, and, as an optional parameter, `NetAbort`. If your movie uses several simultaneous asynchronous operations, you may want to maintain a running list of NetIDs so you can identify and control outstanding Net operations.

Frame Targeting

The capability of displaying multiple frames on the same page—introduced in Netscape Navigator 2.0—is one of the more controversial of Netscape's unilateral additions to HTML. Many people feel that frames are distracting and unnecessary. Other people swear by them.

One of Macromedia's biggest mistakes in version 4 of Shockwave for Director was not anticipating the popularity of frames. To be fair, frames were only a gleam in Netscape's eye at that time, and nobody knew how popular they would be. Although Shockwave for Director 4 movies run just fine within frames, they do not have the ability to target frames. Developers have been forced to work around this limitation with awkward contraptions involving JavaScript, CGI, and the like.

Using Frame Targeting

Macromedia has corrected this limitation in Shockwave for Director 5. The plug-in can now load various pages into alternate frames on the screen, and can even address multiple windows. The following section briefly touches on how to deal with frames, but for a more detailed look at frame targeting, see Chapter 10, "Working with Frames."

```
GotoNetPage uri, target
```

`GotoNetPage uri, target`, enables you to use the frame targetting via the optional second argument. The target parameter is the frame or window name in which you want the page to be loaded.

Here are some examples of calling a frame target:

- "frame2" loads NEWPAGE.HTML into the frame (or window) named "frame2," replacing whatever used to be there. See the following:

  ```
  GotoNetPage "NEWPAGE.HTML"
  ```

- "_blank" creates a new window containing NEWWIN.HTML. See the following:

  ```
  GotoNetPage "NEWWIN.HTML"
  ```

- "win" loads THIRD.HTML into the window named "win." If "win" doesn't exist, a new window named "win" will be created. See the following:

  ```
  GotoNetPage "THIRD.HTML"
  ```

Note that this does not provide for communication between movies. All it can do is cause a new page (html file, director movie, and so on) to be loaded into the target frame or window, replacing whatever used to be there.

Frame Targeting in Practice

Frame targeting facilitates the use of Shockwave for perpetual navigation bars. For example, a site might load up one frame with a fancy Shockwave menu. When you press one of those nice multimedia navigation buttons, a new HTML document is loaded into another frame on the page. The Shockwave movie stays perpetual—never unloading or reloading—as it controls the flow of HTML through the other frames.

A real-world example of frames implementation is shown in the California State Automobile Association's Shockwave sitemap (see fig. 5.7). When you "drive" to the different parts of the site, some descriptive text is loaded into the left-hand frame. This lets the user keep the same Web page open longer, anchoring the Shockwave visually and keeping it in RAM longer. It also defeats the problem of double downloads caused by cache cleanup wiping out the Shockwave file. This movie was created by DXM and is discussed in greater detail in Chapter 16, "True Multimedia on the Web: DXM."

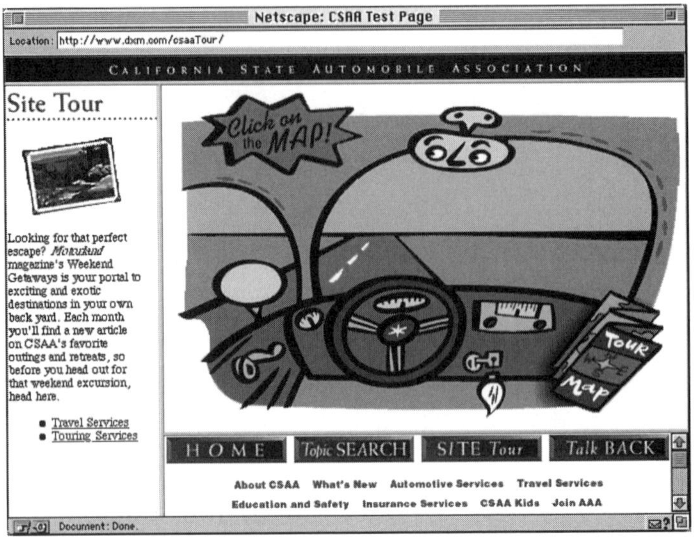

FIGURE 5.7
The CSAA site tour uses frames to provide text information about the different parts of the site. You can view this site on DXM's site at http://www.dxm.com/csaaTour/.

In the case of a sitemap, using frames had the side benefit of enabling viewers to preview the branching before committing to a new download.

Writing to the Status Line

In Shockwave for Director 5, a new function is available to set the text in the status area of the browser:

```
netStatus msg
```

This command sets the status area of the browser window to msg.

Status Line in Practice

The `netStatus` command can enable a convenient way to build "balloon help" guides into your interface. You also can use `netStatus` to implement the classic use of the status line—to show the URL name of the hyperlink under the pointer.

We have an example that does both. In Netscape, open the file STATUS.HTM, which can be found in the Chapter 5 folder of the accompanying CD. The movie has three buttons, each with a different click action (see fig. 5.8). Two buttons are for navigation and the third triggers a "beep" sound. All three buttons have a unique status message when the pointer has rolled over them.

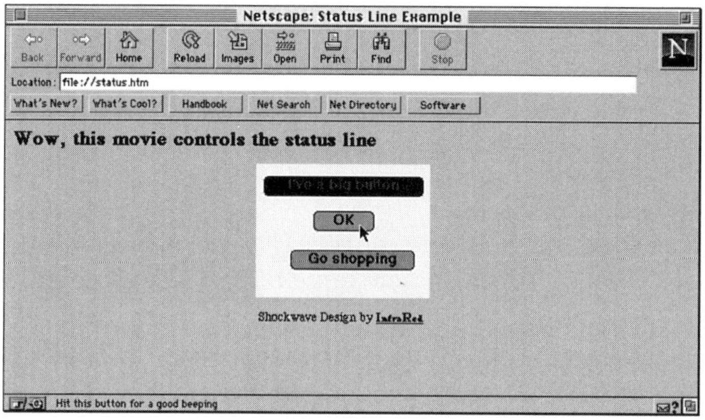

FIGURE 5.8

Rolling over one of these buttons causes a message to appear in the status line.

The source Director 5 file called STATUS.DIR has a specific arrangement to make it work. In it, the buttons occupy the first three slots in the internal cast to facilitate identification of the cast member under the pointer. For convenience, the status message text for each button is located in the names of the button cast members, enabling both a single and simple script to be used to shoot the correct text to the status line, no matter how many buttons we have.

The status line is controlled with the following score script:

```
on exitFrame
  set mCast = the mouseCast
  if mCast > 0 and mCast < 4 then --over a button
    put the name of cast mCast into x
    netStatus x
  else
    netStatus " "
  end if
  go the frame - 1
end
```

When the script executes, it passes the number of the cast under the pointer into the variable mCast. Our three buttons occupy the cast positions numbered 1 through 3. As a result, if the value of mCast is between 0 and 4, then the pointer is over a button. The name of the button cast under the pointer is placed into the browser's status line using the `netStatus` command. If the pointer is not over a button, then the status line is set blank.

New Embed Attributes

When a Shockwave file is invoked from within HTML, it is specified with an `<embed>` tag. Shockwave for Director 5 now supports two new attributes within the `<embed>` tag: the BGCOLOR attribute lets you control the movie's background color while it downloads, and external parameters can be passed into the Shockwave movie from the `<embed>` tag.

Background Color Control

Between the time the Shockwave plug-in is loaded and the movie has been downloaded and started, a blank rectangle with a Macromedia logo is displayed. In 4.0, this area was always white. In 5, it is possible to select the color to be displayed by setting the BGCOLOR attribute in the `<embed>` tag:

```
<EMBED src="movie.dcr" BGCOLOR=#FF0000>
```

The color is specified as a hexadecimal RGB number, with the first two digits setting the red color component, the second two digits setting the green component, and the last two digits setting the blue component. The color specified in the example above would be pure red.

Background Color in Practice

To see an example that uses the BGCOLOR attribute in the `<embed>` tag, open the file BGCOLOR.HTM from the Chapter 5 folder of the accompanying CD. The page is red, and so is the Shockwave window during the download (see fig. 5.9).

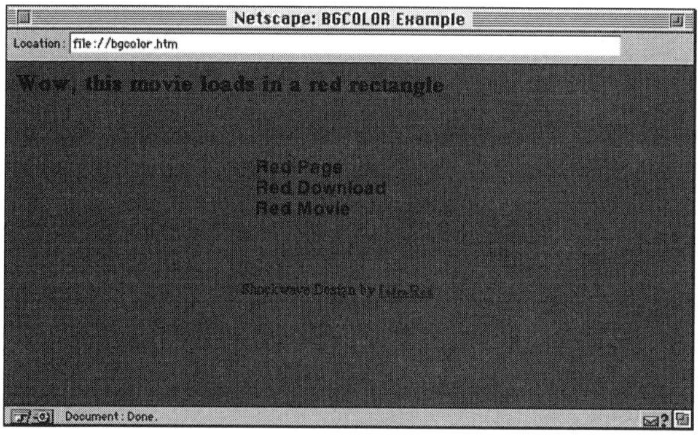

FIGURE 5.9

You can set the background color of the Shockwave window during the download.

The BGCOLOR attribute uses the same color encoding scheme as standard HTML uses (for example, setting the BGCOLOR attribute in the `<body>` tag). This conveniently enables you to use the same hex number for setting both the BODY BGCOLOR and the EMBED BGCOLOR. The example file BGCOLOR.HTM contains the following lines:

```
<body BGCOLOR="FF0000">
<embed src="bgcolor.dcr" height=120 width=460 BGCOLOR=#FF0000>
```

Also notice that we set the background color of the movie itself to red to match the page once it is downloaded. In Director 5, you set the stage color in the Movie Properties dialog box (see fig. 5.10), displayed by selecting Movie: Properties from the Modify menu.

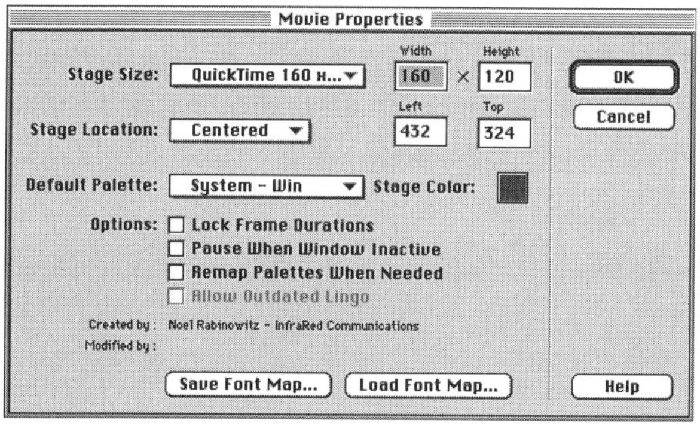

FIGURE 5.10

Setting the stage color of a Director 5 movie is done in the Movie Properties dialog box.

External Parameters

Earlier in this chapter, we saw how saving a preferences file can enable you to maintain state information and pass it into and out of the Shockwave for Director 5 movie. External parameters can be used to achieve similar goals.

An arbitrary number of optional external parameters can be passed into the Shockwave movie from the outside world when the movie loads. This powerful new feature enables you to create smarter, more flexible movies that playback differently depending on external factors. Parameters are passed into the movie by the `<embed>` tag.

Parameter passing is examined in greater detail in Chapter 12, "Talking with the Outside World: Parameters and JavaScript."

The <embed> Syntax to Pass Parameters into Shockwave

Within the `<embed>` tag, external parameters have the general form of name=value, where the =value portion is optional. In the example below, the optional parameter is named, aptly enough, parameter. The parameter value can be a string (as denoted by the "" marks):

```
<embed src="parametr.dcr" height=120 width=160 parameter="beep">
```

Or, the external parameter value can be an integer, as in this example:

```
<embed src="pramint.dcr" height=120 width=160 parameter=3>
```

The Net Lingo to Access Parameters

To access the values of the external parameters within your Shockwave file, you use the following Net Lingo functions.

```
the externalParamCount
```

This function returns the number of external parameters that were passed in from the `<embed>` tag.

```
externalParamName(n)
```

If *n* is an integer, this function returns the nth parameter name from the external parameter list. If *n* is a string and if any of the external parameter names matches *n* (case-insensitive), then this function returns *n*. If there is no such parameter name on the list, externalParamName returns void.

```
externalParamValue(n)
```

If n is an integer, this function returns the value of the *n*th parameter from the external parameter list. If *n* is a string, this function returns the value associated with the first parameter whose name matches *n* (case-insensitive). If there is no such parameter value, `externalParamValue` returns void.

External Parameters in Practice

We present a few very simple examples to demonstrate the principle of external parameters in Shockwave. The first movie called PARAMETR.DIR from the Chapter 5 folder of the accompanying CD has the following handler in a score script in the first frame:

```
on exitFrame
  if externalParamName("parameter") = "parameter" then
    set x = externalParamValue("parameter")
    if x = "beep" then
      beep
    end if
    put x into field "Fred"
    UpdateStage
  end if
end
```

The first line checks that an external parameter named "parameter" has indeed been passed into the movie. Then it checks to see if the value was the string "beep," in which case it beeps. Then it updates the text field called "Fred" to display the parameter value.

To demonstrate, we have two HTML files that embed the Shockwave movie PARAMETR.DCR. Each one calls the movie with different parameters, yielding different behavior. Opening the file called PARAMETR.HTM in Netscape yields the result shown in figure 5.11.

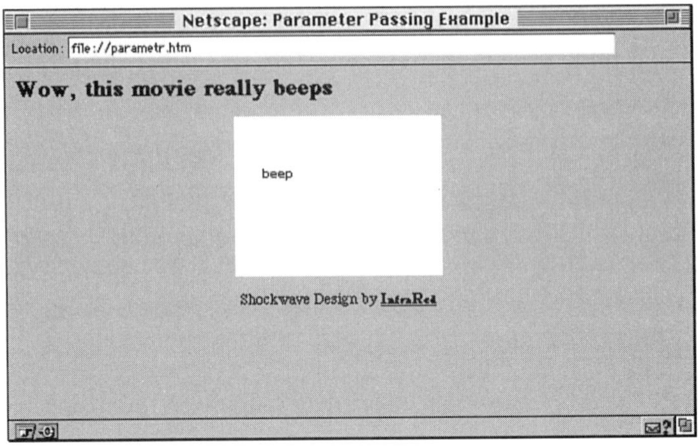

FIGURE 5.11

In PARAMETR.HTM, the external parameter is set to "beep." The movie PARAMETR.DCR responds by beeping.

The `embed` line in PARAMETR.HTM reads as follows:

```
<embed src="parametr.dcr" height=120 width=160 parameter="beep">
```

Yet opening the file PARAMET2.HTM in Netscape yields an entirely different result, shown in figure 5.12.

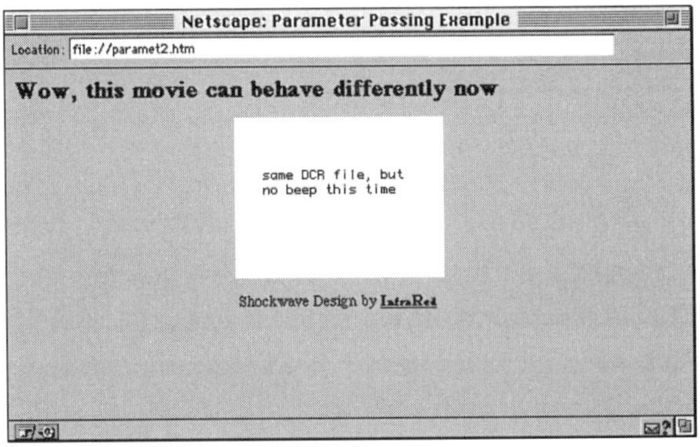

FIGURE 5.12

In PARAMET2.HTM, the external parameter is set to the string "same DCR file, but no beep this time." The movie PARAMETR.DCR responds by not beeping.

The `embed` line in paramet2.htm reads as follows:

```
<embed src="parametr.dcr" height=120 width=160 parameter="same DCR
➥file, but no beep this time">
```

The final example demonstrates the possibility of passing an integer value instead of a string. Open the file PRAMINT.HTM in Netscape and the movie PRAMINT.DCR beeps three times in response to the parameter passed as follows:

```
<embed src="pramint.dcr" height=120 width=160 parameter=3>
```

The profound usefulness of parameter passing may not be immediately obvious. You can begin to see the glimmer of usefulness in Chapter 12, "Talking with the Outside World: Parameters and JavaScript," which shows an example of a Shockwave movie that pulls in various information provided by the user in an HTML form. Of course, even in the example from Chapter 12, the querying could have all been done from inside the Director movie itself. So why bother?

The real power of parameter passing is unlocked when it is used in conjunction with server-side intelligence. In the case of Action Technologies (see Chapter 18, "Advanced Applications: Action Technologies' Metro") Shockwave is used to provide a rich media front end for their Metro workflow management product. The server knows all kinds of relevant information about the state of affairs for each user. External parameters offer a gateway through which we can pass that state information from the server into the Shockwave movie.

The server-side can be programmed with CGI scripts to pass the key information via parameters when it spits out HTML on the fly. The Shockwave movie can be scripted to respond to the external parameters in any number of ways. This represents an immediate advance in the level of functionality that can be achieved with Shockwave.

For example, one could exploit external parameters to create a Shockwave gaming tournament where many users compete for high scores. Each user's name and statistics would be registered on the server's database. Each time you logged in to play a game, your game would be customized according to your name, track record, skill level, and so forth. When you were done with the game, the Shockwave movie would communicate your score and everything else back to a CGI script.

All of this could be accomplished with a goToNetPage command which would pass the information to CGI via the URI in much the same way that HTML forms can be used to submit a search string to a database. When the CGI script gets the information from the Shockwave movie, it can update the server-side database accordingly, and a powerful networked gaming environment is established.

Conclusion

Shockwave for Director 5 offers a multitude of powerful new options for Shockwave developers. In this Chapter we covered the major new features and some simple example applications. See Part V, "Shockwave Solutions," for further discussion of design issues and real examples of new features in Director. See Part III, "Advanced Shockwave for Director," for a deeper discussion on using the new features.

The basic structural changes in the Shockwave for Director feature set comes from the addition of the Support Folder architecture. The Support Folder enables the use of external assets in the form of Xtras, linked media, external casts and locally saved prefernces files. The use of Xtras enables inclusion of customized functions that extend the functionality of Shockwave. Linked media and external casts enable hybrid CD-ROM/Web titles. The use of preferences enables customized user experiences with state memory.

With the addition of the Support Folder architecture, we see Shockwave for Director taking on more flexibility and power. Additional power is obtained with external parameters. External parameters enable your movies to interact with the user and with server-side databases, passing information into the movie at load time. Parameters enable a high degree of customizability, deeper interactivity and move Shockwave more towards becoming a reasonable way to provide client-side intelligence.

The main constraint of using external parameters now is the fact that data is passed through the HTML `<embed>` tag—during the movie load only. Note that in the future, these same external parameter functions may enable access to parameters within other operating environments. As compound application environments mature (such as LiveConnect, ActiveX, OpenDoc, and so on), the external parameter functions will likely be adapted to enable general external parameter access, not just HTML tag access. Realtime parameter access in Shockwave will represent a large quantum leap in the power of the applications that can be created with Shockwave.

Of course, as we all figure out how to best use the new features in Shockwave for Director 5, we look forward to the newer and even more powerful features in store for us in the future.

CHAPTER 6

Shockwave for FreeHand

In this chapter we take on another flavor of Shockwave: Shockwave for FreeHand. This Shockwave for FreeHand primer is constructed in six parts:

- *Explaining Shockwave for FreeHand*
- *Advantages of Shockwave for FreeHand*
- *Solutions with Shockwave for FreeHand*
- *Getting started with FreeHand*
- *Web-specific issues with FreeHand*
- *The Shocking parts of FreeHand*

An Explanation of Shockwave for FreeHand

Shockwave for FreeHand enables you to embed FreeHand graphics images directly into the Web page. Like Shockwave for Director and Authorware, Shockwave for FreeHand has its own file compression utility, also called Afterburner. Similarly, playback or display of Shockwave for FreeHand files is handled by a Shockwave plug-in to Netscape 2.0 or greater. The plug-in will be available for other popular browsers in the near future.

FreeHand, itself, is a popular illustration program comparable to Illustrator or CorelDraw!. With these drawing programs, you create illustrations by manipulating drawing objects such as lines, circles, curves, and so on. Because drawing applications use objects, they enable you to create editable, precise, scaleable, and mathematically compact representations of visual images. This distinguishes them from painting applications such as Photoshop or PhotoStyler, which enable you to manipulate images pixel by pixel.

FreeHand provides powerful control over the drawing objects, or vector graphics. Simple shapes and complicated curves can be created. Line weight and color can be controlled. Objects can be filled with patterns, gradients, and so on. Objects can be scaled, rotated, distorted, grouped, and layered. FreeHand has sophisticated text handling features. And this only scratches the surface of FreeHand's power as a vector-based illustration tool.

Note

In mathematics, a *vector* is a point in space with more than one dimension. Vectors can represent points in a physical space or a function space—a space of mathematical functions. A vector describes not only a quantity, but it also "points" in a definite direction. The speed of your car, for example, is just a one-dimensional number that calculates the total miles traveled per hour, regardless of direction. But the velocity of your car is a two-dimensional vector that calculates both its speed (mph) and direction (degrees from due North).

In drawing programs, individual visual objects are vectors in drawing space. *Drawing space* is the mathematical space spanning the functions that describe all the supported drawn objects. The *vector* is the set of parameters that describe the drawn object, or "point" to the object in the space of drawing functions. In a drawing program, for example, an entire circle can be described by a vector of just three parameters (horizontal location, vertical location, and radius). Additional parameters can be added to the circle's vector, including line stroke width, color of line stroke, color of fill, fill pattern, layer priority, and so on.

Parameterized graphics are inherently compact. The amount of information needed to represent complex objects made up of many pixels like circles, lines, squares, and curves are drastically reduced when these objects are described by vectors. Because the objects are vectors in a function space, it is not necessary to describe every pixel in the image. This brings a great potential for bandwidth savings with vector graphics and Shockwave for FreeHand.

Now in its fifth version, FreeHand's mature and cross-platform code base help make it suitable for porting to the Web environment as a Netscape plug-in. FreeHand is appreciated by designers especially for its fast screen refresh performance in preview mode. This same fast previewing engine is what makes Shockwave for FreeHand an efficient Web plug-in for displaying vectored graphics.

The Advantages of Shockwave for FreeHand

Putting FreeHand graphics on the Web can give your images more communicating power. The following sections discuss three main advantages of creating Web images in Shockwave for FreeHand: scalability, compact file sizes, and the capability to include embedded links.

Scaleable Images

Shockwave for FreeHand images are scaleable. The user can zoom deep into the illustration with just a mouse click, revealing new information in different scales. Scalability, for example, enables you to create an attractive graphic with text information presented at a very scaled down size. This enables you to separate the context from the content. If the user is intrigued by the context, then he can zoom in to get the content. The detailed information is right there, and the user need not link to yet another URL.

The graphic of the "Lotsa Pasta" restaurant's menu, taken from the sample artwork that comes with FreeHand, has been redesigned for Shockwave for

FreeHand (evidence of scaleable viewing on the Web). This image has important information presented at two levels of scaling. The context is set by the large scale design. There is an attractive image, showing a beautiful plate of food, and the title text (see fig. 6.1). One also can clearly see that there is detailed information at a smaller scale.

FIGURE 6.1

This is an imaginary online advertisement for a restaurant done in Shockwave for FreeHand. The large scale of the image is designed to whet your appetite.

The "fine print" information may be easily accessed by the user zooming in with a simple key-and-mouse combination. Zooming in reveals the text of the dishes on the menu at Lotsa Pasta (see fig. 6.2). This scaling gives you more creative options for presenting information in a digestible form. To view this file in FreeHand, open the file PASTA.FH5 located in the Chapter 6 folder on the accompanying CD.

In Shockwave for FreeHand, the image quality does not suffer when scaling in or out. With bitmapped images such as GIFs or JPGs, you cannot scale them up in size too much before image degradation becomes unbearable. This is like the difference between scaling up the font size of screen fonts (bitmapped) as compared to outline fonts in PostScript or TrueType (vectored). At large sizes, a bitmapped screen font becomes jagged and illegible, but an outline font scales smoothly.

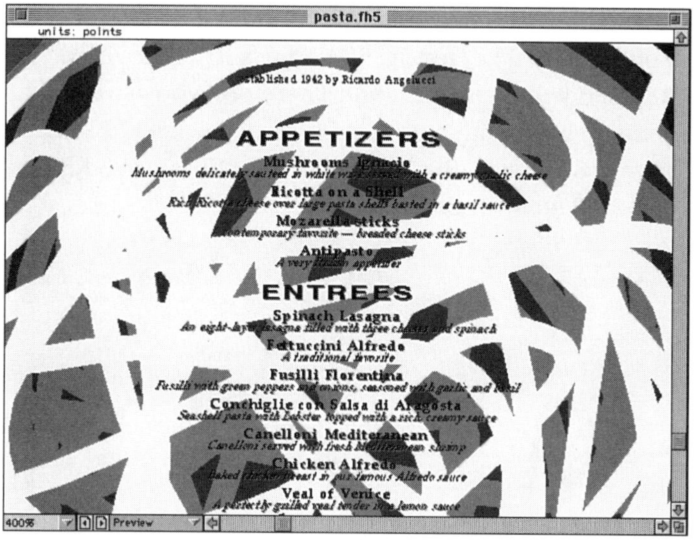

FIGURE 6.2

Zooming into the Festa di Pasta image reveals the delicious dishes on the menu.

Scalability at full resolution is made possible by the vectored (parameterized) nature of Shockwave for FreeHand. The complex outlines of vectored curves, called Bézier curves or béziegons, are mathematically generated based on their anchor points, or handles. Therefore, they can be rendered at any desired resolution or scale. Figure 6.3 shows the Bézier curve of a pretzel. The entire complex shape is generated based upon just five anchor points.

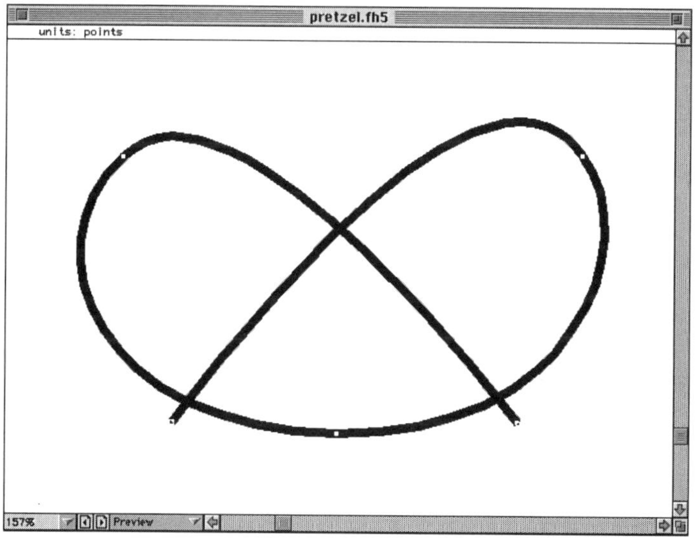

FIGURE 6.3

Whole complex shapes are described with just a few anchor points in a Bézier curve. This pretzel shape is described by just five points.

By adjusting the handle of just one anchor point, you can radically change the whole shape of the béziegon (see fig. 6.4). Only a few bytes of information are needed to encode the anchor point. Therefore, you can see that scalability goes hand in hand with compact file size. The file PRETZEL.FH5, located in the Chapter 6 folder of the accompanying CD, is just 5 KB in size uncompressed and 2 KB compressed.

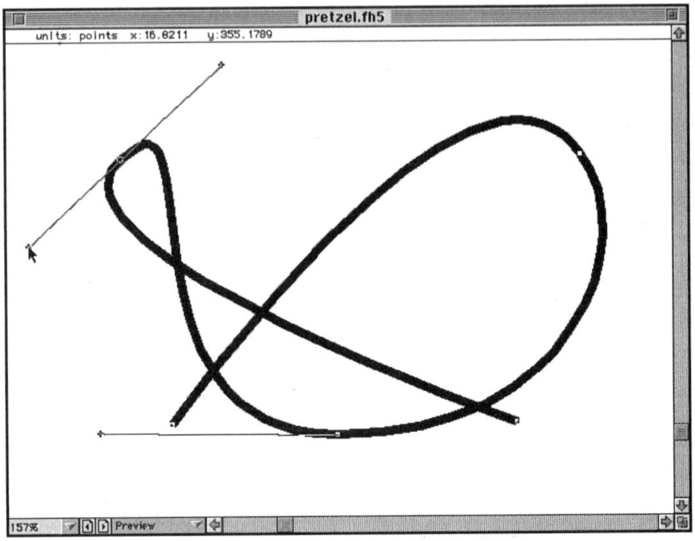

FIGURE 6.4
Changing just one of the handles of a point in the pretzel béziegon has a radical effect on the shape.

Compact File Size

Shockwave for FreeHand images are compact. Because the FreeHand files rely on compact mathematical descriptions to render your images to the screen on the fly, physically large images can take up a very small amount of bandwidth. You are, in effect, exchanging processor time (rendering) for file transfer time (download). With the realities of 28.8 kbps or even 14.4 kbps modems, this tradeoff can result in a tremendous overall speedup in presenting graphical information.

All the flavors of Shockwave have their own file compression to speed the transfer of shocked content across the Web. Like the others and Shockwave for FreeHand, compression is performed by a resource called Afterburner. The Afterburner compression utility can be downloaded free of charge from

Macromedia's website and then accessed from within FreeHand as an Xtra. Figure 6.5 shows FreeHand's Afterburner Xtra. Downloading, installation, and use of all the Shockwave for FreeHand resources are discussed later in this chapter in the section, "The Shocking Parts of FreeHand."

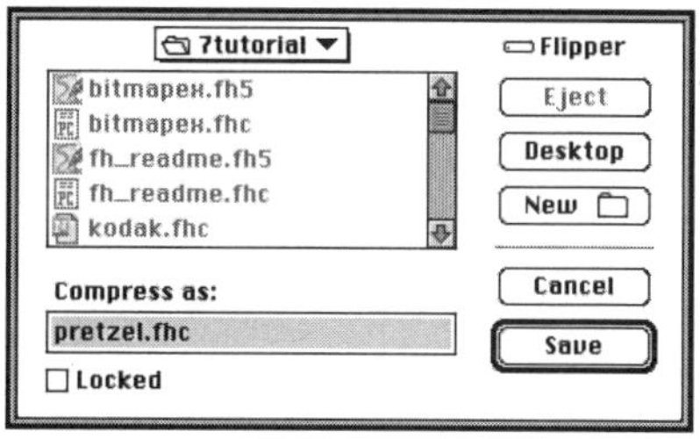

FIGURE 6.5

Compressing Documents for publication on the Web is easy in Shockwave for FreeHand. Just select Afterburner from the Xtras menu and choose a filename and path.

The bandwidth advantage of using Shockwave for FreeHand is obvious when you compare the file size of compressed bitmaps such as GIF files to the file size of the same image in the compressed FreeHand file format. Look in the Chapter 6 folder of the accompanying CD-ROM to compare the two files for the Lotsa Pasta menu graphic seen previously in figure 6.1. The GIF compressed bitmap file called PASTA.GIF is larger than 23 KB. The same image in a compressed FreeHand file, called PASTA.FHC, is only 13 KB. Notice that the text is not legible in the GIF file because it doesn't scale, but in the FHC file, you can zoom in to read the text to your heart's content.

Adding URLs

Objects within Shockwave for FreeHand images can have clickable links to URLs out there on the Web. This provides a simple way to use images created in FreeHand as Web navigation interfaces. The process of creating URL links in Shockwave for FreeHand is easier than doing the same in Shockwave for Director or using image maps.

Adding URL links into your FreeHand graphic is very simple. The URLs are added, edited, deleted, and so on by an Xtra called the URL Manager Xtra. The URL Manager Xtra is a palette that can be opened by selecting Window, Other, URLs. Figure 6.6 shows the URLs palette with two URLs already entered and ready to use. Much like FreeHand's color palette, the URLs palette enables you to drag and drop URL links to your FreeHand objects. (Later in this chapter, the section "Web-Specific Issues of FreeHand," explains how to add URL links to your FreeHand graphics.)

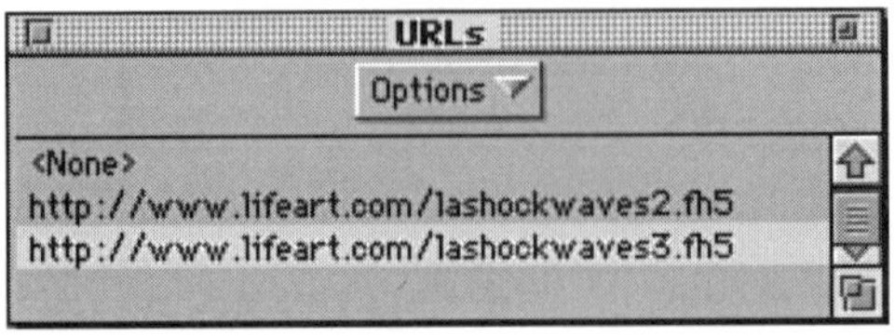

FIGURE 6.6

The URLs palette enables you to manage the URL links in Shockwave for FreeHand.

In the next section, we discuss using Shockwave for FreeHand to solve design problems. The strengths of Shockwave for FreeHand are scalability, compact file size, and embedded links. These strengths lend themselves to solving certain types of design challenges, which are discussed in detail.

Solutions with Shockwave for FreeHand

As we have seen, Shockwave for FreeHand offers several key advantages over bitmapped images. This provides new opportunities to present visual information on the Web. The most direct benefit is enjoyed, of course, by those desiring a way to demonstrate illustrations, as in the case of design firms or architecture firms. These applications alone are exciting, and Shockwave for FreeHand offers even more intriguing possibilities.

Scaleable, linkable graphics in Shockwave for FreeHand can be part of the solution of some interesting design problems, particularly situations that call for presenting a hierarchical complex of information. The classic design challenge suited to Shockwave for FreeHand is the straightforward map. FreeHand is excellent for diagrams and illustrations. FreeHand also is useful for representing and controlling navigation in a complex hierarchical website. Shockwave for FreeHand enables you to present textual information in deepening layers of detail.

Maps

Maps contain large amounts of information—often, too much information to be resolved in the space of a single bitmapped image. Consider that a typical folding map, such as a roadmap, is quite large and dense with street names, landmarks, geography, and so forth. When unfolded, a street map is often larger than the readers entire field of view at a typical reading distance. Therefore, the reader's eye must pan across the map and zoom in on the areas of interest.

The map reading experience relies on jumping back and forth between the visual scales. The large picture orients you to the overall landscape and the small scale contains minute detail. Before the advent of Shockwave for FreeHand, scale jumping in maps could be offered only in the form of a set of interlinked bitmaps. In bitmap-based maps, the simple act of changing scale or panning to an adjacent area of a map requires a whole new download.

Shockwave for FreeHand offers a much more natural and compact solution for presenting maps on the Web. Because it is inherently scaling and panning, Shockwave for FreeHand mimics the map reading behavior that we find so natural in paper maps and avoids the clunky wait-to-see map reading that we find so unnatural with GIFs and JPEGs.

A great example of the usefulness of presenting maps with Shockwave for FreeHand is a series of maps of the campus of the University of California at Berkeley (`http://geogweb.berkeley.edu/CampusMaps.html`). Figure 6.7 shows the map of safety shuttles available on campus. At the large scale, you can see all the routes of the safety shuttles and generally where they go, but you can't read any of the street names or landmark names.

You can zoom in to a particular area of interest on the campus safety map (see fig. 6.8). Now you can read all of the detailed information you need to find your shuttle stop. You also can pan around at this scale to follow a path from one location to another on the campus. And all of this in only one download. The compressed FreeHand file of this map is called UCBERK.FHC and can be found in the Chapter 6 folder on the accompanying CD.

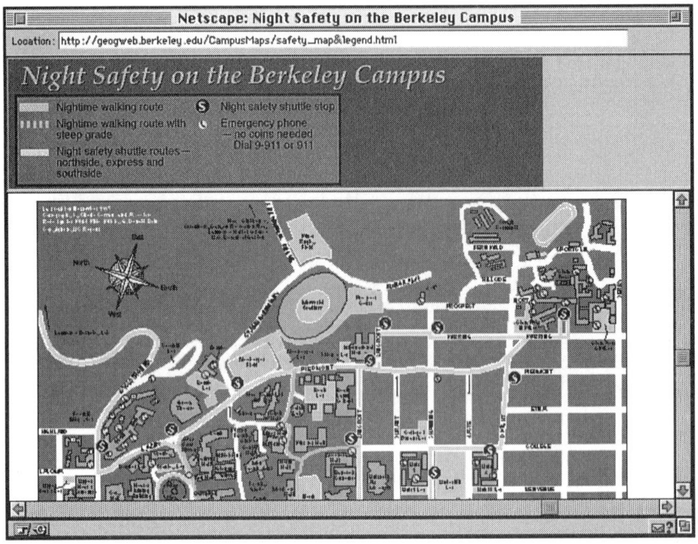

FIGURE 6.7

The safety map of the U.C. Berkeley Campus is available in Shockwave for FreeHand on the Web.

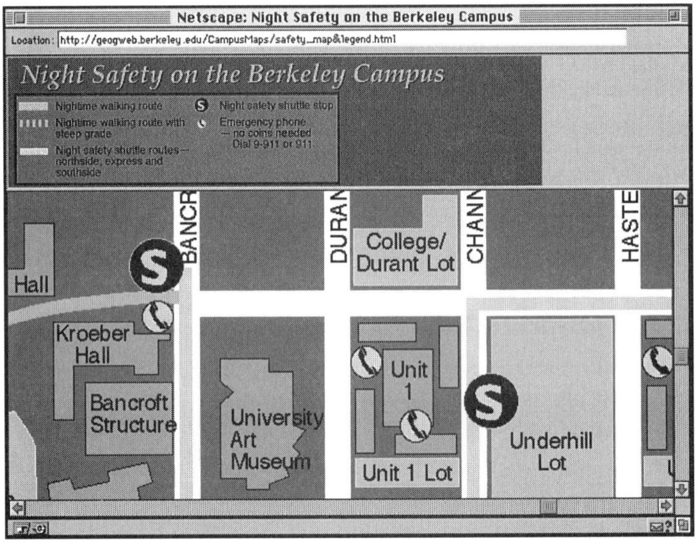

FIGURE 6.8

Zooming into the campus security map enables you to find the locations of the shuttles and safe walking routes.

Diagrams/Illustrations

Diagrams and technical illustrations hold the same promise as maps in Shockwave for FreeHand. The relationship of large-scale structures to the small detail is best conveyed in zoomable graphic form.

Medical illustrations, let's say of human physiology, can contain great amounts of detail. In many cases, the intent of the illustration is to show relationships between the body's different parts. So the ability to view the whole picture as well as closely inspect the details is key to many medical diagrams.

The simple diagram of the human spine made by Lifeart is a great example of the value of using Shockwave for FreeHand (see fig. 6.9). The whole spine can be seen. You can zoom in to see how the vertebrae fit together.

> **Note:** You can find Lifeart's website at `http://www.lifeart.com/lashockwaves.fh5`.

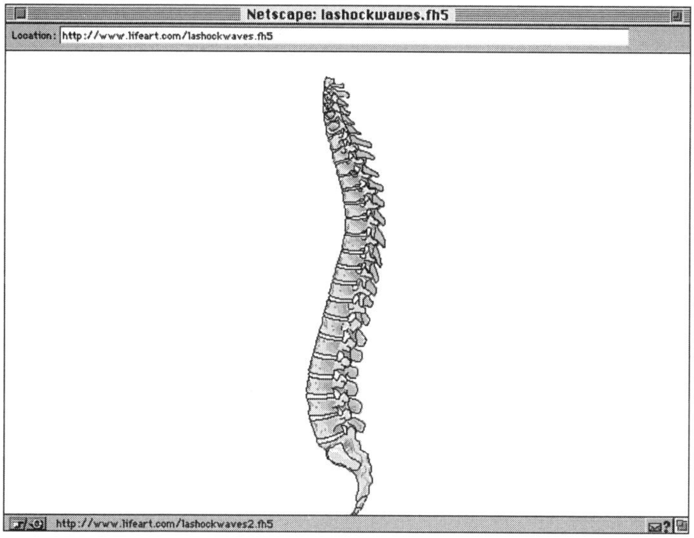

FIGURE 6.9

This is a medical illustration created in Shockwave for FreeHand. You can zoom in to see the bones up close, and you can click to see the vertebrae separately.

The different types of vertebrae have hot URL links, which can take you to detail diagrams of the individual bones (see fig. 6.10). Adding URL links in Shockwave for FreeHand is much easier than adding URL links to GIF or JPEG images. To achieve the same results with JPEG or GIF, you would need to create an image map. Image maps require the bitmap graphic, a map definition file and a CGI script, and only work with absolute path names. And after all that, image maps are not scaleable like Shockwave for FreeHand images are.

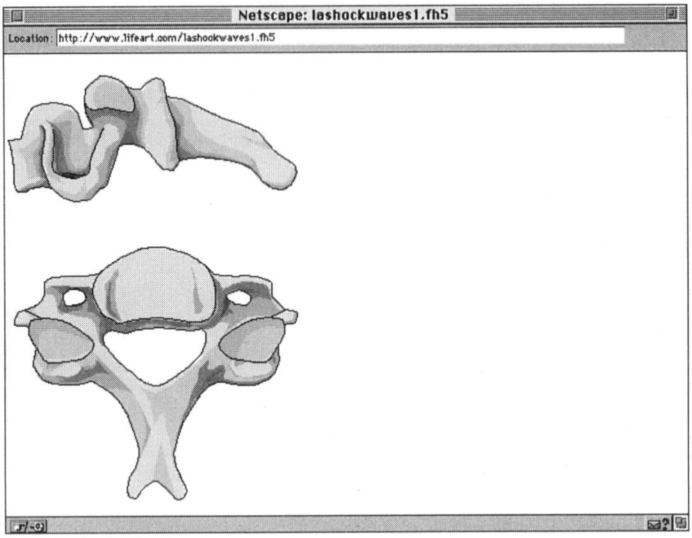

FIGURE 6.10

After clicking on a the spine, you are linked to this detail image of the vertebrae.

To see how these images are put together, you can view the files in FreeHand. The files are called LIFEART.FH5 and LIFEART2.FH5 and can be found in the Chapter 6 folder on the accompanying CD.

Navigation

Navigation is one of the strongest suits of HTML. Hot links are very effective at getting the user from page to page. As sites get larger and more complex, however, the need arises for a global site navigation view. Otherwise, it's easy to get lost—you're unable to see the forest for the trees, so to speak.

Shockwave for FreeHand enables you to visually mirror the structure of your website in the form of a scaleable illustration that contains hot URL links. An example of this is what Kodak did with Shockwave for FreeHand. Just visit `http://www.kodak.com/aboutKodak/aboutKodak.shtml`. Kodak's website is quite large and complex, but with FreeHand, they are able to offer a navigation field that represents the whole nested structure of their site (see fig. 6.11).

The site is represented by an image that evokes a solar system or molecular structure. The home page is central with What's New, Search, What's Hot, and Guest Book closely related. Key departments and site resources are grouped into larger clusters around the home page.

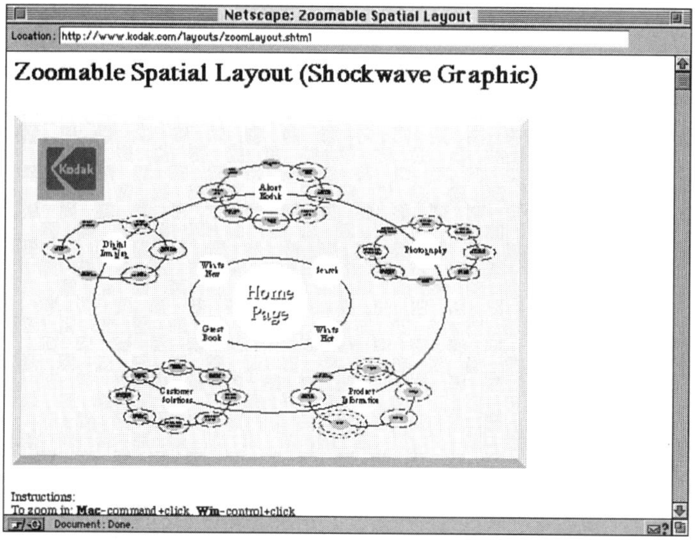

FIGURE 6.11

This is a Shockwave for FreeHand presentation of Kodak's sprawling website. At this scale, the major sections of the site are visible.

These clusters are centers of information about Kodak, digital imaging, photography, customer solutions, and product information. Each subcategory is further subdivided, and as you zoom in, the fine structure comes into focus (see fig. 6.12). And, of course, navigation to the various levels is just a mouse click away.

You can view the compressed FreeHand file KODAK.FHC from the Chapter 6 folder on the accompanying CD.

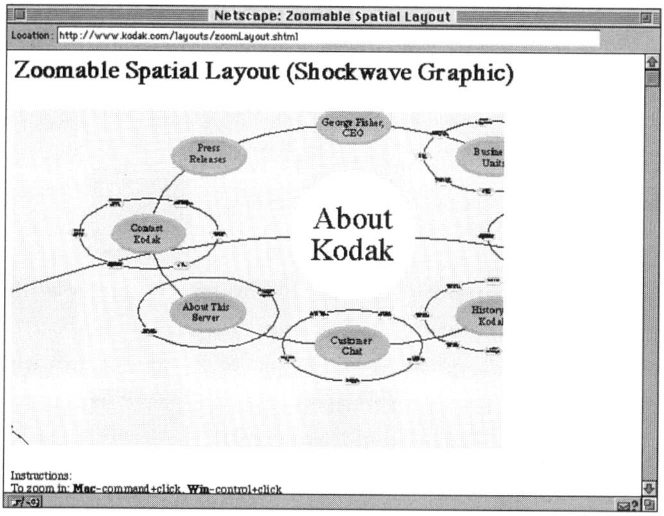

FIGURE 6.12

Zooming into the Shockwave for FreeHand Kodak sitemap reveals the nested structure of their site. Clicking on the various areas will navigate you to different pages.

Websites are prime examples of structures that exist in deepening strata of subdivision or differentiation. Any structure of this kind can be effectively illustrated in Shockwave for FreeHand and Web navigation through that structure easily accomplished.

Text Documents: Scaling Information

Though FreeHand is primarily considered an illustration tool, it has many powerful typographic features. This provides new possibilities for presenting text-oriented FreeHand documents on the Web. In the Festa di Pasta menu, for example, we reduced the size of the text detail to the level of "fine print." (Refer to figure 6.2 shown earlier in this chapter.) As was seen, this allowed the graphical elements to dominate, with the text acting as background information. This is a simple splitting of information into two scales of presentation—graphical at the large scale and text at the small scale.

Scaling is a basic design consideration in all typography. The classic example of the use of scaling in typography is the good ol' newspaper. Several scales of text are used within a newspaper; the two most important text types are the headlines (in large font size) and the body text (in a small size). Scaling the text causes the reader to engage the reading experience at two conceptual scales. At the large scale, the headline text serves as a navigational aid. Newspaper headlines summarize the contents of each individual story and all the headlines on the page form a navigation field, giving quick access to any story.

The large scale enables the reader to prioritize his readthrough. A good headline summarizes the story at a glance and thus facilitates the reading path. Good headlines enable the reader to quickly choose to pass over stories of little interest or to concentrate on the stories of greatest interest. Indeed, the front-page headline aids the reader in deciding which of several newspapers to purchase or read.

Once attracted to a particular paper or story headline, the reader drops down to the lower scale. At the story scale, the read proceeds with key summary information (the lead) and goes on to present further elaboration or detail. If the entire text of a paper were printed at the small scale only, the reader would get lost in a sea of profuse information.

Printed text media continues to refine the use of scaling, but the basic conventions of scaling have been so long established that they are too easily taken for granted.

Scaling is key to the "interactivity" of printed matter, and so to with "interactive" media. The advent of electronic and online media compels the reinvention of the reading experience. Hypertext on the Web has rejuvenated typography, but the process has only just begun. The state of the art is not yet settled. Shockwave for FreeHand offers interesting methods to adapt design conventions to the new possibilities and constraints of the Web. It is a great platform for innovative typography.

One of the major constraints of Web typography is the limited screen real estate generally available. Hypertext links are one way around this constraint, allowing quick "horizontal" movement from point to point within documents. This provides quick access to relevant information one screen at a time. Zoom scaling in Shockwave for FreeHand enables vertical movement between conceptual scales within a document.

So at any given view, the screen can be full of text at all font sizes, creating deep nesting of text detail. The nesting structure itself can convey information by signifying hierarchies and dependencies. Thus, relationship of scale in text can be used as a design element in its own right. A simple application might be heavily footnoted text with the footnotes embedded in tiny print right next to the reference. The user can zoom right into the footnote as they choose.

Almost any document that uses a table of contents or subheadings to guide the reader can be effectively shocked with Shockwave for FreeHand. The document we use as an example is the online documentation of Shockwave for FreeHand (see fig. 6.13). This plain old HTML has four sections that detail how to create FreeHand graphics for the Web.

The shocked version of this site is based on the same text and puts it in zoomable form. The large-scale view summarizes the whole purpose of the document, and section headings steer the user to the information contained in the respective lower levels (see fig. 6.14).

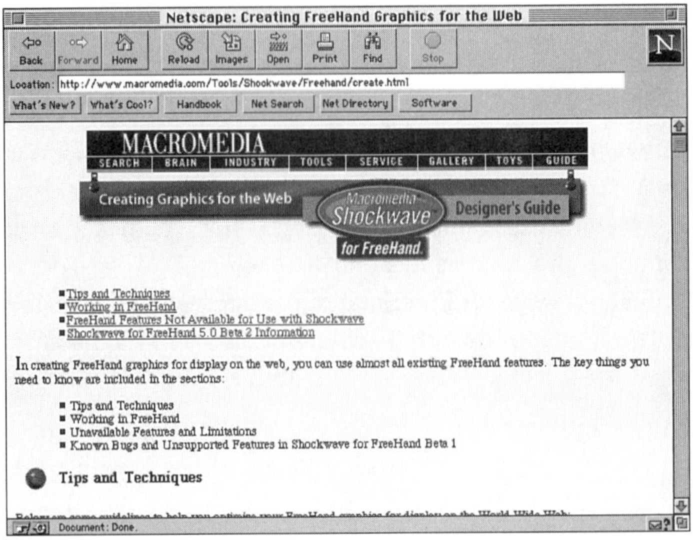

FIGURE 6.13

This is an online FreeHand Designer's Guide done in straight HTML. To see one of the four subsections, you link to another page.

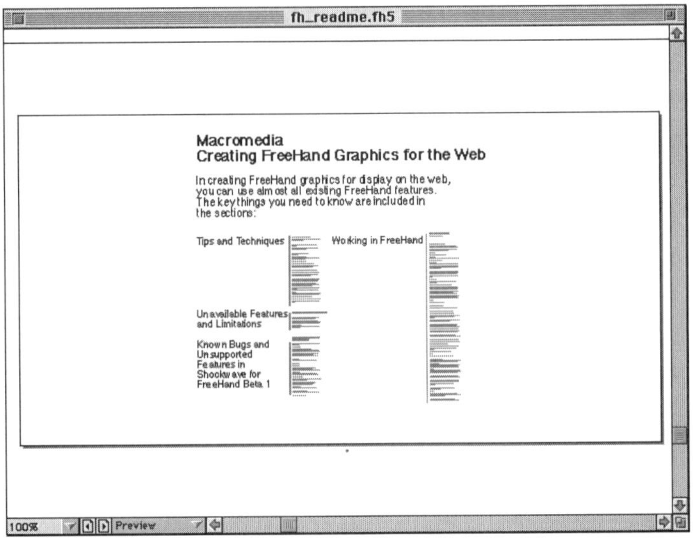

FIGURE 6.14

This is an example of how the same Designer's Guide information can be presented in Shockwave for FreeHand. At this scale, the intro and section headings are visible.

You can zoom in to the section of your choice. When you zoom in, you can read the fine print. To keep you oriented, a vertical section title is positioned to the left of the text column (see fig. 6.15).

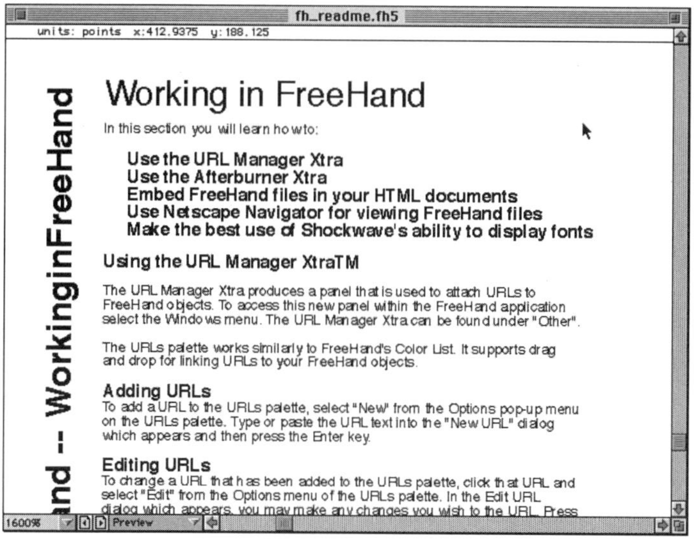

FIGURE 6.15

Zooming into the FreeHand version of the Design Guide reveals the body text of the scaleable README.

You can examine the source file to see how simple it is to work with text in FreeHand. The file FHREADME.FH5 is located in the Chapter 6 folder on the accompanying CD. The process of creating the source file was to copy the text from a text editor and paste it into text objects in FreeHand. Then, size the text using the Scale tool and arrange them using the Arrow tool.

Although icons and other graphically oriented approaches to navigation have become the dominant way to get around on the Web, there is still no substitute for text's ability to compress and convey a dense amount of information. Shockwave for FreeHand may prove an excellent way to combine rich text information with the total visual experience of the Web.

As you have seen, Shockwave for FreeHand is effective at presenting maps, diagrams, navigation, and text-oriented images on the Web. Other powerful applications could include scaleable process maps, organizational charts, flowcharts, and more. Creating imaginative and communicative Shockwave for FreeHand art is just a step away.

In the next section, you will go through a brief primer on FreeHand's tools and capabilities.

FreeHand Features at a Glance

The best way to learn FreeHand is to use it. We have been using FreeHand (see fig. 6.16) for many years now and have found it to be quite intuitive. If you hit an obstacle, you can consult the excellent manuals. This primer is intended to simply highlight the key features, control palettes, and tools in FreeHand for those of you not yet familiar with the program.

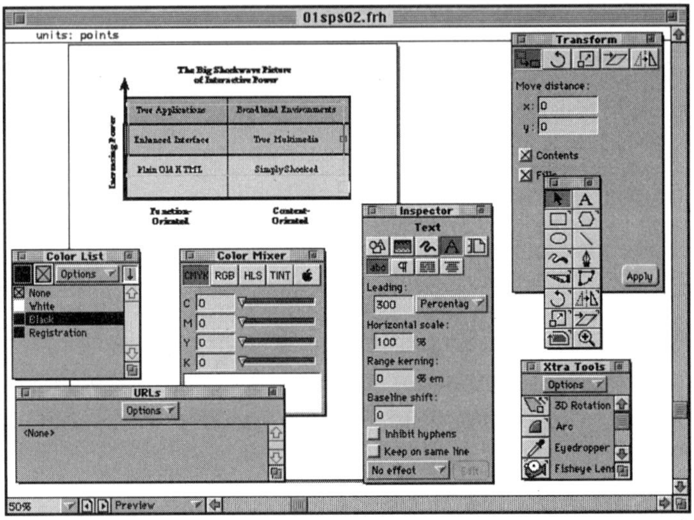

Figure 6.16

This is the FreeHand environment. The graphic we are working on is on the pasteboard, and several palettes are open and ready to be used.

The Toolbox

The Toolbox palette contains two different types of design and illustration tools (see fig. 6.17). The basic drawing tools—Rectangle, Polygon, Ellipse, Line, FreeHand, Pen, Knife, and Béziegon—are used to create graphics. Transformation tools are used to move, rotate, reflect, scale, skew, trace, and magnify. Also included are the familiar Pointer and Text tools.

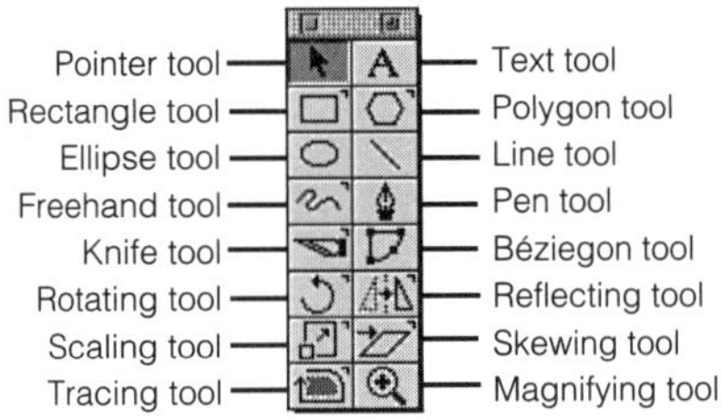

Figure 6.17

The Toolbox palette gives you fast access to FreeHand's drawing and transformation tools.

> **Tip**
>
> If you have a pressure tablet, you can use it to draw with the Freehand tool. Great, expressive lines can be created this way. Double-clicking on the Freehand tool in the Toolbox opens an options dialog box. Try drawing with the pressure tab using the Variable stroke or Calligraphic settings.

Inspector Palette

The Inspector palette reports on everything that happens in FreeHand. Just select any object or text, and the Inspector palette displays all the pertinent information about that item (see fig. 6.18). Using the five major areas of the Inspector palette (Object, Fill, Stroke, Text, and Document), you can numerically or visually adjust any aspect of any part of your design or illustration.

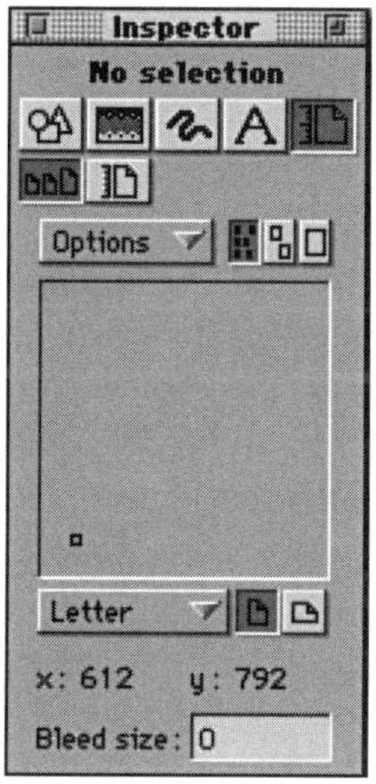

FIGURE 6.18

The Inspector palette provides status information on any object, as well as page settings. This example shows the page settings of a file with a custom height and width. The point size of the page (612×792 points) will be used with the <embed> tag to size the window in HTML.

Xtra Tools

This palette provides easy access to drop-in interactive tools for quickly creating amazing special effects (see fig. 6.19). These special effects can include Fisheye Lens, Eyedropper, 3D Rotation, Smudge, and many more.

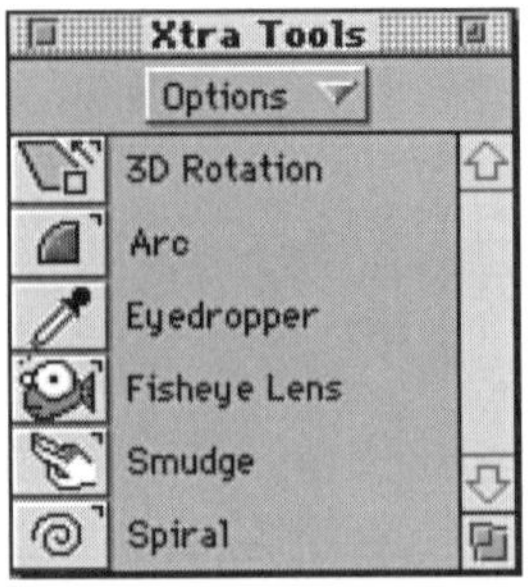

FIGURE 6.19

The Xtra Tools palette provides fast access to the available Xtras.

Color List and Color Mixer

The Color List is similar to an artist's palette of colors. It contains the named spot and process colors that you choose for a particular illustration. All the colors can be changed, reordered, and renamed.

The Color Mixer is used to mix new colors either numerically or interactively; the hues change as you adjust the sliding bars. Using these custom colors is as easy as dragging the color and dropping it onto the object you want to color. (See fig. 6.20.)

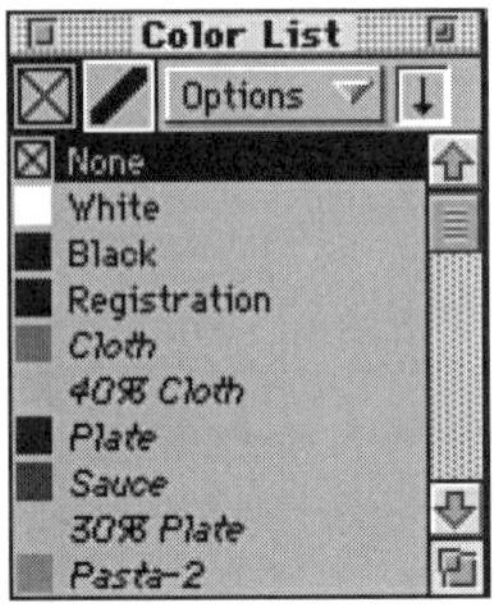

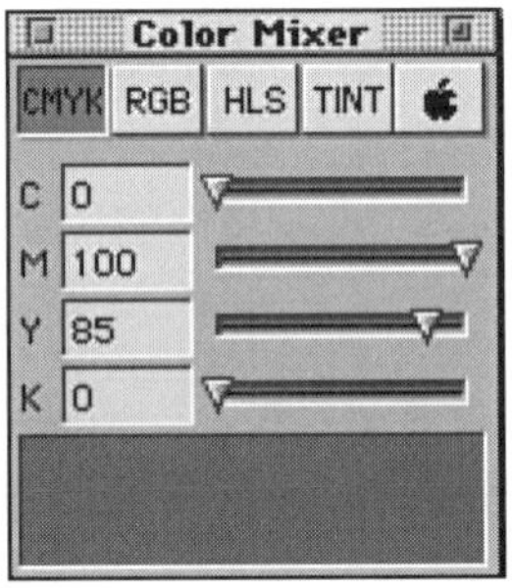

FIGURE 6.20

The Color List and Color Mixer palettes provide fast and easy control over color.

Text

Remember that many of the people viewing your site will not have the same fonts installed in their systems as you. Keep the use of custom fonts to a minimum, or convert them to paths if you want to preserve the look of your graphic.

For reliable control over text and layout, you should use standard cross-platform fonts in your documents. These fonts are Courier and Times. If you wish to use custom fonts in your document and preserve the look of those custom fonts, you will need to use the Convert to Paths command from the Type menu to convert your fonts to path outlines. Doing so will increase the size of your FreeHand document, however, so try to keep your text-to-path conversion to a minimum.

The Shocking Parts of FreeHand

This section puts the "Shockwave" in Shockwave for FreeHand. It contains the technical details you need to know to install and configure the tools for the entire Shockwave for FreeHand environment, from creation tools to server configuration to viewer tools. The section is divided into the following areas:

- Installing the URL and Afterburner Xtras
- Using Afterburner for FreeHand
- Embedding Shockwave for FreeHand
- Serving up Shockwave for FreeHand
- Installing the Shockwave for FreeHand plug-in
- Viewing Shockwave for FreeHand

Installing the URL and Afterburner Xtras

The current versions of FreeHand's URL and Afterburner Xtras for both Macintosh and Windows can be downloaded from Macromedia's website (`http://www.macromedia.com`). Just follow the download instructions posted. Here, we present the installation instructions as they applied at the time of this writing. The install procedure should be substantially the same when you read this, so be sure to revisit Macromedia's site for updated instructions. The downloaded filenames will be different, so don't be alarmed. Also, you might want to refer to the README files and online documentation for up-to-the minute instructions.

Installing and Accessing the Xtras for Macintosh

To install and access the Shockwave for FreeHand Xtras for the Macintosh:

1. After the downloaded file AFAF50.SEA.HQX has been uncompressed, open the folder Shockwave for FH Xtras. This folder contains URLs, Afterburner, XTRASDOC.HTML, and README.
2. Drag the files, URLs, and Afterburner into the Xtras folder located inside in your FreeHand 5.x application folder.
3. Launch FreeHand.
4. To access the URL Manager Xtra, pull down the Windows menu and select Other: URLs.
5. To access the Afterburner Xtra, pull down the Xtras menu and select Compression: Export Document.

Installing and Accessing the Xtras for Windows

To install and access the Shockwave for FreeHand Xtras for Windows:

1. Create a new directory on your hard disk. We suggest you name it "xtrainst."
2. From the File Manager or Explorer, move AWNF50B2.EXE into the directory you created in step 1.
3. Double-click on the file AWNF50B2.EXE. It will uncompress and leave a file named SETUP.EXE.
4. Double-click on the file SETUP.EXE. The Xtras, URLS.FHX, and AFTRBURN.FHX will be installed in the Xtras directory inside your FreeHand 5.x directory.
5. Launch FreeHand.
6. To access the URL Manager Xtra, pull down the Windows menu and select Other: URLs.
7. To access the Afterburner Xtra, pull down the Xtras menu and select Compression: Export Document.

Using Afterburner for FreeHand

Shockwave for FreeHand can use the standard FreeHand file format. You need only add the extension FH5 or FH4 to the filename of the FreeHand document for it to be read by the Shockwave for FreeHand plug-in.

However, when creating graphics for the Web, you'll want to use FreeHand's Afterburner Xtra to compress your documents for faster transfer across the Internet.

To compress your document, complete the following steps:

1. In FreeHand, open the document that you wish to compress. (If you are working on a new document, make sure to save it as FreeHand before you compress.)
2. From the FreeHand Xtras: Compression menu, choose Export.
3. In the File Name field of the Export Dialog box, enter a filename.
4. Click OK.

The compressed file will be named with the extension FHC. Files compressed in this manner are automatically recognized and decompressed by the Netscape plug-in when the file is opened or viewed in Netscape.

When you export a FreeHand document with the Afterburner Xtra, you have the option to "lock" the document so that it cannot be reopened in FreeHand in its compressed format. To lock a document, simply select the Locked option in the Compressed file Export dialog box. Because locked files can't be reopened, be sure to keep a copy of your original, unlocked FreeHand document if you ever intend to edit it again.

To open a compressed file in FreeHand, complete the following steps:

1. From the FreeHand Xtras: Compression menu, choose Import.
2. In the Compressed file Import dialog box, navigate to the compressed file you wish to open.
3. Click OK.

When you import a compressed file, it will be opened as an untitled document. To name the document, you must choose the Save As command from

FreeHand's File menu. You also must save the document before you can export it as a compressed document again.

Embedding

Use the <embed> tag to put your FreeHand graphic into an HTML document.

If your graphics fit on a page that measures 500×400 points, you can specify a width of 500 pixels and a height of 400 pixels in HTML, ensuring optimum display of your graphic.

Your HTML <embed> text for that document would look like the following:

```
<embed SRC="FILENAME.EXT" width=500 height=400>
```

You also can manually force the display of the FreeHand document to a percentage of its size. If you wanted the above file to be displayed in Netscape at 75 percent of its original size, for example, just do a little math and enter width and height numbers that are 75 percent of the original numbers. It would look like the following:

```
<embed SRC="FILENAME.EXT" width=375 height=300>
```

Serving Up Shockwave for FreeHand: Configuring Your Server

Your HTTP server must be configured to recognize and handle Shockwave for FreeHand files. Most servers are Unix-based platforms, although there also are servers that use MacHTTP or WebSTAR software. Once you have configured your HTTP software, you can transfer your Shockwave for FreeHand files to the server.

Configuring Unix Servers

Have your system administrator create an entry in the file that registers MIME types. The administrator will need the following information:

MIME type: image

Sub type: x-FreeHand

Extensions: FH4, FH5, FHC

Configuring MacHTTP Servers

If you are using MacHTTP servers, have your system administrator modify the file MACHTTP.CONFIG. Add the following lines to the file:

```
BINARY .FH4 TEXT * image/x-FreeHand
BINARY .FH5 TEXT * image/x-FreeHand
BINARY .FHC TEXT * image/x-FreeHand
```

Configuring WebSTAR Servers

If you are using WebSTAR, you need to do the following:

1. Have your administrator run the application called WebSTAR Admin.
2. Locate and select your server in the Pick A Server window (your server must be running).
3. Choose Suffix Mapping from the Configure menu. The Suffix Mapping dialog box appears.
4. Choose the following settings:

    Action : BINARY

    File Suffix: .FH5

    File Type: TEXT

    Creator: *

    MIME Type: image/x-FreeHand

The process should be repeated for suffix types FH4 and FHC.

Transferring FreeHand Files to Your Server

You should transfer FreeHand files to your server, via FTP, using a BINARY encoding method. If BINARY encoding is not available or doesn't yield a working transfer, try a RAW data transfer.

When transferring files from a Macintosh, most FTP transfer applications automatically detect traditional Web image file formats (GIFs, JPEGs, and so on) and transfer them using binary encoding (with other files, such as HTML, being encoded as text). These applications might not, however, correctly identify the FreeHand format as an image file. You can ensure that your FreeHand files are transferred correctly by sending FreeHand files separately from other file formats and overriding the FTP application's selected encoding method.

If you don't know how to do this, check the documentation for your FTP application.

Also, some FTP applications (Fetch, for example) provide an opportunity for you to pre-assign encoding methods to files of a certain extension. In Fetch, this is know as "Suffix Mapping" and can be done in the Customize menu. If your FTP application offers this option and you choose to do it, remember to map all three FreeHand file formats (FH4, FH5, and FHC).

When transferring files from Windows, be sure to assign each of your FreeHand files to transfer using the Binary Encoding Method.

Installing the Shockwave for FreeHand Plug-In

The Shockwave for FreeHand Netscape plug-in for both Macintosh and Windows can be downloaded from Macromedia's website. In this section we go through the download and install instructions as they exist at the time of this writing. Note that some of the directions might vary by the time you starting working with them. When you decide to download and install, you should follow the download instructions posted at the website. After you download, read the README files and any online documentation for current install procedures.

Installing the Plug-In for Power Macintosh:

The first step in installing Shockwave for FreeHand 5 is to make sure you're ready.

1. Make sure you have the correct version of the browser you're using. Shockwave requires Netscape Navigator 2.0. (Plug-Ins for use with Microsoft Internet Explorer and other browsers will be available in the near future). If you don't have the correct version of Netscape Navigator, download it from Netscape before you go on.

2. Uninstall any other versions of the browser—all files and directories—completely. The Shockwave for FreeHand installer finds the correct path for the plug-in and Xtras. The installer will get confused by multiple browser copies.

The next step in installing Shockwave is to download NPPF50F1.SEA.HQX from the FTP server:

3. From the Plug-in Center download screen, click the name of one of the download servers listed next to the package you want to download. If the server you choose is busy, choose another one from the list. If all servers are busy, wait a few minutes and try them again.

4. If the server is available, Netscape will immediately begin downloading the file NPPF50F1.SEA.HQX to your hard disk.

   Depending on your Netscape settings, a Save As dialog box might appear. If it does, choose the folder or location where you want to save the NPPF50F1.SEA.HQX file, and then click on Save.

   If your Netscape preferences are set so that the file starts downloading immediately, wait for the file to finish downloading, then locate it on your hard disk. Files downloaded automatically are typically saved in the Desktop folder or in the Netscape Navigator folder on your hard disk.

The next step is decompressing the Shockwave plug-in, which came across as a compressed self-extracting archive. Decompress the plug-in as follows:

5. If you have a helper application for decompressing files, Navigator automatically launches the helper application, decompresses the file, and extracts the archive. It creates a folder called NPPF50F1.SEA.HQX, where it places the Shockwave plug-in and a README document. The folder might include other files for viewing shocked files using Netscape Navigator.

6. If you cannot decompress the file NPPF50F1.SEA.HQX or if you see a saying "No Viewer Configured for File Type" warning from Netscape, choose Save To Disk to save the file into a folder on the hard disk. Then, you can go to the Netscape Utilities Page to download a decompression utility.

The final install procedure is configuring the Shockwave plug-in:

7. Quit your browser.
8. Locate the Shockwave Plug-In package that you downloaded. It's named "Shockwave for FH PPC Installer."
9. If you weren't asked to select the folder where you wanted to save the Shockwave Plug-In package, you'll probably find the folder containing the package either on the Desktop or in the Netscape Navigator folder. If not, use the Finder's Find command to locate it.
10. Double-click the installer icon to launch the installer. Follow the instructions that appear on the screen.

For optimum performance when viewing Shockwave files in Netscape, it is recommended that you increase Netscape's preferred memory partition size. To do this, follow these steps:

1. In the Finder select the Netscape Navigator Application.
2. Choose Get Info from the File menu.
3. In the Navigator Info window, set the Preferred Size to 8000K or more, provided you have enough RAM installed in your computer.
4. Close the Navigator Info window and launch Netscape Navigator.
5. While Navigator is running, select Network Preferences from the Options menu. Set the cache size setting to at least 5 MB.
6. Restart your browser.

To confirm that your plug-in installation was successful, you can select About Plug-ins from the Apple menu. You should see the current plug-in listed in the Netscape Plug-ins window. If you do, then you have installed the plug-in correctly.

Installing the Plug-In for 68K Macintosh:

The Shockwave for FreeHand installation procedure is the same for 68K Macintosh as for the Power Macintosh as described in the previous section. The only difference is the name of the file and the download folder name.

The 68K Macintosh version of Shockwave for FreeHand is called N68F50F1.SEA.HQX and the folder it creates is SHOCKWAVE FOR FH 68K INSTALLER.

Installing the Plug-In for Windows:

The first step in installing Shockwave for FreeHand 5 is to make sure you're ready.

1. Make sure you have the correct version of the browser you're using. Shockwave requires Netscape Navigator 2.0. (Plug-Ins for use with Microsoft Internet Explorer and other browsers will be available in the near future). If you don't have the correct version of Netscape Navigator, download it from Netscape before you go on.
2. Uninstall any other versions of the browser—all files and directories—completely. The Shockwave for FreeHand installer finds the correct path for the plug-in and Xtras. The installer will get confused by multiple browser copies.

The next step is to download it from the FTP server.

3. From the Plug-in Center download screen, click the name of one of the download servers listed next to Shockwave for FreeHand Windows 95 version. If the server you choose is busy, choose another one from the list. If all servers are busy, wait a few minutes and try them again.
4. If the server is available, Netscape immediately begins downloading the file N32F50F1.EXE to your hard disk.

   Depending on your Netscape settings, a Save As dialog box might appear. If it does, choose the directory or location where you want to save the N32F50F2.EXE file, and then click Save. The file N32F50F2.EXE is the compressed self-extracting installer for Shockwave for FreeHand 5.

   If your Netscape preferences are set so that the file starts downloading immediately, wait for the file to finish downloading, then locate it on your hard disk. Files downloaded automatically are typically saved in the Downloads subdirectory inside the Netscape Navigator Program directory on your hard disk.

Note that if you see a "No Viewer Configured for File Type" warning from Netscape, choose "Save To Disk" to save the file into a folder on the hard disk.

The next step is decompressing the Shockwave plug-in, which came across as a compressed self-extracting archive. Decompress the plug-in as follows:

5. Locate the copy of N32F50F2.EXE that you downloaded.
6. If you have not done so already, create a new directory on your hard disk and move N32F50F2.EXE into the folder.
7. Open the directory that contains the compressed file N32F50B2.EXE and double-click on the N32F50F2.EXE icon. (Note: Depending on your Windows settings, the EXE at the end of the filename might not be displayed.) Windows then opens a DOS shell and decompresses the Shockwave Installer.
8. Approximately 10 files will appear inside the directory you created. One of these files will be named SETUP.EXE (or just Setup).

The final step in the installation is to run the installer.

9. Find the file named SETUP.EXE (Note: Depending on your setup the file might not include the EXE extension.)
10. Double-click on the SETUP.EXE icon to launch the installer. Follow the instructions that appear on your screen.
11. Restart your browser.

Installing the Plug-In for 16-bit Windows

The Shockwave for FreeHand installation procedure is the same for 16-bit Windows as for Windows 95 as described in the previous section. The only difference is the name of the file. The 16-bit Windows version of Shockwave for FreeHand is called N16F50F1.EXE.

Viewing Shockwave for FreeHand

Shockwave for FreeHand brings zooming and panning to images on the World Wide Web. This capability is new to most users, so you might want to include any graphic or text that tells your audience how to interact with your Shockwave for FreeHand document. Macromedia provides an instructional graphic file called MAGNIFY.GIF, which can be included in your Shockwave for FreeHand website if you want (see fig. 6.21). The file MAGNIFY.GIF can be found in the accompanying CD's Chapter 6 folder. It also is provided in the downloadable developer's package of the Shockwave for FreeHand plug-in and Xtra.

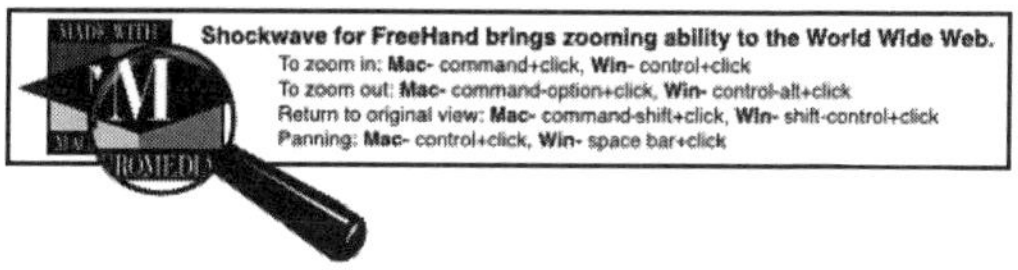

FIGURE 6.21

Macromedia provides this standard instruction image to be placed on Shockwave for FreeHand Web pages. It gives helpful information to your viewers.

Activating Hotlinks

When viewing a FreeHand document in Netscape, the pointer cursor will change into a "pointing finger" cursor any time it is moved over a FreeHand object that has an attached URL. To go to that URL, simply click on the object while the "pointing finger" cursor is visible.

Zooming

Shockwave for FreeHand uses zoom tools similar to those found in FreeHand. After a FreeHand document is opened in Netscape, you may zoom in and out (up to 26,500%), or zoom to a defined area. When active, the Zoom tool looks like a small magnifying glass with a + or – in it, showing whether you are about to zoom in or zoom out.

To activate the Zoom tool in the Macintosh version of Netscape, press the Command key and click your mouse button to zoom in on the desired area. Pressing Command+Option on the Mac will zoom out. If you press Command+Shift and click, the view will return to its original magnification.

To zoom in on Windows, simply click your right mouse button over the portion of the document you want to zoom in on. To zoom out, press the Alt key as you click. You also can press Control while clicking the left mouse button to zoom in and Control+Alt with the left button to zoom out. Shift+Control or Shift+right-click will return the view to its original magnification.

You also can define a rectangular zoom area using the Zoom tool. With the Zoom tool active, just click and drag the mouse to draw the area that you want to magnify. That area will zoom to fill the entire space of the original FreeHand document.

Panning

You can pan or move around within the FreeHand document by dragging it with the Grabber Hand tool. To use the Grabber Hand on Macintosh, press the Control key as you click and drag with your mouse. To activate the Grabber Hand tool in Windows, press the spacebar. The FreeHand document will be moved in the direction you drag.

Web-Specific Issues of FreeHand

This section discusses Web-specific features and design considerations in FreeHand. First, we discuss how to start a Shockwave for FreeHand document and add URL links to your FreeHand document. Then, we delve into repurposing images into FreeHand with the import feature, unavailable features and limitations, and Web optimization issues.

Sizing for the Web

To maintain optimal control over the display of your FreeHand graphics in Netscape, use FreeHand's Page Inspector settings. Open the FreeHand file you want to size for Web publication.

You will need to know the horizontal and vertical pixel size of the image when you embed it in HTML. Because FreeHand does not have a pixel measurement, you need to use points—a roughly equivalent measure. Set the unit of measure to points. When embedded in HTML, the size of the document will be specified in screen pixels; the number of pixels per inch and the number of points per inch are approximately the same (72).

The *page size* is the window within which the document appears in the browser. Therefore, you need to adjust the page size and orientation to fit the objects on the page using FreeHand's page inspector.

1. Select all the objects on the page.
2. Group the objects by choosing Edit, Group.
3. Move the group to the lower left corner of the page.
4. Make a note of the group's width and height as displayed in FreeHand's Object Inspector. These dimensions will be used later when you embed the document.
5. Enter the above measurements as custom page dimensions FreeHand's Page inspector.
6. The object group will now be on a page with the same dimensions. You may ungroup if you like.

Your FreeHand graphic has now been correctly sized for embedding on the Web.

Managing URLs in Shockwave for FreeHand

URL linking is the key Web-specific design element in Shockwave for FreeHand. The instructions for downloading and installing the URL Xtra can be found earlier in this chapter in the section "The Shocking Parts of FreeHand." In this section, we present how to use the Xtra to address, add, edit, copy, apply, remove, and identify URLs in your FreeHand document.

The URL Manager Xtra produces a panel that is used to attach URLs to FreeHand objects. To access this new panel within the FreeHand application, select the Windows menu. The URL Manager Xtra can be found under the Other menu. The URLs palette works similarly to FreeHand's Color List. It supports drag and drop for linking URLs to your FreeHand objects.

URL Addressing

Shockwave for FreeHand supports absolute URLs and relative URLs. Absolute URLs are URLs that include the entire path name and filename for the document (for example, http://eline.com/Infrared/index.html). Relative URLs contain partial path names that are relative to the current folder (for example, index.html). Relative URLs entered in FreeHand are relative to the FreeHand file's location on the server, not the HTML file in which they are embedded.

Adding URLs

To add an URL to the URLs palette, select New from the Options pop-up menu on the URLs palette. Type or paste the URL text into the New URL dialog box that appears and then press Enter.

Editing URLs

To change an URL that has been added to the URLs palette, click that URL and select Edit from the Options menu of the URLs palette. In the Edit URL dialog box that appears, you may make any changes you wish to the URL. Press Enter when you are done.

Copying URLs

You also may duplicate an existing URL. To do so, select the URL you wish to duplicate, and then choose Duplicate from the Options menu of the URLs palette. The duplicate URL will appear with the words "Copy of" appended to the beginning of the old URL. You will need to edit the duplicated URL using the previously described method to remove the words "Copy of" and to make any other changes you desire.

Applying URLs

After the URL has been added to the URLs palette, drag the desired URL selection to the FreeHand object in the same manner as you apply colors in FreeHand. You also may apply an URL to several objects at once by selecting multiple objects on the FreeHand pasteboard and then clicking on the desired URL in the URLs palette. To remove an URL from an object that has already been tagged, either drag the "none" entry to the object or select the object(s) from which you want to move the URL and click "none" on the URLs palette.

Deleting URLs

Clicking on an URL in the URLs palette and selecting Remove from the Options menu of the URL Links Manager removes the URL from the listing. This also will remove the link that the selected URL had to any existing FreeHand objects.

Identifying URLs Used on FreeHand Objects

The URLs palette's Find button is used to determine what objects have been linked to a specific URL. For best results, deselect all FreeHand objects on the pasteboard by pressing the Tab key, then click on an URL and select Find from the Options menu of the URL Links Manager. FreeHand will then display visual selection handles on all objects on the pasteboard that are linked to the selected URL.

URLs may not be added to grouped objects. However, you can add URLs to individual objects in groups. To select an object within a group, Option+click that object. Then, with the object selected, add an URL as you normally would.

Importing Images

Shockwave for FreeHand can combine images created in other applications. This is a useful feature that enables you to repurpose artwork created elsewhere for Internet delivery via Shockwave for FreeHand. Editable Post-script and PICT or TIFF bitmaps can be placed in FreeHand and displayed in Shockwave for FreeHand.

Postscript and Illustrator Images

Postscript is a page description language invented at Adobe that supports vector, bitmap, text, and output control elements. Images are often exported from graphics programs as Encapsulated Postscript (EPS) files. EPS is a standard way to port graphics. Because EPS is not a very compact language for encoding graphics images, Macromedia opted not to support native EPS within Shockwave for FreeHand.

Editable Postscript files, generated in applications such as Adobe Illustrator, can be imported into FreeHand and thus converted into the native FreeHand data type. To import editable Postscript, you first must set the correct import preferences in FreeHand and then use the Place command.

1. Open the Preferences dialog box from the File menu.
2. Select the Category Importing/Exporting and check the Convert Editable EPS When Placed option box.
3. Import an Adobe Illustrator or other editable Postscript file by selecting the Place command from the File menu.
4. Find the desired file using the Standard File dialog box, and press OK.
5. After the conversion is done, the cursor changes to an inverted L-shaped icon. Click on the desired area of the page and the image will appear.

The imported graphic appears in FreeHand as it would in the original application. It is now FreeHand native, so you can edit the component parts of the graphic. You might have to ungroup to get access to the individual objects. If so, select the grouped object with the Arrow tool and choose ungroup from the Arrange menu. Repeat the ungrouping as many times as you have to free all the elements for editing.

Bitmapped Images: If You Don't Care about Scaling...

You can use PICTs, BMPs, and TIFFs in your Shockwave for FreeHand Documents. TIFFs, BMPs, and PICTs can be embedded right in the FreeHand document using the Place command.

The main drawback of using bitmaps is the increase of your file size. However, FreeHand's Afterburner Xtra will compress the bitmap data along with FreeHand's vectored art. Also, using bitmaps hampers the scaleable nature of Shockwave for FreeHand images.

Zooming in on a bitmap placed in a Shockwave for FreeHand file will cause the image to appear pixelated at higher magnifications because of the fixed nature of bitmap's resolution. Therefore, if you are designing a FreeHand document for zooming in and out (such as a map or other scaleable image), try to avoid using bitmaps.

Should you decide to use bitmaps in your Shockwave for FreeHand image, just use the Place command as you did with placing Postscript. To work with your bitmaps in the best quality preview, select Preferences from the File menu. Then, in the redraw category, choose the high-resolution TIFF display.

Using multiple copies of bitmaps is a bandwidth-efficient way to add repetitive textures. Afterburner is very good at crunching down files that contain redundant bitmaps. The file BITMAPEX.FH5 in the Chapter 6 folder on the accompanying CD-ROM, for example, has three copies of the same 640×480 bitmap image, each differently rotated (see fig. 6.22).

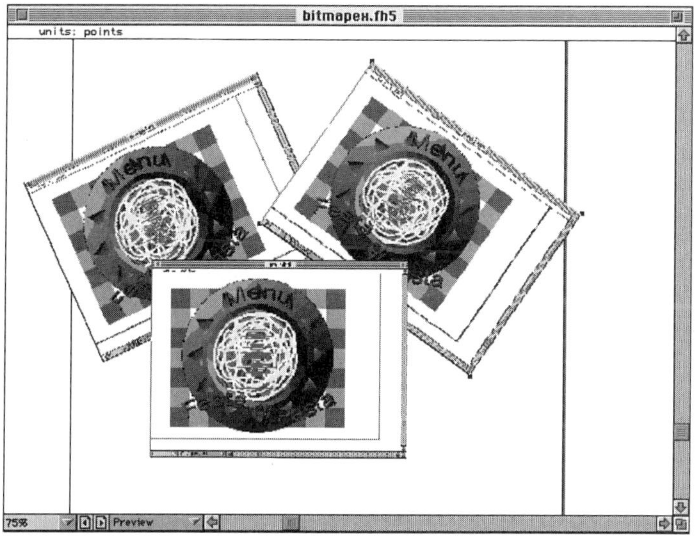

FIGURE 6.22

This Shockwave for FreeHand file has three embedded copies of a very large bitmapped image. The compressed FHC file is a mere 21 KB in size. Tiling bitmaps in Shockwave for FreeHand can be a low-bandwidth way to add a lot of texture.

The source bitmap file, PASTABIG.PIC, is 61 KB. The FreeHand file BITMAPEX.FH5 with three copies of PASTABIG.PIC placed into it is 318 KB. The Shockwave for FreeHand file is a mere 21 KB large.

The main price you pay with using multiple bitmaps as texture is the redraw hit. While FreeHand has a high-performance screen redraw engine for vector graphics, rendering scaled bitmaps to the screen is a much more taxing operation. Therefore, you must decide between risking the impatience of your audience or using a vectored alternative to bitmaps.

Unavailable Features and Limitations

Shockwave for FreeHand does not support all the objects or features that FreeHand is capable of creating. These limitations are as follows:

- The EPS format is not a space-efficient format. Therefore, Shockwave for FreeHand does not support the display of EPS images. Just import editable Postscript with the Convert When Placed option active in the import/export preferences.
- If you have a multiple-page FreeHand document, the page that was active when you last saved from FreeHand will be the page that is displayed in Netscape Navigator. You can view the other pages in Netscape by panning. However, we recommend that you avoid using multiple pages so that you keep file size to a minimum and to ensure that people viewing your page don't inadvertently miss important parts of your graphics.
- A particular FreeHand file may not be embedded more than once in a single HTML document.
- Display of Postscript fills and lines (for example, textured and custom) are not supported. You can get around this using the Paste Inside command. Simply place a bitmapped texture, then Cut and Paste Inside the desired curves.

Of course, you should get the most current versions of Shockwave from the Macromedia website. Read the documentation to find out about the current features, bugs, and limitations.

Optimizing FreeHand Documents for the Web

File sizes and the associated download times are always major considerations when designing for the Web. The following lists contains things you can do to minimize FreeHand file sizes:

- Delete any objects that are not visible in the final graphic.
- Delete unused colors. (This command is available in the Xtras menu under Delete.)
- Delete unused or invisible layers. (This command is available in the Layers palette under Options.)

- Delete items that were placed in the background layer and traced over.
- Simplify complex objects using FreeHand's Simplify command. This command deletes unnecessary points in an object, which can add a considerable amount to the size of a file. (This command is available in the Xtras menu under Cleanup.)
- Keep the use of Paste Insides to a minimum.

Performance on the Web

The two main performance issues in Shockwave for FreeHand are transfer speed (bandwidth) and screen redraw (complexity).

The best test of transfer speed is, of course, to run off the Web. Pull your image across the Web and run within Netscape or other Shockwave for FreeHand compatible browsers running on a baseline machine with the minimum system requirements that you suggest to your users. Test the transfer speeds of your Web server and main target networks. Server and network speeds vary greatly, and with them varies the tolerance of users for your Shockwave files.

If your FreeHand image is intended for zooming and panning, you should test carefully for redraw performance. Very large and complex images can pan and zoom too slowly for your purposes. For quick testing as you develop your image, just zoom and pan within FreeHand. Screen redraw under Shockwave playback is almost as fast as the screen redraw in FreeHand's preview mode. So, if zooming and panning is too slow within FreeHand itself, you should consider simplifying the image.

Conclusion

After completing this chapter, you should have a solid background on using Shockwave for FreeHand. We have shown the benefits of Shockwave for FreeHand and suggested ways you might apply it to various design challenges. Finally we detailed the Web-specific issues and the technology platform of Shockwave for FreeHand. All that remains now is for you to put your creativity to the test and show the world (wide Web) how well you can shock with FreeHand.

CHAPTER

7

Understanding Shockwave for Authorware

Authorware is Macromedia's premium program for computer-based training and information delivery. At roughly $5000, it is intended largely for corporate installations. Because Macromedia offers an aggressive educational discount, however, Authorware has a substantial presence at universities and colleges. These are two types of environments where one usually finds a high-speed internal network (intranet).

Because Authorware is intended for these kinds of installations, Shockwave for Authorware is intended primarily for intranets. There is nothing to keep you from developing Shockwave for Authorware courses for the Internet—and many people have already done so—but the design of Shockwave for Authorware is optimized for intranet delivery. Because of its intranet targeting, Shockwave for Authorware is somewhat more flexible when dealing with concerns such as security and bandwidth than are Shockwave for Director or Shockwave for FreeHand. Shockwave for Authorware enables you to designate certain sites as "trusted," which allows automatic downloading of external content files, such as QuickTime movies, and external code chunks (known as UCDs, or User Code Documents, in Authorware terminology) from that site.

In this chapter we examine the basics of how Shockwave for Authorware differs from Shockwave for Director and FreeHand. We also examine how to make an Authorware movie into a Shockwave for Authorware movie. In the following chapter, we will explore the new network-specific features of Shockwave for Authorware.

Shockwave for Authorware: Maps, Segments, and Trust

In addition to the obvious fact that it deals with Authorware files, there are four ways that Shockwave for Authorware differs from Shockwave for Director:

- It employs a limited kind of streaming, which splits the file into segments of a user-definable size.
- It can, with user approval, automatically download various files such as transition Xtras, external code files, and linked media.
- It requires different files for Macintosh and Windows.
- It uses a separate Afterburner application, rather than a tool Xtra.

These four factors make working with Shockwave for Authorware somewhat of a different experience than working with the other two kinds of Shockwave.

Streaming

A burnt Authorware file results in a map file (with an AAM extension) and a number of segment files. The *map file* is a list of the segment and external files that make up the course. The segment files are the actual material of the course, compressed and split (or segmented). These can be almost any size (4,000–500,000 bytes, which is roughly 4 K–488 K) and are only downloaded as needed. When burning a file, the developer is presented with a dialog box, querying what size segments he wants to split the file into (see fig. 7.1). Larger segments mean less frequent—but longer waits for—downloads, whereas smaller segments force the user to wait more often, but for shorter periods.

By default, the segment prefix for Authorware is the first four characters of the filename. You can choose a different four characters, but is not recommended unless you have a compelling reason (such as pre-existing segments with the same prefix).

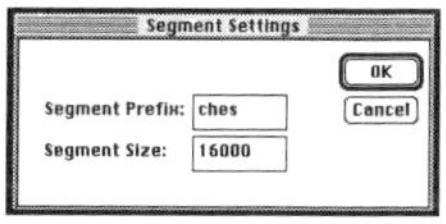

FIGURE 7.1

Segment sizes can be any size between 4,000 and 500,000 bytes.

Because Authorware files usually have a discernible default flow (down the flowline), segments are usually utilized in full. That is, very rarely does a segment end up having to be loaded for the contents of just one icon.

Optimum segment sizes can depend on several variables, including server speed, connection speed, and type of content. Macromedia recommends that you start with a value of 16,000 bytes (the default) and experiment. The segments will not, however, break across icons. So if your first icon is a full-screen bitmap, the first segment will be the size of that bitmap. In the next chapter, we will explore some methods to optimize whatever connection speed you are working with.

The map file is actually a text file that lists which files are appropriate for which platform and how to treat them. A sample map file looks like the following:

```
ver    0   2
get    .
put    DOWNLOAD
seg    mac    math0000.aas    0    63937
seg    mac    math0001.aas    63937    41180
seg    mac    math0002.aas    105117    1245
LIB    MAC    "PIECES.AAM"    "PIECES.PKL"
get    .
bin    mac    "timer.moov.aab"    "timer.MooV"    macbinary,onDemand
```

The first line of the map file is the version of Afterburner that created the file. In this case, that version is 0.2.

The second line indicates the directory in which the segment files are located. Note that in the above example, this is relative to the location of the map file. So in this example, the segment files are located in the same directory as the map file. If your segment files were located in a subdirectory named Segments, one level below the location of the map file, the second line would actually read `get Segments`. You also can specify an absolute URL, so if you wanted to reference the segments in the /AW/Segments directory on the www.corporate.com server; the second line would read `get http://www.corporate.com/AW/Segments`.

The third line tells the plug-in where external files, such as movies, will be downloaded to the user's computer. The default location is a Download folder that's automatically created by the Authorware plug-in when `put DOWNLOAD` appears in a map file. You can get the Shockwave for Authorware plug-in to create a folder with another name by changing the line. For example, `put files` will create a folder called "files."

The fourth and following lines identify the content of the Authorware course. Each content line can identify a segment, a library, or an external content item (such as a movie or sound). Each type of line is divided into columns and has its own format. They are listed in order: segments first, then libraries, and finally external content. External content will produce another directory location line, because the files are often stored in a different directory than segments and map files.

Segment Lines

For segment lines, the format is as follows:

1. Type of content. For segments, this is "seg."
2. Platform. This can be either "mac" or "win." You can have both mac and win versions in the same map file.
3. Segment name. This is the four-character name selected in Afterburner, as well as a four-digit identifier assigned by Afterburner.
4. The start point of the segment, in relation to the beginning of the piece. This number is in bytes.
5. The size of the segment, in bytes. Note that even though the segment size selected for the example map file was 16,000 bytes, the large size of the first segment is much larger than that. This reflects a large bitmap background in the sample file.

Library Lines

For library lines the format is as follows:

1. Type of content. For libraries, this is "lib."
2. Platform. Again, at this point, the platform can be only "mac" or "win."
3. Name of library map file. This indicates the name of the map file containing the library content.
4. Library Name. This indicates the original name of the library.

Note that libraries that are packaged separately must be burned separately.

External Content Lines

External content lines are a bit more complicated, as demonstrated in the last line of the sample map file:

```
bin    mac    "timer.moov.aab"    "timer.MooV"    macbinary,onDemand
```

The format is as follows:

1. Type of content. For external files, this is "bin" (binary).
2. Platform. For external files, this can have any one of the following values:

all	Macintosh and Windows
mac	Macintosh
win	Windows (both 16-bit and 32-bit)
win16	16-bit Windows
win32	32-bit Windows

   Some of these options are not available for different types of files. A windows UCD, for example, should not be downloaded to a Macintosh. A flattened QuickTime movie, on the other hand, can be downloaded for both.

3. Filename on server. This is the filename on the HTTP server, in quotes.
4. Original filename. This the name of the file when linked into the Authorware file. It is in quotes as well, largely because it could contain spaces.
5. Downloading options. This column is optional, but can be very useful to tune the way your Shockwave for Authorware file downloads external content. The options are explained in table 7.1.

TABLE 7.1

SHOCKWAVE FOR AUTHORWARE OPTIONS FOR DOWNLOADING EXTERNAL FILES

Option	*Description*
empty	If you leave the fifth column empty, the file will be downloaded to the user's computer when the Authorware piece begins and deleted when the piece ends. Downloading external files at the start of the piece is usually not the best choice, however, because it can cause long delays for the user.
onDemand	Downloads the file only when the piece calls for it. Many external files that are referenced from icons within Authorware can be downloaded on demand. For external files that Authorware doesn't know about, such as DLLs not

Option	*Description*
	directly referenced within a piece, use the NetDownload function in a calculation icon to download the files when needed. Use onDemand for most external files.
recycle	Does not delete the file when the Authorware piece ends. When the piece starts again, it uses this file instead of downloading it a second time. This setting can save users a lot of time if they run the same piece repeatedly or if several pieces share one external file.
preempt	If a given external file is available on a user's hard disk or CD-ROM drive, this setting tells Authorware to disregard that file and instead look to the network for it. This option can be useful in a few situations—for example, if you provide certain QuickTime videos on a CD-ROM as part of a piece but have put newer versions of these files on the server. This setting means the newer versions will be downloaded.
MacBinary	Creates an AAB file combining the resource fork and the data fork of the file into a single MacBinary file. This preserves the Mac creator and type information and is needed to ensure that movies, Xtras, and XCMDs download properly, because HTTP transfers over the Internet would otherwise not preserve this information.

These settings can be combined by adding additional options, separated by commas without spaces. For more information on these options, see the Shockwave for Authorware developer's guide on `www.macromedia.com`.

Note

Note for Macintosh Developers

Many Macintosh files consist of two parts, called "forks." The first is the data fork, which is common to every platform. The second is the resource fork, which is specific to the Macintosh. HTTP servers, as well as the Unix and DOS file systems do not have resource forks, and do not know how to handle the Macintosh resource fork. Therefore, to upload a Macintosh file with a resource fork successfully, you need to "flatten" it, which means adding the resource fork information to the data fork. The file is then referred to as a *MacBinary file.*

In Shockwave for Authorware, this can be done two ways. When a file is explicitly referenced by the Authorware file, Afterburner automatically flattens the file. When it is not, you must manually flatten it, using the Afterburner File, Flatten command. In either case, the file has an AAB extension added to the original filename to indicate that it is a MacBinary file.

Of course, it is very important to ensure that any external files referenced by your course are uploaded to the correct location.

Trust

The primary concern on the Internet is, of course, security. Nothing makes an MIS manager shiver in his boots more than the thought of people in the company randomly downloading software from the World Wide Web. Things such as UCDs and other external code modules raise the specter-haunting MIS. On the other hand, on an internal network, it is often necessary to have these external code modules to deal with necessary parts of a training course, for example.

Shockwave for Authorware enables the user to assign levels of trust to various Authorware sites. When the user hits a page with an Authorware movie embedded, he is presented with a dialog box giving him the option to "Trust this site" or "Don't trust this site" (see fig. 7.2). When the former is chosen, the Authorware file works just as you would expect; when the latter is chosen, any external file downloading is disabled.

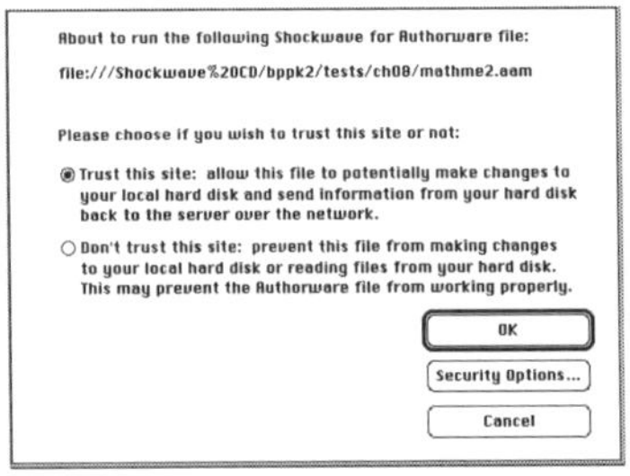

FIGURE 7.2

The user has the option of trusting a site.

> **Tip**
>
> It is important to realize that turning off trusted mode means that even files such as QuickTime movies, which are not actually executables, will not download. This means that files that include any external content will probably not run in untrusted mode at all. This may not be a problem if you are producing content for intranets, because most people do trust their internal MIS people. (If they don't, incorrectly running Authorware courses are the least of their problems.) For Internet delivery, however, it remains to be seen whether people will by default trust unknown sites.

In addition to deciding whether to trust a site, the user can choose among several security options. When a user clicks on the Security Options button of the Trust dialog box, the Security options dialog box appears. The Security options dialog box is separated into several sections (see fig. 7.3). The dialog box shown here is a prerelease version and might not be identical to the final version. The basic components should be the same, however, and it will be helpful to understand what these options mean for developers.

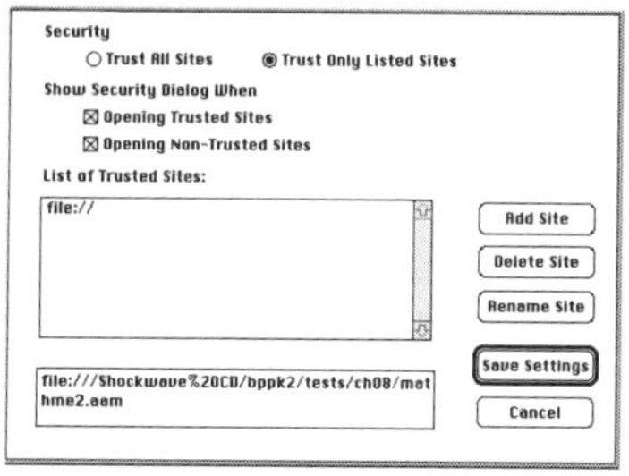

FIGURE 7.3
Understanding the Security options dialog box is helpful for developers.

The first section, Security, would be better termed Security Default. This sets whether every site is trusted (a potential security risk) or whether only listed sites are trusted (a somewhat less serious potential security risk). The default is Trust Only Listed Sites, and it is probably the case that most users will not change this.

The second section, Show Security Dialog When, controls whether the dialog displays when opening trusted or untrusted sites. The default is show the dialog all the time.

The third section is the List of Trusted Sites. A "trusted site" can actually be a site or a specific directory or file. To trust everything on the Macromedia site, for example, you would type `http://www.macromedia.com/` into the text box, then press the Add Site button.

In addition, when running in untrusted mode, there are some Authorware functions and variables that are disabled for security reasons. The disabled functions are

`AppendExtFile`	`JumpPrintReturn`
`Catalog`	`PrintScreen`
`CreateFolder`	`ReadExtFile*`
`DeleteFile`	`RenameFile`

JumpFileReturn	SaveRecords
JumpOut	WriteExtFile
JumpOutReturn	

* ReadExtFile *is disabled only for files on the local hard disk. It will work on files over the network. So the function will work if the file reference begins with "http:",* ReadExtFile(http://www.website.com/file.txt), *for example. If the file reference is a local file, as in* ReadExtFile(c:/data/file.txt), *the call will not work.*

The disabled variables are

DiskBytes	OrigWorkingDirectory
FileLocation	RecordsLocation
FileType	SearchPath

Of course, all these functions and variables will work when the file is run in trusted mode.

This section has given you a basic understanding of the security issues involved and how Authorware deals with them. The following section will take you through the basic steps of making your Authorware movie a Shockwave for Authorware movie.

Basics of Shocking with Authorware

There are two areas you need to concentrate on when using Shockwave for Authorware. The first is designing for the Net; the second is optimizing the process of converting your movies to Shockwave for Authorware. Both categories have slightly different constraints, depending on whether you are targeting intranets or the Internet, but it is best to be aware of the ways to deal with the hardest case (which in this case is the Internet).

Designing Authorware Courses for Shockwave

When designing and developing your Authorware course for Shockwave, you can do several basic things that will make it a much more Net-friendly piece.

These rules will be of utmost importance to those of you delivering over the Internet, but they'll be helpful to those of you who use other delivery methods as well.

- **Keep the presentation window size small.** It is a mistake to depend on users having a screen larger than 640×480 pixels. Netscape in its default configuration takes up 120 pixels vertically simply with its interface. This means that to be completely visible on a 640×480 screen, your piece cannot be taller than 340–360 pixels (depending on the platform). This is a constraint that you will be wise to keep in mind when designing your movies. Unless you know all your customers have monitors larger than 640×480, we recommend creating movies no bigger than the Mac Classic setting in the File Setup dialog (512×342). Therefore, you should keep the window size significantly below that so users can see the whole piece without having to scroll around. A smaller presentations window also allows smaller graphics for things such as backgrounds, which means smaller file sizes overall.
- **Use text instead of audio narration when possible.** Audio takes up very large amounts of bandwidth. Download time almost always take longer than actual playback time. If you were to use an audio narration, it would end up being short bursts of sound followed by longer waits while the next bit downloads. Definitely not a pleasant user experience.
- **Use standard fonts.** If you need fancy fonts, you must bitmap them, which means that they are not editable. With text, it is best to use the standard fonts: Chicago, Courier, Geneva, Helvetica, Monaco, New York, Palatino, Symbol, and Times on the Macintosh and Arial, Courier New, Symbol, Times New Roman, and Wingdings on Windows.
- **Reduce bit depth for sound and graphics.** Images that are more than eight bits deep are almost never worth the download time, especially since many users do not have the hardware to view them. You should try to reduce your images as much as possible. Authorware allows you to assign a foreground and background color to 1-bit images, which is often an excellent way of conserving space. When combined with libraries (see the following item), you often can get a number of different-looking images out of one small download. Unless you have a special need for high-quality audio, it is often best to use 8-bit, 11.025 khz, mono sound files. This is fine quality for voice, and is usually an acceptable trade-off for music.

- **If you have content that is repeated, use libraries.** If you have an image or sound that is repeated in several places in your course, the most efficient way to deal with it is to put that item in a library and use references to it in the course. Simply copying and pasting the icon within the course actually makes a separate copy, doubling the space needed. Using library references, however, adds only a minimal amount of overhead for each copy.
- **Avoid large external files.** QuickTime movies and the like can add an additional dimension of interest to a course, but they tend to be very large. Only in very rare cases do they add enough to a course to be worth the download time. If you have QuickTime movies in your course, examine them carefully to see if they are truly necessary.

  One way to handle the additional download burden is to use a static image from one frame of the movie as a clickable button to download the actual movie. When used with the onDemand setting in the map file, this can enable users to choose whether they are willing to suffer the download time. They must, of course, be running in trusted mode to see the file at all.
- **Avoid UCDs, XCMDs, and other external code items.** For the reasons outlined in the "Trust" section earlier in this chapter, it is often best to avoid external code objects, especially when delivering over the Internet. This unfortunately includes such bread-and-butter items as the Palette UCD or XCMD. Sticking to one palette, therefore, is highly recommended.
- **Check for disallowed functions and variables.** Unless you are sure that your file is always going to be run in trusted mode, you should check through the file to make sure that you don't use any of the disabled functions and variables. The disabled functions and variables are listed in the "Trust" section earlier in this chapter.
- **Use large graphics wisely.** Because large graphics take a long time to download, you should get as much use out of them as possible. So they should be used largely for things such as backgrounds, where they will stick around for a while, or can be put in a library and used repeatedly.

These are some of the basic rules for designing your Authorware presentations for the Web. While it is not absolutely required that you follow these rules, they will make your Shockwave for Authorware website a much more pleasant experience.

EXAMPLE 7.1

Shocking an Authorware Movie

To demonstrate the process of making a Shockwave for Authorware movie, we will use the sample file CHESS.A3M, located in the Chapter 7 folder. (This is a Macintosh file. If you are on Windows, you can use the same file, you simply have to convert it.) There also is an attached library file, PIECES.A31.

Built for Speed

The file CHESS.A3M, which quizzes the user on how some chess pieces move, follows most—but not all—of the rules outlined in the previous section. The presentation window is small (512×342, or "Classic, 9"," after the Macintosh Classic computer's screen size) in Authorware terminology. This will enable us to avoid having the application take up the whole screen when it runs, as well as keep the board small.

Although the chess pieces are used only once in this fragment, we still put them in a library because were we to want to extend this course (and we do), having those graphics in a library would enable us to use them over and over without requiring additional file size.

The only 8-bit image in the piece is the chessboard itself. With it, we use one technique that is not a general rule, but is a good trick to keep in your toolbox. That is, we cut the chessboard in half and use the same image twice—once for the top half of the board and once for the bottom (see fig. 7.4). This means that we are only downloading half as much. In principle, we could actually break this image down to small images, one for each type of square, but that would be more difficult to manage. You will often have to make judgments about the authoring time and effort versus download time.

FIGURE 7.4

Using one half of the chessboard twice reduces the download time by half.

These techniques keep the file fairly small. The total of the library and the Authorware file itself is 246 KB. This is not huge for a file that will be delivered by disk, but is too large for a network course.

Soup It Up

Now we have the file ready to go and it is time to burn it. We first have to package the file. When packaging a file with a library, we have to make a decision whether to package the library internally, or as a separate file. The basic rule of thumb is that if you have multiple files using the same library, it is better to package it externally, whereas if you are using the library with only one file, it is best to package it internally. Although we have only one file in this example, for the purposes of demonstration, we will package it externally.

To package the course for burning, complete the following steps:

1. Make sure the file itself (rather than the library) is the frontmost window.
2. Choose File, Package to display the Package dialog box (see fig. 7.5). Package the file Without Runtime and with none of the other options selected except Use Default Names When Packaging. Accept the default name, CHESS.PKG.
3. Package the file Without Runtime, and with none of the other options selected. When asked, accept the default name, CHESS.PKG.

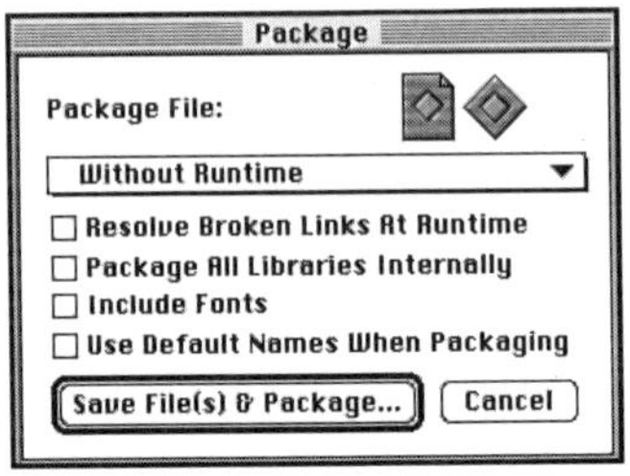

FIGURE 7.5
The Package dialog box.

4. Now open Afterburner. Choose File, Afterburn. Select the CHESS.PKG file and click OK.

If you want to make a version for the other platform, you can follow the same steps with Authorware and Afterburner on the other platform. The only caveat is that you need to select different four-character prefixes for the file and library segments. Then, select all the segment and library references from one of the map files and copy it into the other map file.

You are now ready to take the file for a test drive.

Taking It for a Spin

All that is left to do is embed the piece within an HTML page and try it out.

1. Open the file 7-1.HTM. Add the following line after the line that reads `Enjoy.<p>`:

   ```
   <embed src="chess.aam" width=512 height=342 window=onTop>
   ```

2. Save the file and then open it in your Web browser.

> **Note**
>
> With Shockwave for Authorware, the <embed> tag has one additional parameter, which is the window parameter. It affects how the Authorware file appears in relation to your browser. There are three options for this setting, only two of which work on the Macintosh platform:
>
> - `inPlace` displays the piece embedded within the HTML page in the browser window. You can use `inPlace` only in Windows.
> - `onTop` displays the piece in a separate window on top of the browser window. This makes your piece look more like a separate application. This is the default.
> - `onTopMinimize` displays the piece in a separate window and minimizes the browser. This setting makes your piece look the most like a separate, stand-alone application.
>
> If you are using the `inPlace` setting, there are two additional factors to bear in mind:
>
> - Don't try to use a title bar on your presentation window. (The Title Bar setting is in the File Setup dialog box.) Embedding `inPlace` doesn't allow the display of a title bar. Instead, the height of your presentation window will be reduced by the height of the title bar. This clearly makes for a less-than-ideal user experience.

> ⚡ Avoid using the `ResizeWindow` and `MoveWindow` functions, which, according to Macromedia, "can produce unpredictable results with `inPlace`." Be aware that "can produce unpredictable results" is software-manual-speak for "will probably crash and will probably do so in a spectacularly ugly manner and at the least convenient time."

Summary

This chapter has addressed the basics of Shockwave for Authorware, focusing on how to design your piece to make it as Net-friendly as possible. The next chapter will examine the network-specific features of Shockwave for Authorware, and how you can use them to make your course as Net-savvy as possible.

CHAPTER

8

Developing Shocked Sites with Authorware

Because Shockwave for Authorware is used primarily to provide content, rather than to enhance an already-existing website, developing a shocked site for Authorware consists primarily of developing a Net-friendly Authorware piece (as outlined in the previous chapter) and adding Net-specific features to make the piece as Net-savvy as possible.

In this chapter we will explore the new functions and variables (also referenced on New Riders' website, http://www.mcp.com/newriders), look briefly at ways to ensure the Shockwave for Authorware piece integrates as well as possible with your website, and finally examine an example piece that uses many of the Net-specific functions and variables.

New Functions and Variables

Shockwave has added some new functions and variables and has extended some of the already-existing ones. These additions perform two functions:

- They give Authorware the capability to access the network.
- They provide ways to overcome some of the limitations of bandwidth and security.

The next three sections explore the new functions, extended functions, and new variables for Shockwave for Authorware. These functions and variables are set in bold, with applicable function parameters following in italic.

New Functions

The following three sections describe the new functions for Shockwave for Authorware.

GoToNetPage(*URL, targetName*)

`GoToNetPage` works just like its Shockwave for Director 5 counterpart. It causes the browser to go to another page, identified in the first parameter.

The second parameter can be a window name or a frame name. The second parameter is optional. If you omit it, the browser will load the new page into the current window. Because this is the window in which the Authorware piece is running, the Authorware piece will quit when the new page has completed loading. If you return to the page with the embedded Authorware piece, it will start again from the beginning. If the target is a name that Navigator does not recognize as a valid frame or window name, it will open a new window with that name. There also is a keyword, `_blank`, which will open a new, unnamed window.

One concern that is specific to Authorware is the fact that when Authorware is running `OnTop`, new windows will open up underneath the Authorware piece. Clicking on them will bring them to the front, but it is hardly the most visually appealing construction.

The following code fragment opens the Macromedia home page in a window named "Macromedia." If the window already exists, the page will be loaded into it. If not, a new window will be created. The Authorware piece will continue to run.

```
GoToNetPage("www.macromedia.com", "macromedia")
```

NetDownload(URL)

`NetDownload` downloads the file located at the URL specified onto the user's hard disk. This file can be of any type. The function returns the full path name of the file when downloaded. It will download files to the location you set in the map file. If the map file doesn't have an entry for the file, the file will be downloaded to the Download subfolder of the folder containing the Shockwave for Authorware plug-in (which varies from platform to platform).

The intended use of this function is to provide a way to load files that are not directly referenced by an icon, such as UCDs. You can use it in combination with the `onDemand` setting in the map file to download these files as needed.

The following example downloads the README.TXT file and returns the path name to a variable named string:

```
string:= NetDownload("http://www.company.com/readme.txt")
```

For this example, the path name assigned to string might be C:\NETSCAPE\Plug-Ins\NP16ASW\DOWNLOAD.

NetPreload(IconID@"IconTitle")

`NetPreload` is a function that enables you to take maximum advantage of Authorware's streaming capabilities. When called, this function begins downloading the segment files necessary to execute the icon specified by `IconTitle`. If `IconTitle` is a map, interaction, decision, or framework icon, all icons attached or within `IconTitle` are preloaded.

`NetPreload` is most useful when the user is busy doing something else—reading extensive amounts of text or completing complicated interactions, for example. The function can make the difference between a smooth, immersive experience and a jerky, frustrating experience, but also can be disruptive if used carelessly. Once initiated, the function will complete. This means that if Authorware needs to download another segment in the meantime, the automatic download will be slowed or halted while the preload completes.

`NetPreload` will not work with external files—for example, a QuickTime or AVI movie. This function is best used with display icons containing large bitmaps or sound icons because these are the preloadable icons that take the most time to load.

The return value from this function is meaningless and should be ignored.

Extended Functions

The following two sections describe Shockwave for Authorware's extended functions.

JumpFile and JumpFileReturn

These existing Authorware functions now accept an URL as their first argument. The enhancement enables you to place several Authorware pieces on a server and jump from one to another without leaving Authorware.

The following example causes the current Authorware piece to jump to another piece:

```
JumpFile("http://www.company.com/aware/piece1.aam")
```

Because `JumpFileReturn` requires that records be written to the user's hard disk, it will not work when the user is running in Non-Trusting mode. (For more on Non-Trusting mode, see the section "Trust" in Chapter 7, "Understanding Shockwave for Authorware.")

ReadExtFile

This existing Authorware function now accepts an absolute URL for its argument. To be valid, the URL must begin with `http://servername/` or `file:///`. This example causes the Authorware piece to read the text file MYFILE.TXT and return the file's entire contents as a character string:

```
string := ReadExtFile("http://myserver.com/myfolder/myfile.txt")
```

In Non-Trusting mode, `ReadExtFile` will not take an URL beginning with `file://` as an argument. This is to prevent unscrupulous developers from reading the contents of files from your hard disk.

New Variables

The following two sections describe Shockwave for Authorware's new variables.

NetConnected

This new variable tells whether an Authorware piece is running with the Shockwave for Authorware plug-in. If the piece is running with the plug-in, the value is 1. If the piece is running in the authoring environment or with RunA3W, the value is 0.

You can use `NetConnected` with if-then statements in calculation icons and with a decision icon to branch to different icons, depending on whether the piece is running on an intranet.

This variable is of marginal utility, because it is almost certain that you will not be able to use an Authorware file effectively on the Internet without significant changes, as outlined in the previous chapter.

NetLocation

This new variable tells the URL of the current piece. It is the equivalent of the variable `FileLocation` in the desktop version of Authorware and is equally valuable.

The following example reads in the file MSG.TXT located in the same directory as the Authorware piece:

```
ReadExtFile(NetLocation^"msg.txt")
```

At press time, it was not clear whether this was the final, complete set of variables and functions available for Shockwave for Authorware. Check the Macromedia documentation for any additions or changes.

FileLocation

The one variable extended in Shockwave for Authorware is the `FileLocation` variable. If the course is operating in non-trusted mode, the FileLocation variable will return an empty (zero-length) string. If the course is operating in trusted mode, the `FileLocation` variable will return the location of the plug-in directory on the file system.

Therefore, the author can place the following code at the start of the course in a calc icon to determine the security mode:

```
-- Test for security in trust/non-trust mode.
if FileLocation = "" then
   -- Security is enabled. Operating in non-trusted mode.
   NetSecurity = 1
else
   -- Security is disabled. Operating in trusted mode.
   NetSecurity = 0
end if
```

Integrating Shockwave for Authorware with Your Website

There are several questions you need to ask yourself when you figure out how to shock your site with Authorware:

- How do you prevent users who don't have the plug-in from hitting the dreaded broken plug-in icon?
- Do you want the Authorware pieces to appear as part of the page, or on top, in separate windows?
- What else do you want on those pages?
- What other things do you need to provide other than the Authorware content?

Once you have dealt with these questions, shocking your site with Authorware becomes largely a matter of creating compelling and Net-savvy Authorware content.

Avoiding the Broken Plug-in Icon

There are two ways to prevent unsuspecting users from stumbling across the broken plug-in icon and a confusing dialog box. You can quarantine the Shockwave content in an isolated section of your site and warn the user that she needs the plug-in, or you can use JavaScript to only show the Shockwave content if the user has the plug-in.

Because in most Authorware-shocked sites the Authorware content is the point of those pages, you will most likely want to choose the first method. More information on the second method is available in Chapter 12, "Talking with the Outside World: Parameters and JavaScript."

Quarantining the Shockwave portion of the site means forcing every access to any shocked pages to come through a gateway page. This will warn the user that he needs the appropriate Shockwave plug-in (in this case, Shockwave for Authorware) and tells him how to get it. An example quarantine page is shown in figure 8.1.

FIGURE 8.1

One way to avoid the broken plug-in icon is to add a quarantine page.

Part of the Page or Rising Above?

Shockwave for Authorware gives you two options of how to embed the piece in an HTML page. You can embed the piece as part of the page, like a graphic or Shockwave for Director movie is embedded, or you can embed it so it opens a separate window.

Embedding the piece as part of the page is accomplished by using the `window=inPlace` parameter with the `<embed>` tag. This option is, unfortunately, only available on the Windows platform. In many ways this option seems more familiar to Web users because they are not used to windows randomly popping up out of their browser. It does have the effect, however, of de-emphasizing the Authorware piece. And because you include Shockwave for Authorware pieces at all, they are likely to be the point of the pages on which they appear, this effect might not be desirable.

Embedding the piece so it opens a separate window has two varieties. The first opens a separate window (leaving the browser window alone) and uses the `window=onTop` parameter. The second minimizes the browser window when it opens the Authorware piece and is invoked with the `window=onTopMinimize` parameter. When the Macintosh plug-in runs across a piece embedded `inPlace`, it runs the piece on top without minimizing.

The minimized version can be confusing for novice users and is not recommended. The regular `onTop` version also can be somewhat confusing, but it's a good compromise between possible user confusion and emphasis on the Authorware piece. It is especially recommended when you are opening other windows to display Web pages and the like.

When opening a separate window, the piece obeys the center check box in the File Setup dialog box. Therefore, you can choose whether to have the piece open in the top left corner of the screen or in the center.

What Else Goes on the Pages?

If you are embedding in place on the page, you need to take into account what else goes on the page because it will be visible next to the piece. This text can be anything, but it should not distract from the Authorware piece.

Useful things to include can be quick instructions on how to use the piece or links for the user to follow when he is done. It is important to remember, again, that if the point of the page is the Authorware content, then you should distract as little as possible from that content.

What Other Elements Do You Need to Provide?

When integrating Authorware content into your website, it is important to have all your other ducks in a row as early in the process as possible. If you are depending on external text files, for example, you should nail down their format as early as possible in the development process. You also need to make sure the files are uploaded to their correct location when you go online with the site.

EXAMPLE 8.1

Teach Me Chess: An Authorware Example

In this example, we expand on the chess theme we began in the previous chapter. The file, while by no means a brilliant example of Authorware programming, will serve to demonstrate some of the network-specific features of Shockwave for Authorware.

This file uses the same chessboard and chess piece graphics as the file from the last chapter. In fact, it uses the very same library! This enables us, as we shall see, to leverage the download time of these pieces.

The file does some very simple things. It presents introductory text (in part to give cover for preloading the chessboard graphic) and then presents the user with the opportunity to see demonstrations of the movement of four pieces: pawn, rook, knight, and bishop. After the user is done learning about the movement, he can take a quiz on the movement of the pieces or see a list of chess-related sites on the Web (which is stored in an external file).

The file demonstrates the use of the `NetLocation` variable and the `ReadExtFile`, `GoToNetPage`, and `NetPreload` functions. We will examine the use of each of these in turn.

One other technique is to use custom buttons created in the button library tool (accessible through the Libraries, Buttons menu item). We use the right arrow for the continue button and the stylized X for the button that exits from the current menu. By using a button created in the button library, we gain the same benefits as using the standard library—a graphic downloaded once is used multiple times.

The first network function we use is the `NetPreload` function, which is used in the Preload Board icon, the second item in the flowline (see fig. 8.2):

```
NetPreload(IconID@"board-Top")
```

Notice that we only call the `NetPreload` function once for the board top. This one call is performed in the bishop branch of the Teach me introduction. Any other icons that have that same link to the library source will be instantly displayed because their contents have already been downloaded over the network.

FIGURE 8.2

We use NetPreload in the second icon on the flowline.

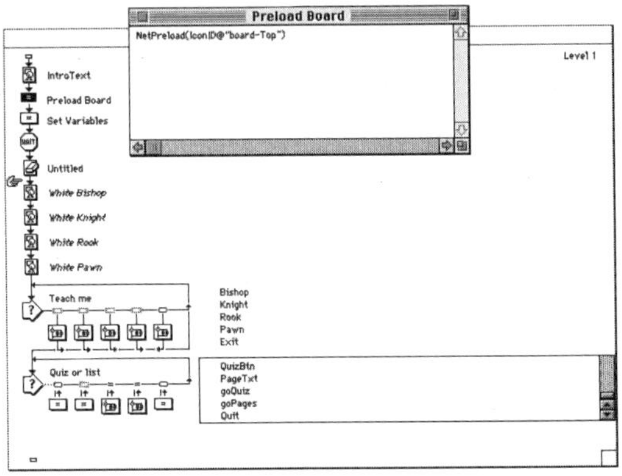

We only use `NetPreload` once, because the only icon we have of significant size is the chessboard.

We use `NetLocation`, `ReadExtFile`, and `GoToNetPage` very close together, in the "goPages" branch of the "Quiz or list" interaction (see fig. 8.3).

In this section of the piece, we first read in the text file containing the list of pages using the `ReadExtFile` function in combination with the `NetLocation` variable:

```
txtVar:=ReadExtFile(NetLocation^"pages.txt")
```

In the interaction that follows, we use an auto-matching conditional to test whether the text variable, `txtVar`, is empty. `txtVar` is the text variable that we use to store the text. If the variable is empty, the file was not read successfully and we need to exit. If it's not empty, we wait at the interaction for the user to click a site name or the exit button.

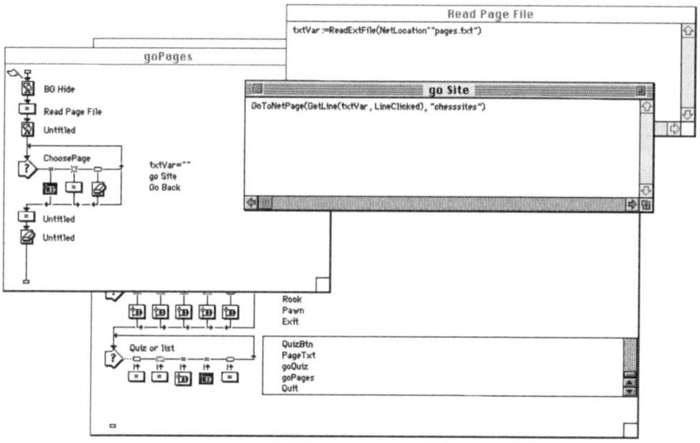

FIGURE 8.3

NetLocation and ReadExtFile are complementary functions.

If the user clicks the list of sites, we extract the line he clicked from the list of sites and open that page in a window called "chess sites":

```
GoToNetPage(GetLine(txtVar, LineClicked), "chesssites")
```

The first time a site URL is clicked, it opens a new window. Subsequent clicks will load the selected page into the window previously opened.

If you open the GoQuiz branch of the "Quiz or list," you will notice that we have included the entire quiz file created in the previous chapter. Because it uses mostly the same graphics files, it requires almost no additional download time to include it.

To maximize loading efficiency, we have packaged this file with the Package all Libraries Internally option selected. This enables Afterburner to distribute the icons among the segments in the order in which they actually occur. The total size of the file is roughly 50 KB!

We have provided a simple HTML file for you, with the piece already embedded, called 8-1.HTM. If you open it in your browser, you should see something along the lines of figure 8.4.

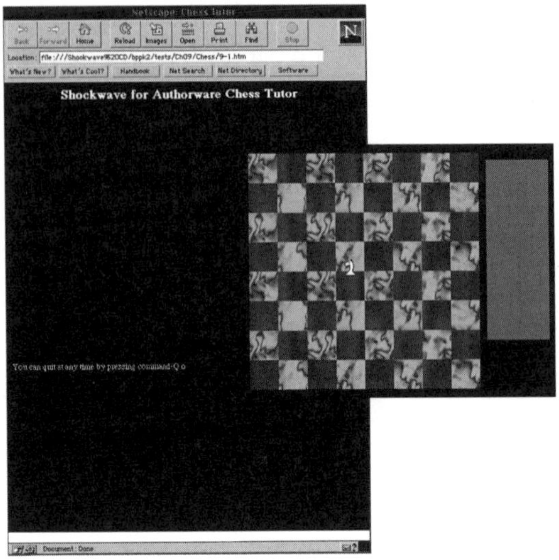

FIGURE 8.4

The Chess Tutor piece is embedded with onTop selected.

Summary

This chapter has provided a quick introduction to the network-specific features of Shockwave for Authorware, as well as how to integrate Shockwave for Authorware into your site.

The next chapter begins Part III of this book, "Advanced Shockwave for Director," in which we explore external casts, working with frames, linked text, and passing parameters to Shockwave movies.

Part III

Advanced Shockwave for Director

Chapter 9

External Casts

One of the most exciting additions to Director 5 is the capability to have multiple casts. In Director 4, each movie was limited to one cast (except for the shared cast, which didn't actually work all that well). Director 5's multiple casts can be internal (contained in the Director movie) or external (separate files). External casts can be shared between both Director movies and Shockwave movies, enabling a developer to use an external cast to store large images that can be shared between movies (see fig. 9.1).

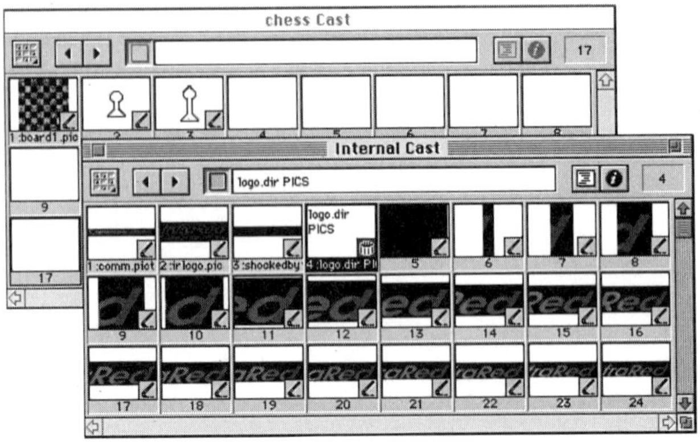

FIGURE 9.1

Movies can use cast members from more than one cast library.

Unfortunately, external casts are subject to the same downloading restrictions: the external cast is not downloaded automatically by Director and the external cast files must be in the support folder. This is the name of the plug-in followed by "folder" on the Mac, and simply the name of the plug-in in Windows. On the Power Macintosh platform, for example, the plug-in is named "NP-PPC-Dir-Shockwave." So if Netscape Navigator is located in the "Netscape" folder on the hard drive named "Internal HD," the full path name of the support folder would be "Internal HD:Netscape:Plug-ins:NP-PPC-Dir-Shockwave Folder." In Windows 95, if the Netscape folder is named "Netscape" located on the c: drive and the plug-in is named "np32dsw," the full path of the support folder would be "c:\netscape\program\plugins\ np32dsw."

Working with External Casts

With Director 5, each movie has a default internal cast, which is contained internally within and has the same name as the Director movie. The default internal cast is equivalent to the cast in Director 4. A movie also can have additional internal casts. Only external casts, however, that have their own file (with a CST extension) can be shared between movies.

Creating an external cast is easy. Simply Choose File, New, Cast (Command+Option+N on Macintosh; Alt+Control+N in Windows) and select the External radio button. You can work with the resulting cast just as you would with the movie's external cast. It is most sensible to name each cast, in addition to its filename, because this enables easier access to the cast from Lingo. To name each cast, choose Modify, Cast Properties, or Control+ click (right-click in Windows) on the cast and choose Cast Properties.

Uses for External Casts

Because Shockwave for Director 5 allows external casts, graphics-heavy portions can be shared, providing the same rich look for several movies on a site. There are two obvious ways to apply this sharing feature: with multiple control panels, which are of different configurations but use the same controls, and with movies that change but use much of the same art (an episodic comic strip story, for example, which would feature similar images of the same characters repeatedly).

Alternatively, a developer could distribute casts on a CD-ROM or floppy disk, with installation instructions. Movies on the Web could then dynamically work with these cast members. America Online and many other services use a model similar to this.

Example 9.1

Two Movies, One Cast

To demonstrate external casts, this chapter will create two control panels that use the same group of cast members. This example is actually well within reasonable size if your audience is on high-speed (corporate or educational) networks. If you are trying to reach a general audience, however, these movies, which weigh in at 60 KB, are probably too big to use as control panels.

The Example Site

For the purposes of this chapter and Chapter 10, "Working with Frames," we will imagine a site with a table of contents page, a home page, a page of information about the creators, a breaking news page, and a help page. Our imaginary site also will have several subdirectories, each with several pages of content. Because an informed Shockwave developer is a Shockwave developer who knows something, we used a fragment of the Telecommunications Act of 1996—not the Communications Decency Act, but one of the more insidious sections. For demonstration purposes, we only fleshed out one subdirectory. These files are located in the Ch9/Site directory. The filenames and locations are detailed in table 9.1.

TABLE 9.1

PROJECT FILES FOR CHAPTER 9 EXAMPLES

Filename	*Description*	*Location on the CD-ROM*
INDEX.HTM	home page	Ch9\Site
TOC.HTM	table of contents	Ch9\Site
HELP.HTM	help page	Ch9\Site
WHO.HTM	creators of the site	Ch9\Site
ALERT.HTM	breaking news	Ch9\Site
DATA3_1.HTM	first data file	Ch9\Site/Sec3
DATA3_2.HTM	second data file	Ch9\Site/Sec3
DATA3_3.HTM	third data file	Ch9\Site/Sec3
DATA3_4.HTM	fourth data file	Ch9\Site/Sec3
DATA3_5.HTM	fifth data file	Ch9\Site/Sec3

The Horizontal Panel

We have created an external cast and the scripts to use it, just for you. Your first task, then, is to link the cast to the movie.

1. Copy the Site directory and its subdirectory to your hard drive.
2. Open a new Director file.
3. Choose Modify, Movie, Casts. This brings up the Movie Casts dialog box (see fig. 9.2).

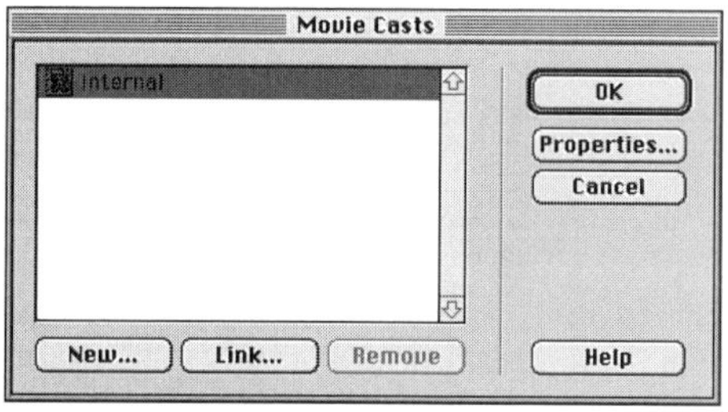

FIGURE 9.2

The Movie Casts dialog box lists the movie's current casts.

4. Click the Link button. This brings up the open dialog box, where you can select a cast. Navigate to the Chapter 9 folder and select the MEDIA.CST file. Click OK.

5. In the cast window, if you are working on a Macintosh, Option+click (Alt+click in Windows) on the cast pop-up on the upper left corner of the window. Select Media. The cast is now open and linked to the movie (see fig. 9.3). Option+clicking (Alt+clicking in Windows) opens the cast in a new window.

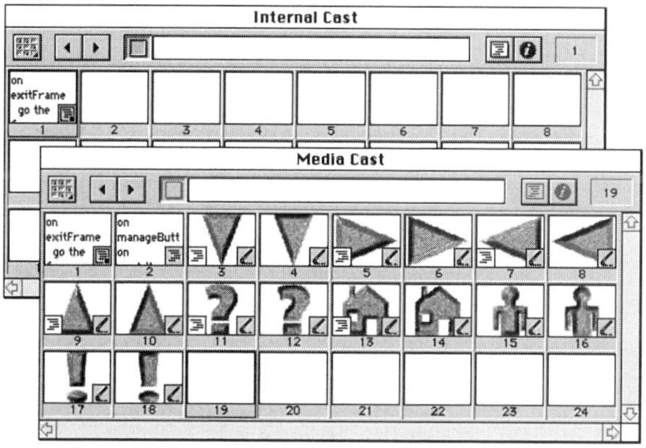

FIGURE 9.3

Option+clicking (Alt+clicking in Windows) on the cast control pop-up opens the cast in a new cast window.

The media cast is set up with scripts to manage the buttons. If a button is clicked, it calls the handler `buttonClicked` with the channel containing the button as a parameter. This enables the downloaded movie to determine what each button does.

Tip

Two things that we do here to optimize ease of editing should be of interest to developers. Though basic techniques, they bear pointing out. First, we use the same script for all cast members. This is important, because it means that we only have to get the script right once. It also means that we can move all the actual functionality to the internal cast, while avoiding repetition of the tedious management of the buttons' up and down states.

Second, instead of repeating the whole script in each cast member, we call a subroutine from each one. This makes changes to the script much easier. If we want to add a click sound, for instance, we can do that by editing only one script, rather than six.

You first use these buttons in a horizontal control panel.

1. In the Modify, Movie, Properties dialog box, set the stage size to 288 × 80, the Default Palette to System-Win, and the background color to gray.
2. Notice that each button shape has two graphic versions. One (the "up" version) is the normal button; the other graphic (the "down" version) will be shown when the user clicks that button. Drag the up versions of all the buttons except the down arrow onto the stage. To follow along exactly, place them from left to right: house, exclamation point, person, and question mark (these are the home, alert, who, and help icons). We recommend placing the buttons in the score in the same order that they are on the stage. This makes them easier to manage.
3. Duplicate the score cells and Option+drag (Alt+drag in Windows) them to frame 2. Select all the sprites and select background transparent in the ink pop-up. Double-click the script channel of frame 2 to open a score script window.
4. In the script window, type the following script:

```
on exitFrame
   go the frame
end
```

5. Drag your sprites to channels 2–5 (so that you can add a background later). Save the file as HORIZ.DIR. Your stage and score should look like figure 9.4.

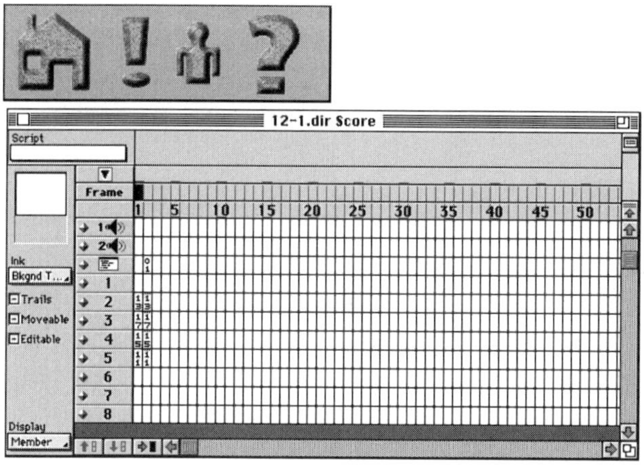

FIGURE 9.4

You should try to order your sprites in the score so that their positions correspond to their positions on stage.

Now you need to make the movie actually do something.

1. In the internal cast, open a new movie script by clicking on an empty cast member and selecting Window, Script.
2. Type the following script:

```
on startMovie
   global gPageList
   set gPageList = ["index","alert","who","help"]
end
```

The following script sets up the list of destination pages. It is important that they be in the same order as the buttons in the score. Add the following handler in the same script cast member:

```
on buttonClicked whichButton
   global gPageList
   set str = GetAt(gPageList, (whichButton - 1))
   GoToNetPage str&".htm"
end
```

Save the file. Your movie is done. Burn the movie by choosing Xtras, Afterburner. Save the file as HORIZ.DCR in the Ch9\Site directory.

You can now embed the movie in the following four pages: INDEX.HTM, ALERT.HTM, WHO.HTM, and HELP.HTM. You also can embed the movie in the contents page, by adding the following line of HTML:

```
<embed src="horiz.dcr" width=288 height=80>
```

To actually run the movie, however, copy the MEDIA.CST file to the [whatever] folder, then open the INDEX.HTM file in Navigator. The cast file must be in the [whatever] folder for [a brief summary of the reason].

The Vertical Panel

To create the vertical panel, you work directly from the horizontal control panel movie. For this example, you add only one new button—the up arrow. This is used to pop up one level to the contents page in the Site directory.

1. Save the HORIZ.DIR movie as VERT.DIR. In the Modify, Movie, Properties dialog box, set the height to 320. Leave the width unchanged.

2. Select the exclamation point in frames 1 and 2 and drag it directly below the home icon. Repeat with the who and the help icons, making sure that you have selected frames 1 and 2 in the score. Drag the up-arrow cast member from the media cast into the score in channel 6. Select frames 1 and 2 and In-Between. With frames 1 and 2 of channel 6 still selected, select Background Transparent in the ink pop-up. Drag the up arrow underneath the help arrow.

Tip

> When moving a sprite, you need to make sure you select every frame in which you want that sprite to move. Selecting all these frames ensures that when you move an object on stage, it moves all copies of that object. If you don't select both frames and then move an object, it will jump around when the movie plays.
>
> If the sprite occurs in frames 1 and 2, for instance, and you move the sprite in just frame 1, when the movie advances from frame 1 to 2, the sprite will jump across the stage. This can reduce the effectiveness of your movie.

3. Choose Modify, Align, and select Align Centers on the second pop-up. Your stage and score should look like figure 9.5.

4. Select Modify, Movie, Properties and set the stage width to 64. In some cases, you might need to move the sprites slightly to make sure they are all on the stage.

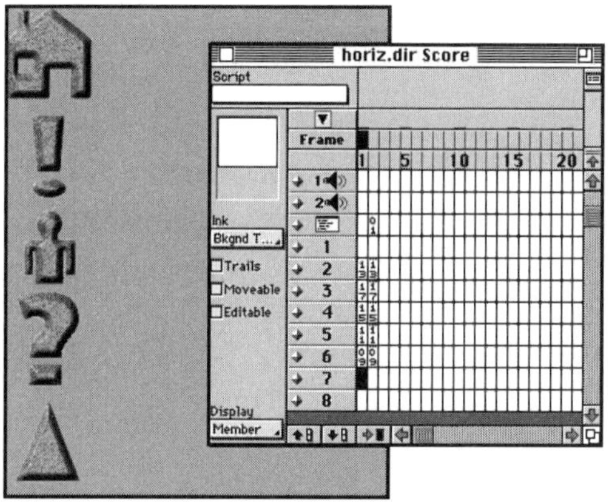

FIGURE 9.5

The sprites are now aligned vertically.

Now you need to modify the scripts to take into account the new button and the changed location of the movie.

1. You need to add the reference to the table of contents page, so you should change the `gPageList` list. The line of the startMovie handler that creates the list should now read

   ```
   set gPageList = ["index","alert","who","help", "toc"]
   ```

2. The only other change you need to make is to place the buttons in the directory above the movie. (Remember that the movie will be located in the Site/Sec3 directory.) Change the `GoToNetPage` command to read

   ```
   GoToNetPage "../" & str & ".htm"
   ```

The movie is now finished. Save it, then choose Xtras, Afterburner and save the file as VERT.DCR in the Site/Sec3 directory.

Each of the data files needs to have the file embedded in it. Because you want the text to flow to the right of the movie, you need to use an `align=left` in the <embed> tag. After the </h2> tag, insert the following tag into each file:

```
<embed src="vert.dcr" height=360 width=64 align=left>
```

Now the example site is operational. A page with the vertical panel should look like figure 9.6.

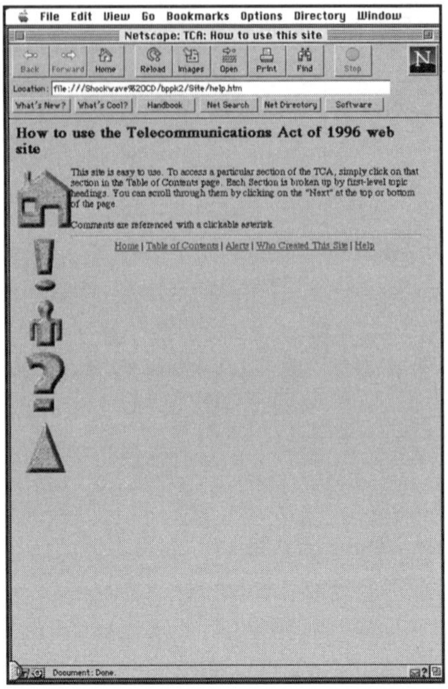

FIGURE 9.6

The site fragment is now operational.

Summary

This chapter has given you a taste of what external casts can do for a site. Making sure external casts are downloaded correctly, however, is still a concern. In Chapter 10, "Working with Frames," you use frames to make the site fragment a little easier to use.

CHAPTER 10

WORKING WITH FRAMES

A big complaint about Shockwave for Director 4 was that the plug-in knew very little about the world in which it existed. Basically, the only thing a Shockwave movie knew about its context was where it was located on the Web server.

In Shockwave for Director 5, Macromedia has addressed this problem to some degree, by adding frame- and window-addressing capabilities and the capability to pass parameters to the movie. Frame-aware capabilities are examined in some depth in this chapter. Parameter passing is covered in Chapter 12, "Talking with the Outside World: Parameters and JavaScript."

Frames and Windows

The capability of displaying multiple frames on the same page—introduced in Netscape Navigator 2.0—is one of the more controversial of Netscape's unilateral additions to HTML. Many people feel that frames are distracting and unnecessary. Other people swear by frames for their capability to compartmentalize Web pages. One of Macromedia's biggest mistakes in Shockwave for Director 4 was not anticipating the popularity of frames. To be fair though, frames were only a gleam in Netscape's eye at that time, and nobody understood how popular they would become.

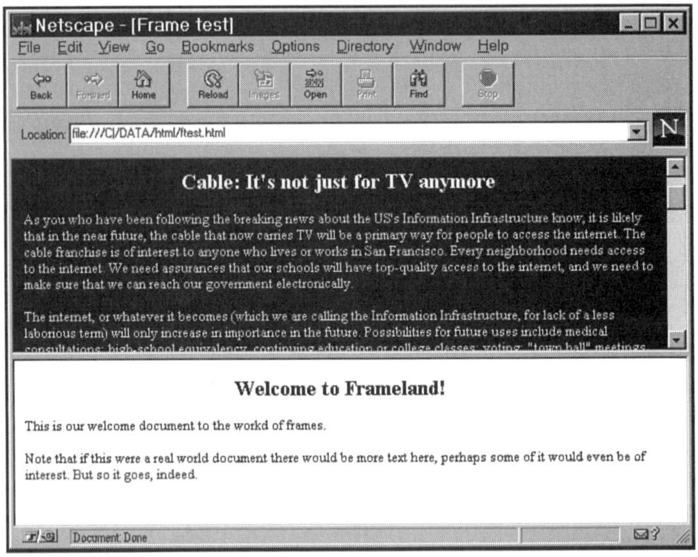

FIGURE 10.1

Frames can be used to divide the html page.

Although Shockwave movies could peacefully exist within a frame, Shockwave for Director 4 did not have the capability to address frames. Developers have been forced to work around this limitation with awkward contraptions involving JavaScript, CGI, and others.

Macromedia has corrected this limitation in Shockwave for Director 5. The plug-in now can load various pages into alternate frames on the screen, and can even address multiple windows. In this section we will touch briefly on how to deal with frames, how people want to use Shockwave for Director with frames, and how to implement frame- and window-aware Shockwave movies.

Creating Frames

Although there are some inconsistencies with the way they work, frames are a fairly straightforward addition to HTML on the authoring side (although the implementation on the browser side in Netscape Navigator 2.0x is somewhat irregular). Frames work somewhat like tables. We will not examine frames in exhaustive detail here, because full, up-to-date information is available on Netscape's website.

> **Tip**
>
> More information on how to use frames is available on the Netscape Web Site at http://home.netscape.com/assist/net_sites/frames.html. Of course, like most HTML, the best way to learn how to use frames is to read the documentation, and then view the source of pages that you like.

The <frameset> Tag

The basic building block of a page with frames is the <frameset> tag, which replaces the <body> tag on an HTML page. The <frameset> tag takes either a cols or a rows parameter. The COLS parameter expresses the way the frame area is divided horizontally; the ROWS parameter expresses the way it is divided vertically.

The values for each of the parameters are expressed in a list. The values can be in one of three formats, which can be mixed. The formats are:

n%	A percentage of the total width or height.
n	A pixel value.
n*	A proportion. Note that for this final type of value, you can add relative weight to each part.

To have a 100 pixel control area at the top of the page, with the rest of the page one big frame, for example, the call would be <frameset rows="100,*"> (see fig. 10.1). To divide your page into two small columns, one on either side with a larger one in the middle, the call would be <frameset cols="20%,60%,20%">.

Or, to have two columns, a small open on the left and a larger one to the right, the tag would be <frameset cols=20%,80%> (see fig. 10.2).

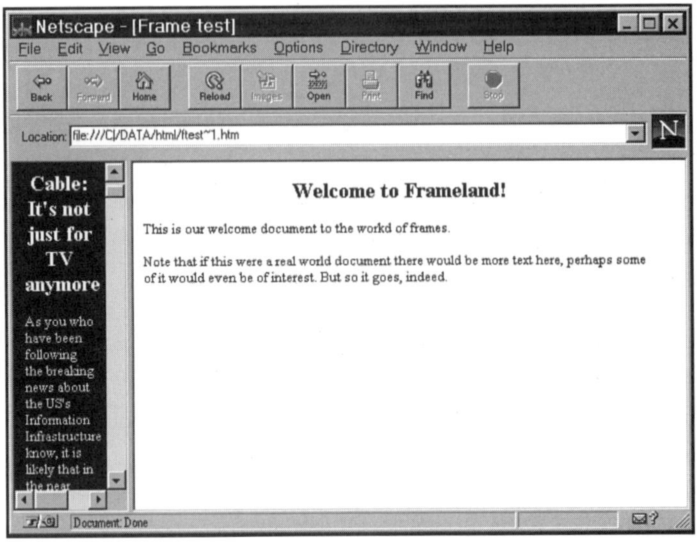

FIGURE 10.2

Specifying proportions with frames is flexible.

Frameset tags can contain frames, other Frameset tags, or `<noframes>` tags. Because the `<noframes>` tag is for browsers that cannot handle frames, none of which can handle Shockwave, we need not concern ourselves with it.

The <frame> tag

The `<frame>` tag is where the actual business of putting information on screen is accomplished. Frames can have several attributes, two of which we will discuss here. For details on the others, refer to the documentation on the Netscape website mentioned previously.

The first attribute, or parameter, of a frame tag is its source file. The syntax for this tag is `src="`*`filename`*`"`. Although the source file can be a Shockwave movie or a graphic, we strongly suggest you use an HTML page, even if it contains nothing but an embedded Shockwave movie. There are two reasons for using a page as source, rather than a movie. First, if you are using a background color on your site, using a page will guarantee that the entire frame has the correct background color; second, some versions of Navigator do not deal well with a page containing only a plug-in object. Although this problem seems to have been solved, it is sensible to be on your guard in case the problem resurfaces.

The second attribute of the frame tag is its name. The syntax for this parameter is `name="name"`. The name parameter is not required but is necessary to load pages into specific frames. We will examine the uses of this tag later in the chapter.

A simple example of the `<frame>` and `<frameset>` tags in use follows.

> **Note**
> This file and the subsidiary files are located on the accompanying CD in the Chapter10 folder as FTEST.HTM.

Note that the `<frameset>` tag goes where the body tag would otherwise go.

```
<HTML><HEAD><TITLE>Shockwave in Frames</TITLE></HEAD>
<FRAMESET ROWS="100,*">
<FRAME SRC="header.htm" NAME="head">
<FRAME SRC="index.htm" NAME="body">
<NOFRAMES>
Get yourself a frame-capable browser!
</NOFRAMES></FRAMESET></HTML>
```

The foregoing HTML page sets up a basic configuration: a 100 pixel header area, with the rest of the page available for information display (see fig. 10.3).

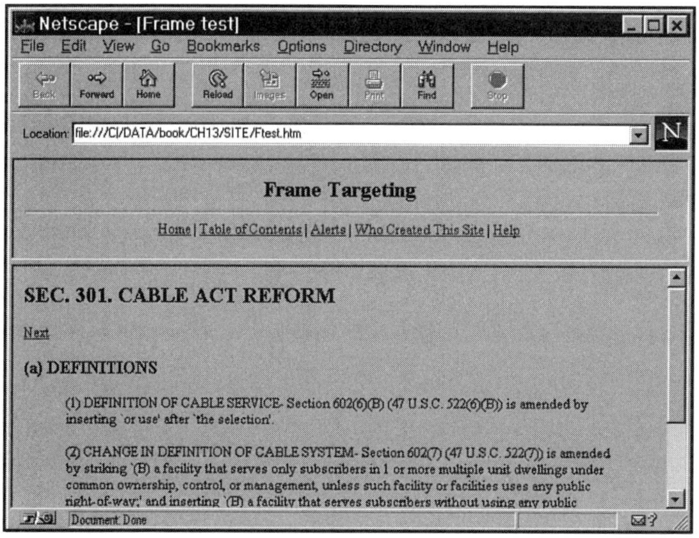

FIGURE 10.3

A basic configuration consists of a main display area and a control area.

A <frameset> tag also can be placed inside another <frameset> tag. This allows for multidimensional grids of frames. The previous example, for instance, could be altered to split the display area into two, as shown in the following example.

```
<HTML><HEAD><TITLE>Shockwave in Frames Example 2</TITLE></HEAD>
<FRAMESET ROWS="100,*">
<FRAME SRC="header.htm" NAME="head">
<FRAMESET COLS="65%,*"
<FRAME SRC="index.htm" NAME="body">
<FRAME SRC="toc.htm" NAME="body2">
</FRAMESET>
<NOFRAMES>
Get yourself a frame-capable browser!
</NOFRAMES></FRAMESET></HTML>
```

This code results in the display area being split vertically into two panes. The dividing line is 65 percent of the distance from the left edge, as shown in figure 10.4.

Note

> You can find the above example in the Chapter 10 folder of the accompanying CD as FTEST2.HTM.

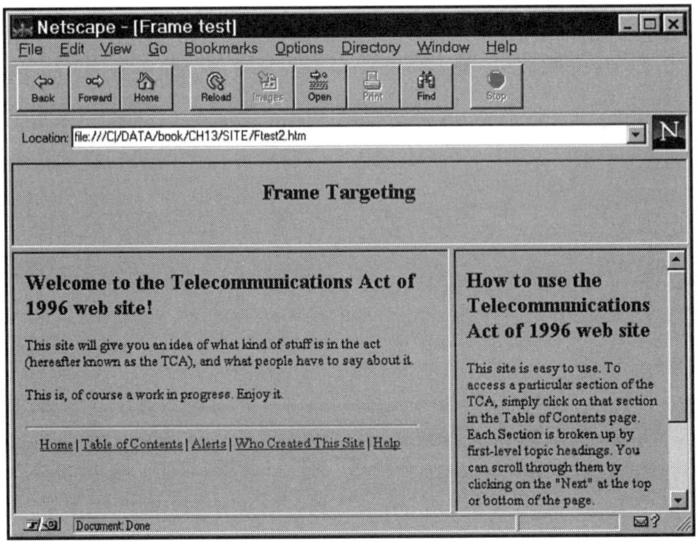

FIGURE 10.4

A <frameset> tag also can be placed inside another <frameset> tag.

Working with Shockwave and Frames

Frames contain HTML pages that can contain anything a regular HTML page can, including Shockwave movies and other plug-ins. The aspect of dealing with frames that is new to Shockwave for Director 5 is the ability to control one frame at a time. A standard configuration in a frame-enabled page, as the foregoing examples show, is to use one frame as a persistent control area, while other parts are used to display the main body under consideration. This is obviously only of use if hrefs can specify a frame target. Netscape, when implementing frames, saw fit to add this capability to Navigator, and now Macromedia has added it to Shockwave.

Frame Targeting Basics

The most common way to address a frame in HTML is to add a TARGET parameter to the anchor syntax. The basic form is <A HREF="url" TARGET="frame_name">. To load a file into the frame titled "body" in the previous example, the call would be <A HREF="who.htm" TARGET="body">.

This same technique works for Shockwave, with slight modifications. The GoToNetPage command has an additional parameter, in addition to the URL, the target. Therefore, the equivalent command to the previous example would be GoToNetPage "who.htm," "body".

There are several issues raised by this addition to the GoToNetPage command. The same Lingo syntax is used to deal with multiple windows under Netscape. If the target is a name that Navigator does not recognize as a valid frame or window name, it will open a new window with that name. There also is a keyword "_blank," which will open a new, unnamed window.

> **Tip**
>
> If your movie opens a new window to load a page you have called instead of loading it into an already existing frame, there is probably a typo in either your **GoToNetPage** call or the frame name in your HTML document.
>
> Be aware that frame names are case-sensitive.

EXAMPLE 10.1

Control Panel Using Frames

Many Shockwave developers want to use frames to provide a way to maintain a persistent control panel. This is quite easy with Shockwave for Director 5.

Note

By this point, we assume that you are familiar with the basics of working with Director and we won't go into extreme detail about the basic mechanisms of the following movie in the main text. For those of you who might be getting in a little over your heads, we will briefly cover the Lingo in the second half of this note. The two buttons on the right will not work in this example, but we will add functionality for them in the second example. For more information on how to make buttons press and unpress and so forth, see the Director 5.0 documentation or our first book, *Macromedia Shockwave for Director User's Guide.*

Lingo is a useful script because it gives you all the functionality of a standard push button. The button goes down when you push it, up when you move the mouse off of it, and activates only when you release the mouse button over the button.

Because the button needs to react immediately to the click of the mouse, it starts on mouseDown, rather than the default mouseUp. The script immediately enters the main control loop, which repeats while the user holds down the mouse button.

The control loop first checks to see whether the mouse is over the last sprite clicked, using the rollover (`the clickon`) function. If so, it sets the flag "pressed" to true and hides the shadow sprite, as well as moves the foreground sprite to make it look as if the button is pressed. Because the shadow sprites are immediately behind the button sprites, they are in channel the clickon - 1. Then the control loop calls updateStage, to display its work.

If the mouse is not over the button, the loop reverses the previous actions. The loop continues to do one or the other of these things until the button is released.

When the button is released, the script checks the "pressed" flag. If the flag is TRUE, then the mouse button was released while the mouse was over the button. In that case, the script needs to restore the original "up" state of the button, by showing the shadow again. It also then needs to execute the button script (which is the goPage script detailed in the following section). If the flag is not TRUE, it needs to do nothing but exit the script, because the button is already in its "up" state.

The movie we will be working with in this example is FPANEL.DIR. You can find it in the Chapter 10 folder on the accompanying CD. The button images are 1-bit versions of the buttons from the previous chapter's example. The HTML example pages are essentially the same as in the last chapter. However, we've added a couple and have listed them below.

Filename	*Description*	*Location*
HEADER.HTM	Blank page in which to place the control panel	Site
FTEST.HTM	Two-frame framework page	Site
FTEST2.HTM	Three-frame framework page	Site

Open the FPANEL.DIR movie. Open the cast window. There you will find a movie script called "buttonWerks." This script starts out with `on manage button`. Basically what the score is doing is managing the nominal "up" and "down" state of the buttons. To make the movie actually do something, we need to add a script that loads a page into a frame. Because we will need to deal with more than two frames (in the next example), we will genericize this command as much as possible. Open a new script cast member and add the following script:

```
on goPage pageName, whichTarget
   GoToNetPage pageName&".htm", whichTarget
end
```

After typing the Lingo into the script window, press the enter key on the far bottom right-hand side of your keyboard. This adds the script and recompiles all Lingo and closes the script window. Because we have used only the name of the page and not the name and extension, in our arbitrary naming of cast members, we must add ".HTM" to the name of the cast member to use in the `GoToNetPage` call.

Now that we have our function put together, we need to actually call it.

1. Open the score script in the cast member named "buttonWerks."
2. In the section that is commented "button selected," add the following script after the `updateStage` command:

   ```
   goPage (the name of member(the memberNum of sprite the clickon)),
   "body"
   ```

This script extracts the name of the cast member of the sprite that has been clicked on, and passes it along with the target "body" to the goPage script examined earlier.

3. Save the file as FPANEL.DIR.
4. Select Xtras, MacroTools, Afterburner, and save the file as FPANEL.DCR.
5. Next, open the HEADER.HTM file in a text editor and replace the <h2>Frame Targeting</h2> line with:

```
<embed src="fpanel.dcr" width=400 height=80>
```

6. Save the file, then open the FTEST.HTM file in your browser and click the buttons. See the happy frames!

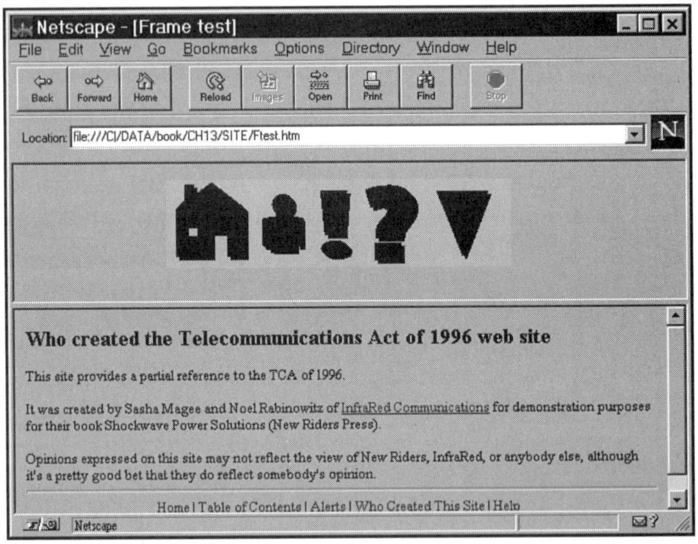

FIGURE 10.5
The Shockwave control panel loads pages into the appropriate frame.

Adding a Third Frame

Now we will add a (more or less gratuitous, if truth be told) third frame to the page and, of course, use our movie to control it. We will make the new frame contain either the help or contents page, while the other pages will occupy the original "body" frame.

Open the file FTEST2.HTM in your browser. Note that there are three frames now. The new frame is named (imaginatively enough) "body2." The "body" frame retains its name, so that we don't have to change that part of the movie. We can now move to the Director movie to add functionality to the buttons conveniently awaiting a purpose. Quit your browser.

1. Open the file FPANEL.DIR in Director. In the cast, open the "buttonWerks" movie script.
2. Find the `on manageButton` handler.
3. Change the line that reads:

   ```
   goPage (the name of member(the memberNum of sprite the clickon)),
   ➥"body"
   ```

   so that it now reads:

   ```
   goPage (the name of member(the memberNum of sprite the clickon)),
   ➥"body2"
   ```

   The only change—in case you missed it—is the addition of a "2" to the target parameter.
4. Close the script.
5. In the score, Select sprite channel 10 frames 1 and 2. This is the foreground sprite of the rightmost button onstage. Repeat with the sprites in channel 12. Remember to select the sprites in both frames 1 and 2.
6. Save the file. Select Xtras, MacroTools, Afterburner, and save the file as FPANEL.DCR.

Helpfully, because we are using the same HEADER.HTM file, it already has the movie embedded in the page. Open the FTEST2.HTM file in your browser again. It should look like figure 10.6, and the buttons on the right should load pages into the right frame.

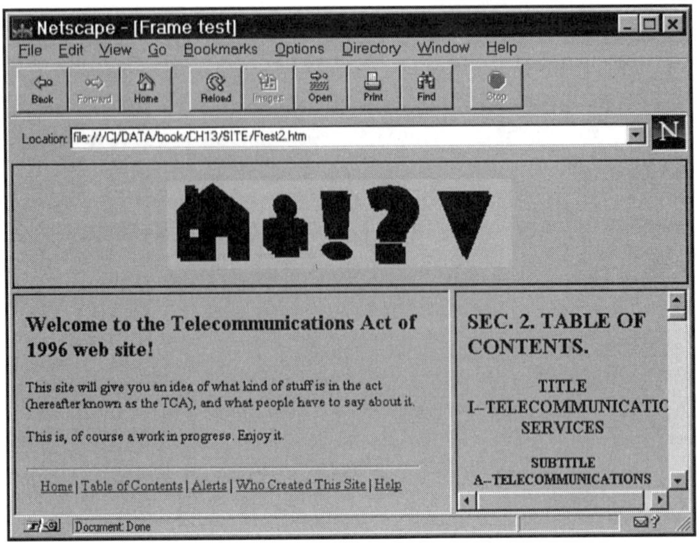

FIGURE 10.6
Shockwave movies can even control multiple frames.

Conclusion

Frames are the first step in making your Shockwave for Director 5 movies aware of their surroundings, and integrating them more effectively into your website. Chapter 12, "Talking with the Outside World: Parameters and JavaScript," takes this one step further by explaining how and why passing parameters to Shockwave movies can be a tremendously powerful technique, especially when combined with JavaScript.

Chapter 11

Linked Text

The ability to read external text files with the GetNetText command is one that adds quite a bit of power to Shockwave for Director. It allows developers to have things such as high score lists and daily messages and create Shockwave movies that can be made to do different things without actually editing the movie. Although the GetNetText command is not as powerful as the FileIO Xtra that comes with the Director application, it can be a very useful tool.

External text, while powerful, can be very tricky. There are several things you should keep in mind when using this feature of Shockwave for Director. The first thing necessary to consider when dealing with external text is that because GetNetText is asynchronous (that is, other operations can go on while the command completes), there are additional commands that are necessary to get the full benefit of GetNetText.

The second thing to realize is that the `GetNetText` command does not work on a local machine. Macromedia has disabled it when the URL does not begin with `http:` to prevent developers from sneaking around and reading private information off the user's hard drive. This can make it very difficult to test without access to an HTTP server. We have provided an external cast that contains stubs that will simulate the operation of these commands on a local file.

Teach Your Movie to Read

The basic outline for the procedure of reading text from the network reads like this: First, you call `GetNetText` with the filename, then call `NetDone()` repeatedly until it returns true, and then use `NetTextResult()` to find the results.

To read in the contents of a file called SETTINGS.TXT in the same folder as the Shockwave movie, for example, the handler would be:

```
on readSettings
   global gFlag
   GetNetText "SETTINGS.TXT"
   set gFlag = TRUE
end
```

Then,

```
on idle
   global result, gFlag
   if gFlag then
       if NetDone() then
           put NetTextResult() into result
           set gFlag = FALSE
       end if
   end if
end
```

This is a fairly bare-bones example. It will only work for one operation at a time, and it doesn't actually do anything with the text except put it into a global variable called result.

Often you have multiple files that need to be read simultaneously, as in the case where you have a settings and a daily message file. This procedure is detailed in the last section of this chapter.

EXAMPLE 11.1

Using Text Files to Create a Control Panel

One of the challenges of using Shockwave is that the network is a quickly changing environment. It can be difficult to use Shockwave movies in this environment, because they constantly have to be adjusted for new files and new directories. It can be an especially severe problem when the Director developers and the Web administrators are in different departments. This is one area where using external text files can be most effective. We will show a simple example of how to use an external text file to provide a customizable control panel.

Each link will have a name, a description, and an HREF. As an arbitrary limit, we will provide the ability to have up to five possible links in the movie. This is an arbitrary limit and could easily be 10 or more.

> This movie is an adaptation of a project we did for Action Technologies. For more information on that project, as well as Action Technologies in general, see Chapter 18, "Advanced Applications: Action Technologies' Metro."
>
> *Note*

The movie TXTPAN.DIR is located in the Chapter 11 folder on the accompanying CD. The final version of the movie, TXTPANEL.DIR, also is there. The movie, in its current state (see fig. 11.1), consists of five text fields (named dept1 through dept5) that will serve as buttons and a status field, named (imaginatively enough) "status." It also contains a tiled background, which is obviously non-functional (but pretty!). The movie in its current state does nothing; it merely goes to the last frame and loops there, displaying some empty text fields. Our first task is to make the movie read in the text file, SETTINGS.TXT, which contains the names, descriptions, and destination pages of the links in the movie.

FIGURE 11.1

The movie in its initial state does nothing but display the tiled background.

The format of the SETTINGS.TXT file is up to five lines, each of which contains the name, description, and destination of each link, separated by semicolons. Optionally, each line can have a comment at the end, marked by a pound sign (#). For illustration, the contents of the included file are

```
Engineering;Where stuff gets done;ENGINE.HTM
Sales & Marketing;Promotions, advertising, etc.;MARKET.HTM#this
section will be split into two
Technical Support; If you have any problems...;TECHSUPP.HTM
MIS;Computer and Network Concerns;MIS.HTM
Management;The people who tell us what to do;MANAGE.HTM
```

1. Because in the process of testing this movie it will very likely end up being saved with text already in the fields, you will add a `startMovie` handler to clear them before they are displayed. Open a new movie script cast member and add the following script:

```
on startMovie
   repeat with i = 1 to 5
       put " " into field ("dept"&i)
   end repeat
   put " " into field "status"
end
```

2. Reading in the file is fairly simple

```
on initText
   global gFlag
   getNetText("SETTINGS.TXT")
   set gFlag = true
end
```

3. We add the variable `gFlag` so that when the file is successfully read in, we do not need to continue checking to see whether it is done. To check whether it is read in, add the following handler:

```
on walkFrame
   global gTextThing, gFlag
   if gFlag then
       if netDone() then
           set gTextThing = NetTextResult()
           parseText
           set gFlag = FALSE
       end if
   end if
end
```

This script first checks to see whether the flag variable set in the previous example is true. If so, it checks to see whether the latest network operation is done. Because the only one you call is the `GetNetText`, that is the one that `NetDone()` with no parameter checks. If the operation is done, the handler does three things.

a. It first puts the text result into a global variable called `gTextThing`.

b. It then calls `parseText` to deal with the text result.

c. Finally, it sets the flag variable to true so that it doesn't need to check to see whether the file is read completely any more.

4. The `parseText` handler is the one that does the actual text manipulation and fills the text fields:

```
on parseText
   global gTextThing, gDescList, gLinkList
   set gDescList = []
   set gLinkList = []
   set gTextThing = cleanText(gTextThing)
   set the itemdelimiter = ";"
   repeat with i = 1 to the number of lines in gTextThing
       put item 1 of line i of gTextThing into field ("dept"&i)
       setAt gDescList, i, item 2 of line i of gTextThing
       setAt gLinkList, i, item 3 of line i of gTextThing
   end repeat
end
```

This handler declares two new list variables, `gDescList` and `gLinkList`. These variables will be used to store the description and destination pages that correspond to each link. The handler calls `cleanText`, which strips out any comments (see the code example in step 5). It then sets the `itemDelimiter` to a semicolon. Use a semicolon—not the default comma—in this example. That way, the user can use commas in the description or link name.

The handler then cycles through the lines in the text file (allowing for the possibility that the user has fewer than five links) and performs the same action on each line. It puts the first item (everything before the first semicolon) into the dept*n* field corresponding to the current line of the text file. Next, it takes the second item of the line and puts it into the appropriate slot in the list of descriptions. Finally, it slots the third item into the appropriate place in the list of destination pages (`gLinkList`).

Tip

When using items in Director, there are two things to realize: The delimiter can only be one character, and an item does not include the delimiter character. Thus, in the case of the line **`Engineering;Where stuff gets done`**; ENGINE.HTM (where the **`itemDelimiter`** is ";"), item 2 is **`Where stuff gets done`** without any semicolons.

5. The `cleanText` handler is an example of one that can be used repeatedly. We define it as a function (in other words, we return a value, rather than manipulating a global variable) so that we can use it more than once.

```
on cleanText textToClean
   set tempItem = the itemdelimiter
   set tempText = ""
   set the itemdelimiter = "#"
   repeat with i = 1 to the number of lines in textToClean
       put item 1 of line i of textToClean & RETURN after
tempText
   end repeat
   set the itemdelimiter = tempItem
   return tempText
end
```

This function takes a text chunk and strips out anything after the first `"#"` in a line. The function first stores the current `itemDelimiter` in a temporary variable. This is not strictly necessary in the current movie, but is good Lingo programming practice because storing the delimiter allows us to restore it at the end of the handler. The function next initializes a blank text variable to contain the result string. Next, it sets the `itemDelimiter` to `"#"`, which is the comment character. The function then walks through the text chunk line by line, takes the first item of each line (all the characters before the first `"#"` character), appends that item, and returns it to the result string. The function then restores the original `itemDelimiter` and finally returns the text result.

6. Except for the `startMovie` handler, none of these are actually called yet in the movie. In the script channel of frame 1 of the score, you need to add the following script:

```
on exitFrame
   initText
end
```

7. In the script channel of frame 2, add the following:

```
on exitframe
   global gFlag
   repeat while gFlag
       walkFrame
   end repeat
end
```

   This will repeatedly call the `walkFrame` handler, which checks to see whether the network operation is done. When it is, the movie advances to the next frame.

8. The third frame already has a score script. You need to add a script to manage the status line. Edit the script in frame 3 to read as follows:

```
on exitFrame
   checkroll
   go the frame
end
```

9. Finally, of course, you need to add the `checkRoll` script:

```
on checkRoll
   global gDescList
   repeat with i = 2 to 6
       if rollover(i) then
           put getAt(gDescList, (i-1)) into field "status"
           exit
```

```
        end if
    end repeat
    put "" into field "status"
end
```

This is a fairly standard rollover script. It checks each of the text sprites to see whether the mouse is over it. If it is, it puts the appropriate description in the status field and exits (see fig. 11.2). If the mouse is not over any of the text fields, it blanks the status bar.

FIGURE 11.2

The status bar updates for each menu item the mouse is over.

10. The final script you need to add is the actual button script. Select all the button sprites and add the following score script:

```
on mouseUp
   global gLinkList
   goToNetPage getAt(gLinkList, the clickon - 1)
end
```

This retrieves the appropriate destination page from the list and goes to that page.

The movie is now ready to be burned and uploaded. Be aware that because `GetNetText` does not work with file: URIs, the movie will not work locally, even when embedded in a Net browser. It must be uploaded. This is very awkward when you are trying to test it. In the next section, we will demonstrate scripts that simulate the network text operations locally. This will enable you to test things like text parsing.

Utility Scripts

Using Director's external casts feature, you can easily create a cast file containing scripts that simulate the network Lingo operations. This file can be linked to your Director movie for testing purposes, then unlinked before uploading. We have included such a cast file, called UTILS.CST, in the Chapter 11 folder on the accompanying CD. We will briefly walk through these scripts so that you can understand how they work and the ways that they are liable to differ from the actual network Lingo operations.

The first is the `GetNetText` command:

```
on GetNetText fname
   global gUtilTemp, gUtilID
   if NOT listP(gUtilTemp) then initUtils
   set t = FileIO(mNew, "read", the pathname & fname)
   setAt gUtilTemp, gUtilID + 1, t(mReadFile)
end
```

This script substitutes a `FileIO` command for the network operation. `FileIO`, of course, is not an asynchronous operation. Therefore, we need to simulate that aspect of the network command. The values returned by the `FileIO` calls are stored in a list (`gUtilTemp`) and are indexed by `gUtilID`.

The script first checks to see whether the list of results exists yet. If not, it calls the `initUtils` handler:

```
on InitUtils
   global gUtilID, gUtilTemp
   set gUtilTemp = []
   set gUtilID = 0
end
```

The `initUtils` handler merely initializes the variables. Note that it sets the index variable to 0, not 1. The reason for this will become clear in a moment. `ListP()`, which checks to see whether a variable is a list, will return false with an uninitialized variable, but will return true even with an empty list. Once the `GetNetText` handler has made sure the variables exist, it creates a new `FileIO` object. It then reads the file and puts the result into the results list. Note that it places it in location `gUtilID + 1`. This is because `gUtilID` increments before returning a value, as we shall see in the next handler:

```
on NetOperationID
   global gUtilID
   set gUtilID = gUtilID + 1
   return gUtilID
end
```

The actual network Lingo `NetOperationID()` function returns an arbitrary value. We need to have a value that also can serve as an index to the results list. So we simply add one to the `gUtilID` to make it a unique, but still indexable value. Note that we increment the value before returning it. Although it is not documented in Macromedia's manuals, nothing in a handler, after a return command, executes.

The next two commands are slightly more complicated. The `NetDone()` and `NetTextResult()` commands must both work with and without a parameter:

```
on netDone ID
   global gUtilTemp
   if the paramCount = 0 then return (getAt(gUtilTemp,
count(gUtilTemp)) <> "")
   else return GetAt(gUtilTemp, ID) <> ""
end
```

Our version of `NetDone()` essentially always returns true if the command was successful. This is an incomplete simulation of the network version, of course, because the latter has a network delay. It might be desirable to add a user-configurable delay into this handler, but because network delays are inherently unpredictable, it makes little sense to do that either.

Tip

> The only real solution to dealing with network delays is to program defensively. Always assume that the text file will take twice as long as you think reasonable to become available. The most sensible way to deal with network delays is to loop an animation or provide text or something similar to keep the user busy while he waits for the file to load.

`NetTextResult()` also can take a parameter or can be called without:

```
on netTextResult ID
   global gUtilTemp
   if the paramCount = 0 then return getAt(gUtilTemp,
count(gUtilTemp))
   else return GetAt(gUtilTemp, ID)
end
```

If there is no parameter, this handler simply picks the last result off the end of the list. If there is a parameter, it assumes it is a network operation ID and selects the corresponding item from the result list.

The final two simulated commands are `GoToNetPage` and `GoToNetMovie`:

```
on GoToNetMovie destFile
   go to movie the pathname & destFile
end

on gotonetpage dest
   put "going to "&dest
end
```

Because `GoToNetMovie` exists to give the Shockwave developer the ability to go from one movie to another—"Just like on a local disk," in the words of one developer—it is ironically appropriate that we simulate this command with the original command. There is no Director equivalent, however, for `GoToNetPage`. We have added this handler as a debugging tool. It simply puts the pagename into the message window.

These utility scripts should give you a way to test your movies in Director without script errors popping up all over the place. It is best to keep in mind, however, the following caveats:

- These utility scripts do not take into account network delays.
- These scripts are by no means robust. There is very little error checking. If you get a bunch of "handler not defined" errors or something similar, you probably are using an incorrect filename.
- There are several network Lingo commands which are not simulated here: `NetError()`, for example.
- Netscape has a limit to the number of connections it can have open at any one time. (This number is 4 by default). Each `GetNetText` call will grab and hold a connection until a corresponding `NetDone()` call is made. These scripts do not take that into account.

These handlers are useful for debugging your scripts before actually burning them and embedding them in HTML pages. Sometimes you will need to use multiple text files in the same movie. The next example demonstrates the additional concerns that are raised by using multiple text files.

Example 11.2

Using Multiple Text Files

Often, it is desirable to use multiple text files in the same movie. For instance, in our previous example, you might also want to add an additional message that changes daily. To reduce the possibility of adding errors to the main interface with each daily message, it is advantageous to make the daily message a separate file.

We will use the previous example and add to it a separate message file called MSG.TXT.

1. The first thing you need to do is make space for the message in our admittedly less-than-optimally-efficient layout. You do this by selecting Modify, Movie, Properties and changing the stage height to 180 pixels, from 150. Because you want the message to stand out, you will not extend the tiled background to cover this area (see fig. 11.3).

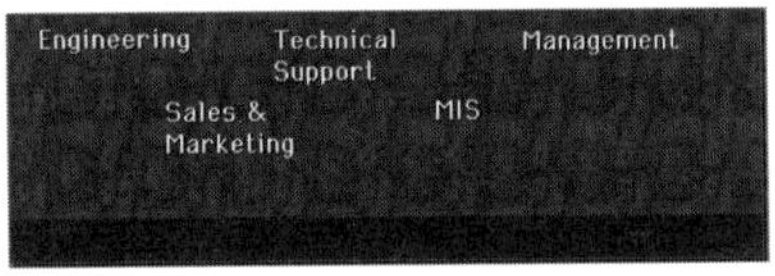

Figure 11.3

Because you want the status message to stand out, you don't extend the background to cover the whole stage.

2. Next, you need to go to frame 3, drag out a new text field (approximately 330 pixels long) and name it "message." Set the font and size to Geneva, 18 pt., bold.

3. To add the code to read in the file, open the movie script cast member called "textMaster." Rewrite the `initText` handler so that it reads as follows:

```
on initText
   global gFlag, gFlag2, gID1, gID2
   getNetText "SETTINGS.TXT"
   set gFlag = true
   put NetOperationID() into gID1
```

```
    getNetText "MSG.TXT"
    set gFlag2 = true
    put NetOperationID() into gID2
end
```

This handler reads in two files, assigning each one a unique ID. It also sets a flag for each operation.

4. Next, you need to adjust the `walkFrame` handler to deal with two text files. Rewrite it to read as follows:

```
on walkFrame
    global gTextThing, gFlag, gFlag2, gID1, gID2
    if gFlag then
        if netDone(gID1) then
            set gTextThing = NetTextResult(gID1)
            parseText
            set gFlag = FALSE
        end if
    end if
    if gFlag2 then
        if netDone(gID2) then
            put NetTextResult(gID2) into field "message"
            set gFlag2 = FALSE
        end if
    end if
end
```

The first half of this handler does essentially the same thing as it did in the previous example, except that it specifies which operation it is taking the text result from. The second half of the handler checks to see whether the message text is read and then dumps it straight into the message text field.

5. The `exitFrame` handler needs to be adjusted to take into account the second text file:

```
on exitframe
    global gFlag, gFlag2
    repeat while (gFlag or gFlag2)
        walkFrame
    end repeat
end
```

6. The movie is now ready to run. Something you can do that will add interest to it, however, is to make the message scroll across the stage. You can do this fairly easily. Select all the sprites in frame 3, and Option+drag (Alt+drag on Windows) to frame 100. Select the "message" sprite in frame 100, and select Modify, Sprite, Properties. Set the sprite's horizontal position to –330. Select the sprite in the same channel in frame 3, and set the horizontal location to 560. Select all the channels except the script channel and In-Between.

7. You now need to adjust the rollover script because it currently is set to loop on frame 3. You want it to go to frame 100, and then return to frame 3, checking the rollover in every frame. Delete the script in frame 3, and select the script in frame 100. Change the line that reads go the frame to read go loopstart. Drag out a marker to frame 3 and name it loopstart. Finally, select the script channel in frame 3 and add the following script:

```
on exitFrame
   checkRoll
end
```

The movie is now ready to be burned and embedded. It should look similar to figure 11.4.

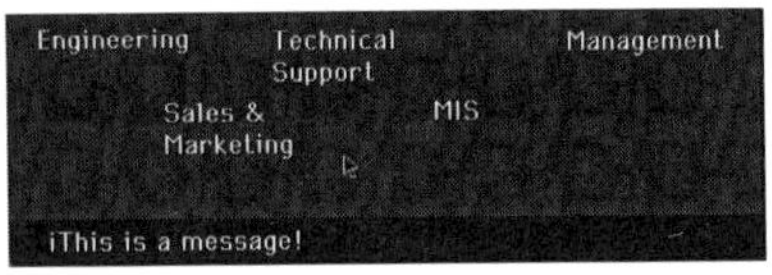

FIGURE 11.4

The message and the menu items are separate text files.

EXAMPLE 11.3

Advanced Text Manipulation

One of the advantages of Shockwave is that it can provide deeper access to your site. It is difficult, in HTML, to provide an intuitive interface which allows access to pages more than one level deep. In the final exercise of this chapter, you will expand our previous example to provide submenus for each of the major topics. In the process, we will demonstrate one method for creating complex text settings files.

Each submenu will be a text field, with an arbitrary limit of four lines. Each submenu item will have an attached link and a description, just like the original movie. Because the panel can have from one to five main menu items and each submenu can have from one to four items, you need to lay out the text file slightly different than before. You will separate the file into several text blocks, each marked by a begin and end line. The first block will be the list of main menu topics, and each following block will be a list of the submenu items in order corresponding to the main menu. A sample submenu block from the example file on the accompanying CD called SETT2.TXT would be:

```
begin
Exec Management; very important people;EXEC.HTM
Middle Management; moderately important people;MID.HTM
Project Management;not-so-important people;PROJECT.HTM
end
```

Adding Submenu Sections

Rather than walk you step-by-step through a rather laborious process, we will outline the highlights of the change from the previous example to this. The resulting file is available on the the *Shockwave Power Solutions* CD as TX3PAN.DIR. We have colored the script lines in the movie file that have changed from the previous example red for easy reference.

1. To prepare the movie, you first need to create five new text field cast members, named sub1 through sub5. These are the cast members that will hold the submenus.
2. Drag out a marker to frame 105 and name it "1." Extend the background past frame 115.
3. Drag the cast named "dept1" onto the upper left corner of the stage. Make sure the sprite is in channel 3.
4. Drag the cast named "sub1" to the stage near the top, approximately halfway from the left. Move the sprite to channel 8.
5. Option+drag (Alt+drag on Windows) the "status" sprite (channel 7) from frame 100 to frame 105. Next, draw a filled rectangle that covers the left half of the textured portion of the stage. Color it dark blue and set the ink to Add. The stage should now look like figure 11.5.

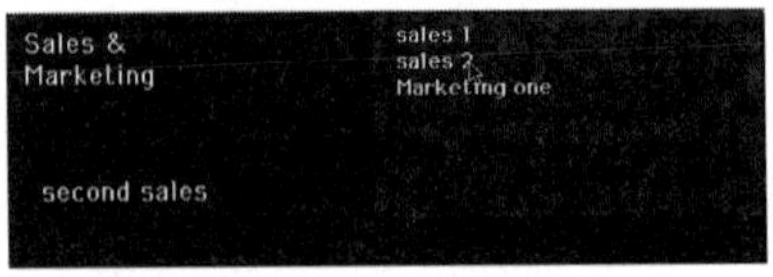

FIGURE 11.5

We dim the left hand part of the stage slightly to emphasize the active portion of the screen.

6. Select frames 105 and 106, channels 1–12, and choose Modify, In-Between. Select the script channel in frame 106 and type the following script:

```
on exitFrame
   checkRoll2
   go the frame
end
```

7. You will create the `checkRoll2` script shortly. Now, select the sprite in channel 3 and give it the following score script:

```
on mouseUp
   go "loopStart"
end
```

This allows the menu name to serve as a button to the main menu.

8. Select the sprites in channel 8 and add the following script:

```
on mouseUp
   global gSubSelect, gSubLinkList
   goToNetPage GetAt( GetAt(gSubLinkList, gSubSelect), the
mouseLine)
end
```

This handler pulls the appropriate list of links from the list of lists of links (which we will create below), using two variables. The first is `gSubSelect`, which is the number of the current submenu; the second is the mouseline, which is the line of the text field the mouse is over. The score should now look like figure 11.6.

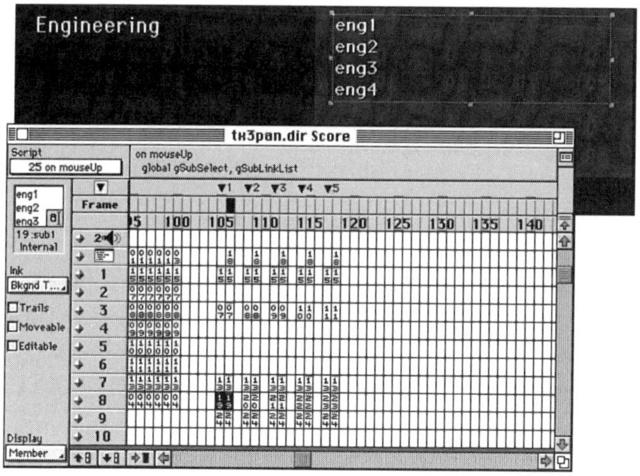

FIGURE 11.6

Each submenu has its own score section.

9. Before you go on to the process of reading in the text, you need to change the main menu. Select the sprite script assigned to the main menu items and change it to read:

```
on mouseUp
   global gSubSelect
   set gSubSelect = (the clickon - 1)
   go marker (the clickon - 1)
end
```

Reading in the Text

Because the "begin" and "end" lines are merely markers and can have any number of blank or comment lines in between them, you need to discard them. You do this by walking through the text variable and hacking out lines until you come to the first "begin" line. After the block following the begin is read, you repeat the process until the next begin line. This method, while not particularly pretty, has the virtue of maintaining our place in the file. The handler you use to do this is `hTrim`:

```
on hTrim thingie
   set tempThing = thingie
   repeat while true
      if word 1 of line 1 of tempThing <> "begin" then
         delete line 1 of tempThing
```

```
        else
            delete line 1 of tempThing
            exit repeat
        end if
    end repeat
    return tempThing
end
```

This handler makes one test: does the first line of the variable contain only "begin?" If so, it deletes the line and then exits. If not, it deletes the current line, which makes the next line the new first line. Then, it checks the new first line. As you will see in the next handler, this makes parsing the text simple, because you are always dealing with the first lines in the variable.

The `parseText` handler changes pretty drastically in this version. Although you did not actually remove them from the text file, the HTML links attached to the main menu items are now ignored. The `parseText` handler now reads as follows:

```
on parseText
   global gTextThing, gDescList —,gLinkList
   global gSubDescList, gSubLinkList
   set numMenus = 0
   set gDescList = []
   set gSubDescList = []
   set gSubLinkList = []
   set gTextThing = cleanText(gTextThing)
   set gTextThing = hTrim(gTextThing)
   set the itemdelimiter = ";"
   repeat with i = 1 to 5
       if line i of gTextThing = "end" then exit repeat
       put item 1 of line i of gTextThing into field ("dept"&i)
       setAt gDescList, i, item 2 of line i of gTextThing
       set numMenus = numMenus + 1
   end repeat
   repeat with j = 1 to numMenus
       set gTextThing = hTrim(gTextThing)
       set descTemp = []
       set linkTemp = []
       repeat with i = 1 to 4
           if line i of gTextThing = "end" then exit repeat
           put item 1 of line i of gTextThing & RETURN after field
```

```
("sub"&j)
            append descTemp, item 2 of line i of gTextThing
            append linkTemp, item 3 of line i of gTextThing
        end repeat
        delete line (the number of lines in field ("sub"&j)) of field
("sub"&j)
        append gSubDescList, descTemp
        append gSubLinkList, linkTemp
    end repeat
end
```

This handler first declares two new global variables, `gSubDescList` and `gSubLinkList`. You also are dropping `gLinkList` because the main menu items no longer actually link to HTML pages. You add a new local variable, `numMenus`, that will be used to count the number of main menu items. We initialize the empty lists.

Because you still need to be able to comment the file, you still call `cleanText()`. Next, you need to get to the first block of text, so call `hTrim()`.

You treat the first block much the same as in the previous example, except that you ignore the third item in each line, if any, because you do not need to link from the main menu. You also keep a count of the number of menu items. Therefore, if you need to add more things to the settings file, you can do so at the end because the handler will only read in settings for actually existing submenus.

The next chunk of code is entirely new. For each main menu item, you do the following:

1. Clear out the variable up to the first submenu block with `hTrim()`.
2. Initialize two temporary lists: one for descriptions and one for links.
3. Fill in the data for each submenu.

   Because it was decided (arbitrarily) that each submenu can only have four items, you repeat from 1 to 4. Note that to allow more items per submenu, the 4 in this repeat loop is the only one you need to change.
4. In the repeat loop, check to see whether you have hit the end of the block. If so, exit the repeat loop.

5. Next, add the first item of the line and a return to the appropriate text field. Then, put the second item of the line (the description) into the temporary description list.
6. Add the link to the temporary link list.
7. When you exit the repeat loop, you have an extra line in the text field, because you have added a trailing RETURN. Delete that last line to avoid script errors.
8. Finally, add the temporary lists onto the end of the global lists.

This loop is repeated once for each item in the main menu. The final script you need to add is the `checkRoll2` script:

```
on checkRoll2
   global gSubSelect, gSubDescList, gSubLinkList
   if rollover(8) then
       set x = the mouseLine
       if x > 0 then
           put getAt( getAt(gSubDescList, gSubSelect), x) into field
"status"
       end if
   else if rollover (3) then
       put "Go Back to Main Menu" into field "status"
   else
       put " " into field "status"
   end if
end
```

This script first checks to see whether the mouse is over the submenu field. If it is, it immediately sets the temporary variable x to the `mouseLine` (see the following Tip for an explanation of this and the following step) and checks to see whether x is greater than 0. If so, it retrieves the appropriate status line value from the list corresponding to the current submenu.

Tip

> We set the **`mouseLine`** to a variable instead of using it raw to avoid an embarrassing script error. Because Lingo (while faster than in previous versions) does not execute instantly, the **`mouseLine`** variable can change during a handler. When the mouse is over a sprite but not over a text line (over the border or after the last line, for example), the **`mouseLine`** variable returns –1. This is the reason for the **`mouseLine > 0`** check. What can (and inevitably will) happen if the **`mouseLine`**

variable is used raw is that after the check to ensure that the mouseLine > 0, the user will still be moving the mouse. Also, when we try to retrieve the appropriate status text, Shockwave will look for item –1 of the list. This is, of course, an out of bounds index and will result in an error.

If the mouse is not over the submenu field, the script checks to see whether the mouse is over the menu item name. If it is, it puts the handy "go back to main menu" message into the status line. Finally, if the mouse is not over either sprite, it clears the status line. The movie is now ready to be burnt and embedded in a page. Feel free to experiment with comments after a line (remembering that `"#"` is the comment character) or between blocks.

Summary

In this chapter we have delved into the use of external text files. This survey has been by no means exhaustive, but should give you an idea of what is possible using external text files.

The next chapter details one of the most exciting additions to Shockwave for Director 5—the capability to pass parameters to movies from the HTML page. This can be combined with the text reading features described in this chapter for incredible power.

CHAPTER 12

Talking with the Outside World: Parameters and JavaScript

As we mentioned earlier, one of the major complaints about Shockwave for Director 4 was the plug-in's inability to communicate with the outside world. A movie knew nothing about where it was located or in what page it was embedded. This has changed in Shockwave for Director 5 with the ability to add arbitrary parameters to the <embed> tag. This enables Shockwave developers to do things as simple as use the same button three times to go to three different pages instead of using three different buttons, or as complex as adjusting the display of each movie to the user's last actions, as discussed in Chapter 18, "Advanced Applications: Action Technologies' Metro."

The capability to specify parameters also provides ways for Shockwave for Director to interact with Java and JavaScript. As we shall see, you can create responsive, aware Shockwave components for your website by combining it with JavaScript.

In this chapter we will touch on the additional power that the capability to specify parameters adds to Shockwave for Director. We will begin with a brief button example, demonstrating the most basic use of the parameter capability. We will then show an example of the integration of Shockwave and JavaScript by creating a smart version of the Action Technologies' Porter movie discussed in Chapter 18, "Advanced Applications: Action Technologies' Metro."

Basics of <embed> Parameters

When a Shockwave title is invoked from within HTML, it is specified with either an `<embeded>` or `<object>` tag, which allows optional parameters for the Shockwave title. External parameters have the general form of `name=value`, where the `=value` portion is optional. For example, the following line specifies an additional parameter dest with a value of "pt.htm":

```
<embed src="bbutton.dcr" height=64 width=64 dest="pt.htm">
```

Additional parameters are, of course, useless without a way to access them from within Shockwave. The following functions allow access to those parameters:

- **`the externalParamCount`**. This property contains the number of external parameters. The number of external parameters includes all parameters, including the `src=`, `width=`, and `height=` parameters, as well as any others. The Lingo fragment putting the `externalParamCount` into field `result` in the case of the example would put the value 4 into field `result`.

- **`externalParamName(n)`**. If *n* is an integer, this function returns the *n*th parameter name from the external parameter list. If *n* is a string, this function returns *n* if any of the external parameter names matches *n* (case-insensitive). If there is no such parameter name, `externalParamName` returns void. Given the example above (`<embed src="bbutton.dcr" height=64 width=64 dest="pt.htm">`), putting `externalParamName(3)` into field `result` would put `width` into field `result`. Putting `externalParamName("width")` into field `result` would also put `width` into the result field.

- **`externalParamValue(n)`**. If *n* is an integer, this function returns the *n*th parameter value from the external parameter list. If *n* is a string, this function returns the value associated with the first name that matches *n* (case-insensitive). If there is no such parameter value, `externalParamValue` returns void. This is probably the most useful function. As we shall see in the next section, the Lingo fragment `GoToNetPage externalParamValue("dest")` applied to the example would go to the "pt.htm" page.

> **Note**
>
> According to Macromedia, in the future these same functions might allow access to parameters within other operating environments. In other words, these functions allow for general external parameter access, not just HTML tag access. This would allow, for instance, command-line parameters on Windows.
>
> The capability to handle external parameters has the potential to be the beginning of the campaign to give Director the capability to interact much more fully with the outside world, both within Shockwave and in general.

EXAMPLE 12.1

Simple Button Management

One of the most common uses for Shockwave is as an interface. By using Shockwave, developers can give their websites interfaces that act like the desktop applications we are all used to, adding items such as audio cues or buttons that actually go down when you click them. One of the barriers in Shockwave for Director 4 was the inability to reuse pieces of the interface that have already been downloaded. To make a button go to a different place, a new copy of the movie had to be downloaded with a different destination page hard-coded into the file. The ability to specify parameters, however, allows a single movie to be reused repeatedly, without the additional download time and without having to maintain multiple copies.

Our simple example button movie does only two things, but it does them reasonably well, and in a reusable fashion. This example is included on the accompanying CD in the Chapter 12 folder and is called BBUTTON.DIR; see figure 12.1 for the example movie embedded in a page. The example movie is not the absolute simplest case, because we have taken the opportunity to demonstrate the `NetStatus` function as well, but it is by no means a complex movie.

In the example movie, the unpressed version of the button is cast member 1 and the pressed version is cast member 2. Also, the button is placed in channel 1 of the movie.

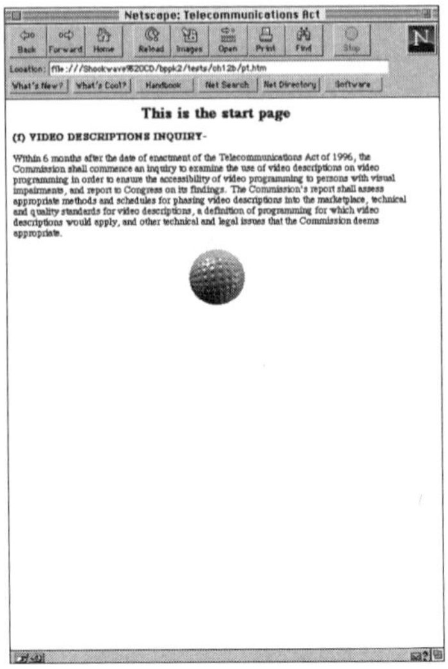

FIGURE 12.1

In Shockwave for Director 5, how a movie is embedded in the page can control what it does. For example, the same button can be used to go to a different page every time it is embedded.

The only graphics in the movie are the pressed and unpressed versions of the golf-ball-looking sphere, which was created in Kai's Power Tools 3.0 (see the following Tip for details on how to use KPT 3 to create round buttons). The score of the movie is only two frames. The movie will write the destination page to the status line when the mouse is over it, and it will go to the destination page when the button is clicked.

Tip

Kai's Power Tools 3.0's Spheroid Designer is a useful tool for creating round buttons with a 3D look. The steps for creating these buttons are straightforward:

1. Select a square or circular area in Adobe PhotoShop or other compatible application.
2. Select Filters, KPT 3.0, Spheroid Designer.
3. Create a Spheroid to taste, or use one of the presets. Make sure that the primary light source of the spheroid you select is from the upper left. Apply. This is your unpressed button graphic.
4. Make a new selection of the same size and shape as the previous one.

5. Open the filter again. It will open with the same settings as when you selected apply.
6. Click on the curvature button to find the curvature of the sphere you have just applied (see fig. 12.2).
7. Drag left on the curvature control until the curvature is the same amount below 0 as the original was above.
8. Apply.

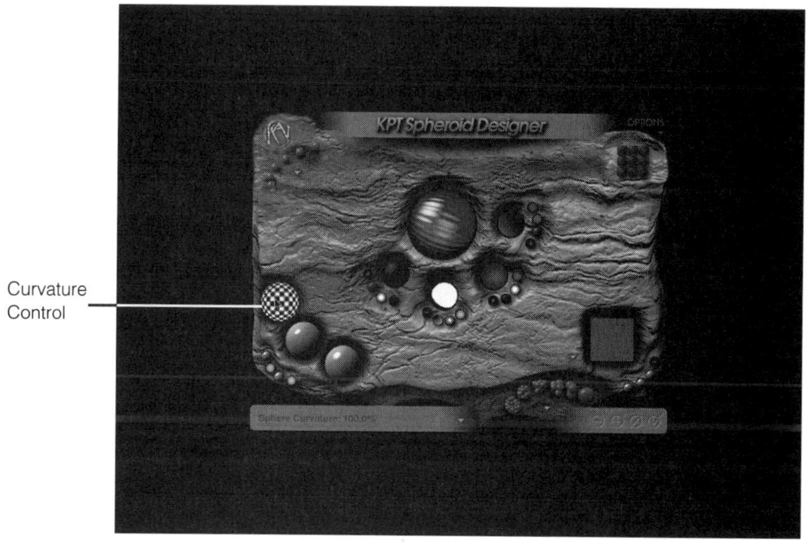

FIGURE 12.2

The curvature control determines how much the spheroid bulges.

Unlike all the other examples in this book, we will begin by embedding the movie, rather than ending the example that way:

```
<embed src="bbutton.dcr" height=64 width=64 dest="pt2.htm">
```

Note the dest=`"pt2.htm"` parameter. This is what allows the movie to do the voodoo that it does so well. It is used in both of the scripts in the movie, as we shall see.

The first part of the movie is the sprite script that we have added to the button graphic:

```
on mouseDown
   set up = 1
```

```
    set down = 2
    set destPage = externalParamValue("dest")
    set the membernum of sprite (the clickon) to down
    repeat while the mousedown
       if rollover(the clickon) then
          set the membernum of sprite (the clickon) to down
          set pressed = TRUE
          netStatus destPage
          updatestage
       else
          set the membernum of sprite (the clickon) to up
          set pressed=FALSE
          netStatus ""
          updatestage
       end if
    end repeat
    set the membernum of sprite (the clickon) to up
    updatestage
    if pressed then goToNetPage destPage
end
```

The basic button-management functionality of this script is similar to the one explained in Chapter 10, "Working with Frames." The new elements focus around the fourth line: `set destPage = externalParamValue("dest")`. This line searches the parameter list for a parameter named `"dest"`. Assuming the file was embedded correctly, it finds the parameter and assigns the value of that parameter (in this case, `"pt2.htm"`) to the variable named destPage.

When the mouse is over the button, it puts the destination page into the status line and erases it when the mouse leaves the button. When the mouse button is released (if it is over the button), the movie goes to the page specified in the embed parameter. The next script, `checkRoll`, is called in the score script in frame 2:

```
on checkRoll
   if rollover(1) then netStatus externalParamValue("dest")
   else netStatus ""
end
```

This script simply checks to see whether the mouse is over the button, and if so, puts the destination page into the status line. The one deficiency of this script, and of the previous one, is that the page name put into the status line is only a relative URL, not an absolute URL. So instead of seeing "http://www.company.com/Directory/pt2.htm" in the status line, you just see "pt2.htm." In the next example, we will remedy this concern.

Working with JavaScript

In the 2.0 version of Navigator, Netscape introduced a scripting language called JavaScript, which enables Navigator to construct documents on the fly. In combination with the capability to specify parameters, this provides Shockwave for Director 5 developers with a very powerful tool to get the maximum leverage out of their movies. In version 3.0, Microsoft will be adding JavaScript to their Internet Explorer product as well. For the purposes of the rest of this chapter, we will refer to the host browser as Navigator, but everything should be equally true for Internet Explorer as well. For more information on JavaScript and how to use it with Netscape Navigator, we suggest Tim Ritchey's *Programming JavaScript for Netscape 2.0*, available from New Riders.

One of the objects built into Navigator is the "location" object. This handy object contains the location of the current file, which enables us to pass the location to the Director movie. This is an excellent way to provide a full path name in the status line, solving the shortcomings of the previous example.

> The code in this example will only work for situations in which the Shockwave movie is in the same directory as the HTML page in which it is embedded and is calling a page in that same directory. It is certainly possible to take into account movies and destination pages in different directories, but that is left as an exercise for the reader.

Warning

To pass the current location to the Shockwave movie, we need to replace the `<embed>` tag from the pt.htm page with the following script:

```
<script language="JavaScript">
<!--
document.write("<embed src='cbutton.dcr' height=64 width=64
```

```
➥dest='pt2.htm'
loc='"+location.href+"'>");
//-->
</script>
```

The `document.write()` method writes the text supplied to the HTML page as it is loaded into the browser. Because the literal text we supply needs to be enclosed within double quotes, we use single quotes for the quotes within that literal text. In JavaScript, the + character is the concatenation operator (equivalent to the "&" character in Lingo). The `href` property of the location object contains the full path name of the HTML page.

The result of this script will be to pass the full path of the HTML file to the Shockwave movie as the `loc` parameter. We now have to modify the movie to handle the new parameter.

To use the previous example as a starting point, save it as CBUTTON.DIR. The final result is on the accompanying CD as DBUTTON.DIR, with the lines of Lingo that have changed conveniently colored red, for easy scanning.

Because the process of extracting the appropriate parts of the location name are moderately complex, we will add a `startMovie` handler to do it once, and therefore avoid repeating the process:

```
on startMovie
   global longDest
   set destPage = externalParamValue("dest")
   set locName = externalParamValue("loc")
   put the itemDelimiter into tID
   set the itemDelimiter = "/"
   delete item (the number of items in locName) of locName
   set longDest = locName & "/" & destPage
   set the itemDelimiter = tID
end
```

We maintain the simple page name as destPage, but we also put the `loc` parameter into the variable `locName`. We never actually use either of these parameters outside this handler, so we don't need to make them global variables. We will extract the relevant parts of the one variable, called `longDest`. Because the path name that was passed to the movie includes the name of the HTML page in addition to the directory path, we need to strip that out. We know that the page name is everything after the last slash ("/") in the path name, so we set the itemDelimiter to the slash character, and delete the last item. The variable locName now contains the path name of the directory containing the files. Deleting an item also deletes the itemDelimiter character, so we concatenate the path name of the directory with a slash character and the page name to create the longDest variable.

In the JavaScript we just wrote, the value of the dest parameter is "pt2.htm" and the value of the loc parameter is the full path name of the HTML page. If, for example, the path of this page is "http://www.company.com/Directory/pt.htm," then this will also be the value of the loc parameter.

The startmovie handler will initially set the locname variable equal to the loc parameter. Using the "/" as an item delimiter, it will then delete the last item in the path name as it appears in locname. Now the locname variable would contain "http://www.company.com/Directory". The startmovie handler then sets the longDest variable to the values of the locname variable and dest parameter (with a "/" added between them) to give a full path name to our destination page, "http://www.company.com/Directory/pt2.htm."

The checkRoll handler also needs to be adjusted to write the full path to the status line:

```
on checkRoll
   global longDest
   if rollover(1) then netStatus longDest
   else netStatus ""
end
```

Finally, we need to change the mouseDown script attached to the button sprite:

```
on mouseDown
   global longDest
   set up=1
   set down=2
   set the membernum of sprite (the clickon) to down
   repeat while the mousedown
      if rollover(the clickon) then
         set the membernum of sprite (the clickon) to down
         set pressed = TRUE
         netStatus longDest
```

```
            updatestage
         else
            set the membernum of sprite (the clickon) to up
            set pressed = FALSE
            netStatus ""
            updatestage
         end if
      end repeat
      set the membernum of sprite (the clickon) to up
      updatestage
      if pressed then goToNetPage longDest
   end
```

In both of these last two scripts, the only change is the reference to the global variable `longDest` and its substitution for `destPage`.

EXAMPLE 12.2

Santa's Little Helper: JavaScript and Shockwave

As seen in the previous example, JavaScript and Shockwave can be combined to make reusable movies. An additional—and more powerful in the long term—use for this combination is providing Shockwave movies with the capability to retain state information. Shockwave for Director 4's inability to handle this kind of information was a major barrier to using Shockwave for network-based applications. For a discussion of this and related issues, as well as the genesis of this example movie, see Chapter 18, "Advanced Applications: Action Technologies' Metro."

The principles in this section could be equally effectively applied to a combination of Shockwave and CGI scripts. The principles are the same, but CGI scripting involves additional complications that are not Shockwave-specific and are outside the scope of this book.

To demonstrate the communication between JavaScript and Shockwave, we have put together a whimsical Christmas-themed adaptation of the porter movie from the Action Technologies' Metro application, which responds to the user's input on a form. The metaphor is not completely seamless, but the movie demonstrates the way Shockwave can respond to JavaScript's input.

The JavaScript Wrapper

There are two HTML pages in this example. The first is a straightforward form, located on the accompanying CD as METR_PAR.HTM:

```
<html><head>
<title>JavaScript Form Test</title></head>
<body bgcolor=#000000 text=#ffffff>
<center><h2>This is the request page</h2> </center>
<form name="gift" action="tst.htm">
Who are you:
<INPUT TYPE="text" name="uname" VALUE="" SIZE=20><p>
Whaddaya Want? (You can ask for up to three items, separate them with
➥semicolons):<p>
<INPUT TYPE="text" name="what" VALUE="" SIZE=50><p>
<INPUT Type="submit" name="submit1" value="gimme!">
</form></body></html>
```

The form has two text input areas, named "uname" and "what." As you will see, the name of the text areas is not used, but they are required. The important thing is that as the page itself points out that the items requested are separated by semicolons. When experimenting with this example, you will want to try three, two, and one items because the movie reacts differently to different numbers of requested items.

The first key to this example is the action parameter of this form. It calls a file called TST.HTM, and it appends the text entered into the fields to the call to the page. Figure 12.3 shows the form.

The second page contains actual JavaScript. To understand how it works, we need to address the basic functioning of forms. When the submit button is pressed, the browser calls (the equivalent of a `GoToNetPage` command in Shockwave) the file specified in the action parameter. It appends the values entered in the `<input>` controls to the filename in the general format:

```
?firstInputName=value&secondInputName=value&...
```

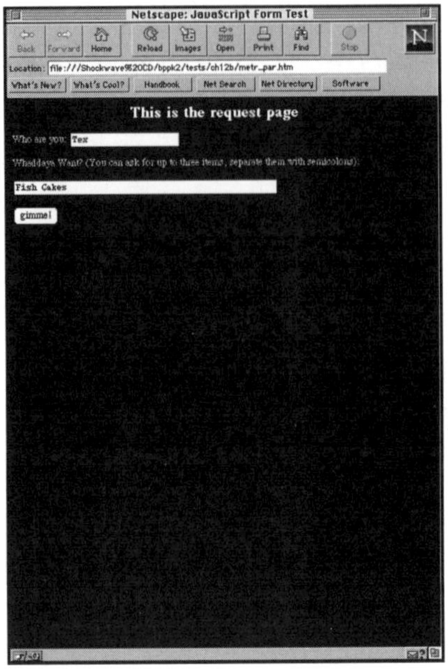

FIGURE 12.3

This example starts with a basic HTML form.

In the case of the form already shown, if the user enters the data shown ("Tex" in the uname field and "Fish Cakes" in the what field), the value sent would be:

```
pathname/tst.htm?uname=Tex&what=Fish+Cakes&submit1=gimme%21
```

The browser replaces spaces with the + character, semicolons with the escape sequence `%3B`, and exclamation points with `%21`.

> **Note**
>
> These latter two substitutions (`%3B` for semicolons and `%21` for exclamation points) are called *escape sequences* and are used because not every application can handle these characters. Other characters also have equivalents. Sharp-eyed readers might have noticed the `%20` in the location line in some of the screen shots. This substitutes for a space in directory names.
>
> For more information on which characters result in escape sequences and what those sequences are, check an HTML reference like the *HTML Sourcebook*, by Ian Graham.

The submit button also has a value, which Navigator displays as its label. In this case, we will ignore the value of the button.

The page simply declares a JavaScript function, adds a title and a header, and then finally calls the JavaScript function:

```
<html><head>
<script language="JavaScript">
<!--
function makePage()   {
   var bigQ = location.search;
   var t = bigQ.indexOf("=");
   var u = bigQ.indexOf("&", t);
   var p1 = bigQ.substring(t+1, u);
   t = bigQ.indexOf("=", u);   u = bigQ.indexOf("&", t);
   var p2 = bigQ.substring(t+1, u);
   document.write("<embed src='cnfrm.dcr' height=175 width=592
who='"+p1+"' what='"+p2+"' BGCOLOR=#000000>" );
   }
//-->
</script>
<title>JavaScript Form Test</title></head>
<body bgcolor=#000000 text=#ffffff>
<center><h2>This is the destination page</h2>
<script language="JavaScript">
<!--
makePage();
//-->
</script>
</center></body></html>
```

The function `makePage()` is the guts of this page. It first puts the contents of location.search into the variable `bigQ`. The search property is the text after the "?" character in the call to the page. If the input is the same as the previous example, it would be `uname=Tex&what=Fish+Cakes&submit1=gimme%21`. Obviously this is a big chunk to bite off, so the script then chops this up into its constituent parts.

We first need to find the value of the `uname` parameter. We know that it will be after the first `=` character, so we need to find the first occurrence of `=` in the string `bigQ`. Fortunately, JavaScript provides a method that is built into all string objects, called `indexOf()`. The `indexOf` function takes one or two arguments. The first is the character to find the index, or position, of in the string. The second argument, if used, is the position in the string at which to start searching. The search starts at the first character if the second parameter is not used. The method returns an integer representing the position of the first occurrence of the character after the start position.

> **Tip**
>
> Because JavaScipt is an object-based language, methods and properties of objects are referred to using the format *object.method* or *object.property.* Therefore, `location.search` indicates the search property of the location object, and `bigQ.indexOf()` represents the `indexOf` method of the string object `bigQ`.
>
> For a full list of JavaScript built-in objects and their methods and properties, refer to the Netscape JavaScript documentation or a reference such as Tim Ritchey's *Programming JavaScript for Netscape 2.0.*

We store the location of the first `=` character in the variable `t`. The next thing we need to find is the position of the first `&` character, which marks the end of the first value. This index we store in the variable *u*. We now use the `substring` method of the string object to extract the information we want and put it into the variable `p1`. The `substring` method takes two parameters, the start and end indexes of the substring. For some reason, the string returned from this function includes the character at the start position, but not the one at the end. In other words, the line `string.substring(5, 8)` returns characters 5–7 inclusive of the string. Because we don't want to include the `=` character in the value we pass to the Shockwave movie, we start the substring at `t+1`.

To extract the second value, we repeat the indexing functions, as well as the substring, taking the ending point of the last search as our starting point this time. We put the result into variable `p2`.

Finally, we use the document.write method to construct an `<embed>` line, passing the parameters `p1` and `p2` to the movie as who and what respectively. Note that we use single quote characters to enclose the parameter values in quotes. Assuming the same input as before, the result of this `document.write` call should be:

```
<embed src="cnfrm.dcr" height=175 width=592 who="Tex"
➥what="Fish+Cakes" BGCOLOR=#000000>
```

The Porter-Santa Shockwave Movie

Now that we have prepared the environment, we need to create the CNFRM.DCR movie. We have actually created the movie for you, and the burned version is located in the Chapter 12 folder on the accompanying CD. Unfortunately, we cannot make the unburned version available, but we will provide the code you need to make the file work. The file has seven text fields, named `"current"`, `"gift1"` through `"gift3"`, and `"greet1"` through `"greet3"`. There are three separate animations, They are located at markers "1," "2," and "3," corresponding to the number of gifts requested. All three greetings always play, but (obviously) the number of gift fields used depends on the number requested.

The first thing we need to do is clean up the parameters passed in, so we need a handler that massages that data. For example purposes, we will assume the `<embed>` tag reads as follows:

```
<embed src="cnfrm.dcr" height=175 width=592 who="Tex"
➥what="Fish+Cakes%3B+tartar+sauce" BGCOLOR=#000000>
```

The handler we use to clean the text is called (conveniently mnemonic), `cleanText`:

```
on cleanText thingy
   repeat while true
      put offset("%3B", thingy) into tOff
      if tOff = 0 then exit repeat
      delete char tOff to (tOff + 2) of thingy
      put ";" before char tOff of thingy
   end repeat
   repeat while true
      put offset("+", thingy) into tOff
      if tOff = 0 then exit repeat
      put " " into char tOff of thingy
   end repeat
   return thingy
end
```

The first loop looks for the escape sequence that the browser substituted for the semicolon characters when passing the form data to the page and replaces that sequence with the semicolon. The second loop does the same thing with the + character that replaced spaces. The handler then returns the cleaned string. The loops repeat until the offset of the string fragment to be cleaned out is 0, which means that the string does not contain the fragment.

To use the cleaned up data, we use the `parseParams` handler:

```
on parseParams
   set who = cleanText(externalParamValue("who"))
   set what = cleanText(externalParamValue("what"))
   put who into field "current"
   set the itemdelimiter to ";"
   put "Hello, "&who&", I'm here to take your gift request." into
   ➥field "greet1"
   put "I've got it. I'll send to the big guy now." into field
   ➥"greet2"
   put "Thank you. Your request is under way." into field "greet3"
   set x = the number of items in what
   repeat with i = 1 to x
      put item i of what into field "gift"&string(i)
   end repeat
   go string(x)
end
```

This handler uses the who and what variables to store the cleaned data from the parameters of the same name. It next puts the name the user entered into the `"current"` field, and into the appropriate place in the `"greet1"` text field. The other two greeting fields are the same regardless of user input.

Because we have reinserted semicolons between the requested gifts, we just need to determine the number of items in the string to know how many gifts the user requested. This number is put into the variable *x*. We then put each item into the `"gift"` fields. Finally, the script goes to the marker with named the number of the gifts requested. The CNFRM.DCR movie in action is shown in figurc 12.4.

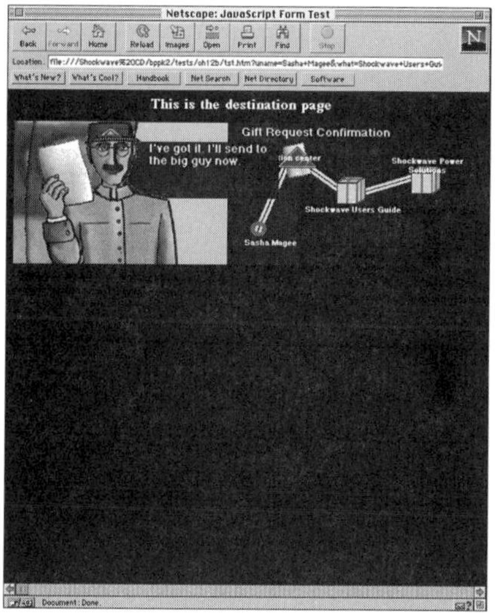

FIGURE 12.4

The movie CNFRM.DCR adjusts for the user's input.

Conclusion

In this chapter we have explored the use of Shockwave for Director 5's parameter-handling capability to reuse movies without redownloading as well as to interact with JavaScript. The next chapter begins Part IV: "Industrial-Strength Shockwave," which provides some techniques that you can use to make any Shockwave file more efficient and fit better into your website.

Part IV

Industrial-Strength Shockwave

CHAPTER 13

Detecting the Plug-In

One of the major barriers to the adoption of Shockwave has been the inability of the browser to detect the presence of the plug-in. Website hosts were forced to work around this problem by warning users that their site required Shockwave, or worse, by maintaining two versions of their site—one with Shockwave and one without.

Although Netscape provided a scripting language for Navigator 2.0, called JavaScript (which has since been adopted by Microsoft for its Internet Explorer product), the version of JavaScript included in 2.0 was not capable of discerning which plug-ins were installed.

With Netscape Navigator 3.0 and Microsoft Explorer 3.0, however, this problem has been fixed. Both applications provide ways to test for the appropriate plug-in with JavaScript. JavaScript also can determine which version of the browser the user is running and react to that specific version. The problem still remains, however. There is no way to tell whether a user running Netscape 2.0 has the plug-in.

Those caveats aside, we will now examine how to check the version of the application and test for the plug-in with JavaScript. Although we assume no knowledge of JavaScript for this example, we strongly suggest you check out Netscape's basic JavaScript documentation. A further excellent source for the JavaScript basics is Tim Ritchey's *Programming JavaScript for Netscape 2.0*, available from New Riders.

Determining the Version of Navigator

Strictly speaking, we don't care what version of Netscape Navigator we are using, except we do need to ensure that it is version 3.0 or higher. And at this point, we really don't care about whether it's Navigator or Internet Explorer.

Both products have a global object called "navigator," which contains information about the name of the application and its version. We could retrieve the version number of the application from the navigator object if so desired, but this is not the most efficient method to determine the version. Because the version is contained in a string, we would have to do extensive pattern matching, including matching for beta versions and dot releases. We also would need to special-case any other browser that implemented JavaScript as well. This is clearly something we do not want to hassle with if avoidable. Conveniently enough, we can avoid it.

In Navigator and Internet Explorer 3.0, the navigator object gained several new objects as properties. These include the mimeTypes object and (most importantly) the plug-ins object. The plug-ins object is the key to being able to determine whether the Shockwave plug-in is present. Therefore, we really need to test to see whether the object exists. Fortunately, JavaScript gives us a way to do that. The following script tests to see whether the plug-ins object exists:

```
function checkForThree() {
   for (var prop in navigator) {
       if (prop == "plug-ins") return true
       }
   return false
}
```

The for...in statement is a useful one. It enables you to walk through the properties of navigator without knowing how many there are, or in what order. This is especially important because you need to make sure the script will work if the navigator object changes.

Note

Functions in JavaScript are declared using the function command. Once a function is declared, it can be called by another script on the same page. Because a function needs to be declared before it is called, functions are usually declared in the `<head>` portion of the HTML page. Declaring a function establishes the function name, parameters (if any), and the actual logic of the function:

```
function functionName (parameters) {
   do something...
   ...
}
```

The `{}` characters (often called curly brackets or curly braces) delineate the extent of a function or control loop. Thus, in the preceding example, the outer set of curly braces mark off the beginning and end of the function, while the inner set marks off the extent of the for...in loop.

Three things you need to be especially aware of when writing JavaScript code follow:

- JavaScript is case-sensitive. This means that you must be very careful to use upper and lowercase characters appropriately. To the JavaScript interpreter, "Function" and "function" are completely different commands.
- Lines in JavaScript have no termination character. This means that each line is interpreted separately. Make sure your editor doesn't break lines arbitrarily, or you will end up with many errors.
- To keep the user's browser from trying to interpret the JavaScript code as HTML, you need to comment out the script code using the HTML comment combinations: `<!--` and `-->`. You also need to keep the JavaScript interpreter from trying to interpret the closing comment combination as a

JavaScript line by commenting it out using the // combination, which indicates a JavaScript comment. Thus, a template for the script section would be:

```
<script language="JavaScript">
<!--
actual script code
//-->
</script>
```

Be aware that in the for...in construction, the variable (in this case prop) contains the string that is the name of the property. A script that is useful for examining an object is as follows:

```
function showProps(object, name)   {
   for (var prop in object)
      document.write(name+"."+prop+" = "+object[prop]+"<P>")
}
```

Figure 13.1 shows the output of the previous function called as `showProps(navigator, "navigator")`.

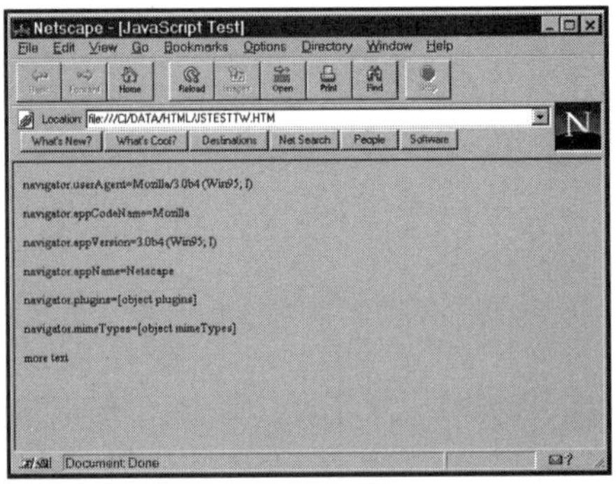

FIGURE 13.1

The showProps function displays the properties of the navigator object.

To show how the `checkForThree()` function can be used in a quick way, we have included the following HTML page:

```
<html><head>
<script language="JavaScript">
<!--
function checkForThree() {
   for (var prop in navigator) {
       if (prop == "plug-ins") return true
```

```
    }
    return false
}
//-->
</script>
<title>Which Version of Navigator are you Using?</title></head>

<body>
Your version of Navigator is:
<script language="JavaScript">
<!--
if (checkForThree()) document.write(" 3.0 or greater")
   else document.write(" 2.0x")
//-->
</script>
</body></head>
```

The result will be a page with the text "Your version of Navigator is: 3.0 or greater" (or "2.0x", if you have that version). This is obviously of limited utility, but when combined with the methods examined in the next chapter, it can be the means of avoiding the dreaded broken plug-in icon. Next, we will learn how to determine whether the plug-in is present.

Determining Whether the Plug-In Is Present

There are several ways that you can check for the presence of the Shockwave plug-ins. They all involve iterating through the navigator plug-ins object, checking each plug-in. We will use the plug-in's name, rather than the mimeTypes it can handle (which is another common way of dealing with this). This decision is somewhat arbitrary, because either method, in the current world of Shockwave, will work equally well. Searching for the name, however, seems to be the method that will be the best in the long term. This is true because we have to deal with multiple versions of the plug-ins anyway.

The basic technique for checking for a plug-in is to walk through the list of plug-ins, checking each name for a match with the desired plug-in. The basic `checkForPlug-in` function follows:

```
function checkForPlug-in(plug-inName) {
   for (i=0;i<navigator.plug-ins.length;i++) {
       if (navgator.plug-ins[i].name == plug-inName) {
           return true
       }
   }
   return false
}
```

This script walks through the list of plug-ins (the property `navigator.plug-ins.length` tells us how many plug-ins there are) and matches each one against the supplied plug-in name, which is contained in the parameter variable `plug-inName`.

> **Note**
>
> The for loop in the previous example is the equivalent to the Lingo repeat with command. The first parameter of the loop, **`i=0`**, is the starting value. The second parameter is the ending, or limit value. The third is the step increment (in this case, i increases by one each time through the loop). The parameters are separated by semicolons.

The functioning of this script, of course, depends on the page designer supplying the correct plug-in name. The easiest way to find out the name of a plug-in is to choose the About Plug-Ins menu item (under the Apple Menu on the Macintosh or under Help on Windows) and check the name that Netscape gives the plug-in. In figure 13.2, for example, we see the About screen portion for the Shockwave for FreeHand plug-in. The name in this case, as you can tell from the figure, is "Navigator FreeHand Plug-in."

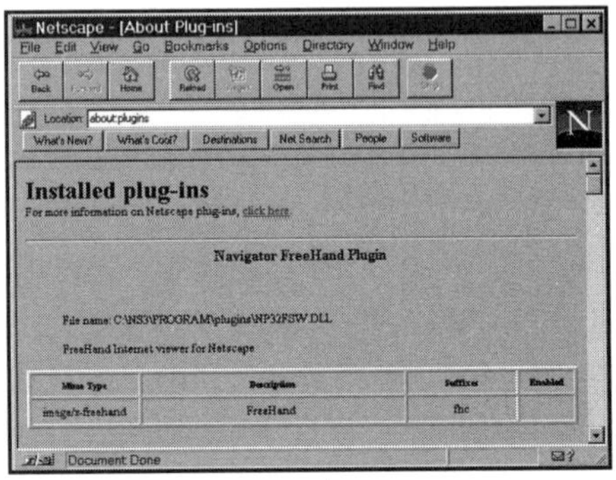

FIGURE 13.2

Selecting About Plug-Ins gives you a list of the installed plug-ins.

The names for the three Shockwave plug-ins at press time (we suggest you confirm that these are the names of the current versions) are:

Plug-In	*Name in Netscape*
Shockwave for Authorware	Shockwave for Authorware Plug-In
Shockwave for Director	Navigator Director Plug-In
Shockwave for FreeHand	Navigator FreeHand Plug-In

When the Plug-In Is Not Present

The meat of this question, of course, is how to use this to substitute an image if the user doesn't have the plug-in. Assuming you have declared the above function in the `<head>` section of your HTML page, the script fragment to embed a Shockwave for Director movie or an image would be:

```
if (checkForPlug-in("Navigator Director Plug-in"))
   document.write("<embed src='MOVIE.DCR' width=400 height=300>")
else
   document.write("<img src='IMAGE.GIF' width=400 height=300
  ➥alt='Image for those without the Shockwave for Director
  ➥Plug-in'>")
```

Note that when using nested quotations (quotes within quotes), you alternate double and single quotes. The following is a sample page (on your CD as 13-1.HTM), which will load either the static (GIF) version or the Shockwave for Director version of the InfraRed Logo:

```
<html><head>

<script language="JavaScript">
<!--
function checkForThree() {
   for (var prop in navigator) {
       if (prop == "plug-ins") return true
       }
   return false
}
```

```
function CHEckForPlug-in(PLUg-inName) {
   for (i=0;i<navigator.plugins.length;i++) {
       if (navgator.plug-ins[i].name == PLUg-inName) {
           return true
       }
   }
   return false
}
// -->
</script>
<title>InfraRed Communications</title></head>

<body BGCOLOR=#000000 TEXT=#FFFFFF LINK=#FF0000 vlink=#8E2323>
<center>
<script language="JavaScript">
<!--
if (checkForThree())    {
   if (CHEckForPlug-in("Navigator Director Plug-in"))
       document.write("<embed src='IRLOGO.DCR' width=464
       ➥height=60><p>")
   else
       document.write("<img src='IRLOGO.GIF' width=464 height=60
       ➥alt='InfraRed Communications'>")
   }
else {
document.write("<img src='irlogo.gif' width=464 height=60
➥alt='InfraRed Communications'><p>")
document.write("<em>WARNING: You are not using the latest version of
➥Netscape Navigator. We Suggest you go to")
document.write("the<a href='http://www.netscape.com'>Netscape web
➥site</a> and obtain the latest version</em>")
}

//-->
</script>
<noscript>
<img src='IRLOGO.GIF' width=464 height=60 alt='InfraRed
➥Communications'><p>
<em>WARNING: You are not using the latest version of Netscape Navigator.
➥We Suggest you go to the <a href='http://www.netscape.com'>Netscape web
➥site</a> and obtain the latest version of Navigator</em>
<p>
</noscript>
```

```
<h2> InfraRed Communications</h2></center>
In a real home page there would be more text here, but this is just an
➥example so there is not.
</body></html>
```

This page is an agglomeration of the script fragments we explained earlier in this chapter inserted into a full HTML page. In addition, we provide a `<noscript>` alternative for those folks using a non-JavaScript (and hence non-Shockwave) capable browser.

The part of this script in the `<head>` section simply defines the two functions examined earlier. The page then defines a title and then begins the body section, defining the page colors. Note that the first line of the `<body>` section is a `<center>` HTML tag. Because we want whatever ends up displaying (whether it is a Shockwave movie or a GIF) to be centered, we put the script after the tag.

The script checks to see whether the browser is Navigator or Internet Explorer 3.0. If so, it checks to see whether the Shockwave plug-in is installed. If the plug-in is present, it embeds a movie. If not, it displays a GIF (see fig. 13.3).

FIGURE 13.3

If the plug-in is not present or the user is running a pre-3.0 version of Navigator the page displays a GIF file instead of the movie.

If the browser is not one of these versions, the script displays a GIF with a message that the user should get the latest version of Navigator. Note that if the browser is JavaScript-capable but is not version 3, we can be confident that it is version 2.0x of Navigator.

The next section is the `<noscript>` section. If the browser is not capable of dealing with JavaScript, it will execute this section of the HTML code. Here, we also display an image and add a message urging the user to obtain the latest version of Navigator. Finally, the page displays the remaining HTML.

Conclusion

This chapter has examined the basics of using JavaScript to avoid the dreaded broken plug-in icon that occurs when the user does not have the appropriate plug-in.

We have only touched on the possible reactions to the growing combinations of browsers and plug-ins that are proliferating on the Web. As Macromedia releases new versions of the Shockwave plug-ins, Netscape, Microsoft, and other companies release new versions of their browsers and other variables rear their ugly heads, the ability to negotiate the appropriate version of the HTML page will become more and more important. Mastery of the JavaScript basics we have covered here will greatly increase your ability to create a positive experience for visitors to your website.

In the next chapter, we examine some of the more complex ways JavaScript and Shockwave can interact to create more personalized Web pages.

CHAPTER 14

ADVANCED COMPRESSION ISSUES

In this chapter we take on advanced concepts and techniques in data compression for Shockwave.

Several strategies for file size reduction have been detailed in other chapters. These strategies are concentrated on authoring practices that finesse more content out of lightweight elements like QuickDraw objects, ink and color, or scripted interactivity. These practices free you from reliance on bandwidth-heavy elements such as bitmaps, sound, and video.

Advanced compression enables you to take on the bandwidth hogs, giving you the understanding and the tools you need to put your rich media on a bandwidth diet. Your bitmaps and audio and digital video will never wear the same jeans again.

This chapter is divided into four major sections:

- Conceptualizing compression
- Compression in the Shockwave environment
- Techniques for precompressing bitmaps
- Techniques for precompressing audio

The first section, "Conceptualizing Compression," gives a conceptual framework for understanding and analyzing compression. If you want to concentrate on advanced techniques, tips, and tricks for file compression in the Shockwave environment, you can skip ahead to the next section.

Conceptualizing Compression

This section discusses the key importance of compression, touches on information theory in simple terms, shows a fresh way to visualize data compression, and details lossless and lossy schemes. This prepares you to handle compression in the Shockwave environment with greater sophistication.

The Importance of Compression

What is compression? As discussed in earlier chapters with reference to Afterburner, *data compression* is the process of reducing digital information. In the most basic sense, compression technologies reduce the size of data.

So why all the fuss about compression? Because a staggering portion of our economy is reliant on digital information. With ever more types of data stored and transmitted on ever-growing networks, file compression has become a key area of research and development. Certainly data compression has been a major component of the overall success of the Internet and continues to be a vibrant area of innovation on the Web.

Why is compression so important on the Web? The answer is simple—time and money. From a user's standpoint, time is of the essence. Users want the desired information as fast as they can consume it. Personally, I know that if any computer process makes me wait at all, it is simply not fast enough.

Given a fixed rate of data transfer, a compression of file size yields a proportional savings in the transfer time.

For an information service provider, data compression brings a two-fold benefit. First, when data is compressed, the users of that service enjoy faster access to their data. Second, compression allows more services can be offered to a larger audience at the same time.

Information service providers invest big capital into meeting the bandwidth requirements of their data plant. Outlays for data servers, data storage and backup, internal network routing, and inter-network connections are just a few. All must keep pace with the bandwidth requirements of network traffic. Data compression enables us to serve more network traffic with less bandwidth requirements.

Given a fixed rate of network traffic, a compression of the average data stream yields a commensurate capital savings.

The imperative of the marketplace has compelled tremendous advances in the field of information theory and in practical methods of compression. Other technologies, such as data streaming and network caching, also help maximize user time and network resources. Generally speaking, streaming and caching work together with compression technology, and will play a growing role in the Shockwave environment. Right now, Macromedia is still developing their approach to streaming.

Streaming is a great technology challenge for multimedia on the Web. Ideally, a streaming version of Shockwave would allow you start the playback of a movie before the whole download finished (fast-play). You would need control over the order that cast members are sent across the network, much like the Lingo command `preloadCast` allows Director to control the order that the cast is loaded into RAM.

Even if it were possible to provide absolute control over the cast download sequence, you still don't know the order you'll need to deliver the media. In a Shockwave for Director kiosk, for example, there might be several choices from the main menu and users can decide on their own which branch to follow. They might decide on a branch that is not yet loaded, putting you back to the original bandwidth problem. In this sense, non-linearity is the bane of streaming.

Shockwave for Authorware approximates streaming by offering *segmenting*—breaking down large movies into easy-to-download chunks. Authorware movies are object-based, constructed like branching flowcharts. This facilitates segmenting in Shockwave for Authorware. Director's frame architecture is not so easily adapted to segmenting.

Our speculation shows that a hybrid approach might be called for to provide streaming in Shockwave for Director. The combination of fast-play capability with streaming of continuous media types such as audio and digital video would solve the major streaming needs.

For the near-term, the saving grace of Shockwave for Director is the fact that files are cached locally and handled automatically by the Netscape browser or as linked media in a support folder. But even with the coming of broadband networks—data streaming in Shockwave and better caching methods—there will always be a need for data compression. The more you know about compression, the better.

The underlying mathematics of data compression is beyond the scope of this book and we are not experts in this field. But as providers of compressed data to the Web, we find it important to have some knowledge of information theory. This helps us work creatively with compression and take advantage of compression technologies as they emerge.

Entropy and Compression

The principles of file compression are related to the concept of entropy. Entropy is the subject of a vast amount of academic inquiry and debate. For most people, the mere mention of the word "entropy" is enough to make them run away screaming in a fit of confusion. But entropy is not a hard concept to grasp conceptually.

Entropy cuts across many realms of experience. Therefore, it is in some ways easier to recognize and characterize than it is to quantify or measure. From the steam in your teapot to the clothes in your messy room, you'll recognize entropy when you see it. This section is a qualitative discussion of entropy and compression using words and pictures instead of equations.

So what is entropy? Typically, it is said that *entropy* relates to the quantity of randomness or disorder in a system—more disorder means higher entropy.

We have been warned by the second law of thermodynamics that in a closed system of matter and energy (such as the universe), entropy tends to increase. And with the ultimate increase of entropy disappears the available energy of the universe—its final fate, one of cold random chaos, known as heat death.

The notion of entropy can be applied to information, as well as matter and energy. Before the universe freezes, however, we can at least take advantage of information entropy to compress our data. The entropy or disorder in a file can be interpreted to mean the amount of information it contains.

Disorder and Information Entropy

How is "disorder" related to "information"? In this context, the information in a file is the amount of unique data words needed to make up the file. An orderly file, such as {1111111111111111}, contains very little information and few details, so to speak. Because it is orderly, each additional bit contributes little new information. Such a data file is said to be in a *low entropy state*. It is patterned, predictable, and orderly.

In a disordered file, such as {1001011010111000}, the bits are noise-like, unpredictable, non-repeating, and full of details. The file is comprised of many unique data words. Because it is disordered, each additional bit contributes a lot of new information. This type of file is said to be in a *high entropy state*. It is chock full of information because it is unpatterned and disorderly.

Probability and Information Entropy

How is probability related to information? A high entropy file also is said to be in a more probable information state; low entropy files are said to be in a less probable information state. You can confirm this idea yourself. If you generate a binary data file at random, it is very unlikely to be a low entropy file such as the one represented in the right half of figure 14.1. A file generated at random, in all probability, will be a high entropy file like the one represented in the left half of figure 14.1.

Figure 14.1

A random (higher entropy) file is shown on the left. A patterned (lower entropy) file is shown on the right.

We created a little Director movie called RANDOM.DIR (in the Chapter 14 folder on the accompanying CD) which generates a random pattern. If you run it and watch it generate patterns over and over, you will see that the vast majority of the patterns generated are disordered, such as on the left side of figure 14.1. Therefore in practice, we see that of all possible information states, the disordered states are more numerous than the ordered ones.

In a low entropy file, the large structure of data is more unique because it has a highly patterned or improbable structure. Low entropy files have non-unique sub-parts; the data words are more interchangeable.

In a high entropy file, the large structure of the data is less unique because it has a more probable or random structure. High entropy files have sub-parts that are more unique; the data words are non-interchangeable.

Lossless Compression: Reversible Transformations

Lossless compression is achieved by removing the orderly (redundant) information in such a way that it can be restored later based upon the disorderly (unique) information that remains in the smaller compressed file.

Lossless compression is a reversible data transformation. Reversibility means that the source file can be exactly recovered from the transformed file. In a reversible data transformation, the file might change, but the net information contained in the file does not. This means that the total entropy of the file does not change under lossless compression.

In order to compress the size of a file reversibly, you must somehow increase the entropy per bit because less data has to carry the same net entropy. In lossless compression, data is destroyed (compressed), but entropy is not. Thus, a greater compression rate requires a greater increase in the entropy density.

Afterburner applies lossless (reversible) compression to the bitmaps in Shockwave files in much the same way that Stuffit or PKZIP work. The total entropy of the source file is the same as the total entropy of the Afterburned file—only now the entropy is more dense (more entropy per bit).

Let's try a lossless compression of the checkerboard and the randomly generated bitmap patterns seen in figure 14.1. Note that we are no longer talking about binary data files. Instead, we are talking about bitmapped representations, which also have similar compression characteristics.

First, to make the most accurate compression, we saved the two bitmaps in Encapsulated PostScript (EPS) format because bitmaps in EPS are saved in a more one-to-one format (as opposed to PICT, which removes some redundancy). See the files PATTERN.EPS and RANDOM.EPS in the Chapter 14 folder on the accompanying CD.

Compressing the two bitmaps using a ZIP utility (we used MacZip and zipped the data fork only) yields the following results:

TABLE 14.1

LOSSLESS COMPRESSION OF RANDOM.EPS VERSUS PATTERN.EPS

Before Compression		*After Compression*	
RANDOM.EPS	44 KB	RANDOM.ZIP	3.0 KB
PATTERN.EPS	44 KB	PATTERN.ZIP	1.5 KB

Notice that the randomly generated image is twice the size of the patterned image when compressed with lossless compression.

> **Note**
>
> Some Mac users might get confused and frustrated that their files are not shrinking. On my Macintosh hard disk, for example, the file RANDOM.ZIP equals 4 KB and PATTEN.ZIP equals 4 KB. But the preceding table shows RANDOM.ZIP to equal 3.0 KB and PATTERN.ZIP to equal 1.5 KB. How can this be?
>
> The secret behind this mystery is that the Finder reports file size based on the block allocation size of your hard disk. Consequently, files might appear larger than they really are. But fear not. You can get the true file size from the Finder by selecting the file and pressing Command+I. For Windows users this is not an issue. Both the Windows 3.11 File Manager and the Windows 95 Explorer show the true file size.

Visualizing Entropy

Compression ratios alone do not tell the whole story about compression. In our search for simple tools to analyze the entropy within our files, we discovered that (believe it or not) Photoshop was the cool tool for the job. When used in conjunction with the pattern recognition built into your own eyes, Photoshop enables you to visualize entropy quite well.

Photoshop opens and displays many types of graphic files, but it also can convert any raw data into a bitmapped representation. In Photoshop's File: Open dialog box, you can open any type of file. Just select the Show All Files option and choose Raw from the Format pop-up. In older versions of Photoshop, you have to use the command File: Open As to open a file as raw data.

Opening raw data converts the bytes of the file into a sequence of gray level (0–255) pixels laid out in a rectangular bitmap of arbitrary height and width. Because each byte of source becomes a pixel in the bitmap, the width times the height in pixels is equal to the file size. Photoshop tries to guess at a factoring of the source file size into a nice width and height.

If the file size is a prime number (it has no whole number factoring) or the file has no large factors, Photoshop then requires you to choose a width and height. You must calculate a whole number width and height whose product comes closest to the file size without going over.

After the file is converted to a bitmap, you can assess the entropy of the file by simply looking at it. If it looks regular, structured, patterned, periodic, and so on, then it has a low entropy density. If you can't recognize much large-scale patterning, that's because it is a file with a high entropy density. High entropy density files resemble the random static noise such as what appears on an untuned television screen.

Using our trusty random and pattern files, we demonstrate entropy analysis in Photoshop. First, we open the two source EPS files—not as EPS, but as raw data. This allows us to see into the data structure. When opening the EPS files as raw data, we chose width=273 and heigth=150 to come close to the source file size without going over.

Comparing the two source files (see fig. 14.2), you see immediately that they are both fairly patterned. After some examination, you also see that the image of RANDOM.EPS is more disordered than PATTERN.EPS. From this you can infer that both files are in a low entropy density state and that the file RANDOM.EPS has higher entropy than the PATTERN.EPS file.

FIGURE 14.2

This visualization of the random and the pattern EPS files reveals regularity and structure (low entropy). Which one seems more disordered (higher entropy) to you?

Next, we open the two corresponding compressed ZIP files as raw data as well. The images of the two compressed files show few visible patterns or regularity of any kind. About the only qualitative difference that can be seen is that one is larger than the other, but they both seem similarly disordered. From this we infer that the ZIP files are in a state of high entropy density (see fig. 14.3).

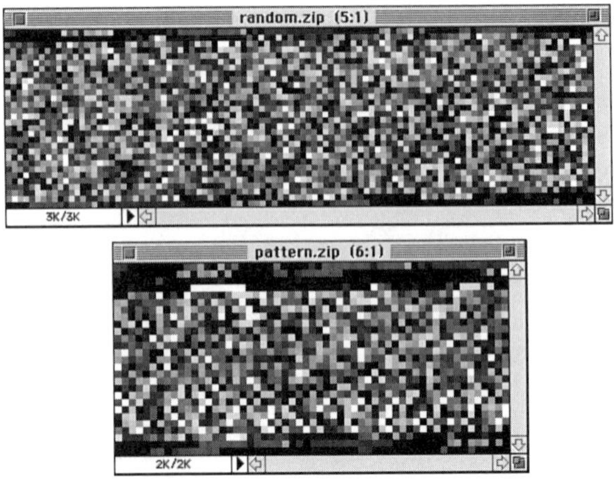

FIGURE 14.3

The compressed ZIP files appear much like static noise. They are both in a very disordered (high entropy) state.

Besides visual inspection, we use the histogram tool to analyze the entropy further. Select Histogram from the Image menu to get a graph of the data spectrum. The histogram plots the occurrences of each gray in the bitmap. Figure 14.4 shows the histograms of the original EPS files. Notice that most of the bytes fall into just a few bands. This means that certain 8-bit data words are repeated very often.

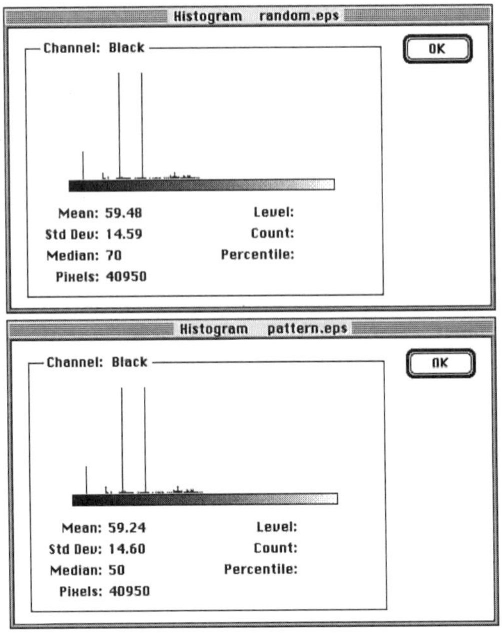

FIGURE 14.4

Histograms for the uncompressed EPS files reveal that few unique 8-bit data words are present. This is a very improbable (low entropy) state.

The histogram can be likened to a glossary of all the 8-bit data words in the file. Because the histogram shows how the 8-bit data words are spread, it tells us something about the entropy of the file. Redundancy or patterning (low entropy) in a file often shows up in a spiked or irregular histogram. The spikes in the histograms in figure 14.4 confirm that the EPS files are low entropy.

A truly random (high entropy) file would have nearly equal amounts of every 8-bit data word and, thus, a more flat histogram. Take, for example, the histograms of the compressed ZIP files (see fig. 14.5). Notice how much more spread out they are than the histograms of the uncompressed EPS files. A wide variety of data words are needed to make it up the file. This is an indication that the ZIP files are high entropy.

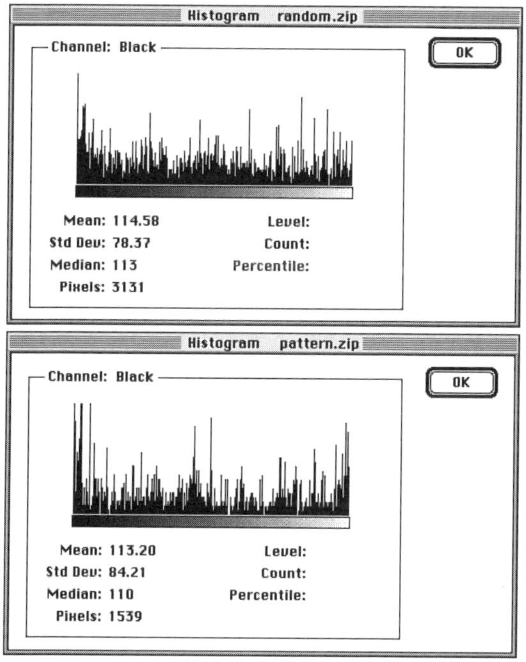

FIGURE 14.5

After compression, the data is spread among more unique 8-bit data words. The data is compacted into a much more probable (high entropy) state.

The histogram function in Photoshop tells us nothing about the randomness of patterns larger than 8-bit. You can see in figure 14.2 (shown earlier) that much of the redundancy or regularity in the PATTERN.EPS file occurs in chunks of several pixels (bytes). A histogram showing the count of larger data words, say 24-bit or 32-bit data words would be needed to compare the difference between RANDOM.EPS and PATTERN.EPS.

Using Photoshop to analyze entropy has other limitations as well. For instance, it is a very subjective and qualitative tool. Although it was not designed to analyze entropy, and despite many limitations, it is surprising how much you can visualize and learn about entropy using Photoshop. This is perhaps more a testament to the inherent pattern recognition ability of the human eye. And with that, we take you back to compression.

Entropy and Compressibility

What is the relationship between entropy and compressibility? We've just seen in practice that a more ordered file (PATTERN.EPS) compresses more than a less ordered one (RANDOM.EPS). If you like, you can confirm that this relationship generally holds—files with lower entropy density are more compressible.

Our trusty example files exemplify this (see fig. 14.6). Indeed, when using lossless compression, the file with higher initial entropy density (RANDOM.EPS) is less compressible than the one with lower initial entropy density (PATTERN.EPS).

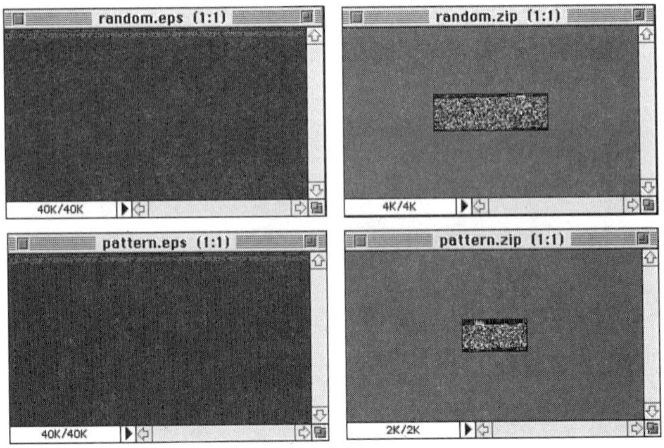

FIGURE 14.6

PATTERN.EPS compresses more. It has less total entropy than RANDOM.EPS.

What happens if you apply lossless compress to a compressed file? You might guess that even after lossless compression, there still might be some redundancy or pattern remaining; therefore, a compressed file also might be compressible. Testing multiple compression, we get the following results:

TABLE 14.2

MULTIPLE LOSSLESS COMPRESSION

	Before Compression	*First Compression*	*Second Compression*	*Third Compression*
RANDOM.EPS	44.27 KB	3.14 KB	3.06 KB	3.32 KB
PATTERN.EPS	44.32 KB	1.54 KB	1.56 KB	1.82 KB

You can see this for yourself. The series of ZIPed files are in the accompanying CD's Chapter 14 Folder. After the second round of compression, both files are actually getting larger. The lossless compression utility is having a hard time increasing the entropy density past a certain point. It seems the files have approached some saturation of entropy density, at least within the language of the ZIP compression scheme.

Because compressing a file packs the same information entropy in a smaller number of bits and because we see that there is a definite limit to compressibility, we conclude that there is some inherent limit on the entropy carrying capacity of binary data. Indeed if there wasn't such a limit, we could conceive of the absurdity of a lossless compression that makes files disappear altogether. Any lossless compression algorithm (no matter how efficient) and every file (no matter how predictable) has to have an ultimate limitation on compressibility—entropy itself.

After lossless compression packs the file's entropy to saturation, you can only shrink it further by reducing its total entropy. This requires somehow destroying information in an irreversible way—lossy compression.

Lossy Compression: Irreversible Transformations

Lossless compression reduces file size by trading redundant information for higher entropy density with no net change in entropy. Lossy file compression reduces file size by trading unnecessary information for entropy headroom resulting in a net decrease in entropy. Lossy compression irreversibly degrades information present in a file. When employing lossy compression, it is a good practice to keep backups of all your source material in case you need to rework anything.

Good lossy compression schemes remove information that is unnecessary for the given purpose. In the case of perceptual media (images, moving images, and sound), unnecessary information is that which is least perceptible to the human senses. Lossy compression schemes for perceptual media preserve as much perceptive fidelity as possible by strategically redistributing entropy to the key sensitivities of human senses.

Applying lossy compression to the source media files throws out information in the less sensitive areas, giving you more sensory bang for your entropy buck. Lossless compression might reduce the file size outright or just reduce the entropy density of your file allowing higher compression ratios under lossless compression and, therefore, shorter downloads.

Smart application of lossy compression in Shockwave production can significantly reduce download time while preserving the sensory impact. Precompressing your bitmaps and audio and digital video with a perceptually based lossy scheme can enable you to pack more content into your Shockwave movies.

With the compression primer out of the way, we now give an overview of compression in the Shockwave environment.

Compression in the Shockwave Environment

This section is an overview of the advanced compression techniques available in the Shockwave environment. The compression techniques are introduced by media type, starting with bitmap compression and audio compression. We conclude this section with a more detailed introduction to compression issues for digital video.

Bitmap Compression for Shockwave

You are familiar with Afterburner by now. It is the lossless compression scheme for all flavors of Shockwave. Afterburner employs a type of lossless compression similar to ZIP and Stuffit. It performs run-length encoding and creates a glossary of data words. It is a fast compressor and an even faster decompressor.

Of all the media types contained in typical Shockwave movies (all flavors), Afterburner has the greatest effect on the bitmapped media. Afterburner's efficiency varies greatly depending on the regularity and order within the bitmap image. You can infer from the earlier discussion of entropy that continuous or regularly patterned regions of color compress the best and noisy chaotic many-colored images compress the least.

A great strategy for improving Afterburner's efficiency is to precompress the bitmapped image with a lossy compression scheme. This means removing information, reducing the detail in your bitmaps, flattening out irregularities, restricting the color range, and so on.

The first line of lossy attack is color-depth (bit-depth) reduction. Reducing bit depth, say from 16 to 8 bits, can be done with or without dithering. A non-dithering bit depth crunch maps each 16-bit pixel's color to a color in an 8-bit palette. This straight truncation of color information can look pretty bad as subtle gradations are lost, washed into areas of flat color. (See the section, "Bit-Depth Reduction and Dithering," later in this chapter for visual examples of reducing bit depth in images.)

Dithering uses the average color of 8-bit pixel groups to more closely approximate the exact color of the 16-bit original. Dropping a 16-bit image to 8 bits cuts the file size in half, but it does not necessarily cut its total entropy in half. As you might guess, non-dithering can often yield more entropy savings than dithering. Non-dithering preserves less visual information and creates a more uniform (lower entropy) file. Dithering preserves more visual information with groupings of many different colors, creating a more noisy (higher entropy) file.

Additional compression can be achieved by applying blurring to the image. This tends to smooth the image, removing some noise. With judicious use, blurring can destroy a fair amount of entropy while preserving image quality.

> **Tip**
>
> A more advanced form of compression is Cinepak. This QuickTime-compatible compressor is usually used for digital video, but it can be used to apply lossy compression to still PICT images as well. As you will see in the section, "Techniques for Precompressing Bitmaps," Cinepak can offer great flexibility in trading image quality for bandwidth.

Afterburner provides lossless compression of as much as 70 percent or more. The many lossy compression techniques for bitmaps give you the creative control over bandwidth that you need to maximize the impact of your Shockwave movies.

TABLE 14.3

LOSSY COMPRESSION OF BITMAPS IN DIRECTOR, AUTHORWARE, AND FREEHAND*

	Compression	*Quality Loss*
Bit-depth reduction with dithering 16 bits to 8 bits	30%–50%	Medium
Bit-depth reduction No dithering 16 bits to 8 bits	40%–70%	Large
Blurring	5%–15%	Small
Cinepak	15%–25%	Small

**Compression is the Afterburned savings when you precompress.*

Audio Compression for Shockwave

Macromedia has always stated that Afterburner does not compress the audio portion of DIR files, but only compresses the bitmaps. We are not sure why they make this disclaimer, especially when it is not really true. Afterburner compresses the entire source file, in much the same way that files are compressed using ZIP or Stuffit. Any data in the source that is compressible will in fact compress under Afterburner.

But because sound is chaotic, non-repeating, and noisy (high entropy density) to begin with, audio files are generally less compressible under lossless compression than are bitmaps. Therefore, Afterburner often has a lesser effect on the sound portion of the Director or Authorware files.

The large data size of audio requires us to apply severe lossy precompression to sound files used in Shockwave. A huge file savings is achieved by reducing the sampling rate and bit depth of the sound file. A source file sampled at 44.1

khz/16 bits (CD-quality) can be shrunk to one eighth the original size by reducing it to 11.025 khz/8 bits. This rather drastic process is called *down-sampling* and it comes at the expense of high-frequency response and signal-to-noise ratio, resulting in a serious reduction of fidelity. (See "Precompressing with Sampling Reduction" later in this chapter for examples.)

Down-sampling should be applied with a high quality dithering algorithm. Down-sampling audio with dithering sounds much better than truncation and usually doesn't cost much additional bandwidth in the final burnt movie. You can perform good down-sampling in Sonic Foundry's Sound Forge, or Macromedia's Sound Edit 16 or Deck II. On the Mac, shareware such as SoundHack or Apple's MoviePlayer are fine, too.

There are several lossy compression schemes for audio on the Internet such as µ-Law, au, MACE, IMA, MPEG, and so on. These perceptually based lossy compression schemes exploit in various ways the special characteristics of audio signals and the peculiarities of human psychoacoustics to concentrate entropy on the most sensitive parts of the audio.

In choosing among audio compressors for Shockwave, our main criteria is cross-platform compatibility, sound quality, and compression efficiency. The only real choice at this time is IMA audio compression, which (although there are several drawbacks) does provide nice-sounding 4:1 compression of audio sampled at 44.1 khz/16 bits.

After crunching in Afterburner, IMA audio compression offers equal or greater bandwidth savings than down-sampling to 11.025 khz/8 bits and IMA sounds so much better.

We feel that IMA compression is only a taste of things to come for audio compression. The future promises more efficient, better-sounding, and standardized schemes. But in certain applications, IMA audio compression gives you an excellent solution today to the vexing problem of audio in narrowband Shockwave.

Finally, using redundancy within your sound loops can help achieve better compression ratios. Longer sound loops like background music should be composed of a few small building block loops.

TABLE 14.4

LOSSY COMPRESSION OF SOUND IN DIRECTOR AND AUTHORWARE*

	Compression	*Quality Loss*
Down-sampling with dithering 44.1 khz/16 bits to 11.025 khz/8 bits	40%–50%	Large
IMA 4:1 Compression 44.1 khz/16 bits to 44.1 khz/4 bits	40%–60%	Small
Redundant loops	25%–50%	None

**Compression is the Afterburned savings when you precompress.*

Digital Video Compression for Shockwave Primer

Shockwave for Director 5 supports external media such as QuickTime movies. Even under enormous compression, the file sizes for digital video make audio files seem like guppies. Shockwave delivery of digital video is only feasible for high-speed connections such as 1.5 Mbps Ethernet LANs, cable modems, or even faster connections.

Shockwave does not yet stream digital video across the Net, which means that the whole digital video cast member has to download before Shockwave for Director can play it. Support for external casts in Director 5 provides interesting solutions to the digital video problem. It is possible to create a hybrid application in which lightweight media is pulled off a Web server and heavyweight media is pulled locally from a CD-ROM or hard drive. An example of digital video as a linked cast is given in Chapter 5, "Shockwave for Director 5."

The compression techniques for digital video under Shockwave are more or less the same as compressing video for a single-speed CD-ROM. Cinepak compression is highly recommended for its decompression efficiency and image quality, even at compression high ratios.

AUTHORS' NOTE

The following are some tips for compressing digital video:

1. Compression starts with acquisition. Obtain the best generation and format for any preshot material you are using.
2. Shoot your own footage in the best format possible to keep noise to a minimum. Chroma and luma noise can hamstring Cinepak efficiency.
3. Light your set well to avoid needing to gain up the camera.
4. Minimize the texture and motion on the set and in your subject—no finely textured backdrops, wind-blown trees, and so on. Use a solid-colored wardrobe.
5. Digitize the material at the highest available data rate to avoid JPEG artifacting. JPEG noise reduces Cinepak efficiency.
6. Adjust your TBC settings or tape output levels to spread the chroma and luma signals. Cinepak compresses the dynamic range, so you want to fill it to maintain more signal to noise.
7. Use After Effects to resize the video window of your final edited piece. Don't use Premiere to resize because its algorithm adds artifacting, which will reduce Cinepak efficiency.
8. Try a Gaussian Blur in After Effects or Premiere to smooth out JPEG and other signal noise. This will increase Cinepak efficiency.
9. Use MovieShop to perform final Cinepak compression. Adjust cropping and Frames per Second as needed. Set the Data Rate to 100 KB/sec for single-speed CD-ROMs and 200 KB/sec for double-speed CD-ROMs.
10. If your QuickTime movie has an audio track, use IMA audio compression. You can convert to IMA in MoviePlayer or MovieCleaner Pro.

For other QuickTime tricks, MovieCleaner Lite is an excellent shareware tool for the Mac. MovieCleaner Pro has more handy features, including support for IMA audio compression. We use MovieCleaner Pro or MovieCleaner Lite to refine our movies for Director and Shockwave for Director. You can download MovieCleaner Pro at `http://www.terran-int.com`.

Director often skips or stutters at the beginning of video playback. To get around this problem, apply a First Frame Hold to your movie using Movie-Cleaner. This advanced setting slows the frame rate for the first frame, keeping it on screen long enough for Director to get up to speed. This does not add file size and is perfect for movies that fade in or start from a still image.

For movies that start or end in a still image, you can use MovieCleaner to maximize image quality of the first and last frame. Use the advanced video setting High Quality First/Last Frame. This gives more bandwidth to the first and last frame and makes sure the last frame is a keyframe.

The next section details the techniques for precompressing bitmaps for Shockwave. The emphasis is on bit-depth reduction and Cinepak with some discussion of filtering.

Techniques for Precompressing Bitmaps

When precompressing bitmaps with lossy compression, you have to consider the impact on Afterburner efficiency. Precompression might yield huge savings in the DIR file size, for example, but add little savings in the DCR. Or conversely, precompressing bitmaps might yield no change in the DIR size, but significant savings in the DCR file. The only way to know is to test through to the Afterburner stage.

Bit-Depth Reduction and Dithering

The most basic lossy scheme for precompression of bitmap images is color-depth reduction. The reduction of 16- or 24-bit images to 8 bits is a technique of great concern to all Web designers. The added download time of 16- or 24-bit images is considered an unwarranted extravagance, so 8-bit color depth is king on the Web. The same holds true in Shockwave. The bit depth of bitmap cast should never exceed 8 bits unless there is a very compelling reason to do so.

The big concern when reducing from 24 or 16 bits down to 8 bits is dithering. Dithering often yields a higher quality image than non-dithering. Dithering generally preserves more visual information, more complexity, and wider color range—thus more total entropy. This means that precompressing with a dithered bit-depth reduction will generally cost you bandwidth after post-compression with Afterburner.

Non-dithered reduction truncates the color information, mapping the 16-bit color to the closest equivalent color in an 8-bit color palette, simplifying the image file more than dithering does. If you can get away with it visually, using a non-dithered bit-depth reduction can save significant bandwidth in the final Afterburned file.

Compare the difference in compressibility between a dithered and non-dithered bit-depth reduction. We created a textured background using KPT Texture Explorer in Photoshop. The original 16-bit image is shown in figure 14.7. The file BG16BIT.PIC can be found in the Chapter 14 folder on the accompanying CD.

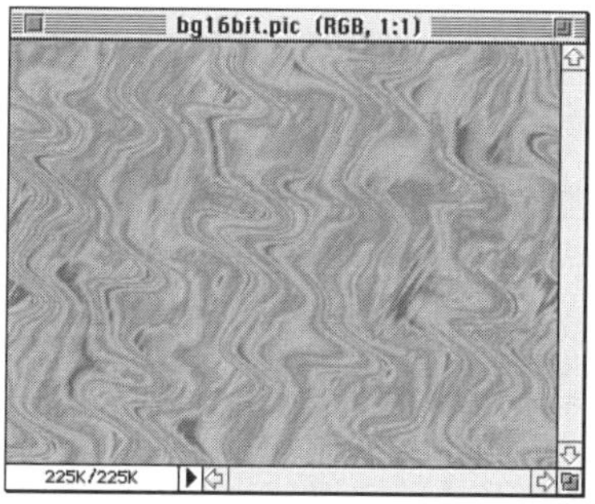

FIGURE 14.7

The test background is shown here in 16-bit color depth.

We then precompressed the image to 8 bits with both a dithered and a non-dithered bit-depth reduction. Bit-depth reductions of both types can be done in Photoshop, Debabelizer, Director, or other programs. The following section includes the steps for dithering in Photoshop.

Dithered Bit-Depth Reduction in Photoshop

Bit-depth reduction in Photoshop is done by simply changing the Mode from RGB to Indexed Color.

1. Open a 16-bit file in Photoshop.
2. Select Mode: Indexed Color.

3. Choose 8 bits, System Palette, Diffusion Dither.
4. Click OK, and then Save As a new filename.

We applied dithered bit-depth reduction to the file BG16BIT.PIC and named our dithered file BGDITHR.PIC. Both files can be found in the Chapter 14 folder on the accompanying CD.

Photoshop can do the reduction non-dithered as well—simply choose None instead of Diffusion in the Indexed Color dialog box. In our travels we have found, however, that Photoshop is not as good as Director at performing non-dithered bit-depth reduction.

Non-Dithered Bit-Depth Reduction in Director 5

Bit-depth reduction in Director 5 is either done upon import or with the Transform Bitmap command. The following steps show how to reduce color depth upon import.

1. Open Director 5 and select File, Import.
2. Select your 16-bit image file and click on Import.
3. In the Import Option dialog box, choose 8 bits, whichever palette you are using, and Remap Colors.
4. Click OK, and then Save As a new filename.

If you want to reduce bit depth of a 16-bit image already in a Director 5 movie, choose Modify, Transform Bitmap and select the same settings as in step 3.

We applied non-dithered bit-depth reduction to the file BG16BIT.PIC and named our dithered file BGTRUNC.PIC. Both files can be found in the Chapter 14 folder on the accompanying CD. Comparing the resulting image quality of the two methods (see fig. 14.8), we see that the dithered image is truer to the original. The non-dithered image, however, is not bad.

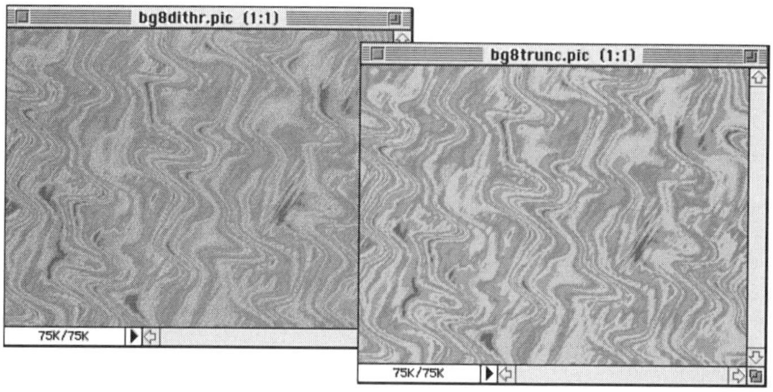

FIGURE 14.8

This is a comparison of image quality under bit-depth reduction. The dithered 8-bit image is on the left and the non-dithered 8-bit image is on the right.

We now compare compressibility under Afterburner compression. We created two Director files containing only the 8-bit image (BGDITHR.DIR and BGTRUNC.DIR in the Chapter 14 folder on the accompanying CD). Comparing the final file sizes of these compressed DCR files, we see that the DCR with the dithered image is 33.3 KB and the non-dithered is 26.7 KB, for a 20 percent file savings. See figure 14.9 to visualize the difference in the source files and what happens in the compression process.

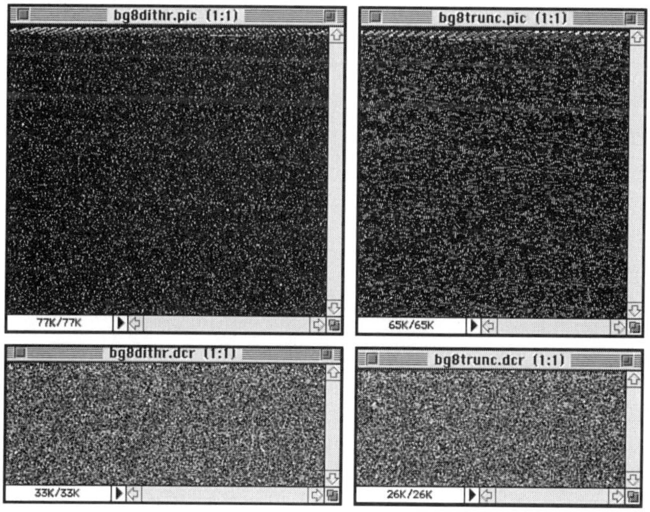

FIGURE 14.9

Visualize the difference in compressing the dithered image (left) and the non-dithered (right). The movie with the non-dithered 8-bit image compresses to a smaller DCR file.

Notice that the rate of compression is nearly the same in the two files. The key difference was in the precompression. Because the non-dithered source PICT was smaller (smaller in size and total entropy) than the dithered, the final non-dithered DCR was smaller as well.

As always, you should experiment with the different tools at your disposal to find the best balance between quality and compression

Finally, when your project necessitates the use of dithering, try to smooth the source file with a slight Gaussian Blur in Photoshop. This can reduce the complexity and thus the size of the compressed final file. Also, always avoid double dithering. Dithering an 8-bit image to a palette different than the one it was first dithered to not only degrades the image quality, but it can seriously increase the noise in the file and thus increase the final size.

Beyond bit-depth reduction, a further degree of lossy compression can be achieved by applying more advanced techniques such as Cinepak compression.

Cinepak Compression

In this section we detail the Cinepak procedure used by George Williams of the Multimedia Production group at Andersen Consulting. We let him describe the process in his own words because he was kind enough to share this technique with us. See Chapter 17, "Immersive Retailing and Simplified Menu Metaphors: Andersen Consulting" for a broader case study of the Shockwave work of George Williams and Andersen Consulting.

> **Note**
>
> What is Cinepak compression? Cinepak is the most popular software-based CODEC for digital video. Cinepak yields high compression rates for digital video and offers efficient decompression even on slower machines. It is a standard CODEC included in QuickTime (Mac and Windows) and AVI (Windows), as well as other platforms. Cinepak is supported by most major video games and multimedia software tools. Cinepak is licensed by these many software companies from Radius, so it comes at no extra cost to the developers or the public. Visit the Radius website for more information on Cinepak: `http://www.radius.com/`.
>
> How does Cinepak work? Cinepak uses a vector quantization algorithm, compressing both within and between frames. It is a software-only CODEC, so you don't need any special hardware for compression or playback.

Why does Cinepak work for static images? The Cinepak compressor is usually used to output QuickTime or AVI movies, but as we have shown, it can compress an image even when outputting numbered PICT files. Cinepak does lossy compression on each frame before it removes interframe redundancy. In effect, when we output PICT with the Cinepak compressor, we are exploiting its own precompression stage.

Cinepak compression results in a PICT with lower entropy—more patterns, more order, and less information.

George's Premiere Cinepak Technique

George Williams: The idea of using Cinepak compression for Macromedia Director files came about while the Creative Services department was working on VR interfaces.

The interfaces were initially seen as mockups for applications that would later use QuickTime VR (QTVR). Drawing heavily from the Apple Computer methodology for QTVR, the department began to work on finding the right data rate and color palette combinations for specific needs (knowledge and work in video compression made this a painless operation).

This example is a background image from an immersive sales environment. I was a part of prototyping at Andersen Consulting using Shockwave. [See figure 14.10. The file AC_RAW.PIC can be found in the Chapter 14 folder on the accompanying CD.]

FIGURE 14.10

The background image created for a prototype sales environment based on Shockwave.

As in this example, if a movie has a large background image, it really pays to compress the file while keeping most of the image quality. The reason is simple. The more visual information in the large image, the higher the perceived quality and value of the movie overall. This is not so much a set rule as a reality of corporate multimedia.

The basic thinking behind using Cinepak is that the user or audience needs only as much visual information as is necessary to transmit the desired information. Cinepak removes some visual information along with file size, but we can still offer an appealing image.

Applying our Cinepak technique to the source file AC_RAW.PIC produced the image shown in figure 14.11. (The file AC_CIN24.PIC can be found in the Chapter 14 folder on the accompanying CD.)

FIGURE 14.11
The same background image—but precompressed with Cinepak.

After compressing the source with Cinepak, importing the images into Director and compressing with Director had almost a 15 percent reduction in file size without much loss of image quality. In Shockwave, bandwidth reduction is key, so even a 15 percent savings is worth your time.

TABLE 14.5

COMPRESSION WITH CINEPAK

Before Compression	*After Compression*
AC_RAW.DIR 89.6 KB	AC_RAW.DCR 54.5 KB
AC_CIN24.DIR 88.1 KB	AC_CIN24.DCR 46.6 KB

AUTHORS' NOTE

George is absolutely right. Using Cinepak to precompress the file can yield significant file size reduction in the final. You can see what's going on in the visualization of the four files in question (see fig. 14.12). Here, the use of Cinepak has reduced both the size and the amount of information (entropy) density in the precompressed DIR file. Thus, Afterburner is able to crunch the precompressed file more.

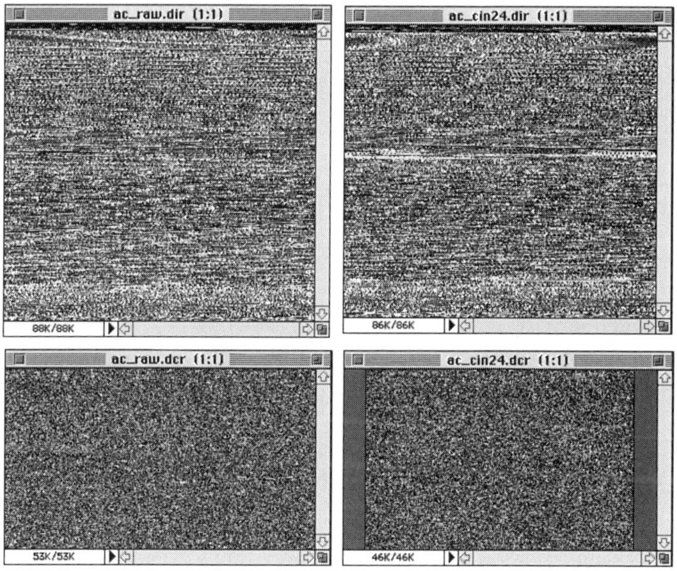

FIGURE 14.12

Compare the Afterburner efficiency with the raw image on the left and the precompressed image on the right. Afterburner is more efficient on the Cinepaked image.

Step-by-Step Cinepak for PICTs

Before you compress a bitmap using Cinepak, check the color depth. Predithering at the start will affect the amount it can be compressed. In some cases, reducing the amount of color information up front by dithering can increase overall efficiency. Beware, however. When Cinepaking, you'll save it as a 24-bit image and then dither it back to 8 bits once in Director. If your source is a dithered 8-bit image, this will mean double dithering with a possible loss of efficiency. We advise testing on both a high bit-depth source and an 8-bit dithered source.

The following steps show how we compressed the demonstration image:

1. Import the original PICT into Premiere. The image appears in the Project window.
2. Drag the PICT from the Project window to the leftmost part of the Video Track of the Construction window.
3. Drag the out-point of the work area (the yellow ribbon at the top of the Construction Window) all the way to the left so that the work area has a one frame duration.
4. From the Make menu, choose Movie.
5. Use the following settings:
   - Output: Work Area as Numbered PICT Files.
   - Check the Video option box. Set the size based on the actual dimensions of the image. (You'll have to deselect the 4:3 aspect default ratio.)
   - Target: Full Frame Size.
6. From Compression options, use the following settings for their background image:
   - Compressor: Cinepak and Millions of Colors.
   - Quality: High. (This setting can have significant impact based on file size and image quality.)
   - You can usually ignore the Frames Per Second, Key Frames, and Data Rate options. (Data Rate can sometimes have an effect on final image quality and file size.)
7. Name the file and save it.
8. Import the compressed image into Director as 8-bit dithered.
9. Do your usual Director magic.
10. Compress with Afterburner.

Note that you might have to try the method several times before you get the desired balance between image quality and file size. I have found that file size savings are most noticeable when you have a lot of small images, such as frames of animation within a larger background image.

For Mac developers who own DeBabelizer, the process is only one step and, thus, a little quicker. Simply open the original PICT and Save As: QuickTime, still using the same Cinepak settings we described in the Premiere technique. For multiple images you can use the batch processing built into DeBabelizer.

This form of compression is initially misleading. In Director, the movie containing the Cinepak PICT image is approximately the same size as its counterpart that contains the uncompressed image. Still, compressing the movies with Afterburner reveals a difference of approximately 15 percent. This difference depends on the overall size, the richness of the color palette, the complexity in the original image and, in some cases, the data rate set in the compression options.

More on Cinepak and Other Lossy Schemes

We hope that you enjoy great compression using the Cinepak method as described by George Williams. As George suggests, it is advisable to try various combinations of settings and always keep source files in full depth/resolution when conducting tests.

We at InfraRed have found the production process most efficient when working in straight 8-bit dithered images until near the final stage. We like to make changes to artwork on the 16- or 24-bit original, dithering upon import as we go. When the design becomes finalized, we begin precompressing with Cinepak to melt out every last kilobyte we can.

George's example uses Cinepak in a minor trade of quality for bandwidth. But there is a very wide range of quality and compression available in Cinepak. For example, we followed George's step by step, but chose Lowest Quality in compression options. The resulting file AC_LOW.DCR (in the Chapter 14 folder on the accompanying CD) is 58 percent smaller than the DCR with the uncompressed image. Look at the file AC_LOW.PIC to compare image quality.

The greatest challenge of precompressing is to choose the right method and settings—and to have the patience to experiment. For instance, you can output Cinepak in grayscale, 8-bit color, or 24-bit color. Always choose the minimum acceptable depth. Cinepak does a great job on many images, but it is not great for every type of image. Therefore, you might want to try other available compressors like the animation compressor, JPEG, and so on.

You also can pre-filter the image before you precompress with Cinepak. For instance, using Gaussian Blur before you use Cinepak can save additional bandwidth. We took the source AC_RAW.PIC and applied a Gaussian Blur with a radius of .8 resulting in the file AC_BIR_8.PIC. Then, following the earlier Cinepak technique step by step yields an additional two percent savings over non-filtered.

Precompression with Cinepak gives you more creative options. Used by itself, Afterburner is a blunt instrument. Precompressing with the wide range of quality and data rate settings in the compression options dialog box enables you to closely refine the expenditure of bandwidth within your movies. Precompression techniques become even more significant with larger and more complex movies where smart bandwidth rationing is more critical.

In the following section, we discuss precompressing the audio portion of your Shockwave files.

Techniques for Precompressing Audio

Before delving into precompressing audio, let's review the basics of digital audio. Digital audio files encode a numerical representation of sound waves. The analog sound signal is digitized, or "sampled," converting its amplitude into a number at fixed intervals of time. The file is later turned back into an analogous voltage wave by digital-to-analog converters, then the voltage wave is amplified in order to drive a loudspeaker cone that creates sound waves in the air. The resulting audio fidelity depends on the sampling frequency and the bit depth of the digital audio file.

The sampling frequency (samples per second) multiplied by the bit depth (bits per sample) gives the data rate of the digital audio (bits per second). Stereo audio on CDs are two channels of 16-bit numbers sampled 44.1 thousand times per second (44.1 khz/16 bits). This yields a bitstream of more than 1.4 million bits per second (1.4 Mbps), or nearly the speed of an Ethernet connection (almost fifty times the speed of a 28.8 kbps modem).

So for the Internet, we have to compress the bitstream. This trades fidelity for bandwidth. At best, the highest audio frequency that can be represented digitally is half the sampling frequency. Therefore, any decrease in the sampling frequency decreases the high-end response accordingly. Reducing the bit depth adds noise, roughly doubling the audible noise content for each bit of amplitude resolution removed.

In Shockwave, some compression is accomplished when you use Afterburner.

What Does Afterburner Do to Sound?

As we have said, contrary to popular belief, Afterburner does indeed compress the audio portion of a Director file. The extent to which the audio data is patterned, regular, repeating, and noise-free is its compressibility under the lossless compression of Afterburner. To demonstrate the compression of audio by Afterburner, we take a little sound loop we composed for a Shockwave movie for Apple Computer's OpenDoc Web page (APREV.AIF in the Chapter 14 folder on the accompanying CD).

After importing into Director and compressing with Afterburner, we indeed observe substantial savings in file size. To make this point more precise, we correct for the portion of the DIR and DCR file that is not related to the audio by subtracting the data size of an empty DIR and DCR file respectively.

TABLE 14.6

AFTERBURNER COMPRESSES AUDIO

Before Burning		*After Burning*	
EMPTY.DIR	1.0 KB	EMPTY.DCR	0.4 KB
APREV.DIR	33.4 KB	APREV.DCR	22.8 KB
audio portion	32.4 KB	audio portion	22.4 KB

As you can see, the file savings is 10 KB, or a very noticeable 69 percent. For some sounds, the Afterburner compression is substantial. But even with bandwidth savings from Afterburner, the audio still eats too much bandwidth at 44.1 KB/16 bits. You need to drastically precompress the audio before it gets to Afterburner.

Precompressing with Sampling Reduction

The simple way to precompress audio is to reduce the sampling frequency and the bit depth, otherwise known as down-sampling. Taking audio sampled at 44.1 khz/16 bits down to 11.025 khz/8 bits is an eight-to-one savings in raw file size and about the same in burnt file size. Down-sampling is a very straightforward process and there are many tools to choose from.

Using dithering when down-sampling is advised because it sounds better and does not cost much bandwidth. We use two different sound files to demonstrate this. One is the synthesized sound loop done for Apple's OpenDoc Shockwave page; the other is a guitar loop sound taken from a promo video we posted for Macromedia's Extreme 3D. All movies contain a sound that was down-sampled to 11.025 khz/8 bits.

TABLE 14.7

DITHERED AUDIO IS ONLY A BIT LARGER

Dithered and Burned		*Truncated and Burned*	
APL_DITH.DCR	22.933 KB	APL_TRUNC.DCR	22.929 KB
GTR_DITH.DCR	30.863 KB	GTR_TRNC.DCR	30.913 KB

As you can see, the file size difference is less that two tenths of a percent. If you compare the sound quality of the corresponding AIF files, we think you will hear the clear benefit of dithering

We have performed down-sampling on Macs with SoundHack, Deck II, SoundEdit 16, and MoviePlayer, and for Windows we've used Sonic Foundry and have been satisfied with the sound quality of the dithering in each.

Precompressing audio by down-sampling, even with dithering, is a brute-force method that yields acceptable results—there is a noticeable and annoying whining noise and loss of highs that accompanies down-sampling. Down-sampling removes information linearly; it does not differentiate between more and less sensitive audio information, nor does it capitalize on the natural structure of the audio signal.

But fear not, IMA compression can rescue us from the indiscriminate hand of down-sampling.

Precompressing with IMA

IMA audio compression takes 16-bit audio files and compresses them at a 4-to-1 ratio with very little degradation of sound quality. The IMA compression standard uses adaptive differential pulse code modulation (ADPCM). In ADPCM, each audio sample is represented by the difference between its true value and a predicted value. IMA compression is a bare-bones version of ADPCM. It has no complex prediction scheme, but rather just uses the decoded value of a given sample as the predictor for the next sample.

Oversimplifying slightly, IMA is adaptive differential PCM, just without the adaptive part. The sound wave is represented by the difference between adjacent samples (at 4 bits per sample) rather than a fixed value for each sample (at 16 bits per sample). IMA compression exploits the natural tendency in audio data for each sample to be close in value to the previous sample. Erroneous encoding is minimal because large separation between samples is relatively rare.

IMA compression is incorporated into the Mac platform in QuickTime 2.0/2.1 and Sound Manager 3.1. For PCs, IMA runs under QuickTime for Windows 2.0 and Video for Windows. Mac will play IMA compressed QuickTime and IMA compressed AIFFs. Windows only plays IMA for QuickTime.

IMA compression is sleek enough for audio to be compressed and decompressed, real-time or faster than real-time, on both Mac and Windows with no perceptible system drag.

IMA Compression for Shockwave

In IMA for Shockwave, the sampling rate is reduced from 44.1 khz to 11.025 khz just as in the brute down-sampling. But reducing the bit depth down from 16 bits is handled with greater finesse in IMA than just chopping down to 8 bits as we must normally must do. Each 16-bit sample is encoded as a 4-bit difference, twice as efficient as the 8-bit result of the standard down-sampling method.

IMA offers the sound quality of 11.025 khz/16 bits while using the same or less burnt bandwidth than the same sound down-sampled to 11.025 khz/8 bits. This is a tremendous advantage in certain applications of Shockwave.

The constraints of IMA compression in the Shockwave for Director environment are threefold:

- IMA sound imports into Director only on the Mac side and then only when saved as an IMA compressed System 7 sound.
- Director does not loop IMA sounds.
- IMA playback on Macs requires certain system resources.

To incorporate IMA sounds into your movies, you must IMA compress them on the Mac side and save them as a Mac System 7 sound. Director will not import an IMA compressed AIFF file. Once inside the Director movie, it plays on Mac and Windows.

You cannot use IMA compression on a looping sound in Director. Until this limitation is removed, IMA sounds can only be used for one-shot sound effects such as narration, warnings, events, and so on.

On the Mac, either QT 2.0/2.1 or Sound Manager 3.1 must be installed to play back IMA compressed sounds. If not present, you will get either garbage or nothing. In Windows there are no software or driver requirements; all the code necessary to decompress IMA sound is built into the Shockwave plug-in.

Authors' Note

IMA stands for Interactive Multimedia Association. This is a non-profit professional society. You can find IMA on the Web at `http://www.ima.org`. If you want more technical information on IMA audio compression, you can purchase the "IMA Digital Audio Doc-Pac" from the IMA. Here's some of what they say about their nifty audio compression:

"The IMA Reference Algorithms for ADPCM compression and decompression are an implementation of adaptive quantization with fixed prediction. The specific implementation of the quantizer adaptation using table-based lookup was offered by Intel/DVI® as an open standard for use by the IMA.

"This algorithm encodes only the difference between consecutive samples, allowing a wide dynamic range to be maintained with a minimum data bandwidth. It is applicable to all four of the DATWG approved sample rates.

> **"The IMA compression algorithm assumes the original sample is a 16-bit two's complement variable. The new sample is the resulting 4-bit ADPCM sample."**
>
> **And so you get to enjoy great sounding 4:1 precompression of audio in Shockwave. Pretty cool, huh?**

Taking a closer look at IMA's effect on the files reveals some interesting characteristics of IMA compression.

IMA Audio Compression at a Glance

We have an ensemble of three example audio files: the synthesized Apple OpenDoc sound, the guitar sound, and a generic voice-over sound. After IMA compresses the sounds, they sound much better than dithered down-sampling yet they are about the same size, or even smaller, when burnt.

TABLE 14.8

IMA COMPRESSED SOUND IS THE SAME SIZE OR SMALLER THAN DITHERED DOWN-SAMPLING

Down-sampled to 11.025 khz/8 bits and Burnt	*IMA Compressed at 11.025 khz and Burnt*
APL_DITH.DCR 22.9 KB	APL_IMA.DCR 16.1 KB
GTR_DITH.DCR 30.9 KB	GTR_IMA.DCR 22.5 KB
VO_DITH.DCR 12.3 KB	VO_IMA.DCR 13.7 KB

IMA compression of both musical sounds yielded much greater file savings than in the voice-over sound. The voice-over was in fact slightly larger when IMAed and burned than dither down-sampled and burned (but it sounds great). Figure 14.13 is a visualization comparing IMA compression and dithered down-sampling of the Apple OpenDoc sound.

Figure 14.14 is a visualization comparing IMA compression and dithered down-sampling of the voice-over sound.

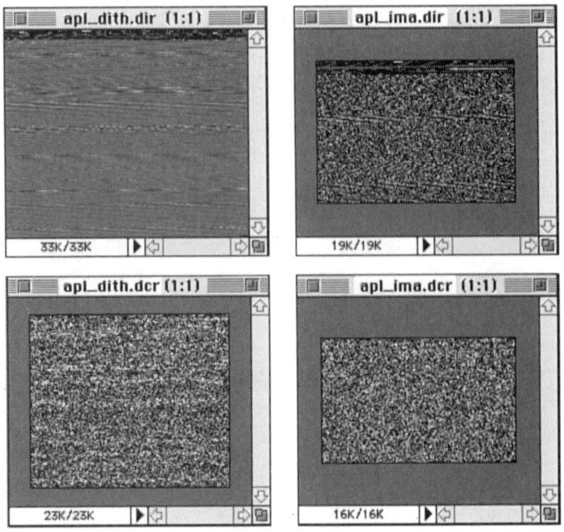

Figure 14.13
The synthesized music when IMA compressed (right side) burns down to 70 percent the size of the dither down-sampled file (left side) and still sounds twice as good.

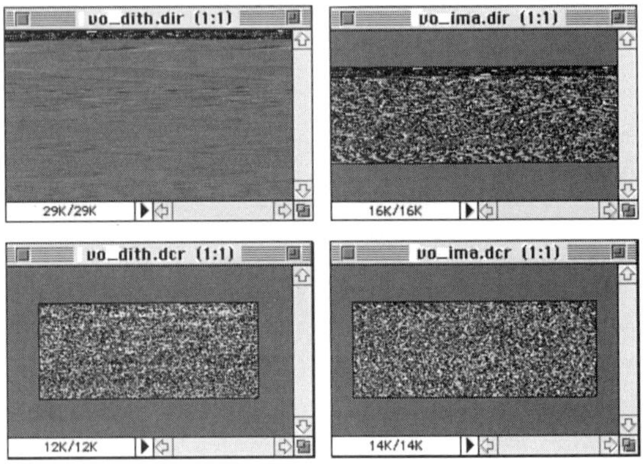

Figure 14.14
In the voice-over file the dithered file (left side) burns better than the IMA compressed (right side). IMA, at nearly the same size, sounds far better.

The dithered voice-over allowed greater Afterburner efficiency than the dithered synthesized music. With each audio file you encounter, there will be different compression characteristics. But overall you will find that IMA compression is a great advance over normal down-sampling.

IMA Compression Using MoviePlayer

There are several ways to compress audio in IMA. We skip techniques for IMA compression in Windows because you can't import IMA audio into Director for Windows anyway. You can use Macromedia SoundEdit 16 version 2 or Terran MovieCleaner Pro. The following list is a step-by-step guide for IMA compression for Shockwave using Apple MoviePlayer 2.0 or 2.1:

1. In order to create IMA compressed audio on the Mac, you need QuickTime 2.1. You can get it from Apple's FTP site if you don't have it. (`ftp://sam.austin.apple.com/Apple.Support.Area/Apple.Software.Updates/US/Macintosh/System/QuickTime`)
2. Open your source AIFF file in MoviePlayer. Use the highest resolution source you have.
3. Choose File, Export, and click on the Options button.
4. In the Options dialog box, choose the following:
   - Compressor: IMA 4:1
   - Rate: 11.025 khz
   - 16-bits Mono

   Click OK. This returns you to the Save dialog box.
5. In the Save dialog box, choose Export File as: Sound to System 7 Sound.
6. Name the file and click OK.
7. Open your Director 5 movie and import the System 7 sound file you just saved.
8. Enjoy your liberated bandwidth.

Audio-intensive applications of Shockwave are a perfect venue for IMA compression. This applies much more to Shockwave with heavy narration or one-shot sound effects. Even at this stage of the game, there are plenty of powerful uses for IMA compression.

Precompression via Audio Redundancy

The last method of audio compression we discuss is redundancy. Short sound loops are a staple in Shockwave production. Sound is such a bandwidth sponge, that keeping sound loops extremely short is imperative. But, no matter how cool that sound loop is, the same sound playing over and over, ad infinito, comes dangerously close to being boring, or worse, annoying to the viewers.

Loops are too often not musical enough. Music is built upon patterns of repetition and variation. Having just one short sound loop (let's label it loop 'A') limits you to building a song pattern of A-A-A-A-A-A-A and so on. But what if I want a more interesting song? I want my song to be structured Verse-Chorus-Verse-Chorus-Bridge-Chorus-Bridge-Verse-Chorus-Chorus. Or, how about the Blues? One type of Blues, known as 12-Bar Blues, is built on a basic chord progression I-I-I-I-IV-IV-I-I-V-IV-I-V.

You don't even need to know what those symbols mean in order to realize there is redundant information in the patterns—and redundant information means compressibility. You can build longer songs for Shockwave using less bandwidth if the song is composed of redundant building blocks.

We exemplified this using the files from earlier in this section as building blocks for a song. We created a file called REPEATAUDIO using Macromedia Deck II v2.5. In Deck we used the Add Sound to Clipboard Command to import the three files GTR4416.AIF, APL4416.AIF, and VO2216.AIF. Then we copied the sounds from the Library window and pasted them one after another in an interesting pattern in the Tracks window. Figure 14.15 shows the arrangement of the building blocks.

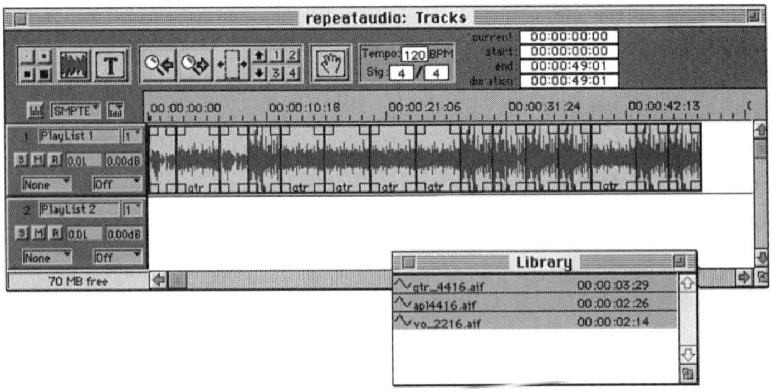

FIGURE 14.15

Our 49-second song was composed in Deck II v2.5 from just three building blocks. The redundancy makes it more compressible in Afterburner.

Then we selected the whole song in the Tracks window and downsampled it to 11.025 KB/8 bits using the Edit: Mix to Disk command. This resulting file, named REPEATING.DIR, is 543 KB and compresses in Afterburner to 271 KB—almost half the size. Compare this rate of compression to a non-redundant sound file of the same duration. The Director file NONREP.DIR contains the non-redundant sound NONREP.AIF. It is also 543 KB, but it only compresses down to 361 KB.

TABLE 14.9

REDUNDANT AUDIO COMPRESSES MORE THAN NON-REDUNDANT

	Unburned DIR	*Burnt DCR*
Non-redundant	NONREP.DIR 543 KB	NONREP.DCR 361 KB
Redundant	REPEATING.DIR 543 KB	REPEATING.DCR 271 KB

So we see that the non-repeating file achieved 25 percent less compression than REPEATING.DCR. You will get even better results if you use shorter building blocks for your songs. Redundant audio files, composed of identical copies of few building blocks offer you many more musical possibilities than the simple sound loops. This enables you to build longer sound loops using less bandwidth.

Conclusion

In this chapter you have gained greater insight into the nuance of information theory and how this relates to compression methods. You now have powerful tools at your disposal to flexibly allocate precious bandwidth to the elements of your Shockwave movies.

In the next chapter, we discuss public broadband networks and high-speed communications in the context of delivering powerful and valuable interactive content using Shockwave.

PART V

SHOCKWAVE SOLUTIONS

Chapter 15

Cosmetic Shockwave and Beyond: Infonautics

This chapter discusses the purpose of using Shockwave in simple cosmetic ways. As exemplified by the Infonautics Corporation's Electric Library, simply shocking a site and adding a Shockwave-enhanced interface can yield certain important benefits. Basic uses of Shockwave also are a stepping stone to providing more advanced immersive environments.

Most of the chapter is derived from an interview we did with Josh Kopelman, the Executive Vice President of Infonautics. The chapter covers the following major topics:

- *Using Shockwave for online information services*
- *Simple cosmetics and enhanced interfaces*
- *Analyzing the impact of Shockwave*

AUTHORS' NOTE

Where does this fit into the Big Picture?

In this chapter, we have Shockwave examples of cosmetic enhancements such as banners and logos. These are today's quintessential basic uses of Shockwave. This type of Shockwave usage falls within the Simply Shocking category in the big Shockwave picture. (See figure 2.1 of Chapter 2, "Power on the Web.") Cosmetic Shockwave is content-oriented. It is primarily used to draw attention to the very fact that Shockwave is being used and, additionally, it is used to add the communication value of animation and sound.

There also is an example in this chapter that falls into the Enhanced Interface category. The example is a shocked navigation bar with rollovers that helps users know what they are jumping to—a function-oriented usage. Also, the chapter ends in a discussion of a hypothetical True Application use of Shockwave.

Infonautics

Infonautics Corporation is a young and exciting company on the Web. They are creating new classes of online information products. Their Electric Library is a fast-growing online information service that provides a new method of online learning and research. Infonautics has invented basic enabling technology and business models that enable them to deliver a high level of value on the Web. Figure 15.1 shows their home page.

Their main Web product, the Electric Library, is a subscription-based tool used by students and researchers on the Web. Its plain-language search engine enables searching of a huge library of books, magazines, newspapers, news wires, maps, photos, art, and literature. The Electric Library is based on Infonautics' core technology called the Electronic Printing Press (EPP). Infonautics licenses EPP to the world's publishing community, allowing them to offer their own custom online information services.

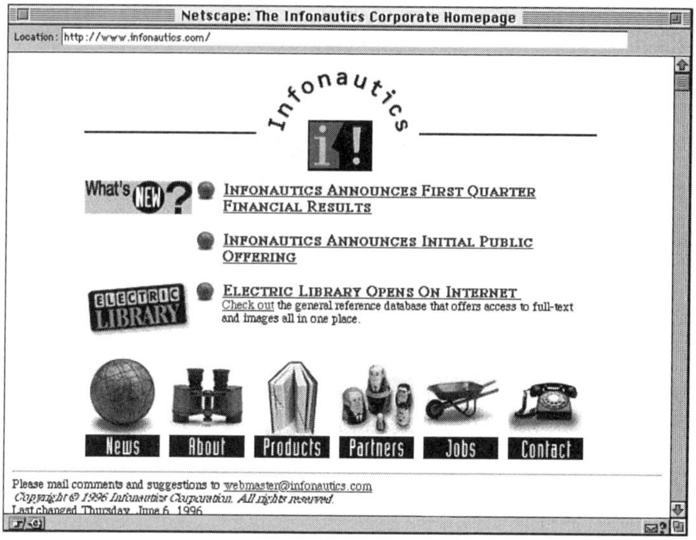

FIGURE 15.1

You can visit the Infonautics website at http://www.infonautics.com/.

The Interview

As part of their technology leadership, Infonautics decided to shock the Electric Library. We worked with Josh Kopelman on the project. Josh Kopelman is co-founder and Executive Vice President of Infonautics Corporation. He supervises corporate development, marketing, strategic partnering, and fund-raising. Josh has an extensive background in the financial development of startup technology companies. Therefore, we really appreciated his perspective on how Shockwave fits into Infonautics' strategy and what benefit they derived from their initial shocking effort.

Infonautics found Shockwave to bring distinct benefits to their Electric Library, even when only applied in very basic applications such as banners and navigation bars. They used Shockwave to help identify themselves as a technology leader and, in some ways, to enhance the user experience. As such, their preliminary experience with Shockwave has proven a success.

In the process, Infonautics discovered several important issues from their "shocking" experience, issues that have longer term implications for their product. The Electric Library movies are good examples of transitional or introductory Shockwave. Josh's comments shed much light onto how these basic Shockwave solutions are today helping to facilitate the goals of Infonautics and why Shockwave offers important future opportunities to provide valued services on the Web.

Shockwave for Online Information Services

InfraRed Communications: First, I just want to get a general background about Infonautics. What do you do? What are your business goals?

Josh Kopelman: Infonautics is an online information services company. We build consumer information services, kind of like Lexus/Nexus, for consumers over the Internet and other online services.

Providing Value on the Web

IRC: And what is your current strategy for maintaining leadership on the Web?

Josh: Currently, we are doing some pretty heavy marketing and customer acquisition on the Web. We have a highly trafficked website and we are attracting customers through a variety of partnerships, paid advertisements, print advertising, and a number of methods.

IRC: In what ways have you found the Web a facilitating technology for your business?

Josh: The Web is not just a facilitating technology for our business, it is our business. Our business model is based on providing value for consumers over the Internet. Our whole product is premised on the fact that there are millions of people now on the Web and that the Web is a great distribution and delivery platform for our content.

IRC: What kind of design challenges or interactive challenges do you face when trying to provide value on the Web?

Josh: We face that which is faced by a number of sites—wanting to make your site look appealing and visually inviting. You want it to be dynamic so that there is always something new. You want it to be engaging so that people sort of bookmark you and come back. But you also don't want it to be overwhelming. You can't just throw stuff up there. It really has to be refined and elegant, sleek and informative, and entertaining. And that's what it takes to be a very good sales piece for us.

Plugging In to Shockwave

IRC: Why have you made Shockwave a part of your Web strategy?

Josh: We felt that Shockwave as a technology, while it is still emerging, has a number of connotations. First, it helps to define us as a leading technology company. The fact that Shockwave is still emerging and evolving means that by having it on your site, you are clearly letting people know you are serious about this. This isn't just throwing up ten pages to see if anyone knocks on your door.

We also think that it provides us with a lot more interactivity than just straight HTML, JPEG, and GIF. Shockwave enables us to reinforce our branding message, sleekness, and elegance of the site.

IRC: Now have you thought about using other interactive technologies like Java or anything else?

Josh: Sure. And I don't think they are mutually exclusive. I don't think the goal of the website should be just to go down a checklist and say "Yes, I use all of these things." I think that if you have the need, then Shockwave and Java could work very well hand in hand.

The fact that Shockwave is still emerging and evolving means that by having it on your site, you are clearly letting people know you are serious about this.

IRC: So what kind of criterion were most important to you when you were planning to provide more attractive content with Shockwave?

Josh: There were a number of elements. Everything from an installed base to ease of use. Initially, the concern regarding Shockwave was the question, "Are there enough of the plug-ins installed and is there a large enough audience?" We have been pleasantly surprised about that.

IRC: What have you found specifically about the installed base? What proportion of your users are going to the Shockwave site?

Josh: I don't know offhand the exact proportion, but I can tell you that it is a larger number than we had all expected. I think Shockwave also keeps people in the site longer. Not just because it is a larger file to download, but because it shows a higher commitment level for someone to click on a Shockwave site. And it gives us more ability to use the attractive technology in a sales way, in a way to inspire more questions and more interest in the product.

Shocking the Electric Library

IRC: So can you describe the particular use of Shockwave that is currently on your site?

Josh: Currently, it is primarily in a cosmetic role. We have shocked everything from animating our product logo to putting rollover buttons in our main navigation menu to animating some of our sales buttons. For example, our animated 'Free Trial' button helps us to lead our consumer to take advantage of our free trial offer. It is now an animated flashing Shockwave button that really has a punch to it.

Simple Cosmetics and Enhanced Interface

Let's take a break from the interview to examine in some detail the shocked Electric Library and other simple cosmetic uses of Shockwave.

Simple Cosmetics in the Electric Library

The shocked Electric Library uses the same interface, look, and feel as the unshocked. The banner is animated in Shockwave. The "ELECTRIC" letters enter from top and bottom and then are pushed aside by the word "LIBRARY." Then it settles on a subtle loop where the letters shift upward like a wave moving through the banner (see fig. 15.2). The file ELIB_BNR.DIR (and DCR) can be found in the Chapter 15 folder on the accompanying CD.

In shocking the Electric Library, Infonautics wanted to build an attractor button for the free trial link. The movie ELIB_FRE.DIR can be found in the Chapter 15 folder on the accompanying CD. The button is much more appealing than a static one in that it zooms in at the start, it wiggles, and it has different color down state (see fig. 15.2).

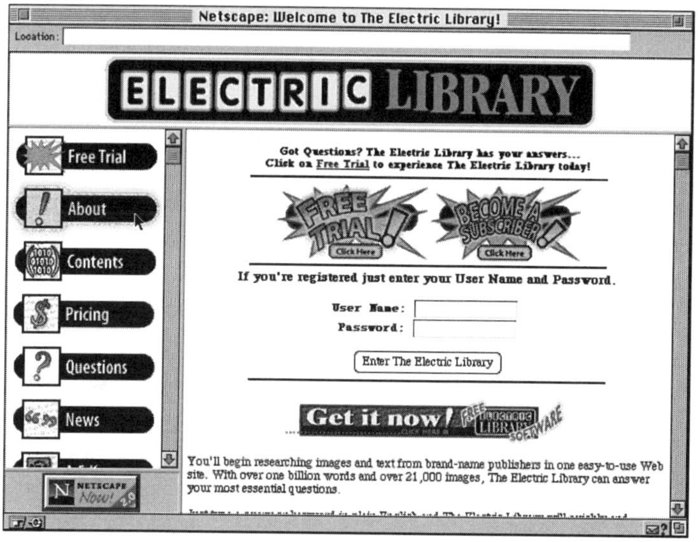

FIGURE 15.2

The shocked Electric Library site has an animated "Free Trial" button. Inside the Electric Library, the logo banner is shocked with a simple, but attractive, animation. The perpetual navigation bar also is shocked with a nice rollover highlight.

The more interesting part of the shocked Electric Library is the perpetual navigation bar. The shocked navigation bar adds an active rollover highlight. One could argue that it takes on more than cosmetic significance as it enhances the overall feel of the navigation. So this moves a bit beyond a Simply Shocking solution toward an Enhanced Interface solution. (See figure 2.1 in Chapter 2, "Power on the Web," for the Big Shockwave Picture.) The perpetual navigation bar ELIB_MNU.DIR can be found in the Chapter 15 folder on the accompanying CD.

> **Note**
>
> To keep a perpetual navigation bar in one frame and use it to load contents into another frame, you need the capability to target frames. Frame targeting was not built into Shockwave at the time Infonautics shocked their site, so they had to invent a fancy workaround using Java Script and CGI scripts. Now, frame targeting is supported in the `goToNetPage` Lingo command in Shockwave for Director 5.

Other Banners

Another example of how a simple cosmetic movie can really add to a page is our very own InfraRed Communications home page movie. For us, clearly it is important to demonstrate Shockwave itself. Simply Shocking the InfraRed banner helps identify us as a Shockwave provider. But it adds to the message as well.

The ingredient it adds is a touch of humor. The key to humor is timing, and timing is a natural gig for a time-based medium such as Shockwave (see fig. 15.3). Using Shockwave, we set up our straight line—We know more about Shockwave than anybody else…—then a slight delay, and deliver the punch line—…for the time being. The joke implies our awareness of the changing nature of our art and proves that we can sit back and laugh at ourselves sometimes. This joke is impossible to tell without Shockwave.

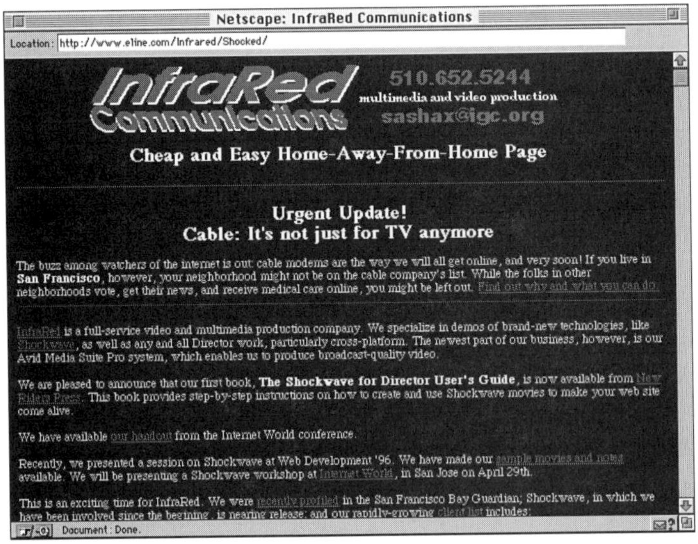

FIGURE 15.3

Like the Electric Library banner, the InfraRed Communications banner movie is a cosmetic enhancement to the page. It adds interest and humor.

Having text cycle through and animate lets us communicate more of our character and allows us to tell really bad jokes about ourselves, which we love to do. To see the movie, open the Director file IRLOGO.DIR, or open the page locally in a Shockwave-enabled browser with the file HOME.HTM. Both files can be found in the Chapter 15 folder on the accompanying CD.

Having examined the simple cosmetic uses of Shockwave, we return to the interview to hear Josh's evaluation of Infonautics' Shockwave experience and his views on future developments.

Analyzing the Impact of Shockwave

IRC: So have you found that Shockwave has increased the value of your site?

Josh: Oh, I believe so, both from an overall branding perspective but also as a possible source of customer acquisition.

IRC: What kind of production or technology issues were raised with Shockwave and how do you see that evolving?

Josh: I think the biggest issue is the fact that currently there was no way for us to automatically detect the plug-in. For example, we currently automatically detect what browser you are using through CGI, so we can use some advanced browser technology—everything from frames to a variety of other things.

There is no ability for us to detect whether someone has a Shockwave plug-in or not currently. What that means, therefore, is that we can't use our Shockwave home page as a default home page for people who have Shockwave. It has to be a reactive choice of the user. I think that was clearly our number one concern. From what I have been hearing, I think that problems will probably disappear in the next six months.

> Josh is absolutely right. And sooner at that. Plug-in detection is now possible in Netscape 3.0 using Java Script. See Chapter 13, "Detecting the Plug-In."
>
> *Note*

Planning for Immersive True Applications

IRC: What are your future plans in relation to Shockwave or other interactive technologies? Are you going to try to move into more content-based immersive applications or keep the uses cosmetic?

Josh: Right now, we are still looking at some other cosmetic approaches and I think in the future we will be bringing it more into the content side. As a content aggregator, we don't necessarily create most of the contents that we provide to our users. We're repackaging it, so I don't necessarily see us as the one's that are creating Shockwave. I think that eventually, some of our content providers will be providing us with Shockwave content.

IRC: Do you see the user interface of the Web being a satisfactory one or would you like to see that evolve into something more immersive?

Josh: I don't think anyone sees it as being satisfactory right now. But I think the one thing that it has going for it is the billions of dollars of investments that people are pouring into it. So if you look at the speed of change and the speed of improvement, it's really revolutionary as opposed to evolutionary—the rate at which it is growing. I am encouraged by all those things.

Homework Helper: A True Application with Shockwave Potential

IRC: Six months, or a year down the road, are there any exciting opportunities for Infonautics to use interactive media like Shockwave as a way of front-ending or packaging your online product?

Josh: Yes, clearly. We are looking at all of those things. We are actually examining whether it is possible to use Shockwave as an interface to our entire database or not.

We have a product that is currently available on Prodigy that is based on a C++ type application. That application has a lot of advanced functionality that we had to strip out of our current Web product. The reason we had to do that was because we were constrained by the boundaries of HTML.

While it is not possible to use Shockwave, Java, or other technologies to do that today, they clearly offer the nearest-term promise of delivering on that. They offer us the promise of being able to bundle and deliver all the functionality which we have built without having to strip it down to the lowest common denominator HTML.

IRC: What kind of functionality might that be?

Josh: Everything from animations within the product, to multiple documents simultaneously, to better navigational tools, to including sound into specific parts within the service. The ability to have some more client-side intelligence on a higher level. One of the biggest constraints right now is that all the processing and all the intelligence really has to reside on our servers. We would much prefer to be able to build client-side or desktop-side applications which would have some of that intelligence.

Authors' Note

The application that Josh is referring to is the Infonautics Homework Helper. Homework Helper is an extensive online general reference library for kids. Using Homework Helper, students can pose a question in plain English and launch a comprehensive search of the Infonautics database (see fig. 15.1). It is a type of application that can today be delivered only through a proprietary online service with client software installed on the user's machine, in this case, Prodigy, or a stand-alone subscription service.

The Electric Library is a Web front end to the same database as the Homework Helper, yet is a considerably different user experience. The difference is in the searching intelligence and the fast responding immersive interface. For instance, the student can tell the Homework Helper about themselves so the searches will know more of the educational context and thus produce more relevant findings.

The HTML-based Electric Library cannot easily handle these preferences, but with Shockwave it could. Shockwave is an opportunity to provide a database front end on the Web with a set of features that more closely approximates one like the Homework Helper. Shockwave is fast becoming a viable platform for True Applications on the Web, offering most of the graphical user interface and some of the client-side intelligence that products like the Homework Helper now provide.

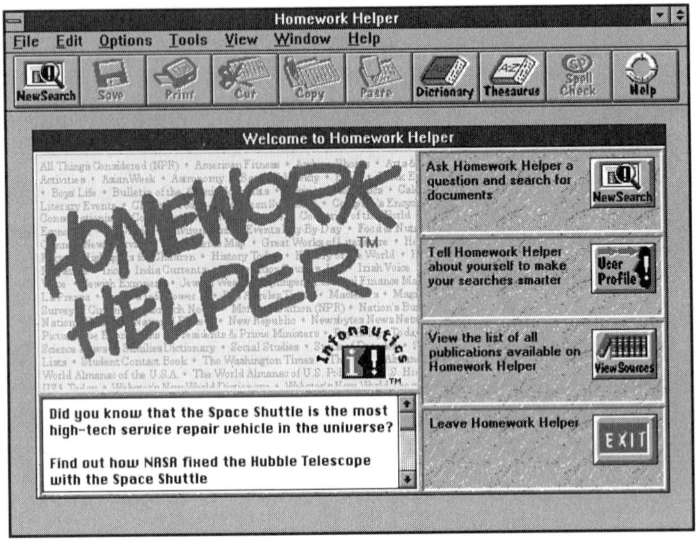

FIGURE 15.4

The Infonautics Homework Helper is available through Prodigy or as a stand-alone application. The straight Web can't deliver the same functionality. Shockwave could be used to provide much of that missing functionality to a broad Web audience.

Getting Beyond HTML Constraints

IRC: Have you seen any other interesting or thought-provoking solutions that are based on Shockwave today?

Josh: It's funny, but it grabbed my imagination after seeing some of the games that use Shockwave right now. While clearly we are producing a reference tool, not a game, gaming was the application that most opened my mind to the possibilities Shockwave offers us to improve our site.

It doesn't even look like you are using the Internet anymore.

Based on this fact—looking at it from a very high level—it doesn't even look like you are using the Internet anymore. The Internet becomes a communication transport, not necessarily a navigational construct. Thus, you are freeing yourself from a lot of the constraints that are forced on you by the very fact that there is a Web navigation paradigm and a Web functionality set.

The prospects depend upon the growth of the Shockwave base and also on the growing bandwidth of connection speeds. But with using Shockwave, you could potentially deliver a high-quality experience without having to be constrained by the lowest common denominators of HTML.

Conclusion

Ultimately, information services such as Infonautics live and die, in large measure by the information value they can provide their subscribers. The perceived value of an information service is based on answering questions and searches in a quick and satisfying way and allowing the user to navigate the information once it is identified. Much of this value comes from the user interface—measured by how responsive, intuitive, easy, fun, and smart the front end is.

Using the Web as a front end has tremendous advantages in providing value, primarily universality and ease of access and use. This comes at the expense of total control over the user interface. Shockwave holds great promise for overcoming the limitations of HTML in part, or all, of the user interface. The experience of Infonautics is indicative of how basic applications of Shockwave can lead to intermediate ones, and then to advanced uses that begin to provide the types of value today seen only in full-blown applications.

CHAPTER 16

True Multimedia on the Web: DXM

This chapter examines some more advanced uses of Shockwave. The examples, shocked by DXM, demonstrate successful design solutions for True Multimedia on the Web. Then, there is a bit on sound for the Web and on looking ahead to broadband solutions.

A majority of this chapter is pulled from a talk we had with Lee Swearingen, a principal owner in DXM (a San Francisco-based multimedia production company). The discussion spans the following topics:

- Using Shockwave for an immersive advertisement
- Creating a site tour with Shockwave
- Using Shockwave in Web games
- Sound for Web multimedia
- Local storage and bandwidth

AUTHORS' NOTE

Where does this fit into the Big Picture?

The Shockwave applications shown in this chapter are media and interactivity rich, highly self-contained, and content-oriented. This type of Shockwave usage falls within the True Multimedia category in the big Shockwave picture. (See figure 2.1 in Chapter 2, "Power on the Web.")

In all three sample Shockwave movies, the interactive experience for the user is steady and extended in time. Their immersion is focused on the Shockwave content, fully dependent on the Shockwave content. Three important varieties of True Multimedia—interactive advertisements, site tours, and games—are typified in the DXM examples.

This chapter's concluding issue of local storage and broadband relates to possibilities for creating broadband environments with Shockwave.

DXM and the Interview

DXM is a multimedia design and production company that develops products and provides services, such as Shockwave production. Founded in 1995, DXM is growing quickly and has an award-winning team of experienced designers and producers. The principals, Kathy and Lee Swearingen, have published several books and magazine articles on the subject of Director and Shockwave for Director. Figure 16.1 shows the DXM home page.

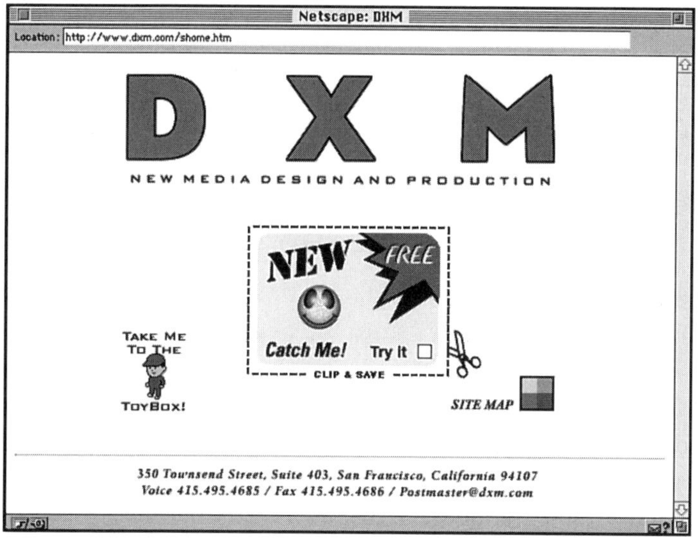

FIGURE 16.1

You can visit the DXM website at http://www.dxm.com/, and from there you can get to their shocked site.

Prior to cofounding DXM, Lee Swearingen was the head of Macromedia's Creative Services for several years. He produced many of their award-winning Showcase CD-ROMs. Lee's point of view on Shockwave is grounded in a design sense that comes from his years of multimedia experience.

Creating True Multimedia for the Web

Shockwave is nearly an ideal way to provide true multimedia applets on the Web. With Shockwave you can deliver interactive advertisements, site tours, games, presentations, training pieces, cartoons, demonstrations, and so on to the broad Web audience. These types of small stand-alone applets are very compelling, sometimes even addictive.

DXM has created very well-designed true multimedia pieces that take great advantage of low-bandwidth techniques and provide lots of fun. We certainly gained knowledge from the discussion of their experiences in designing them. One of the nice qualitites of true multimedia Shockwave pieces is that they really almost speak for themselves. But there is much to be learned by letting the designer explain the design process and describe the solutions in their own words.

From Big CD-ROMs to Tiny Advertisements

InfraRed Communications: What do you do at DXM?

Lee Swearingen: DXM is a design and production company providing interactive multimedia for the Internet. We all have a CD-ROM development background. We've worked on titles for T/Maker. I did the Macromedia Showcase CDs versions 1 through 4.2 and a bit on 5.0 when I was over there.

Kathy Swearingen [also a principal owner in DXM] was a product development lead at T/Maker doing children's titles. So we come out of the CD crowd, and it was easy for us to transfer our skills and resources and reuse a lot of the same Lingo code, even some of the games that we had already created in Director and apply them to the Internet using Shockwave. Of course, now the challenge is to keep the file size extremely small. So we've gone all the way from doing full-blown CD-ROM stuff all the way down to doing Shockwave at 30 KB to 100 KB.

1996: Year of Web Enhancement

IRC: What are the concerns that your clients are addressing when they put Shockwave on the Web?

Lee: I think our clients want Shockwave because they want to add something new to their sites. In 1995 everyone was rushing to get their Web sites up. In 1996 and beyond, people are rushing to enhance them and add sounds and animation, graphics, and interactivity to their sites. This keeps them interesting and fun, especially as the bandwidth continues to grow.

The clients want to add Shockwave because it is something that they have heard about. They think it's neat. There is a certain novelty to the whole thing. They also don't really know what it can do, so we have to educate the client quite a bit and tell them what can be done. They are concerned about the end-user having the plug-in installed, so that is an issue. I just heard that Macromedia is up to four million downloads. Hopefully, they are all installed and working.

Those are the issues so far. I think they are also concerned about different bandwidths of their customers. Some clients actually don't care if the movies are larger, because their users are all connected. For example, in a project we did for Informix, we had a file that was 200 KB. To them that was no problem and they didn't even understand why it was an issue. But other clients are trying to appeal to a broad mass audience of end-users at home with 28.8K modems. Actually we don't even focus on speeds below 28.8K.

The Immersive Advertisement Application: Levi's

IRC: Can you give an example of a client of yours who really made excellent use of Shockwave, taking advantage of the immersivity of the technology in a way that really benefitted their website?

Lee: Sure, one thing that we did for Levi's is an interactive ad that goes with a billboard ad campaign they're doing. There is a billboard in San Francisco that has the big bull's-eye pattern. [See figure 16.2.] We adapted that in Shockwave and added a cool sound and a hypnotic animation. We did that with color cycling and custom palettes. It has an effect on your eyes; it causes walls to go wavy; and also if you continue staring at the center, it fuzzes out the entire background. But so far it is not a permanent effect—we're hoping nobody gets a seizure looking at it. [The file LEVIS.HTM in the Chapter 16 folder of the accompanying CD can be viewed in a Shockwave-enabled browser.]

Lee: Levi's was really a promotional Shockwave movie that fit really nicely into the style or the look of their ad campaign.

IRC: Yeah, and it certainly is an immersive ad. In fact, I think I've been hypnotized!

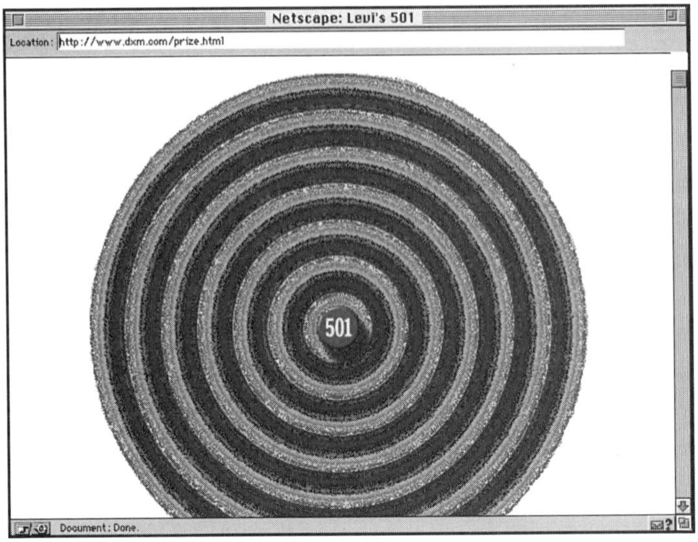

FIGURE 16.2

DXM's Shockwave adaptation of a Levi's billboard ad. The rings cycle inward in a hypnotic animation. When you wake up, you have an inexplicable urge to buy jeans.

The Site Tour Application: California State Automobile Association

Lee: Another slightly more practical use of Shockwave was for the California State Automobile Association (CSAA) and we used Shockwave to give a site tour. [See figure 16.3.] The interface for the site tour is the inside of a car, of course. There's some nice details like the eyes in the rear-view mirror follow the cursor and there are some fun honking sounds.

Note

> The CSAA tour is not on the CD-ROM because it relies on CGI for frame targeting and thus doesn't run locally. We encourage you to visit the CSAA site tour at `http://www.dxm.com/csaaTour/`.

Inside the car there is a road map that shows all the different sections of CSAA's site and gives a rollover icon for each. [See figure 16.4.]

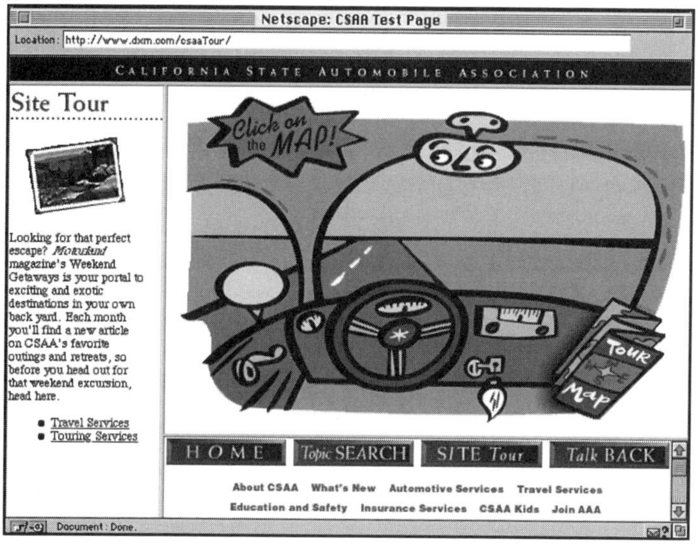

FIGURE 16.3

The CSAA site tour uses the metaphor of a road trip. You can view this site on DXM's site at http://www.dxm.com/csaaTour/. The first thing you do is click on the map.

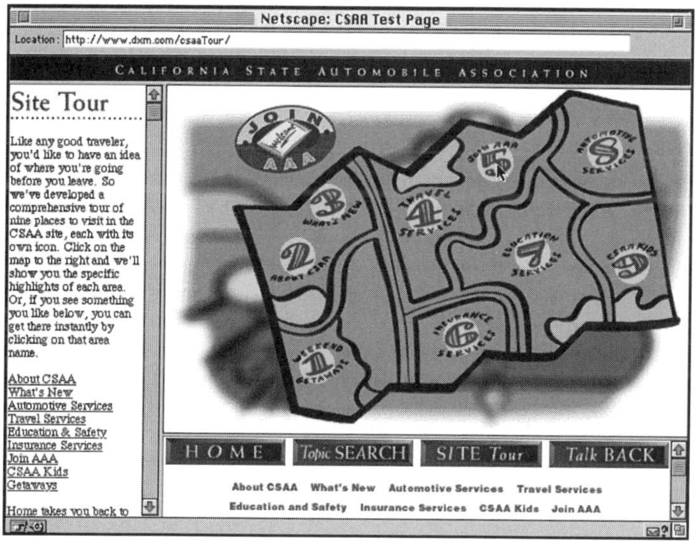

FIGURE 16.4

The road map in the CSAA site tour shows all the sections of the site. The preview icon changes when you roll over the different sections.

When you click on a section of the map, the car sorta virtually travels there—the trees and billboards go by. Because this is CSAA, the car metaphor worked nicely and fit in well with their site. After 'driving' you 'get there' in your little car, and more information appears on a roadside billboard about what is in that section. [See figure 16.5.] You can go to that section if you choose exit. Meanwhile, the movie triggers the frame on the lefthand side to update. So now there is even more text about what's in that section of the site.

Let's say you clicked 'What's New' on the map, the car drives to that billboard and the frame on the left updates with details and links in the news portion of the site. It's like previewing down another level in the hierarchy without having to commit to a download.

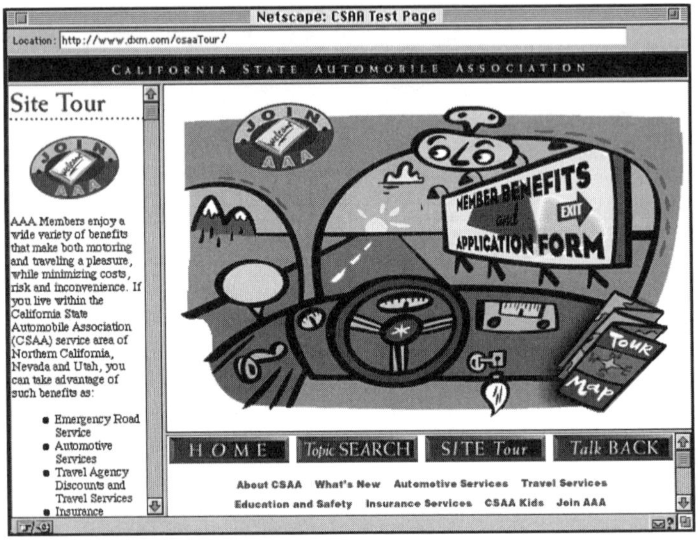

FIGURE 16.5

The roadside billboard marks your "arrival" at a section of the site. You get a preview describing the section in text in the lefthand frame. You can then exit the tour and actually jump to that part of the site, or go back to the map for more about other sections.

A Multi-Frame Solution

IRC: Because you did this in Shockwave for Director 4, you needed a complicated workaround for targeting frames using JavaScript and CGI. But because that is no longer a problem in Shockwave for Director 5, let's talk about the design concept. What was the benefit of putting the CSAA movie into a multi-frame interface?

Lee: The benefit of doing it this way is that the Shockwave file stays loaded in memory. This file is fairly large so we didn't want people bouncing around too much, loading and reloading. With the frames solution, once you are in the site tour the file is in memory, and because you don't unload the movie until you leave altogether, it stays in memory regardless of how the user sets the cache preferences in his browser.

> **Note:** Targeting frames in Shockwave for Director 5 is discussed in Chapter 10, "Working with Frames."

Even if users don't have the cache set high enough, it doesn't get wiped out. Otherwise, depending on your settings, you may wipe out your cache by going to another page and then coming back. I think everyone's had the frustration of loading a big Shockwave file and the first click takes them somewhere else. Then they have to reload to go back.

With the frames solution, once you are in the site tour the file is in memory, and because you don't unload the movie until you leave altogether, it stays in memory regardless of how the user sets the cache preferences in his browser.

So I think frames are good for keeping the Shockwave movie anchored. We also let the user know if they are going to leave the Shockwave section. If you click on the roadside billboard, it takes you out of the Shockwave page. But we put up a warning first. We bring up a dialog box that states "You are now leaving the site tour." You can either hit OK to advance to that section or you can hit cancel to stay in the tour.

Reactions to the Site Tour

IRC: I really like this site tour. Can you describe CSAA's reaction?

Lee: CSAA was really pleased. For one thing, they really had no idea what you could do with Shockwave. We were fortunate in that they gave us the freedom to advise and come up with the idea and push what we felt would work. They trusted us to do that and it paid off for them in the long run, because we know more about the concerns of keeping the file size down and making it a pleasurable experience overall. Most clients will not have that kind of background.

IRC: So how did you read their minds to implement a Shockwave solution that fit what they wanted to communicate?

Lee: Well, we had a few brainstorm meetings and discussions. We actually approached them with the idea of doing a site tour. We wanted to do a Shockwave site tour, so this was a good application. CSAA had just launched their site and they thought they could get a little more exposure and traffic for their site by using Shockwave.

We had some meetings and bounced three or four ideas, and then they really liked this one. Now CSAA has just put the tour up on their site, so we are just as curious as you are to see what kind of reaction it gets. But internally at CSAA, everyone is very pleased. The shocked site tour is nice for CSAA because, not only do the end users use it, but they use it for internal purposes. For example, they can use it for a quick presentation anytime or if they are at a trade show. They can go to the Shockwave site tour and in a multimedia way show what is on their entire website. So it ended up providing a two-fold function—one use for individual visitors and another for CSAA's own promotional uses.

IRC: Why is Shockwave a more effective way of presenting a site overview than non-shocked page?

Lee: If you look at it from a strictly functional point of view, possibly a text outline is just as effective, perhaps even more functional of a way to present a site overview. But unshocked site tours in general are fairly boring. Most people don't go there unless they just want to see a text outline of the site.

CSAA wanted their site to be unique and fun and entertaining. They appeal to families. They have a broad market and so their site is family-oriented and appealing for children as well. Additionally, the car metaphor, the dashboard, and the traveling metaphor really fits with their service. They just felt that doing it in Shockwave fit the overall objective of making it an entertaining site.

The shocked site tour is nice for CSAA because, not only do the end users use it, but they use it for internal purposes. For example, they can use it for a quick presentation anytime or if they are at a trade show.

IRC: It seems to me that with a site tour like the one you did for CSAA, it actually becomes fun to find out all about the site for no other reason than to use the interface.

Lee: Yes, and the other thing that it makes you notice is that there are nine very distinct sections of the site. Users tend to focus better because each billboard has something unique about it. Normally, in a site outline, users might read it, but they'll probably just skim through it and won't pay much attention. But doing it the Shockwave way, through entertainment value, you really encourage users to explore what is on the site.

The Gaming Application: Fireboy on Ice

IRC: One of the great advantages of Shockwave is that you can provide immersivity. The gaming application of Shockwave is quite immersive in the sense that one can easily get carried away and spend hours of the day playing these games. In fact, I've spent some time playing your game Fireboy on Ice.

Lee: Fireboy on Ice has been kind of interesting. I mentioned that we had a background in Director so Shockwave is a nice transition for us. The same is true for a lot of CD-ROM developers. They have already created their titles using Director. Something like 80 percent of the New Media Invision Award winning titles, or some very large percentage, were created with Director. It's really the standard.

Online CD Title Previewing

Lee: So you have this huge base of a lot of entertaining stuff that is already in Director. So getting it on the Web is easy. We actually see this as a whole new application area for Shockwave—using the Web as a way of previewing your CD-ROM titles. Many developers have had the experience of not being able to get their products onto the shelf. And customers are frustrated, afraid to buy CDs, because they are not able to try them out before they purchase. They might read a review, but there is no free way to see what the game is really like.

We actually see this as a whole new application area for Shockwave—using the Web as a way of previewing your CD-ROM titles.

I think the Web and using Shockwave will allow you to preview games before you purchase the CD-ROM. It also broadens distribution for those smaller developers who can't get their titles on the shelf at all. It gives them a way of broadcasting or publishing their work to a global audience literally overnite, especially if the product already exists. They just FTP it up to the server and everyone can look at it.

Fireboy on Ice

Lee: So Fireboy on Ice is an example of this. It was originally created by a Japanese developer, Toshimitsu Takagi. He created a product called "Movie 100," which was a lot of little Director files that he made. We had a personal relationship with him and asked if we could create a Shockwave version of Fireboy. So we took his CD-ROM version and reworked it. We made the file size much smaller, repositioned the layout of the game, and posted it on the Web. [See figure 16.6.]

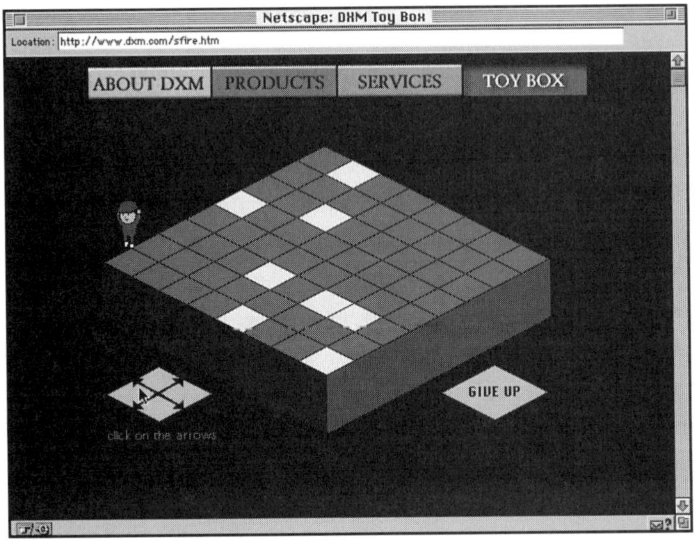

FIGURE 16.6

Fireboy on Ice is an arcade-style game created in Director and repurposed for the Web in Shockwave.

We have had a great reaction so far to Fireboy. We have links on our site to his site in Japan. All of a sudden, he has opened up his work to an American audience which he never had before. Now he is getting a lot of new traffic of people coming from America to see his stuff. In fact, he just did an English version of his site to accomodate all the new American visitors. [See Takagi's work at `http://www.d-craft.co.jp`.] That is part of how we see games going.

IRC: Tell me a little about the game.

Lee: The name Fireboy on Ice is translated from Japanese. You use the arrow buttons on the left to walk the character from the righthand corner to the opposite corner. As you walk through, everything is just fine until you hit one of the trap doors and fall screaming into the pit. You start again on the right and you try to remember where the trap doors are and go around them. You want to get to the opposite side in as few tries as possible. [You can play Fireboy by going to the DXM website or by viewing the file FIREBOY.HTM in the Chapter 16 folder on the accompanying CD.]

One thing that we need to work on is a better payoff. Right now, when you win, Fireboy just jumps up and down three times. We should also add a scoring mechanism and the number of tries. But you do have to remember where the trap doors are and go around them. You can give up and it will show you where the trap doors were, but it shuffles the traps for the next turn. There is no way of cheating.

AUTHORS' NOTE

Actually, after an intense interrogation, Lee did admit that there is a way to cheat. If you use the arrow key fast enough and jump really quickly, it doesn't activate the trap door, so you just sail right past the traps to the other side. But what fun is that?

IRC: So what kind of conclusions have you drawn from the Fireboy on Ice experience?

Lee: Well for one, it was really exciting to collaborate with someone in a another country. Fireboy proved that you can really use Shockwave to broaden your exposure to a home audience. I think it was also a very smooth transition going from his original CD-ROM version to a Shockwave version. It is very straightforward. We basically just made it smaller and juggled the layout for a 640×480 display. Oh yeah, and we did some Lingo work and some palette work, and probably a zillion other little things that take time but are by no means impossible.

I think that is the ultimate challenge to the Shockwave designer—how to stretch the media elements and use Lingo or whatever you have to do to entertain the user.

IRC: What does the success of Fireboy on Ice tell you about the uses of Shockwave itself?

Lee: We have gotten feedback from e-mail, from strangers who think Fireboy is cool. People find out who we are and they say, "Oh wow, you did Fireboy." I think it has definitely gotten us exposure and generated some excitement.

We also did show that you can have an engaging and entertaining experience with Shockwave on the Web. The file is 50 KB; it downloads quickly. So with minimal media, a couple of small sounds and a small animated loop, we can create an engaging experience. I think that is the ultimate challenge to the Shockwave designer—how to stretch the media elements and use Lingo or whatever you have to do to entertain the user. I think that we did succeed in that area, or Takagi did at least.

Online Arcades

Lee: We've had a chance to be part of an emerging trend in online gaming—online arcades. Rocket Science came to us because when they did an announcement relating to Cybercash. They wanted to create an online arcade-type system which works with Cybercash. You could have mini-transactions of 25 cents or 50 cents to pay as you play. There is no overhead or transaction fee. I think it is based on the Cybercash wallet, where you prepay a certain amount and then it just debits a certain amount with no surcharge. So that really allows you to have virtual on-line arcade. So Rocket Science came to us for Fireboy because they wanted to do a press release, but they had no examples, no games. So we agreed and then a Fireboy screen shot actually ended up in USA Today.

Sound for Web Multimedia

IRC: I noticed in all your work, there is great attention paid to the audio. Can you tell us about your new sound effects CD-ROM?

Lee: Sure, we just produced a product called the Earshot SFX, a multimedia sound effects library for multimedia developers. We have a friend that does Hollywood sound effects so he has a huge archive of his own original work that he repurposed and reworked into a multimedia library. We spent endless hours downsampling all the sounds to 11.025 khz/8 bits, as well as 22 khz/8 bits, to really gear it toward the developer and make them cross-platform AIF files.

Because our market consists of multimedia developers, we felt it would be good to create a website to go with the product. So we are using Shockwave on the Web to promote the earshot product. [Go to DXM's Shockwave site to find out more about Earshot. Try http://www.dxm.com/sproduct.htm.]

Earshot is totally geared toward the developer. One thing that is relevant to Shockwave developers is that Earshot has very small, tiny sounds, and a lot of them loop. We even have sine waves, triangle waves, and other waveforms that are just one cycle of the wave. You loop them in Director. They play as long as you want, but only take a fraction of 1 KB. They are about 250 bytes I think, and we did four octaves with different instruments so you can create little pianos or other simple instruments. You can even add decay to the notes with the Lingo command `sound fadeOut`. [You can see a demo of the looped sound waves. Use a Shockwave-enabled browser to open SOUNDS.HTM from the Chapter 16 folder on the accompanying CD.]

> **Tip**
>
> You can use many of the sound effects on the Earshot collection for free. DXM has kindly agreed to let us include more than 50 MB of their sounds on the accompanying CD. Just look in the Earshot folder and use any of the sounds royalty-free in your projects.

IRC: We want to thank you and Kathy and DXM for letting us put so many of your cool sounds on the CD-ROM of this book. I'm sure they'll come in handy for our readers. Can you describe the sounds that I am going to hear?

Lee: There you will find a selection from various categories of Earshot. Feel free to use them royalty-free for your projects. We hope you enjoy them, and if you would like to purchase the full product, that information is in there as well. The Earshot compilation has more than 2,000 studio quality sound effects on a double CD-ROM set for Mac and Windows. It's a real time-saver that meets the special sound needs of new media developers.

Local Storage and Bandwidth

IRC: Is there anything else you would like to add about Shockwave or, looking toward more advanced applications, things like that you see on the horizon?

Lee: Well, we are very interested in storing media locally, either off CD-ROM or the user's hard drive. With Shockwave for Director 5, you can do this. We're considering what some alternative applications could be.

IRC: For the sake of argument, what would be the purpose of external media?

Lee: If you had a Shockwave application with certain media elements like sound, animations, or video that you want to refer to or to play, then you can get them to the user on a CD-ROM. Say you had a weather program, for example, and you had a CD full of tornadoes, lightning, thunderstorms, birds chirping on a sunny day, or 3D maps, whatever. You could have all that media stored locally on the user's hard drive or CD and trigger those sequences based on real information coming off the Web, like the weather service, in this case. All you're doing on the Internet is simply retrieving a small text string and avoiding the bandwidth issue altogether, and that text string could trigger whatever you like.

Creating a really low-bandwidth, high-quality Shockwave movie is a lot like painting with a single-hair paintbrush. Every little detail counts, and that can be very time-consuming.

IRC: On the bandwidth issue, how do you see Shockwave applications changing in response to broadening of the pipes?

Lee: I try to use my imagination and look at a page that today loads very slowly. Now imagine what it would be like if it was much, much faster. That's broadband. Seriously though, I think you would really end up with something like interactive television. You know the cable modem's bandwidth is roughly the equivalent of a CD-ROM. At that speed you really could have a very rich multimedia experience on the Internet, so we are really looking forward to that and hoping that it happens very soon.

Of course, we all think about what advantage that offers over traditional CD-ROM delivery. I think the biggest advantage to having the Internet behave like one big CD-ROM is the fact that it's all changeable and live. You can publish something today, then change it and tweak it tomorrow, for real-time updates. Nothing is physical, it is all virtual and networked.

IRC: How do your clients think about bandwidth?

Lee: Well, creating a really low-bandwidth, high-quality Shockwave movie is a lot like painting with a single-hair paintbrush. Every little detail counts, and that can be very time-consuming, and I think in some ways clients expect a lot. They don't really know that multimedia is new to the Web or they don't realize it's a big deal. At trade shows they come by and don't even notice. Maybe it's the first time that they've seen the Web so why shouldn't it be animated?

I hope that clients appreciate the amount of detail that goes into creating good quality, low-bandwidth movies. They see the end result and it looks just as it should be. But it is not evident how much work went into making it so small and it is precisely that fine-detailed work that affects the bidding and the pricing. They actually cost a little more than what you would expect sometimes.

IRC: Does broadband solve that problem? Can you see in a few years just throwing bandwidth at your designs?

Lee: Well, fifty percent of the people may end up with cable modems in five years, but there will still be 50 percent with 28.8k. I think things will probably have to be scaleable. So it's a very good experience for us as developers to learn all the tricks to keep the file size down and then we'll grow with the bandwidth.

It's funny that we used to do multimedia for floppy disk distribution where we had to squeeze everything into one megabyte. Now we're squeezing to 30 KB to 100 KB, so that experience was great. When CD-ROMs came along, we lamented that all our floppy-sized techniques were useless. But now it is coming in really handy again. And it is also part of the strength of Director. There are a lot of tools in Director—patterns, tiles, and things—that were really there from way back when it was running on a Mac Plus. Those tools and techniques have suddenly become very valuable again.

Conclusion

We have seen in the DXM pieces that, with clever design, you can really pack an interactive punch into some very small Shockwave movies. And we have talked about some specific design techniques and design goals that shape the True Multimedia uses of Shockwave. As more and more interactive content appears on the Web in this form, the demand for designers to create innovative and memorable True Multimedia will grow as well.

With content such as the Fireboy on Ice game, we can begin to see the promise of using Shockwave as a vehicle for creating and delivering multimedia demos today, and with the coming of broadband, we can clearly see Shockwave becoming a viable channel for delivering actual titles in the near future. For those who have already used Director to create multimedia content, Shockwave can immediately be exploited for promotion and marketing to the broad Web public. We have also seen that Shockwave can not only complement CD-ROM content, but with the Levi's hypnotic ad, we see that Shockwave can be made a facet of any advertising campaign.

CHAPTER 17

Immersive Retailing and Simplified Menu Metaphors: Andersen Consulting

This chapter examines general interface issues for the corporate Web and offers case studies of two very interesting design challenges: immersive retailing and simplified menu metaphors. The content is from a discussion we had with George Williams, a multimedia producer with Andersen Consulting's San Francisco office.

The dialogue addresses corporate intranet and Internet goals, the immersive retailing example of "Basement One," and the simplified menu metaphor example of the "Internet Primer."

Authors' Note

Where does this fit into the Big Picture?

In this chapter we discuss applications that play with immersive user interfaces and metaphors other than the desktop. The immersive sales environment, "Basement One," is intended to be become a sprawling collection of movies that create a dynamic world of interesting characters who wear the products. The movies on their own are content-oriented and could be categorized as True Multimedia in the Big Picture. (See figure 2.1 in Chapter 2, "Power on the Web.") However, the movies are not on their own. They are the multimedia part of an online sales environment—a True Application on the Web—and that is how we properly think about them in the Big Picture.

The Shockwave "Internet Primer" movie also is an example of a True Application. It uses Shockwave to enhance the function of online training. It constitutes a valuable resource that can be used repeatedly by the end user.

Andersen Consulting

Andersen Consulting is a global management and technology consulting organization whose mission is to help its clients change to be more successful. The organization helps its clients link strategy, people, processes, and technology. Figure 17.1 shows their home page.

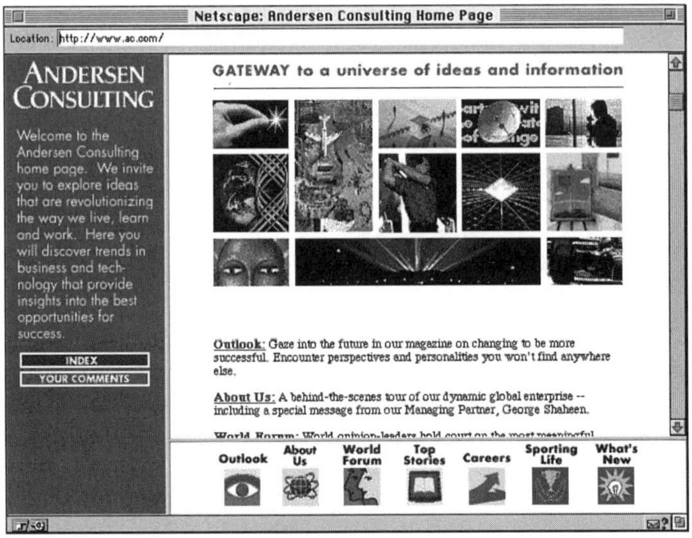

Figure 17.1

You can visit Andersen Consulting's website at http://www.ac.com/.

The Interview

To find out more about late-breaking Shockwave trends on the Web, we spoke to George Williams, a multi-talented multimedia producer for Andersen Consulting's San Francisco office. George's work is focused on Internet projects and pushing the Shockwave curve with Andersen's clients. Some of his work is on the front end, helping make sales by demonstrating the repackaging of the client's information as Shockwave media.

George helps to educate clients on the new Internet and intranet technologies. He is involved in producing micro-kiosk applications using Shockwave. This enables the client to previsualize the possibilities of Shockwave in a browser situation. George then implements these new ideas, having shown what is possible conceptually and technologically. George has produced a whole lot of high-powered multimedia and Shockwave.

The penetration of Shockwave solutions into the corporate Web lexicon is facilitated by consulting firms, such as Andersen, and expert multimedia producers such as George Williams. We found George's perspective highly instructive in two respects.

First, he identifies key features of corporate decision-making logic and the needs of average intranet users. He shows how these factors condition interface design and how Shockwave can provide solutions.

Second, George relates two specific Shockwave implementations that he developed. One is an online immersive retailing model that is personality-oriented as opposed to product-oriented. The other is a menu metaphor that offers intuitive navigation through a text-heavy presentation.

Corporate Intranet and Internet Goals

IRC: What do you do at Andersen in terms of Web work overall?

George: Overall, we do website management in a very comprehensive way. We start by going through a whole process of talking to the firm and with the client about what their goals are, about the changing technologies, and then getting graphic designers to execute the design. We always try to implement new technologies and so we get programming teams, if necessary. Finally, we maintain the sites as well.

IRC: Who are some of the bigger clients who are doing interesting things?

George: We have Sega and the Dial Corporation to name a few. These involve, especially Dial, secure transactions for their intranet work.

Designing for Business Goals

Noel: What business goals of your clients have you found most important—what they consider their Web strategies? What sort of business goals are driving their plans?

George: A lot of it is actually just trying to be first. At this point that is a big part of their goals when they see something that's new. They can also see cost savings, although they are not too sure where those come in necessarily.

There is a great big learning curve. So in many ways they are not too sure what a strategy would even be. They don't completely understand what this is all about. So that's where we come in.

One basic concept that we encourage is that our clients, by using the Internet in whatever form, can implement part of what is often called the paperless office concept. In that they can access information anywhere and use it like a large database. That's the general focus. Plus there are a lot of opportunities for certain types of transactions that take place almost instantaneously without having to worry about tracking paper.

Noel: Can you describe some technical and design challenges your clients face or that you at Andersen face when implementing a plan for them on the Web?

George: One of the big issues is security, issues concerning the firewall. People are always worried about hackers. They've read headlines. Though they are not to sure what that it's all about, they do know they don't like it. Security tends to be the biggest technical issue.

The design issues often involve concept. What is it exactly they are trying to achieve? They have to be brought back to square one. There are certain constraints such as screen size, low resolution, bandwidth, and those types of things. There are certain things you should avoid and certain things you might want to consider in terms of design or presenting product or services.

What is Shockwave Good For?

IRC: What clients are making the most use of Shockwave at this point and what are they doing with it?

George: At this point it's very new and it is something that we are just now introducing as a possibility. The specific uses have involved pulling information from different locations on the Net, such as financial data. That kind of thing.

IRC: So making calls to external text files and presenting that information live?

George: Yes.

IRC: So why is Shockwave particularly well suited to that? Can't that be done with some other kind of technology?

George: Well in fact, that is very interesting, because some people have fallen in love with Java even though they are not quite sure what Java is. Often the two are misunderstood as interchangeable technologies, which of course, they are not.

What people like about Shockwave is the ease of providing a nice-looking front end. It doesn't look like the usual plain vanilla desktop. You can do some interesting things with it fairly quickly, whereas with Java, you really have to be a good programmer to get the same results within a certain time frame. We have clients right now who are looking to Andersen to see what can be done with it on their site. That is part of the work I do with some of these educational pieces to show what's possible.

Andersen is promoting Shockwave because it is seen as new technology. A certain amount of the benefit is the prestige of being first. But there is deeper value in the new technologies coming out. It is part of a general push for multimedia. So Shockwave is seen as just an extension of a multimedia trend. It is finally sinking in that multimedia still doesn't exist in many areas. And when displaying information, people are able to absorb information much quicker with multimedia than with more traditional interfaces.

> *What people like about Shockwave is the ease of providing a nice-looking front end. It doesn't look like the usual plain vanilla desktop. You can do some interesting things with it fairly quickly, whereas with Java you really have to be a good programmer to get the same results within a certain time frame.*

IRC: What are the key areas on the intranet that you think multimedia makes the most sense in?

George: That would be training, first of all. It has been talked about in some database applications, but the jury is still out until we know better how that can work. At this moment, prototyping of virtual reality [VR] environments is a good application of Shockwave.

Virtual Reality Environments

IRC: Can you go into that a little bit? VR prototyping of what? Why are you presenting VR information using Shockwave?

George: One, it's very difficult to implement otherwise—at least at this point—with other technologies out there, including QuickTime VR. Given the reality of corporate life, Shockwave is just simpler to work with. It is easy enough for someone to drop in a Shockwave plug-in and then be able to access Shockwave content verses QuickTime VR. QuickTime VR has many advantages, but it isn't as clean a package.

Getting the users up and running is a major concern. There have been some cross-platform issues with QuickTime VR. Using Shockwave to simulate a VR setup frees you from using any kind of QuickTime at all. It is very, very simple to use this Shockwave in the front-end. You see a picture of a very simple object in a virtual space. You point to that object. It opens up and you can access information and then Shockwave will call out to the Net or your intranet and pull information into that space. Then you can see that information and be happy.

That is basically what it is. I have had conversations recently with some managers from the east coast offices about implementing that type of thing in-house at Andersen, because we're finding that the present LotusNotes setup, used for internal communication, is being used less and less. People have to go through so many different submenus and submenus that they're not using the damn thing at all. They are just sending voice mail and faxes. So the systems they had set up to form an internal communication database is kind of ineffective simply because people can't get through the interface.

Dump the Desktop for a Friendly Web

IRC: How does Shockwave address those obstacles?

George: In this instance it would be Shockwave as VR interface. In the situation just described, you'd see objects that represent various databases to interact with. And because it is Shockwave, it is easy to maintain and update the bitmapped images very quickly.

IRC: Right. And now you will be able to externalize the graphics with the release Shockwave for Director 5. So, what communication problems or challenges facing Anderson's clients can be solved by using Shockwave on the Web? What can be done with Shockwave that really can't be done easily any other way?

George: I would say making the Web friendlier. Most people have some flavor of the Netscape browser. But for a lot of people that's still not a friendly enough environment. With Shockwave you can tailor the front end, throw in the company logo or other defining things, and produce something that is tailored to the corporate culture very easily. That way the interface is closer to the level of most users at that time.

IRC: So what sort of production technology issues come up in developing these sort of Shockwave front ends? What do you have to do at Andersen or what do your clients have to do to pull that off?

George: A lot of the work is actually more theoretical. It involves a lot of discovery and design work. Distilling information down to what they need to know right away. We are discovering how Shockwave can best display that information and in what form. Also, how do we make this a standard thing so that people always know to look at a particular area of the screen to find something familiar.

In essence what we are doing and what the clients are asking for is a front end that fits on top of the desktop, one that is an extended or a simplified environment. They are also saying that with the Internet and with these new ways of accessing vast amounts of information there is no particular reason to stick with the desktop metaphor. In fact it has been a big surprise that when people are offered alternatives to the desktop they prefer those.

IRC: What type of alternatives can you give to the desktop using Shockwave?

George: One alternative to the desktop is the VR metaphor—which seems to be more popular than I expected. One can imagine many types of menu structures using different types of hierarchies and different ways of displaying information.

My favorite alternative has been sort of turning the menu structure inside out. Right now the menu starts at one level and you move inside and down to get the information. I'd like to see an alternative where information is brought up to you and you keep track of where information came from as opposed to where you've gone.

Technology is at the point now where it makes sense to have a smarter interface, one that knows something about the way people operate and has a certain amount of artificial intelligence. We are trying to come up with something that meets people halfway so they don't have to change the way they work or the way they think about information. Because of the corporate setting, they don't have time. They want to open up something and have it help them do their job.

Noel: Can you explain what types of work processes can be enveloped in a Shockwave front end using these various metaphors you described?

George: A lot of library functions. Certain types of internal database functions where people need to access certain types of database functions all the time. In the case of consultants, they are looking at different industries and having a thousand different bookmarks doesn't quite work for them. They need something simpler and that can anticipate based on what they accessed in previous sessions. Kind of like an active agent, but staying inside the program itself. This tracking information will be kept in a text file. Shockwave will mainly access that and so by the time it is actually talking to you, it kind of knows what you want already.

Shockwave is Changing the Intranet

IRC: As far as intranet stuff goes—corporate training and so on—how do you envision technology like Shockwave for Authorware and Shockwave Director changing the way people are trained in the work place the way information is disseminated inside corporations?

George: By providing a simple front end that people can access. This will allow people to access training information or entire training programs that can be maintained and updated fairly simply and will not require special workstations in certain locations. If you have a browser and you have access to the Internet, you could be trained at your own pace.

A consultant from Andersen was looking at a training piece that I'd done and said he thought I should put it on the Web with Shockwave. He didn't realize that it was already shocked. He was interacting with this Shockwave thing for quite a while before he realized what it was, because in many ways, it is that transparent.

IRC: Have you gotten any feedback from users of Shocked websites that Andersen has been a part of?

George: They're excited that they can see things move and hear music. They like the ability to interact in real-time instead of pushing a button and waiting for another page to come up in the more traditional static website. A funny story was when a consultant from Andersen was looking at a training piece that I'd done and said he thought I should put it on the Web with Shockwave. He didn't realize that it was already shocked. He was interacting with this Shockwave thing for quite a while before he realized what it was, because in many ways, it is that transparent.

The direction we seem to be going in is online tutorials, starting with tutorials about the Internet itself. We have a demo that talks about the Net, what you can do with it, and "Oh, by the way, you are looking at this in Shockwave." Let's talk about that after we look at a Shockwave design that was shown very successfully yesterday at one of the corporate sites in

Arizona. It's an example of using Shockwave to create an immersive retail environment.

Immersive Retailing: The "Basement One" Example

IRC: Can you talk about the two sample movies from the immersive retailing environment and what you were trying to do with them?

George: The two movies are for an upscale, yet still hip, retailer. We have changed the name to "Basement One" for the purposes of this interview. The idea is that instead of going to a virtual mall, which many people are doing or talking about and which isn't really new anymore, instead you go into a space where you meet interesting people who happen to wear the products that are sold by a particular retailer.

The characters have stories that change quite frequently, either daily, weekly, or what have you. They do interesting things and their lifestyles are intriguing. They are people you would want to know more about. As you find out more about them, you also find out about the various fashion products. It is much more of a soft sell and it is much more lifestyle oriented as opposed to product oriented.

The Shocked Environment

The "Basement One" environment that George and Andersen made is an interactive sales environment. In "Basement One" the main attraction is the characters. The main menu is a menu of characters. Clicking on the characters tells you who they are and something about them. For example, in Figure 17.2 we meet Orlando Rodriguez. To view the "Basement One" main menu, play the movie DEMOSHK1.DIR in Director, or open DEMOSHK1.DCR in a Shockwave-enabled browser. These can be found in the Chapter 17 folder on the accompanying CD.

Figure 17.2

The "Basement One" environment presents alluring characters, their lifestyles, and the fashions they wear.

If you really like the characters, you can find out what is happening in their world. Figure 17.3 is from the movie that tells about Orlando's life. To view the Orlando movie from "Basement One," play the movie DEMOSHK2.DIR in Director or open DEMOSHK2.DCR in a Shockwave-enabled browser. These can be found in the Chapter 17 folder on the accompanying CD.

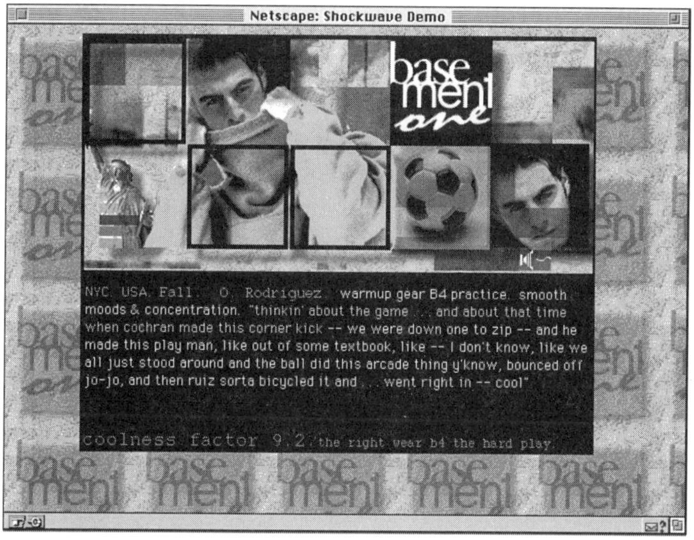

Figure 17.3

The Orlando movie shows how the immersive sales environment engages the viewer.

In the Orlando movie, you read about his recent soccer game. You can see the crucial play by clicking on the FUTBOL_CLIP. And, yes, you can even pick the color of his shirt.

The Challenge of Attractive Packaging

IRC: On the "Basement One" piece, maybe you can spell out the design challenge and why you came up with this particular package. Can you talk about the communication you were trying to achieve with it?

George: To design something that would be attractive to the target market—people within a certain age range who fit into a certain demographic of income. Of course, these would be people who tend to use the Internet in general.

It had to be something attractive. In its most basic form, there is a lot of text, probably too much text in my view. The text area takes up almost half the actual screen. I'm a bit frightened by that. But there is enough going on above that and also the text has many colors which carry different meanings as well.

I think people might stick around. It certainly has been the case so far. People just sort of go in there and click on things seeing what happens and being surprised that things actually do happen. People like that there is some music in the background. People stay there and they are engaged. That was the idea. And the selling aspect of it gets done in the text or some of the active areas.

IRC: What kind of feedback are you getting?

George: Other clients and some of the managers within the company who were very skeptical of the idea were pleasantly surprised when they saw it. And I was surprised that they were pleasantly surprised, in fact. These are people who are just really not graphically oriented and are leery when they see a lot colors and other things. They see that as fluff. In the case of the "Basement One" piece, they saw it as something very, very serious and something that should be considered.

They had not seen anything like this before and they thought maybe we could be first or one of the first to take this approach with some of our clients. Also, they saw this as a way to change the face of the company to some extent, you might say. The company is seen as progressive in terms of design, but when it comes to other areas such as technology, they do not have any presence at all. This seemed to be the way to bridge those two areas and also to give them "youthful" presence online as well.

Designing for Performance

IRC: What techniques did you use in making the movie with Director? What tricks did you use?

George: There were no special animation tricks per se. We used standard puppetSprite techniques. I got a small audio loop and also made the sound of the soccer ball being hit. It is actually a drum hit, which was doctored a bit in SoundEdit 16.

The critical thing here was performance. It had to perform very well. People could not have any questions about why something was not happening immediately.

First of all, for the sake of performance, I found that I had to reduce the number of puppetSprites. This meant redesigning the movie, as everything originally took place in one frame. It seemed too much overhead. I was running this on a PowerMac 8500, and it was still very slow. The waveform volume icon changed so slowly when you changed volume you could almost count the number of seconds. There was also bad delay with the color changing on the sweater.

So we broke everything out into separate sets of frames to make it work better. The critical thing here was performance. It had to perform very well. People could not have any questions about why something was not happening immediately.

In order to get reliable performance, I had to go with the simplest and the most basic Lingo solution.

Designing for Interactivity

IRC: How did you decide what level of interactivity to include? Were your goals based around interactivity primarily or was it a secondary concern?

George: I had several goals. It first had to be engaging and offer a certain amount of interactivity. It had to have audio in some capacity. The audio was changed in the last minute. At first there was a talking character, but the movie became too large. So that was dropped. It had to have sound even if nothing more than just a click sound. There had to be something happening in the audio. The background music was the way we got that.

There had to be some kind of animation and so you get that in the soccer game. The soccer game is my favorite piece because I know how the animation was put together. Everything was faked and yet, in some of the frames, it looks almost like real animation. Also very critical, there had to be some color changes on the sweater because that was the product being highlighted. So then the nature of the story was why would this character be wearing a particular sweater? What was happening?

It became kind of like writing the little scenario in reverse. We wrote the scenario to fit those design considerations.

Designing for Bandwidth

IRC: Who is your audience and how do you decide on the file size?

George: The audience would be consumers who are not using ISDN for sure. People most likely still using 14.4 modems, a few 28.8, but we are looking for lower speed and that meant having a smaller movie size. The movies had to be under a 180 K. That was very critical.

IRC: What was your approach to bandwidth control?

George: A lot of that bandwidth control was done in the audio. That's the biggest single chunk of any of these movies, so we downsampled and shortened them.

There is only really one big image and that's the background. I knew I had a lot of leeway with the bitmap images, because I can always compress them.

It's standard procedure for us to put our bitmaps through Cinepak compression either in Debabilizer or Premiere. We've found that the differences in size can be as little as 30 percent, or sometimes as much as three to one, depending on how much image quality you are willing to sacrifice. [See Chapter 14, "Advanced Compression Issues," for a more detailed tutorial on the Cinepak compression technique.]

The key with "Cinepaking" your bitmaps is to do it as your last step before importing into Director. Do all the image processing first. Recompressing an image that has already been compressed will look bad and hurt your compression ratio.

First, we make the images in Photoshop. I should note here that the backgrounds of the two "Basement One" movies both come from a single Photoshop file with at least 20 different layers. That way we are able to keep everything in registration, so to speak, without worrying about shifting elements. I make the layers that I want to have Cinepaked visible and do a Save As PICT. I usually change to indexed color first with diffusion dithering and adaptive palette, because the images come out cleaner.

It's often faster to Cinepak in Premiere than Debabilizer, because we are not really using a batch mode. In Premiere, the interface is very simple and everything is right there and I can compress it right away.

The key with Cinepaking your bitmaps is to do it as your last step before importing into Director. Do all the image processing first. Recompressing an image that has already been compressed will look bad and hurt your compression ratio. Cinepak compression is a feature that Premiere does very well. And a lot of people don't really use it, but we use it an awful lot to control bandwidth.

Lessons from "Basement One"

IRC: What about future uses of Shockwave? What did the "Basement One" prototype indicate to you and to Andersen's clients?

George: They are starting to see that they should take Shockwave seriously, that it really is more than something for animated logos. They can manage information in some very interesting ways both for Internet uses and intranet uses, which is more the direction they are going in right now.

I know of several developers who put up websites and have really been surprised that people had a lot of trouble using what was there. They made a number of assumptions and found out those were not exactly correct. A lot of wrong assumptions centered on the interface itself. Things like hot spots, for example. They just assumed people would go to the right space and click on something and would know what happened afterward, where we have never made that assumption.

We really assume people are computer illiterate and we work backward from that assumption. So rather than build on what Apple and Microsoft have done [with the desktop—auth] we have tried to reevaluate. What is it people are doing and what is the simplest way for them to do it? Then we go from there and come up with some interesting results.

That reevaluation is why we care a lot about interface metaphors as more and more people start using the Internet.

IRC: What metaphors have you found the most friendly and intuitive?

George: We found that there are two. For some applications there's the VR metaphor, although there are some problems using that in Shockwave—largely file size. But it seems to be the one that people get the easiest. But let's talk more about simple menu metaphors.

Simplified Menu Metaphors: The "Stairstep" Example

George: Here we are taking a fresh look at the menu metaphor. Our goal is to take different levels of information and array those levels in a much simpler form. So you are not going through a pull-down menu, then another menu coming off that, and maybe another one. On the Mac side, that may not seem like an issue, but in Windows the various branches can cause people to become lost very easily. So what we have done is to pull the information up and we sort of track where it came from and indicate that in a very simple way. To make it even easier, we do a complete reformat of all the information being used so you only have a very set number of levels to begin with.

The "Internet Primer" Movie

IRC: What do you mean by pulling information up and letting people know where it came from? Do you have an example?

George: Yes. Recently, a client of ours, Dial Corp., was interested in offering an Internet primer to the users on their network. They wanted to use a multimedia form because they see that's the direction in which things are going and for their own employees it allows them to soak up information much quicker. That's the rationale for the application.

The "Internet Primer" piece was initially a presentation, then redesigned for single users, and then a Web application. I call it an application, even though in a way, it isn't quite. It's somewhere between a presentation and application.

Nonetheless, we set up some very simple stairstep icons. They looked like stairsteps with arrows at the end. By doing a simple rollover, you give a little dialog in different parts of the screen based on how important the information was. A dialog comes up and it would be very visible telling you what the stairstep was.

It tells you about the level at which you are accessing information. At the top level are the different sections you could go to. If you go down to the next level, you are not yet accessing the information but you are getting a preview of what is underneath. Clicking will bring up the deep information, and if you go down to the third stairstep level, you would have something else. The stairstep icon would change color all the while. We found out it was very easy for people to deal with.

The navigation issues are different in the "Internet Primer" piece than in "Basement One." It is not about selling. It's about data access and retrieval and information management in general. The client is not too sure what the possibilities are with the different technologies. It is still often the case where they still ask about Shockwave and Java as if they were interchangeable.

So I've used this as an opportunity to show them what is possible with Shockwave. It is not a splashy application of Shockwave, but rather a plain vanilla information management piece that just has a very nice front end. Those have been very successful so far.

AUTHORS' NOTE

The stairstep metaphor is used in the "Internet Primer" movie that George and Andersen made for Dial Corp. It is intended as an informational training for managers and others using Dial's corporate intranet. The primer discusses the Internet itself, a brief history, a dictionary of terms, and a discussion of the Internet's uses. To use the primer, play the movie INTRA_NV2.dir in Director, or open INTRA_NV2.HTM in a Shockwave-enabled browser. Figure 17.4 shows the interface.

The navigation interface is a very intuitive and interesting one. The stairsteps take you to deepening levels of the exposition. At each stairstep level there is 'horizontal' movement across topics and 'vertical' movement into topics.

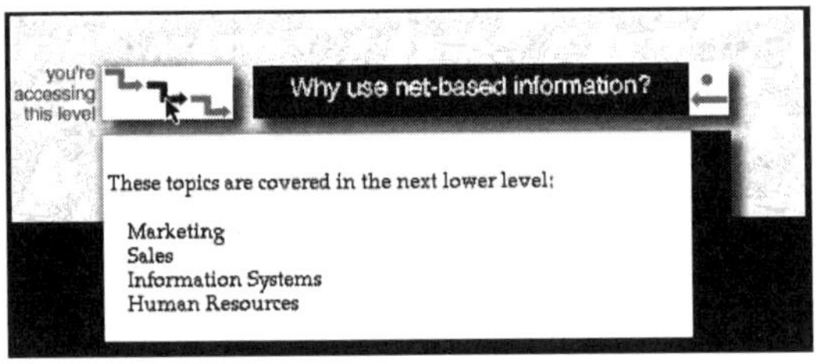

FIGURE 17.4

The "Internet Primer" is an interactive training piece created in Shockwave for Director. It uses a stairstep metaphor for simplified navigation.

Why the Stairstep Metaphor Works

IRC: What makes the stairstep metaphor approach easier to use?

George: Well first of all, the stairsteps are all visible at once. Whereas if you are using a standard menu, you really don't know what is underneath that menu unless you know the application or program very well. In this particular case, we are talking to the entire corporation, which means not just MIS people, but a lot of consultants, middle managers and their secretaries will view it as well.

Even though all these people had used Windows, when it comes to on-line information on the Internet or even on a LAN, people don't like to go to a lot of levels. They want it to be right there. The stairstep solution was a way to collapse the information and simplify it and make it very visual so you can always see just by looking at the stairstep where you are. And by having just three levels you don't have to count. It's either the top, the bottom, or the middle. So it's very simple even for people who are not very visual per se.

IRC: How can Shockwave be used to move further in that direction?

George: At this point, a lot of the navigation has to be hard wired in. We have to make sure that the text that comes up does reflect where information is coming from. The initial use was to have everything internal to a movie so it was very simple that way. This particular piece was, in fact, designed for pulling text files off an intranet that would have a certain location and would be able to look at where they were coming from and check against an internal database in the movie itself. So future versions of this metaphor will be smarter and more aware of other things on the Net.

Shockwave in the Controlled Environment of the Intranet

IRC: Do people on these intranets resist installing Netscape and Shockwave in fear of support headaches?

George: Really so far we have not had much trouble. I think because it is an intranet, it is a controlled environment. The company has essentially said "We will all use Shockwave," so people don't question that since it comes from the top. People who take care of upgrading machines just go through and make the necessary changes to all the machines which they are having to do anyway because everyone will be running Netscape so they just do it in one operation.

Conclusion

George has elaborated on specific user interfaces made in Shockwave that address some very basic goals on the Web. The goal of drawing users on the public Internet into immersive sales environments is served in a very subtle and elegant way using the lifestyle-oriented method. The goal of providing menus or information hierarchies for corporate intranets is facilitated by level indicators that have simplified metaphors like the stairstep.

These applications are extremely valuable examples for Shockwave developers. The examples go a long way to scratching the surface of multimedia user interface design issues for the Web.

CHAPTER 18

Advanced Applications: Action Technologies' Metro

This chapter discusses the integration of Shockwave solutions into Web-based software applications. This chapter also examines how Shockwave solutions are intimately related to basic communication challenges in a world with too much information. Here we discuss the Web as a medium for coordinating work and navigating through vast informationscapes, and how immersive user interfaces can be designed. The bulk of this chapter is derived from a discussion we had with Rodrigo Flores, the vice president of Product Management with Action Technologies. The dialogue spans the following topics:

- *Work coordination tools for the Web*
- *Action's Shockwave solution in detail*

- State memory and contextualizing information
- Preliminary results and lessons from the shocking of Metro
- Using Shockwave to design information spaces

AUTHORS' NOTE

Where does this fit into the Big Picture?

In this chapter we see Shockwave incorporated into the user interface of a Web-based workflow management system. Action Technologies' Metro is a powerful system for coordinating the work of the many people and departments within companies or groups of companies. The Shockwave user interface component adds to the functionality of the Metro software by making it easier and more fun to use. This solution is really the defining one for the True Applications category in the Big Shockwave Picture. (See figure 2.1 in Chapter 2, "Power on the Web.")

Relative to today's standards, Metro is a very high-level application of Shockwave. The Shockwave movies in Metro are sitting on top of what is already an advanced application of HTML. As part of the software package, the Shockwave elements are intended to convey the Metro metaphor, adding to the ease of use and fun. The net result is a more immersive work tool.

Action Technologies

Action Technologies is a software company that produces tools for the coordination of work. In years developing coordination systems, they have distilled a great deal knowledge about the way people work. Action has created important models of the work process itself. They use their patented "workflow" model in their powerful software products. Action boasts an impressive installed base of customers using their work coordination systems. Figure 18.1 shows Action's home page.

Early in 1996, Action Technologies contracted us at InfraRed to create a Shockwave component of Metro, their inaugural work coordination product for the Web. Shocking Metro gave Action Technologies the distinction of offering the first true Web application with an integral Shockwave user interface. In the course of our collaboration with Action Technologies, we found them to be a particularly innovative brain trust. I think it is safe to say that the Metro project taught us all important things about designing user interfaces with Shockwave. You can see what Action is up to at `http://actiontech.com/`.

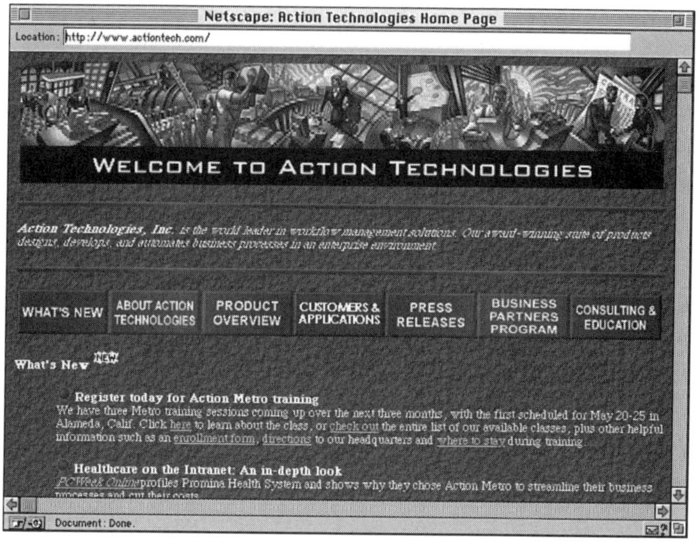

FIGURE 18.1

You can visit Action Technologies' website at http://www.actiontech.com/.

The Interview

The Shocking Metro project was managed by Rodrigo Flores, Action's Vice President of Product Management. Rodrigo manages the design and production of Action's products. In leading the development of Metro, Rodrigo and his team grappled with the complex issues in delivering a powerful work process management tool over the Web.

In many ways, Action is out in front with Metro. They were first to market with a Web-based workflow system and the first true Web application with a Shockwave UI option. Rodrigo Flores was a key force behind Action's success with Metro and all their products and in his interview, he was kind enough to share some of his perspectives on using Shockwave for coordination and navigation applications on the Web.

Coordinating and Navigating the Infostorm

To best use Shockwave's potential, it is important to understand the underpinnings of that potential—the basic nature of its advantages and limitations. This enables you to identify how to use Shockwave to break out of some of the Web's confinements. Rodrigo's comments are important here in that he has clearly identified these strengths and limitations through the process of creating a groundbreaking Shockwave application.

Furthermore, there is an underlying methodology and analysis contained in Rodrigo's comments, which we expect you will find useful to think about. Rodrigo raises several important themes in relation to Shockwave. Among those are the following:

- Working within technical constraints
- What you can do with state memory
- Contextualizing work and information
- Contending with the problems of universality
- Engaging metaphor development
- The value of dense interactivity

Because work coordination is the very crux of Action's products, it is not surprising that Rodrigo brings out some very enlightening approaches to user interfaces and trends in presenting information and navigation. The process of Shocking Metro took us to some of the limits of what Shockwave could do, revealing deeper implications for coordination, navigation, and immersive user interfaces.

And, finally, we see why Shockwave constitutes a powerful prototyping environment for applications that rely on strong immersive metaphors in the user interface. In the actual practice of Shocking Metro, Shockwave revealed itself as an important vehicle for development and delivery of multimedia user interfaces for Web applications.

Work Coordination Tools for the Web

InfraRed Communications: First, can you explain what Action does in general, if you can summarize it?

Rodrigo Flores: Well, we produce and sell software for the coordination of people—groups of people, teams of people. We provide the software on the major groupware platforms such as Lotus Notes, MS Exchange and, of course, the Web. We also provide the same coordination and development tools for the major SQL environments such as MS SQL Server, where people develop in Visual Basic.

Metro then belongs to the class of tools that we call collaboration and coordination products. These are tools for individuals or groups of people to work together to manage their work, track their deadlines, figure out where things are, who's going to do what next, who's behind, and tools to remind them via e-mail. That's our business essentially. Coordination tools.

IRC: So, what strategy were you pursuing when you provided these tools in an HTML front end?

Rodrigo: With Metro the main thing is to provide coordination and work management tools that would require no client software. Going on the Web meant that people using Mac and Windows and Unix and everything could now participate and coordinate work without having to install software, learn software, or do a whole bunch of expensive operations.

All they have to do is buy Metro and a server, and now they can begin to work together, manage projects, track deadlines, manage commitments. All this using the Internet as the network and the Web and HTML as a front end.

Metro in Action

Let's break from the interview for a minute and take a quick look at what Metro does. Let's take a typical case of a large corporation that integrates work processes from various departments under Metro. Each department, such as Human Resources, Information Services, Customer Support, and so forth, has customizable forms for frequent processes. Thus, you can streamline the communications for individuals and groups. Metro enables each person to instantly access the status of all their requests and commitments.

In Metro you initiate, send, and receive request forms, and track the status of the requests and commitments in the Metro Workbox. Figure 18.2 shows Metro's Workbox page. A form can be a common one, such as a request for sick leave, or any ad hoc request that would come up in the course of managing a special project. Your workbox can sort your requests to zero in on a particular range of commitments or requests.

FIGURE 18.2

This is Metro's workbox full of work.

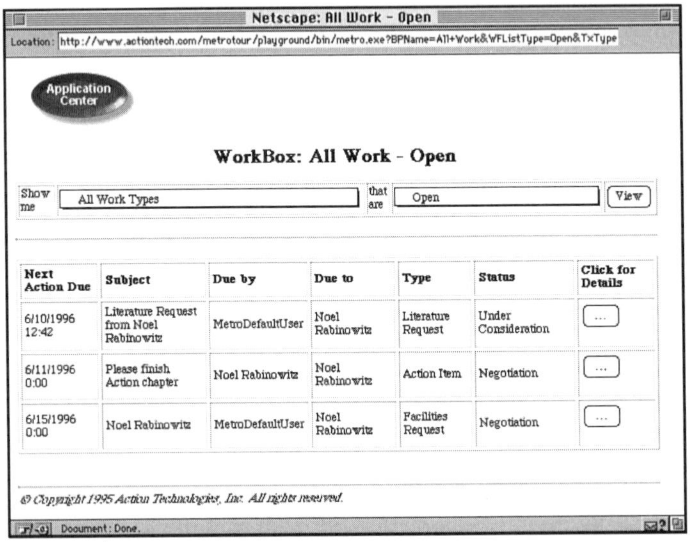

The main navigation center in Metro is very horizontal. Because Metro can coordinate work in large organizations with many departments, the main navigation center is a sizable field of buttons. Figure 18.3 shows the main navigation center in the unshocked version of Metro. Each company department might have many standard form pages. This means that the main menu or button field needs to have more than fifty links—quite a messy page. Alternatively, the hierarchy could be split into an additional menu level—also not a great solution because this adds to navigation time. Another possibility is to use Shockwave for the main navigation menu.

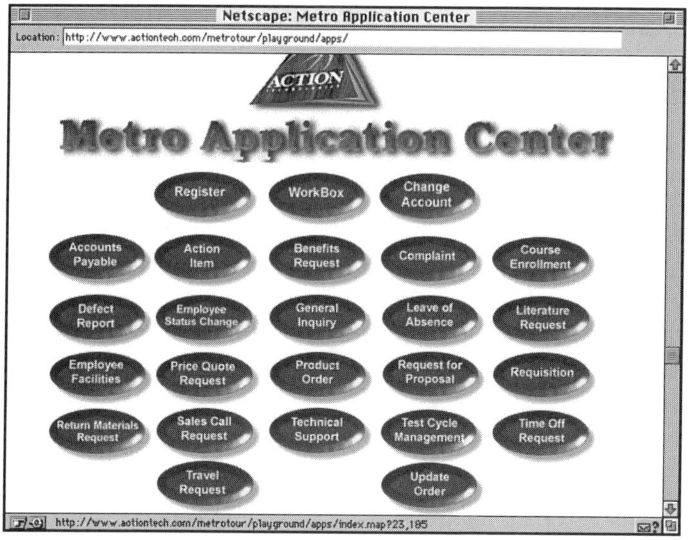

FIGURE 18.3

This is the main navigation center of Metro in the standard version. The button field really can't get any bigger.

Metro's main navigation menu in the Shockwave version is so much more compact and cool to use. It has an immersive environment metaphor of a Metro system with each department as a metro line; each form is a station stop. The main navigation movie is like a central station with all the lines available on a map. Figure 18.4 shows the Metro map.

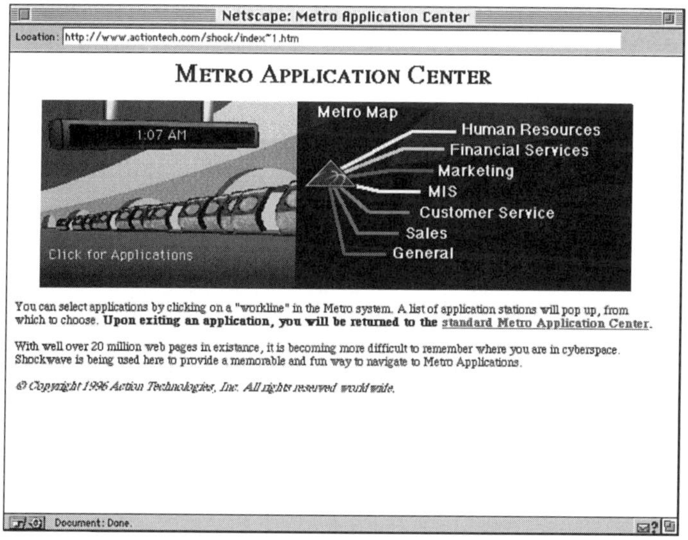

FIGURE 18.4

This is the main navigation center of Metro in the Shockwave version. Users can navigate to up to 70 customizable locations in just two clicks. A rollover status line tells you where you are going before you go there.

Instructions are given in a status line as you roll over departments and forms. All of the location names, status messages, and the URL links are contained in an external customizable text file.

Metro's Shockwave interface is much more interesting to use than the straight HTML version. The metaphor of the Metro system conveys a sense of motion, of travel and "connectedness," and it's fun. For instance, when you choose to go to a particular location, the doors of the Metro train close and the train leaves the station, taking you to your destination as the target page loads. You really feel like you are getting somewhere. Furthermore, jumping to any location is just two quick clicks away, so it is much faster to use.

A demo version of the Metro main navigation movie, METR_NAV.DIR, can be found in the Chapter 18 folder on the accompanying CD.

Trends in Coordination Tools

IRC: Have you seen a general trend of corporate work applications to be front ended on the Web?

Rodrigo: Yes. In fact, this might be interesting to you. This week in *PC Week* [May 7, 1996], there is an article "Health Group Gets Interactive Treatment." That health group, Promina Health Systems in Atlanta, is a customer of ours. A huge group—nine hospitals with thousands of employees—is streamlining its work process on an intranet, all based on a Web front end.

We are seeing two trends with our Web products. One consists of people who want to provide communication, collaboration, and publishing tools to everyone in their company regardless of the platform and regardless of the training they have. They are essentially saying, "Gee, we put Netscape Navigator or MS Internet Explorer on every desktop." Now we can provide these people with a number of tools very simply, because they don't have to be a distributor. It's done very cheaply, because they don't have to buy for every desktop, and—put in a more friendly manner—because I don't have buttons and pull-down menus. I can use graphics. I can use fun stuff and, therefore, reduce my training costs, for example.

So we are seeing a lot of movement toward people using HTML front ends for collaboration and coordination in the intranet. That's one trend.

There is a second trend and one that I think is the most exciting. Because of the fact that the Internet infrastructure is already there, people are beginning to form communities of interest. Like in the example of Promina Health Systems, now you can tie your doctors, your hospitals, your HMOs, your labs—all of which are independent companies, independent places, and buildings—all into one common process. And that process is based on how we serve the patients better, basically.

Twenty years ago, only General Motors could afford to even talk about putting a network into place. Now, two guys who want to form a company can get onto a local provider and essentially use the Internet as their own private network.

You couldn't convince them to buy the same type of software. You couldn't convince them to plug in wires and construct a network. The cost and training would be too prohibitive. But, basically, I can say everybody has a browser, everybody is on the Net. It's free, so they can assume that it is a common platform. Once you assume a common platform, then you can do some interesting things—if you have tools like Metro.

So those are the two trends—the intranet and economic communities of interest.

Moving to the Web

IRC: So, was ubiquitousness the main factor prompting Action's movement into the Web-based products?

Rodrigo: There are two pieces to that. One is the ubiquitousness of the TCP/IP network to begin with as the fundamental design. Twenty years ago, only General Motors could afford to even talk about putting a network into place. Now, two guys who want to form a company can get onto a local provider and essentially use the Internet as their own private network at a cost of $19 for unlimited hours a month, or free from AT&T for five hours.

So today, for $20, you are buying the networking capacity that GM may have paid millions for quite a few years ago. I don't know that people understand the economic leverage that provides. Really, you are getting the same thing from that point of view. So, ubiquitous TCP/IP networks is number one.

Number two is that the Web is a common platform for navigating, for publishing information, and for front-ending a variety of different systems. So those are the two phenomena that work together. You put those two together and you see there is some interesting stuff that is possible and necessary to develop.

HTML's Limited Interactivity and Stateless Protocol

IRC: What have been some key design or technical challenges that Action faced in putting together your Web strategy and your products into an HTML front end?

Rodrigo: Well, there are a bunch of challenges. But for the purposes of this conversation, the main challenge is the lack of interactivity, or the one-shot CGI limitation. The Web can front-end any system through CGI or one of the new APIs. But so far, it's a one-shot interactivity. You can press a button and you can link to a new page. And while that makes design really simple in some ways, you just don't have a lot of options.

Right now you can get some interactivity on the Web but it requires you to click... page, and click... page forever. You are essentially in click hell.

The problem with one-shot interactivity is when you need more complex interaction with a customer. It's when you need to give them more choices. When you need to tailor the environment to fit their world a little better, it becomes very difficult. The fact that the Web is based on a stateless protocol means that it is very difficult to have it remember who you are.

For example, maybe the browser can remember what my favorite font color is. But if I'm looking at my workbox in Metro, what was the last view I was looking at? What if, for example, I'm a time-oriented person and I want to manage time? I should be able to go into Metro and see time views all the time.

If I'm a project person, I want to see project views. But Metro in that way, and the Web overall, will just not remember those state variables. It just has the views that it has. But if you can remember state, you can remember where you can go and what you can do. You can customize the interactivity. So we find that lack of interactivity and statelessness are a few of the main challenges today.

Making the Web Remember to be More Interactive

IRC: So in what directions is Action moving to address those two problems—interactivity and state memory?

Rodrigo: Well, there are only a few things you can do. Shockwave was one aspect of that. In the Metro project, one of the things we did is to let the user get a very rich interaction. And you can get a lot of information that is changing based on the state of where you are in the workflow or where you want to go next. This interaction occurs in very little real estate without the high cost of having to download three or four pages.

So in a very compressed time, with compact real estate, and dense click experience, if you will, we give people a lot of information and a lot of navigational tools. Shockwave certainly drives that. We will probably be doing that with Java also, maybe JavaScript, but certainly Java.

Another aspect to our approach to the state problem is going to be our development of what I'm calling Membership services, so that in some way when you log onto Metro via the Web, it remembers things about you that are particular to you as a member of the application. Other people are talking about directory services right now—ways to find things on the Web like the Yellow Pages and White Pages. But I think membership services are going to be one of the hottest areas of growth on the Web.

We want to remember a lot about our customers and our users. And not just like what they wear but what they've spent with us. And maybe customize what we offer them next in a commercial selling environment. Or in a views setting, we want to know where they were last—especially given the fact that a lot of people come in from modems.

IRC: They don't have the time to hunt.

Rodrigo: That's right. I don't know if some of that will be done in the client. You see that Netscape Navigator 3, for example, has a new feature so that if you are downloading a file and you lose your connection, it will resume the download where it left off. This is very important. So that is what I mean by remembering. In this case it is easy for Netscape, because they are right in the front of the client. It is a little harder for those of us who live on the server side.

Action's Shockwave Solution In Detail

IRC: Focusing on Shockwave, what did Shockwave specifically offer as solutions to those problems?

Rodrigo: I'm not a graphic designer or anything. But remember, even before we hired you [InfraRed—auth], the question really was that certainly we wanted animation capabilities because that's kind of fun. Right? And believe it or not, fun was a part of the design position. We wanted to do something that was fun and interesting and eye-grabbing. So then Shockwave rose to the top.

But fun was not the only reason because you can make fun by putting the Joke of the Day, too. So, the next aspect of it is the amount of navigational information we wanted to present to the user but in a friendly and intuitive way. That's where the idea was when we started working on it. We spent a lot of time working on the metaphor for Metro.

AUTHORS' NOTE

Rodrigo is not kidding. The Metro metaphor took us a long time and many versions to develop. Action's goal for Metro was to communicate a sense of connectedness, of people working together, of simplicity and confidence in the workflow, and fun. Our job as Shockwave developer was to try to interpret these communication goals and translate them into a metaphor that worked transparently as a user interface.

Because the product is named Metro, we first tried a Metropolis metaphor made out of skyscrapers with subdepartments in each building. But this was entirely too literal to be fun—the last thing people in office buildings need is a constant reminder that they are in an office building. We didn't even show our tests to the team at Action.

We then tried the Metro train metaphor and developed a proof of concept. Figure 18.5 shows an early draft of the Metro Center Station. It became clear right away that the Metro train metaphor had the potential to embody the project goals, and was particularly good at representing the flow of information and easy navigation.

In this version of the Center Station movie (METR_OLD.DIR located in the Chapter 18 folder of the accompanying CD) the train itself was a movable navigation bar. Each car was essentially a button representing the different departments you could navigate to. When you clicked on a given department, the car door opens and an image appears in the background symbolic of the department in question. Or, instead of clicking the cars, you could click on the map of the Metro system at the top. Also just for fun, the whole train could be dragged back and forth like a little toy.

A majority of this specific implementation was dropped in later drafts. Together with Action, we concluded that the moving train was a distraction and that having each car represent a different destination was a mixed metaphor (because that's not how trains work). We also threw out the map on top and decided that having a representative image for each department was too arbitrary, and so on. We raise these details to illustrate just how much trial and error is involved in building an application's user interface around a novel metaphor. Flexibility and experimentation were key to the process.

Rodrigo: Incidentally, I think metaphor design is another hot job of the next ten years. Because as people begin to use Shockwave, and VRML and blah-blah, really the design of metaphors and the carrying out of good metaphors is going be hot. Because they're not real environments, they are virtual. Whatever you design is not going to be real. If you put a cup on my screen, it's not a real cup. It's a metaphor for a cup. Metaphor designers—people who come up with good metaphors that are intuitive and that people can navigate with—are going to be valuable.

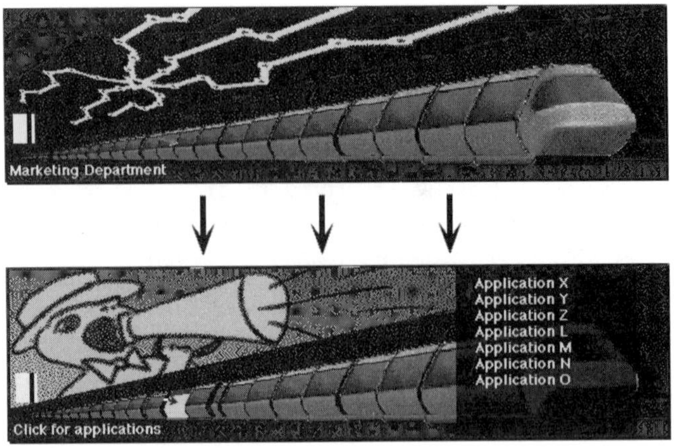

FIGURE 18.5

Early drafts of the Metro train proved that the overall metaphor could work well. The image of this draft shows how clicking on a train car pulls up a background image and the submenu. This specific implementation of the interactivity was reworked entirely in later versions.

As people begin to use Shockwave, the design of metaphors and the carrying out of good metaphors is going to be hot. Metaphor designers—people who come up with good metaphors that are intuitive and that people can navigate with—are going to be valuable.

So Shockwave was a way to explore this. Could we have done it with something else? When we started calling around, we asked ourselves, "Could we do it with Java today?" Well yeah, sort of. But it is too expensive, too difficult. At this moment, Java's really not appropriate to explore this kind of thing. It may be sometime, but it's not right now.

The third thing, and it's mainly a minor thing but it concerns me, is the compact real estate. The fact is, right now you can get some interactivity on the Web but it requires you to click… page and click… page forever. You are essentially in click hell. You are navigating through page and page after more pages to get what you want. When, in fact, what was really needed was to have those choices available in a very small real estate. And that's the other thing that Shockwave did.

IRC: Can you please elaborate on how you apply the term "real estate" in this context?

Rodrigo: For me, real estate is the page. Real estate is the X,Y coordinate. And that's tied to time dimension because loading a page is a very expensive operation. While loading a Shockwave applet can be rather slow sometimes, the fact is if you are smart and you put in a lot of interactivity, it can save your user a lot of loading back and forth of pages.

Loading pages is an expensive operation on the Web because you've got to unload a page. There is a unload cost. So you load, then unload a page. The thing has to go get the new tags and you have to get the new graphics. And graphic designers have gone wild on the Web. And all of this just so you can get what? One more choice? It's very limited.

So time compression is very important to me. Maximizing the amount of information in the package. Now, you put it all together. You have metaphors, small real estate; you have interactivity. You can therefore compress a tremendous amount of information in a way that is friendly, fun, easy for you to digest. Hell, it's really easy and powerful.

The Shocking Part of Metro

Rodrigo: For example, the man we put at the end of the Metro movie lets you have some idea about what the process is. It doesn't make you an expert on it, but you now know something about it. And you didn't have to read "Reengineering the Corporation" and subscribe to the *Harvard Business Review* to understand what the process was and why it was important. You understand that when you submit a form, the Metro Porter takes it from you and he takes care of it. You now know something more. You can take more ownership of the process. (See figure 18.7 later in this chapter to see the Metro Porter character.)

We presented the shocked version of Metro at AIIM [Association for Information and Image Management] and gave public demos and people liked it. AIIM is the largest industry event for document imaging and document management. [AIIM is the place to be for vendors of workflow systems.—auth] There were people there talking about imaging and rasterization and they were talking about TIFF files and document management and corporate standards. And then I have my little guy come out and say his things and it was really a breath of fresh air.

Using Shockwave to Instill Confidence

We'll step away from the interview again to take another look at Metro. One of the design goals in the shocking of Metro was to instill confidence in users when they initiate a work process. Too often, after submitting forms in HTML, you get a static screen with some canned message like "Your form has been received." When you submit a form in the unshocked version of Metro, it acknowledges receipt with the page shown in figure 18.6.

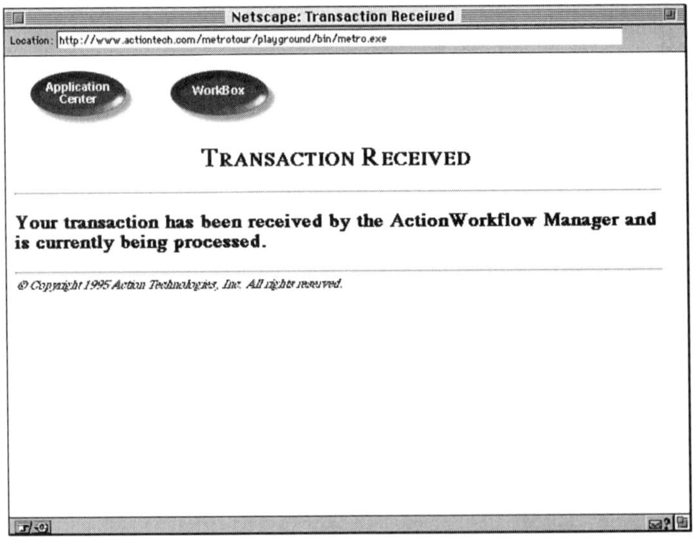

FIGURE 18.6

After you submit a form, you receive this confirmation page in the unshocked version of Metro.

Action Tech wanted to use Shockwave so that Metro would instill more confidence that your form is being handled properly, as opposed to just lost in the vast, heartless abyss of the network. Animation is an excellent way to illustrate and confirm such a process. Figure 18.7 shows the porter character we created. When you submit work, the porter comes out of the metro and takes it from you, confirming that he will deliver the information to the proper place. The porter cares; he is responsible and reassuring.

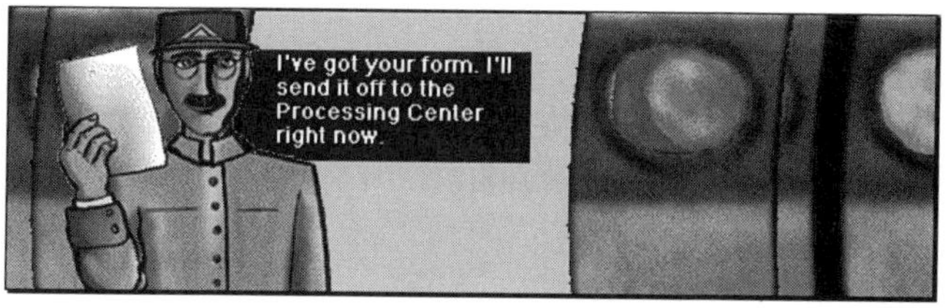

FIGURE 18.7

In the shocked version of Metro, submitting a form brings you to the confirmation movie. The porter acknowledges receipt of your forms and assures delivery.

Even though he is not real, for some reason it is easier to entrust your work to the responsibility of an animated character like the Metro Porter. The immersive nature of Shockwave allowed Action Tech to confer the character of confidence, trustworthiness, and professionalism into Metro with animated cartoons. Using an anthropomorphic user interface quite literally put a more human face on the work process.

A demo version of the Metro Confirmation movie, METR_CON.DIR, can be found in the Chapter 18 folder on the accompanying CD.

Choosing Shockwave for Speedy Development

IRC: What criteria were you weighing when you chose between technologies to deliver the interactive part of it?

Rodrigo: As I said, we didn't really look for too many other technologies, though I certainly assume that there were other things. But for me the more important thing was whether it had a certain ubiquity, whether it supported some number of platforms. If it was Windows alone, it was not enough. Believe it or not, a lot of people are doing animation plug-ins, but they are not doing it for a sufficient number of platforms.

And there was speed. Shockwave was there. Nobody else was there at that particular moment. We could've waited. But there were two other agendas hidden underneath. One was to get it done quickly, so obviously we would get the splash, the PR benefit, and the uniqueness for being first.

The other issue was learning, like the Japanese companies do with consumer goods. They don't know if it is going to be successful but they know that if they don't attempt the first version of the stereo toilet bowl cleaner, they will never know if that combination works or what the problems are with it.

It is a long road to being a great metaphor designer, to being a great interaction designer, or making it fun and making it easy. It's a long road. I don't think it's a flash of genius kind of thing. It's more of a constant process that you throw yourself into. And since it's a long road, let's get started quickly.

Learning from Experience

IRC: In starting down that long road, what did the prototype Shockwave experience enable you to learn?

Rodrigo: We learned that if you make it fun, people like it. But we knew that already. We learned something about the complexity and the cost of bringing this stuff to life. It's not a trivial thing.

It is going to be interesting. I don't think that we are even at the very beginning of what people are going to do. It has not even begun. Action has taken the very first step in exploring something that I'm guessing will be extremely important.

So what we learned is that we are at the very beginning of the process. We don't really have good language with which to talk about these issues yet. And we learned that the skill sets that we need to produce these kinds of interfaces are much larger than most people think. Advertising agencies have no idea. They couldn't even hold a conversation that makes sense about this. A lot of people think the Internet is "old hat," but they don't even realize this is something that we are still going to be dealing with 20 years from now.

Is it important to learn? Well yeah, I think so. It's good to be well grounded on those things. You could have the conversation because you read *WIRED*, or you can have the conversation because you've done it. And we learned by doing it.

Working with Bandwidth Constraints and State Memory in Shockwave

IRC: The Metro project brought us to the boundaries of what Shockwave can do. Can you describe some of the key limitations encountered?

Rodrigo: There are a few things. Bandwidth is going to be a design constraint in the way that two-, three-, or four-color presses are for graphic designers in print media. Bandwidth is a constraint. But you can view this constraint like it's black-and-white photography. Black and white is a constraint right? But yet you can make great art with it. Now I'm not saying we're making art here, but bandwidth design for 28.8k modems requires a certain art. Maybe in a few years we will design for ISDN speeds, but bandwidth will always be a constraint.

Right now, our basic human media types (which kind of begin and end with television) can consume more bandwidth than anyone can deliver to us in the next three to four years or longer. Certainly for the mainstream, it will be even longer. We are going to be talking about bandwidth issues when we turn the century. Designing around bandwidth means talking with people who know and understand it, have the appreciation, and are still able to do great stuff.

In a way it's like the *I Love Lucy Show*. Look at all the constraints. It was black and white with no retakes and no *Terminator* effects. They didn't even have multimedia, but it's still funny. Bandwidth is part of the medium, and we have to work with it. It's not something that most people really understand. And even when they talk about it, they don't talk about it with love. You don't see the black-and-white photographer hating that constraint, but the bandwidth constraint is here for a while. [So learn to love it.—auth.]

Bandwidth is a constraint. But you can view this constraint like it's black-and-white photography. Black and white is a constraint, right? But yet you can make great art with it.

The second constraint is the state thing. It would be nice to have the Shockwave movies remember things, or know something about where it is or who is using it. We tried to do that. But it's not what I call production ready. There is a lot more we could've done, but for that we would've needed a larger project. This means letting Shockwave movies access different class libraries and different back-end scripts and it's a problem.

In the case of the little man. Right now, when the little man is telling you the confirmation message, we have it hard-coded with the same message for every application and for every state, which is fine. But that state information is available online in real-time. There is no reason why that little man couldn't be engaged in a dialog that reflects the state of the process in real-time to confirm what's going on up to the second. But for that, a lot more integration is needed than we were willing to do and more, I think, than the environment can handle with aplomb at least for the next several months. We'll see. Maybe there are things to revisit as the capabilities change.

AUTHORS' NOTE

At the time of the Shockwave prototyping on Metro, this rather troublesome limitation of statelessness became very important. At that time, the only way to pass a variable or parameter into the Shockwave movie was with an external text file. The text file can be changed and read in, but this is still stateless in that it gives the same behavior for all users at all times.

For Metro, this meant that the porter, who confirms the submission of forms, could only give a single stock confirmation for every type of interaction. This was unfortunate indeed because the server side knows exact details on each transaction and could easily be programmed to pass that data into the Shockwave movie for a far more convincing and specific confirmation.

If every time you hand your assistant a task and they reply with an identical "Thank you, sir, may I have another?" you begin to wonder if they are completely brain-dead. Because of the lack of parameters in Shockwave, the porter only responded with a rather monotonous "Thank you for your request. I will handle it right away." A smarter-seeming agent will echo your request more exactly, like "Yes, I will deliver your request for proposal to the IS Department with a return receipt."

Now in Shockwave for Director 5, parameters can be passed into the movie using the <embed> tag. Figure 18.8 shows the same confirmation movie, but parameterized to give a specific response each time. The porter's words can be passed into the movie by a front-end or back-end script. It can even show a different animation of the work flowing through the Metro system depending upon which work process is being confirmed. It is much smarter and reassuring.

This is demonstrated in the file METR_PAR.HTM, which can be found in the Chapter 18 folder on the accompanying CD. Just open it in Netscape with the Shockwave for Director 5 plug-in installed. Type your name and type what you want for Christmas, click on Submit, and then watch the nice Metro Porter promise to ask Santa to bring you whatever you asked for.

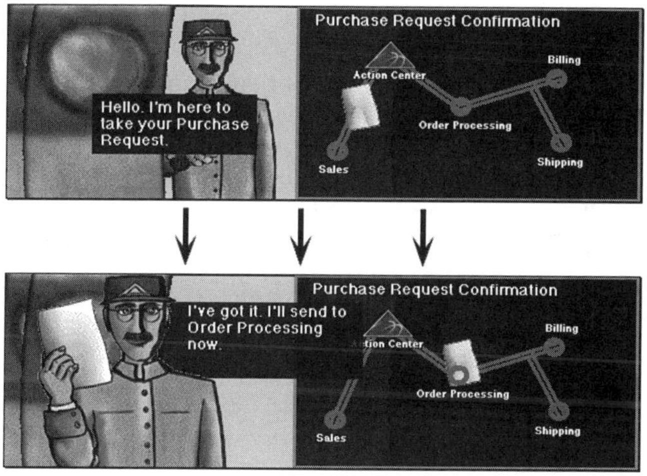

FIGURE 18.8

This is the same confirmation movie as in figure 18.7, but it has parameters that make it smart. The Porter says a specific message, confirming the exact workflow process that you are initiating instead of a 'one-size-fits-all' confirmation.

State Memory and Contextualizing Information

IRC: Now can you describe what value that state information adds?

Rodrigo: Well, this goes beyond Shockwave, but we are living in a world where we are overwhelmed with information. And there is more coming. Just look around my office or yours. Information is everywhere. We have all grown up in a world where the more information you have, the better. And our capabilities of handling information are rather limited. We can read, and so on, and I may be going overboard, but I think the new information technology may lead to the evolution of a new human species.

This idea started with my children. Most people say children don't have any attention span. I think this might be an excellent talent in a world that is overwhelmed with information. The ability to not pay attention. The ability to just filter and get to the essence and move on. The ability to have your information message get to you in micro seconds. We kind of laugh at it. But the days are over where you sit and read your James Joyce book for five weeks. It just doesn't work in our world.

It's very important as we design our work and life environment so that you get down to just the basics—extremely efficient information. And one class of information that is a pain in the neck now and that we spend a lot of time chasing around is status information on our projects and where things are. For example, there is a whole class of meetings that is nothing but status ratings.

You know where you are, but you have to report to others so they know where you are as well. Project management is all about who has it, where is it, what state is it in, is it complete, where are the breakdowns, what are the problems, what is current, what is behind, and so forth. And so there is going to be a need for an action management design—personal action management design.

Personal Action Management

IRC: What do you mean by this concept of Personal Action Management?

Rodrigo: We've seen PIMs (personal information managers), but now we need to talk about PAMs (personal action managers). Look, there's a lot of information out there. Let's get it down to the core things I need to do. I already know what project this is because I started it. Just tell me where it is. I don't need information on what this project is all about. I already know what the project is about because we had the meeting three months ago. But what are we doing with this? What are the problems? In other words, filter it and bring it down to me as relevant questions and information on what I need to do or what I can do.

That is the problem of the personal information manager today. It never has any context. People are fundamentally action beasties. Everything we do is related to what we are going to do next. So the whole reason we need information is to plan for future actions.

The problem is when we get overwhelmed with information. It becomes completely decontextualized from the actions we want to take in the future. We plan based on the commitments that we have made and the problems—for example, commitments—we have broken. So when you have to read through a whole bunch of stuff that has no relevance to you—or you don't know if it has relevance—to get the information you need, you have to recontextualize it to what is going on in your life. Replan your day, week, month, or whatever and then proceed to take action on a number of different fronts given the new context.

Because this is how we handle information, state management, and tracking state, status of actions and commitments then becomes a really great service. So you don't have to do all that reprocessing every time. The state machine or the agent machine ought to know all those things for you and immediately contextualize so you don't have to do all the searching and foot work. You may want to read through all that anyway, but you shouldn't have to.

Profuse Information

IRC: Sometimes it seems the Web is all about wading through information. So a focus of ours is the idea of creating sites with immersivity and powerful resources that draw you in based on how useful they are and how accurately they reflect your agenda, your problems. And how they can get you speedily to the answer.

Rodrigo: Right. The bottom line is that the Web is going to create a huge problem of way too much information. We have all been trained to never say that information is bad. I've never heard it said. Have you ever said that? That information is bad?

IRC: Actually I've said the worst heresy of all. I've said sometimes I hate the Internet! Because it is just too big, too much stuff. It's really a love-hate thing.

Rodrigo: Well, but it's there and now we design around it. It's a constraint. It's our black-and-white picture. The point is the information is out there.

Most people say children don't have any attention span. I think this might be an excellent talent in a world that is overwhelmed with information. The ability to just filter and get to the essence and move on.

Some say that it's worthwhile if we make the search engines better. Well, the search engines can be made to search better, but they can't contextualize it within the concerns that you have. Those search engines will never be able to know that you made a date with two women in one evening—not me because I'm married, but maybe you. This is a big problem and all the searching on the Internet won't solve this problem.

So it's the contextualization, number one, making the search applicable to your concerns. And then being able to act to resolve the world around those concerns. In other words, I've got to change this meeting here. I have to cancel here, reschedule this, set time for this here, all of that. All of that is going to require some system. And that's what we hope Metro does.

And that is why with Shockwave and interactivity, time is premium and compression is premium. It's funny because we can all make twice as much money tomorrow, but we will still have the same amount of time.

IRC: Don't I know it. Time is notoriously not scaleable.

Preliminary Results and Lessons from Shocking Metro

IRC: Now, has the Shocking of Metro made a measurable impact? Is there more interest, more sales, more usefulness, better feedback?

Rodrigo: We certainly have gotten somewhat more interest. In terms of sales, it is kind of hard to measure that. It's one of those things we have yet to see. But it has brought more interest. It certainly gives us a better demo. And in our industry, the demo is half the battle, or the whole battle for some people.

I don't know whether we have achieved all of our goals. It's not a question we can answer until we have half a million people using our stuff and then we will be able to know something. Right now we don't have enough people using this stuff yet to know one way or another. It may turn out to be that people get sick and tired of that little train and the little man. I don't know. But I'm hopeful.

System Integration and Hidden Costs

IRC: A little bit on system integration. Do your clients' IS departments resist the Shockwave part of Metro because then they have to support not only Netscape, but Shockwave as well?

Rodrigo: Well, that is a concern. That's a problem.

IRC: How do you think Macromedia could change Shockwave? Or could Netscape change?

Rodrigo: It would be great if they could bundle Shockwave in with Netscape so it will already be plugged in when you install it. A big problem with Shockwave is the fact that it is not ubiquitous—even though it is free and it is getting there. It means that when you design your pages, you have to do the Shockwave edition and the unshocked edition.

So Shockwave has its negative aspects. Yet this is not Shockwave-specific. Any plug-in, including Java it should be said, that is not ubiquitous, meaning there all the time, is a problem. You have to ask people to go and install it and do it.

This problem is compounded when the technology is not available for all platforms. So then you are forced into designing what we call parallel universes. In fact, we have that problem with Metro. We have to provide a Shockwave version or a non-Shockwave version. So it almost can double your workload.

I believe right now for people implementing Shockwave, and so forth, there is still a hidden price there. And if they knew better, it might not be something people would consider to begin with. So then if you are using it for decoration for your home page, twice the work only means two pages.

But, when you design applications, it's not quite the same issue. Twice the registration, twice the installation, twice the pages, documentation, and so forth. It actually turns out to be quite a bit of work.

The Universality Problem

IRC: Are there any other features or capabilities you would like to see in Shockwave?

Rodrigo: Right now, the biggest problem for me is that universality. It has got to be everywhere. For Shockwave or any similar technology to succeed, it's got to be ubiquitous. Free is good; downloadable is good. It's better than not free, better than not downloadable. But still it puts a crimp on my experience if I have to go to the Shockwave site to download and install.

It would also be easier if Macromedia would allow people to host their own Shockwave plug-in site because right now I have to send my users to the Macromedia site to get it. This throws my users off the experience. It aggravates the whole problem of the Internet where you are trying to get someplace and you get diverted through a whole other zone. It's the equivalent of going to work via a Las Vegas casino. That place is designed to draw attention to ten other things and if you need to get to work, it is not a good thing. Macromedia needs Shockwave ubiquity more than they need people looking at their Web pages.

Challenges in Developing True Applications in Shockwave

IRC: Developing Shockwave applications can be more like true software development, where the Shockwave is more like a client than a piece of pretty art. What problems does that generate?

Rodrigo: Well, maintenance is a problem when you have parallel universes. Right now, Shockwave applets don't know much except to load themselves. For example, this time I want to load this file, but next time I want to load that file. But right now you can't feed Shockwave that parameter. Since the file always has the same name, you have to go back to parallel universes.

I don't think that stuff is really ready for prime time as a development environment for creating applications. I think it has a potential. I think clever people doing a lot of work can make really cool stuff with it. But for the average Joe, it's not a trivial thing.

Bandwidth is another problem that could have interesting solutions. Like dynamic bandwidth allocation, for example. In an intranet like ours at Action Technologies, bandwidth is not a big issue. Then having a version of the applet that is much higher bandwidth and much better color and a lot more friendly is absolutely awesome. Having a lower-bandwidth version and having the appropriate one dynamically load would be interesting. Or having Director produce two versions if you want to—a low-bandwidth and a high-bandwidth.

Using Shockwave to Design Information Spaces

IRC: Finally, have you seen Shockwave used as a solution to other interesting design challenges?

Rodrigo: I've seen lots. But I don't think anybody is trying to do what we are trying to do. I'm not sure why. It's scary and kind of surprising.

But training is certainly a big opportunity on intranets, especially with Shockwave for Authorware. It's an interesting way to deliver training on demand. There are so many different classes of training programs. Large corporations have a very large informationscape that it is very difficult to navigate. So having that kind of thing to navigate through corporate departments, employee orientation and benefits, your HR employee manuals, and so on.

Training is certainly a big opportunity on intranets, especially with Shockwave for Authorware. It's an interesting way to deliver training on demand.

Certainly I can see making a lot of sites more fun and a little more reactive. I think it goes back to this: any application can benefit from Shockwave if you need a very strong metaphor. We have a metaphor now that people think is dominant called the desktop. You have folders and trash cans. Think about it. It has taken 10 years to get to that metaphor on a majority of PCs. Think about pull-down menus and bitmapped icons. It is a whole visual language and objects that we manipulate on a day-to-day basis.

But the desktop metaphor is not appropriate to every application. They are not suited to the purposes of a large variety of applications. They are not appropriate for newspapers, magazines, and many others. People will have to develop new metaphors. And Shockwave, and Director in general, is a great metaphor development environment.

And then maybe later on, once you have created the coolest metaphor, you can do the C++ version because it's portable; it's DLL; it's OLEd. But where are you going to discover metaphors? Investigate them? Research them? I think it's in Shockwave or that kind of environment.

Navigating large internal corporate informationscapes is a major application for design of immersive metaphors. We are seeing people doing VRML virtual reality stuff. And it's very primitive right now. It just an idea, a playful thing. But just the idea that some bank out there is trying to put the lobby of the bank in a virtual environment is interesting as a direction. I'm sure there are other reasons, like they want to be cool and with-it and all that stuff. But there is another aspect of it.

In a world that is overwhelmed with so much reading information, spatial information provides a very rich, very easy kind of interface. We know how to move forward and sideways, to look up and down. So you don't have to train people to do that; they already know it. You can use that pre-knowledge to design the information space or the navigation space. And that's what you are going to need tools like Shockwave for.

Conclusion

The Web is changing the way people work together. Work coordination products like Metro provide powerful tools for synergizing work in complex organizations. Shockwave contributed to Metro's attractiveness, friendliness, and immersion. But more than that, Shockwave showed multimedia's great promise for simplifying coordination and navigation in the swelling complexity of the Web infoscape.

It was exciting to play a role in the prototyping process with Metro, to see how far we could push Shockwave. And in the process, we confirmed that an immersive multimedia interface with a good metaphor could elevate the total effectiveness of a Web-delivered software application. Importantly, Shockwave enabled us to rapidly develop this in a standard platform, at a relatively low cost, and with a small footprint.

The lesson we draw from this experience, and from Rodrigo's comments, is that one must take Shockwave very seriously as a development and prototyping environment for immersive multimedia user interfaces for the Web. To which we would should add that, with many of its key limitations resolved in Shockwave for Director 5, it should prove a more robust delivery platform as well.

We conclude, as Rodrigo does, that we are only at the beginning of a process of reinventing the user interface on the Web. Shockwave is an extremely profound instrument in this reinvention.

Chapter 19

Creating Identity: Organic Online

This chapter covers the basic issues of how the Web is used to create identity. The content is taken from a discussion we had with Tom Wang, a Strategic Planner with Organic Online, Inc.

Our discussion covered the following issues:

- *Communication on the Web*
- *Multimedia and Web commerce*
- *The Internet multimedia technology platform*
- *Shockwave today*
- *The future of Shockwave*

AUTHORS' NOTE

Where does this fit into the Big Picture?

In this chapter we discuss issues that are basic to all levels of interactive power of Shockwave on the Web. In the near-term, this chapter has the greatest relevance for Shockwave solutions in the categories Simply Shocked, Enhanced Interface, and True Multimedia. (See figure 2.1 in Chapter 2, "Power on the Web.") General issues discussed about creating identity on the Web and doing innovative marketing on the Web apply to most any current use of Shockwave as well as the Shockwave solutions of the future.

Organic Online

Organic Online is a full-service Web development company. From conceptualization to realization and refinement, Organic has been providing innovative and solid Web service to some very big clients since 1993. Figure 19.1 shows Organic Online's home page.

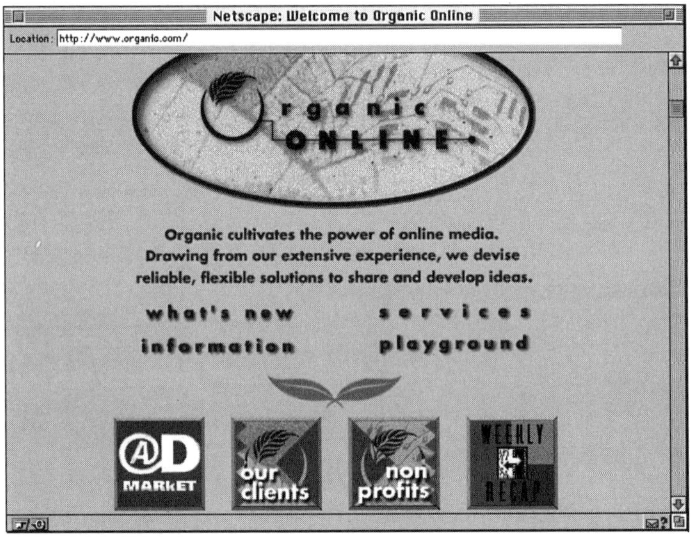

FIGURE 19.1

You can visit Organic Online's website at http://www.organic.com/.

In our experience collaborating with Organic, we have found their staff and management to be super smart. Also of note, the CEO of Organic Online is Johnathan Nelson, a long-standing industry trendsetter. In addition to offering top Web design services, Organic Online embodies substantial expertise in Web marketing and leadership in Web strategy and technology. You can check them out at `http://www.organic.com/`.

The Interview

To get the lowdown on current trends in Web multimedia and marketing, we talked with Tom Wang, Strategic Planner at Organic Online. Tom's focus is on content strategies and new media publishing models for Organic. Tom's job is to amass a knowledge base on industry trends, interactive communications, and Net technology.

Tom uses this knowledge to advise Organic's clients and help them develop their plans for success on the Web. His years of work with Organic's clients provide him with a very realistic perspective on corporate information and communication goals on the Web. From his vantage point, we can see how emerging technologies such as Shockwave can facilitate those communication goals.

Creating Identity on the Web

Engaging in Shockwave production is a significant decision because the resources needed and the market ramifications are considerable. We really appreciated Tom's comments because he explains some terms that are used in the Internet marketing community, the way that Organic's thinks about the Web, and what their clients have learned from their efforts on the Web.

Creating identity means creating several important distinctions. It means distinguishing a target audience and its frame of mind; identifying the tasks in reaching them; identifying how using different technologies distinguishes you from others; allowing the different parts of your organization to be differentiated and reflecting that on the Web; identifying the information you want your audience to see; and distinguishing one's organization as a player in cutting-edge technology. These are some key distinctions that Tom touches on in our discussion.

Communication on the Web

The recurring theme in Tom's discussion is about the business of using the Web to establish identity. Understanding some basic trends in Web communication gives us important context to know how best to use Shockwave, address problematic issues around Shockwave, and position Shockwave content successfully. Knowing how and where to push the curve using Shockwave is related to the basic question of identity.

Business Goals

InfraRed Communications: Tom, what are some of the business goals driving the Web strategies for Organic's clients?

Tom Wang: Most of the clients who are working with Organic now are in an experimental phase. Some more experimental than others. Their objectives vary depending on how intrinsic information is to their business.

Some clients are looking to simply promote themselves. Some clients are trying to lend brand equity to their corporation. Some are trying to provide investor relations information. Some are trying to provide information services.

It's quite a wide range and each objective is unique. If there is a common thread linking Organic's clients, it is that a lot of them already have a cult around their brand.

IRC: Are your clients creating "more cutting-edge applications" using advanced or experimental methods? What are they trying to achieve?

Tom: Some clients are trying to do what is the equivalent of a single-sponsor magazine around their brand, where they seek an audience with a certain psychographic. The Web tends to be good for attracting psychographics.

Psychographics and Relationship Marketing

IRC: What do you mean by psychographics?

Tom: Whereas demographics are things such as age, area code, race, income, and so on, psychographics are states of mind. In some ways people who watch *Seinfeld* are a certain psychographic. They might also be common to a demographic. But there is a certain type of person you all know who watches *Seinfeld* or watches *The Simpsons* and is attracted to the whole world around that.

Psychographics are a frame of mind. Hypothetically, genX [generation X, auth.] is both a demographic and psychographic, though that's a stretch. But in terms of the single-sponsor magazine metaphor, when our clients target an audience, it is a psychographic audience for the most part. They say, "Let's present a 'zine or magazine, whether it's corporate or non-corporate, targeted at a particular audience and have our logo or our brand sponsor it."

Some of the other cutting-edge marketing techniques are relationship marketing, which means building a world for your customer to live in. It's a whole world so that when I buy a widget, not only do a buy that widget, but I buy into everything about the widget. I want to meet other people who buy this widget. I even want to wear a T-shirt that reads, "I buy Widgets."

IRC: Right. And you want to spend time at www.widget.com playing widget games…

Tom: Exactly. Right. That could be an aspect of relationship marketing, too. Relationship marketing is a broader thing. It is a means of forming a dialogue with your customer so you can improve based on their input and not just nod your head but really listen to what they are saying and providing and then alter what you do accordingly.

IRC: How do cutting-edge Web applications help with those marketing strategies?

Tom: Well, the Web is about communications and openness and connecting people together, and if you can facilitate that, you foster this relationship marketing quite well.

Site Segmenting

IRC: Can you get a global sense of how the Web is facilitating or changing the corporate strategies of the companies that are using the Web?

Tom: I think that the Web is often an impetus for companies to reevaluate their communications strategy as a whole. If a company can say whatever it wants to the world, what does it say? That is a tough question.

With a television commercial you have certain issues, but very rarely do you have the unlimited capacity of the Web to provide lots of information. The secret of a bore is to tell everything—and you don't want to be a bore. So what do you tell? That's an interesting challenge for companies.

I have found in speaking with a lot of these companies that it is an impetus for them to reevaluate their communication strategy and company organization as whole. If I am going to create an information architecture and divide it up into five major parts of my company, what are the five major parts of my company? Sometimes it's a horse before the cart, but that is when it gets really exciting and interesting for companies. And you learn a lot about companies through that process.

The Web is often an impetus for companies to reevaluate their communications strategy as a whole. If a company can say whatever it wants to the world, what does it say? That is a tough question.

IRC: So how does this reevaluation usually affect companies' Web strategies?

Tom: Usually it's segmentation. Most companies have a corporate site that serves certain purposes and then they start segmenting. They say, "This part of my business does this; this part of my business does that." They decentralize control.

If my company makes widgets and wagits, is it important that the widgets and wagits have the same look and feel? No, not really. Widgets are for young people and wagits are for old people. So, they decentralize and segment.

Audience Targeting

IRC: So where does the interactive multimedia fit into that? How does the Web help differentiate the audience?

Tom: Well, it's a demand-driven medium. I choose to go here; I choose to go here; I choose to go there. It's a narrowcast rather than a broadcast medium. When I turn on my TV channel, if I turn it on a certain time of the day, I might catch a certain type of message depending on the audience for that show. But with the Web, you ask them, "Are you 20 or are you 30? If you are 20, we are going to give you something for 20-year-olds, and if you are 30, you get something else."

That's why the Web is well suited for psychographics. The Web can ask you, "Are you feeling surly? Are you feeling like you want to waste some time? Or do you want to get some information? Are you shopping for a car? Or do you want to just read a magazine?" That's why interactive multimedia is crucial for narrowcasting.

Web Multimedia and Commerce

IRC: And what about those who are actually trying to sell services directly on the Web?

Tom: You mean trying to get people to spend money on the Web?

IRC: Yeah, spending money on the Web, or even more narrowly, those who are selling information that can only be delivered on the Web?

Tom: Those are two distinct questions. I wouldn't call it selling information. I call it exchanging information. You give us this information and we give you something. You give us your name, your e-mail address, and in exchange we send you postings about something that you are interested in.

Also, information exchange is key to how privacy will work in the future on the Web. You only get as much information as you want and if you don't give your information, then you might not get the full array of services. It is a sort of "give them Venice, but make them pay for Rome" mentality, where you show them something valuable and then you say, "Give me a little information, and I'll show you the Colosseum."

The Web Experience and Direct Commerce

IRC: How about direct commerce on the Web?

Tom: Direct commerce is a tough nut to crack. It's still in the developmental stage. I think the problems are less about security issues and more about marketing. I know that I tell my Master Card over the phone and I send it in the mail and I have it in my wallet lying in my room. Security is an issue, and it's a real issue. There is a lot that needs to be worked out like all the difficulties with encryption, et cetera. But getting people to buy stuff on the Web is a more profound problem.

I think one of the more interesting trends in marketing is experience buying. The closest analogy in the real world is Niketown in Chicago. It's this huge monster museum dedicated to athletes. It's an unbelievable experience. You walk through and when you buy something from Niketown, [it's] not so much that you went in to buy a shoe or a T-shirt, but the purchase is more like a souvenir of your experience.

Madonna is another example of that. Are you buying music when you buy Madonna's music? Well, sort of. You are also buying a souvenir of watching her video and reading about her and all of the whole media event.

I think that is an interesting part of commerce. The things that have been successful on the Web to this point have been things like Virtual Vineyards, which is a boutique-like environment. Otherwise its tough. You have got to offer something really valuable. Value could be a significantly lower price or more selection. Other than that, it's tough for direct commerce on the Web.

IRC: In providing the kind of experience on the Web that you describe, is rich media content becoming an important part of that?

Tom: Sure. That's what I'm getting at. I use Niketown as an example in the real world, but in the virtual world the potential is really unbelievable. VRML [Virtual Reality Modeling Language], for example, is particularly strong as an experience. Experiences that are immersive, most importantly, can mimic the Niketown mentality.

IRC: What are the type of design and technical challenges you face, even the marketing challenges you face in selling this concept to your clients? Is this something they are dragging out of you or are you trying to show them the way?

Tom: You mean for sales on the Web? We haven't been pushing that hard. As I said, the Web is still early. A lot of people are just grappling with the concept that they are on the Web at all. We haven't been pushing that hard. It's a viable and interesting opportunity for them, but it is also a turf war to some degree.

For example, if I am a coffee manufacturer entering the Web, do I let my catalog company handle the online catalog or is it going to be my advertising agency? Or is it going to be my Web server organization? It's a turf war between people to decide who gets the Web responsibility. It gets complicated.

IRC: So how are these turf issues being resolved in the industry?

Tom: T.B.A.—it hasn't been worked out. It is too early in the industry to tell.

The Technology Platform

IRC: Has Organic been toying around with Java or Shockwave or other technologies for delivering rich interactions? And why?

Tom: Yes, we are. Now, why are we exploring new technologies? Now I'm going to get philosophical. Technology is inherently political. When I send an e-mail message and I cc: someone else, that sends a message. When I choose to publish a Web page using a certain type of HTML tag that is not compliant across certain browsers, then that sends a message. Same with new technologies.

To beat a dead horse, the medium is the message. What you do with the medium affects the message you send. It's a reality. Just the very fact that you use Java or Shockwave for a particular effect, or if you implement VRML, sends a message above and beyond how you might implement it. I don't mean to pooh pooh how you implement it, and that is extremely important. But it is also significant that you are using these new technologies—that is a message in and of itself.

The trick is to avoid using these technologies gratuitously.

IRC: Can you discuss what would be a gratuitous versus a non-gratuitous use of rich media?

Tom: I'll give a positive gratuitous first. Gratuitous is not always bad. If I am about to launch a site in a month and the site is not yet up, I might put up a really interesting and evocative Java applet or a unique Shockwave application as a coming attraction. Is that gratuitous? Yes, but does it help? Can it be effective? Sure.

An example of a poor application of a technology would be something that disorients users, something that doesn't really take into account the audience and the objectives of what you are trying to do. If you are a large corporation trying to reach a broad audience and a majority of your site cannot be viewed by them, then you are pushing the technology curve in the wrong direction. You have made a mistake. And you have done something gratuitous to please your upper management and not something to please your consumers and your audience. It offends the audience and it offends me.

Positioning New Technology

IRC: How do you suggest to your clients that they simultaneously push emerging technologies without alienating the users who can't view?

Tom: Well, there are two things you do. One is, you define your audience very carefully and you strive to reach them through your marketing objectives. So clarity of purpose is first.

The second part of it is technological. Have you heard of browser negotiation? Browser negotiation is a quite elegant solution toward solving that. If you come in and your browser talks to my server and my server finds out that it is Java enabled, it will send it a Java applet. If it is not a Java-enabled browser, then it won't.

That is an emerging model, though. Not all browsers are honest to my server, and that complicates things.

IRC: And not all plug-ins are negotiable.

Tom: Yes, which we'll get to a little bit later. That's another solution. There are a variety of solutions; there's not just one—browser negotiation, defining your audience extremely clearly, or relegating or quarantining a particular technology to one particular section. Therefore, that new technology will not disrupt or reduce the overall experience for those who cannot view it.

AUTHORS' NOTE

Please refer to an excellent article on content negotiation: "What Is Content Negotiation? Towards an Extensible Framework for an Ecology of Data Types" by Brian Behlendorf, Organic Online. You can find this article at `http://www.organic.com/Staff/brian/cn/`.

Brian is the Chief Technology Officer at Organic Online. Brian oversees the creation and implementation of new technologies at Organic. He also participates in creative brainstorming sessions with Organic's clients, offering a check on what can or cannot be done with today's and tomorrow's technologies. Brian plays a strong role in the Web standards effort as a member of several IETF and W3C workgroups. He also plays a coordinating role in the Apache HTTP server development project, is a founding father of the Virtual Reality Modeling Language project, administrates Hyperreal, and was chief engineer at HotWired prior to moving to Organic.

Working with Shockwave

IRC: Let's turn to Shockwave. Has Shockwave become an important part of these technologies in your view?

Tom: Oh, sure. Shockwave is definitely important. It is still nascent and still has some things to be worked out, but it's definitely something that people at Organic and people in the Web industry are keeping their eye on.

IRC: What is it about Shockwave that is compelling that interest?

Tom: The immersive effect. When it works, it works extremely well. If I have my browser memory set up with enough megs and I download it and my computer doesn't crash, then it all works together very well. It works within the browser window and it's effective in presenting immersive experiences, interactive experiences, flashy experiences. Then it's fun.

Choosing a Plug-In

IRC: How do you see the competition between emerging plug-in technologies? What is your approach at Organic when advising your clients on those decisions?

Tom: We see Java and Shockwave as tools that are not in competition with one another. When Shockwave was first introduced, it was around the time that Java began to pick up speed, too. There was an enormous debate circulating around our office, the subject of which was "Java versus Shockwave." The conclusion of that debate was that "Java versus Shockwave" is not the issue at all.

That is an improper way to approach these new technologies. They serve different purposes. One is a language. The other a multimedia tool. They are completely different and suited to different applications.

IRC: So in what situation is Shockwave appropriate to use? Now or in the next five months?

Tom: Five months is too far in the Web's future to know for sure. As of May 1996—if Shockwave doesn't change before then—I think that Shockwave is exciting if you are trying to reach a small technically literate audience or you want to develop a section of your site which is extremely cutting edge and quarantined. And then you can really do some great things with Shockwave. But in terms of making my home page Shockwave only, I can't image advising that in good faith. Unless I was building a home page that caters to the special audience of Web designers who use Shockwave.

There was an enormous debate circulating around our office, the subject of which was "Java versus Shockwave." The conclusion of that debate was that "Java versus Shockwave" is not the issue at all.

IRC: What is the single most important criteria that your clients consider when they choose between the multimedia delivery technologies?

Tom: Justification. That would be the single biggest criteria. What is your justification for using this technology and can I see it on my computer? Can the persons making the decisions see it on their computer? If they can't, we tend not to go for it.

Good Applications for Shockwave

IRC: What are some specific applications of Shockwave you have developed for your clients?

Tom: We did a Shockwave application for someone—the example we called positive gratuitous earlier. They were counting down to a website launch, and Shockwave was such a hot technology that people were going just to see Shockwave. So in the countdown period, for three weeks before it launched, Shockwave drew a lot of traffic and got a lot of people to think about this domain. And Shockwave started people thinking about their website as something that would be technologically advanced.

So if I'm a viewer who has spent three minutes on that site that successfully used Shockwave, I may leave the site thinking that I will come back when they do launch. They seem to be doing something quite inspiring and interesting. I might even tell a friend.

IRC: Now when the novelty value wears off and people are used to pervasive Shockwave, what are the types of applications that will take advantage the action use value or added function?

Tom: That is a good question. More your alley than my alley. Shockwave has a wide variety of applications. As for me personally, and I don't know if this speaks for Organic, but I think it does good for flashy-type stuff that's on the very surface of elements. Because it is very difficult to integrate CGI scripts and Pearl scripts with them.

I think it works very well for a tour of the site. Something where I sit back for a minute and they give me a tour of the site. I think the most interesting aspect of Shockwave, to be honest, is that it uses the Web as a distribution medium and not for what it was intended, which is HTML. It might as well be FTP. Your only difference is that it's inline. That is what is exciting about it.

It's like trading cards. The Web is incidental to how it's delivered. So the Web is the best way to deliver it at this time. But I don't really see it, to be honest, as something that will really deeply soak into the fabric of the Web, because the Web is not meant for it. But I think the Web is an excellent distribution tool for it.

IRC: What is it about the Web that makes it an excellent distribution tool?

Tom: Ease of use. That's the reason why Mosaic was so popular in the first place. It is easier to use than FTP, and so it's fun.

I think the most interesting aspect of Shockwave, to be honest, is that it uses the Web as a distribution medium and not for what it was intended, which is HTML.

IRC: Are you aware of Shockwave for Authorware? I think that particular technology begins to break down the barriers to weaving it into the fabric of the Web as you say. And because Shockwave is an open architecture, you can develop Xtras that bridge to other scripting languages and actually begin to use it as a front end for databases and so on.

Tom: That makes it a lot more promising. The only reason that I am tentatively skeptical is because it is healthy to be tentatively skeptical. I'd love it if Shockwave turned out to be the next big thing and soaked into the core of the Web. I'm just skeptical due to some of the problems it is having now. It can't be negotiated. It cannot interact currently with a lot of back-end scripts. It crashes machines a lot. Those are very basic things, but those are important. I see great promise for it. It needs to be worked out so Joe living in Iowa can use Shockwave, too.

Note

Note that early versions of the Macintosh Shockwave for Director plug-in had some stability problems. The current release versions are very stable. As far as we know, most crashing in the current versions of Shockwave for Director is caused by either bad Lingo coding, insufficient RAM allocation on the Mac, or insufficient cache size in Netscape (both platforms). The solution is to know your audience and test movies extensively on typical hardware platforms. If you offer a troubleshooting page, you might include a suggestion such as this: "If crashing in Shockwave occurs frequently, increase the size of the disk cache in Netscape by selecting Network Preferences from the Options menu."

User Response

IRC: Do you have any sense of the users' response to the Shockwave parts of websites?

Tom: Yeah, sure. You see the traffic; the response is visits. Lots of people visit your site when it gets shocked. That's why I say it can be very valuable for positioning yourself as a very technologically advanced brand or publication. I don't mean again to pooh pooh what you do with it, but the fact that you are using it is a message in and of itself. Now how it is implemented is 70 percent of the game. Specifically, how can I see user response to it? Whenever I see a Shockwave application put up by Organic, I see traffic.

The Future of Shockwave

IRC: Let's talk about the future of Shockwave a bit. You have mentioned a couple of shortcomings of Shockwave. What specific capabilities or features would you like to see in future releases and why?

Removing Shortcomings

Tom: Number one, remove Macromedia wallpaper. Second, facilitate browser negotiations. Third, ensure interoperability with the majority of operating systems—that is to say, do not crash my computer. Those would be the three that stick out in my mind.

IRC: What about integration with back-end scripts?

Tom: Yes. I would even put that as number four. You are right, that is a major problem. But those three are so big that I would deal with those first.

Now, I don't mean to take the legs out from under Shockwave. I think it is an extremely intriguing, immersive, and interesting technology that has a very exciting potential. But the Web is a cross-platform medium. In order for Shockwave to be a long-term success and not to get lost in the shuffle of 100 other plug-ins, it needs to facilitate cross-platform presentation.

IRC: Why is the [Macromedia] wallpaper a problem?

Tom: I think it is more of a problem from the developer's side. I've seen developers act very violently to that. They hate it. They think that it is unfair. They think that it takes creative control away from them.

Let's say I'm designing an immersive experience for an audience and one of the criteria is they have to sit and look at a Macromedia logo and there is no way to change that! At least with a the Netscape browser, for example, if I don't want to look at the 'N' on top I can remove it. I lose something when I remove it, which is all these neat little tools at the top of my browser. But I can remove it if I want to. You can't remove it with Shockwave. That's terrible.

IRC: But there are implementations to work around some of these problems and presumably Macromedia and Netscape will react to user feedback and make changes.

Tom: I know. Well, I should be really clear in saying that I'm not ragging on Shockwave. I want to be perfectly clear that Macromedia has made a huge contribution to the Web. Shockwave is one of those contributions. It is tremendous and exciting. I look in terms of my daily bookmarks and I have the Shocked Site of the Day as one of them. Make no mistake of how impactful it is to the Web community. I'm just trying to be very realistic about the implementations.

If I come to a page and I see a broken icon, I will leave and I will never come back. That's me personally, and I would venture that is true of a lot of people.

IRC: Sure. And those are the questions of the day. Creative control is key. Stability is key. Negotiation is key. Fear of the broken icon is a major obstacle.

Tom: Right. If I come to a page and I see a broken icon, I will leave and I will never come back. That's me personally, and I would venture that is true of a lot of people. I haven't seen any workarounds to the lack of browser negotiation. I hope to see it implemented at the system level.

Assumptions about the Technology

IRC: Looking down the road with Shockwave, assuming that those four problems you mentioned are fixed and also assuming broadband, what are the future uses of Shockwave?

Tom: Assuming broadband and that those problems get fixed, the potential for Shockwave is astounding. As Macromedia often says, "You have a tremendous base of people who know how to create these great applications." Assuming those basic problems get solved, wow! Great.

But that's such a big assumption. It's like asking me to assume encrypted safe transactions work on the Web and assume the bandwidth issue gets solved and assume that HTML style sheets become adopted. Therefore, what do you think the future of the Web? Those assumptions really are the crux of the future of the Web.

IRC: I'm assuming that if there is a profitable solution, then someone will find it.

Tom: I don't know if that is true about negotiation. I am sure the wallpaper thing can be fixed, and I'm sure the crashing of the browser will be fixed. But the lack of plug-in negotiation is a profound problem that needs to be fixed.

> **Note**
>
> Tom's concern about plug-in negotiation was apparently shared by Netscape. With Version 3 of the Netscape Browser, you can determine whether a user has a particular plug-in installed by using a Java script. This technique is discussed in Chapter 13, "Detecting the Plug-In."

Assumptions about the Users

IRC: What are some important groups of users that readily gravitate toward immersive and rich media like Shockwave? What is their psychographic?

Tom: I'm going to make some broad-stroke assumptions. People who live in cities tend to be more forward thinking than those who do not. That is an incredible generalization but true. People who are younger tend to have more free time on their hands and so are more experimental. Those are two examples of types of people who are well-suited for these sort of immersive environments.

Let me try determining it more psychographically. We have to ask, "What is the state of mind of the users who want these sort of things?" People who are interested in other cutting-edge technologies would be one psychographic. And what type of people are interested in cutting-edge technologies? People who, for some reason, think there is something more out there and they aren't getting it right now.

They don't believe that surfing through TV channels is the end-all and be-all and, for whatever reason, their curiosity has been piqued. They are willing to devote some time and some money to find out what this is all about. I would say curiosity and experimental mind sets.

More people's eyes will be opened to the potential of Shockwave when business apps are developed. It takes a few innovators, and it takes some mistakes.

Now to get back to reality, there are just straight-ahead business people. "I want to know if this can help my business run better. How can I help develop relationships with my customers?" That's a more grounded impulse. Those are the types of users and clients who in many ways are driving Shockwave. They want business applications.

Right now, the best Shockwave applications I've seen have been done by individuals who have just put up these whacky shocked sites. That's very interesting. But business applications for Shockwave are very exciting to me.

More people's eyes will be opened to the potential of Shockwave when business apps are developed. It takes a few innovators, and it takes some mistakes.

IRC: Anything else you would like to add?

Tom: I'm looking forward to seeing Shockwave develop. I hope dearly that these problems become addressed and that it evolves into a cross-platform and open-platform complement to Web browsers.

Conclusion

This chapter has only scratched the surface of creating identity on the Web. Web marketing is just in its infancy, but the field is filling and the pace is quickening. Pioneer companies, such as Organic, and sharp thinkers, such as Tom Wang, are forever seeking a competitive edge.

We hope this discussion will facilitate your use of Shockwave in creating identity on the Web. Your Shockwave work can only benefit from the ability to better recognize communication trends as they emerge and project the coming trends on the Web.

CHAPTER 20

Creating Complex Applications: Apple Computer

This chapter addresses the possibilities of incorporating Shockwave as parts of compound applications on the Web. We also discuss the ways in which Apple Computer is using Shockwave publicly and internally. The content is taken from a discussion we had with Carl de Cordova, Network Bear for Apple Computer.

Our discussion covered the following issues:

- *Apple's shockingly large website*
- *Compound applications on the Web*
- *Shockwave and personal Web servers*

AUTHORS' NOTE

Where does this fit into the Big Picture?

In this chapter we discuss both specific examples of Shockwave solutions made for Apple and speculate on solutions made possible by component architecture systems such as Apple's OpenDoc.

The first Shockwave examples presented in the chapter are animated navigation bars, categorized as an Enhanced Interface solution in the Big Picture. (See figure 2.1 in Chapter 2, "Power on the Web.") Then we discuss a prototype online tutorial designed to be used on a regular basis to train tech support staff on Apple's products. This solution has elements of both True Multimedia and True Applications solutions.

Some possible True Applications solutions are discussed in the context of using the OpenDoc environment to create compound documents containing Shockwave parts.

Apple Computer

Figure 20.1 shows the Apple Computers Inc. home page. Ever since becoming one of the first shocked sites on the Web, Apple has been a strong endorser of Shockwave technology and has made Shockwave part of their plan to promote their component software system—OpenDoc. Apple now bundles Shockwave with many of their new computer systems. Apple has a gargantuan website and their Web masters have made significant use of Shockwave and plan even more.

FIGURE 20.1

You can visit Apple's home page at http:// www.-apple.com/.

The Interview

To find out about Apple's usage of Shockwave now and their approach to the technology, we spoke with Carl de Cordova. Carl is Apple's Network Bear. He works with the community of Web masters at Apple to provide standards and implement new technologies. He works to ensure coordination of the Web development efforts of Apple's sub-sites by creating standards and guidelines. We at InfraRed had the pleasure of working with Carl on the production of Apple's debut Shockwave movies that coincided with Macromedia's public release of Shockwave for Director in December 1995.

Shockwave is currently being used mainly to add a certain "coolness" factor, and in some cases, to really prototype and provide unique interactive experiences and resources on the Web. We will see examples of such uses of Shockwave in Apple Computer's site, and some of Carl's thoughts on Apple's experiences with Shockwave.

Carl's comments also look a few steps ahead to get to the crux of some significant long-term trends on the Web and trends in software development. The concepts he raises are of greatest interest to Shockwave developers interested in linking the Web multimedia features of Shockwave to more robust programming tools such as Java. Carl presents stimulating ideas about how Shockwave can be used in the compound documents of the future—using OpenDoc.

We were very intrigued by Carl's perception and what OpenDoc can offer Shockwave developers and what Shockwave can offer OpenDoc developers. This may prove to be a very promising avenue to more tightly integrate Shockwave content and interfaces into custom-made applications.

Apple's Shockingly Large Website

InfraRed Communications: From your point of view, what are some of the goals that Apple is pursuing generally on the Web? What is Apple trying to do out there?

Carl de Cordova: We want to try to get as much information out about what Apple is doing. Make it available so people can find any information that they want to find about the company, our products, and services. And to do that, we have used a distributed process. The groups within Apple who want to put up a website are allowed and encouraged to do that.

We've developed a set of standards for Apple's internal groups putting together websites. We then build these smaller sites into things we call "pods." A pod is our own little term for a place outside the firewall where you can host those sites. Right now we have six pods spread out all over the world—three here in Cupertino [California], one in Campbell, one in Austin, and one in Zeist, which is outside of Amsterdam.

The Distributed Site Strategy

IRC: Why have you adopted a distributed site strategy?

Carl: For one, we are a pretty distributed company. At first we tried to do something like IBM did—establishing an over-arching Web department. All those who wanted to do Web stuff had to go through one department. But because we are more of a distributed type of organization, in some ways we really didn't have a choice but to distribute the Web strategy.

People at Apple are going to do it, especially on the Macintosh. It is an easy thing to do. Once you provide them with a connection and a machine, they are going to build Web pages. So we started encouraging people to build sites. We are providing them with the tools needed and a place to host their things. Then our job becomes working on the back-end problem.

So we have been working with people to make sure that they understand what they are getting into when they put one up, to make sure they have a long-term commitment. We try to keep people from putting up websites and then abandoning them, and so forth. We make sure they have a pretty good business plan for what they are trying to accomplish and where it is going to go.

IRC: So what are some of the goals and business plans? How do you help evaluate those business plans in terms of Apple's overall Web strategy?

Carl: We sit down with the folks at the various pods and look at what kind of messages they are going to be sending, and how the site can best be structured to fit back into what Apple is already doing. One of the problems you've got with a whole bunch of different websites is duplicate efforts. For example, two years ago we put up all the product literature spec sheets. The spec sheets were put up in Austin and they were relatively comprehensive, with a mechanism to update new sheets regularly. Then, let's say that the QuickTime team just decided that they want a website. It is far better for them to point back to those existing resources than to recreate everything from scratch. We have done a lot of that kind of coordinating.

We have also done a lot of work to make sure all the smaller sites also point back into the real Apple site. We have done this by providing a set of templates and standards for the user interface. The standard elements include links to the overall find-it page, an overall map of the site, a master index at the top of various sections, and at the top of the main site. So there is an index system that hopefully contains everything out there.

IRC: It sounds like the main idea is integration and coordination of these different groups and their plans—to make sure that they add into the overall Apple plan.

Carl: Definitely, it is really easy to make simple mistakes if there is no coordination. For example, when a little group decides they are going to do a site, they may get all spun up about it and then create a site where a user can actually get trapped. Where one could literally click on every link and never leave that site.

We want to make sure that doesn't happen. If the first thing someone discovers about Apple is the Cyberdog site, we want to make sure they can get out of the Cyberdog site. Getting into the bigger Apple site has to be very easy and straightforward and fairly uniform across all our sites.

Developing In-House Expertise

IRC: How has using the Web benefited Apple's overall business plan?

Carl: There's a couple of ways. One, having one of the larger websites, very dynamic and complete, it says a lot to our customers about our ability to deal with the cutting edge. Imagine if we didn't have a website. We wouldn't be looked upon as a very cutting-edge company. So there's that piece.

Another piece the Web has been terrific for is developing our expertise internally. We now have a group of about 115 people who know how to run websites and know what this publishing thing is all about. They have learned the ways of running websites by dealing with the challenges. Now we are going through another generation. The first generation was typically at the level just above that of a hobbyist. The Web was kind of an extra job that someone did on the side. Then we went through a period where the Web became an official thing and we were doing it very seriously.

There are hundreds of thousands of people out there who understand how Director works. Being able to leverage off of that is tremendous.

In our current period, those people are changing jobs. Maybe they've run a successful website for a while and now they are moving into more influential positions because they know what they are talking about. They've got the expertise.

We are now helping these people move into jobs where they have impact on products and strategies more at the core of the company's focus on the Internet space. These people are extremely valuable because of their experience.

Shockwave in the Apple Site

IRC: What is Apple doing with Shockwave?

Carl: So far, we have pretty much just been experimenting. We've got about four different pieces that we are running on the main site. [Figure 20.2 shows Apple's home page Shockwave movie. Note that the movie is not currently available on the network. You can view it from the file GAMEBOY.HTM in the Chapter 20 folder on the accompanying CD.]

We jumped on the bandwagon early to do a number of banners and example pieces primarily to show our support for the new technology. We think it is neat. [Figure 20.3 shows Apple's "Web City" Shockwave animated navigation bar.]

FIGURE 20.2

The home page navigation interface, called the "gameboy," is shocked on Apple's main shocked site at http://www2.apple.com/sw/. The menu items and two featured items on the right are nice rollover buttons.

FIGURE 20.3

The "Web City" navigation bar has animations when you roll over the buildings. Here, the politicians are fighting in City Hall.

IRC: Has the Shockwave part of your site measurably increased the traffic, the value, and the usefulness of the site?

Carl: We like to think of it as a very successful experiment. We have kept the majority of the initial Shockwave up on the site. The only other major piece is the training piece that the service training people in Austin did, which I'll talk about a little later. It was done primarily as a technology demonstration piece which we say is fairly successful. I believe it has had 200,000 or so hits over the past couple months [April and May of 1996–auth.]. It was really heavy when the Shockwave plug-in rolled in December.

IRC: Why was Shockwave made a part of the Apple's Web strategy? What were you pursuing in using Shockwave?

Carl: A couple of things. We really like Shockwave. It's a very good technology, a very Mac-like technology. It's taking something that already exists, that's pretty easy to use, and has a full rich set of tools and makes it easy to offer content online. I think the fact that you can take something you have done in the past and move it very quickly and easily to the Net is terrific. There are hundreds of thousands of people out there who understand how Director works. Being able to leverage off of that is tremendous.

The reason why we've included Shockwave in a lot of our Web projects is because we have a ridiculous amount of content laying around on CDs and other places that is done in Director. And we feel that we can move it to the Web fairly easily with Shockwave.

We also feel like it is much more of a useable tool for our users, for Apple's customers, than something based on a programming language. These demonstrations that we are seeing on things like Java are very nice but that is not a very good use of Java to begin with. Java is not very good at easily doing the kinds of multimedia that Director is outstanding at. The reason why we've included Shockwave in a lot of our Web projects is because we have a ridiculous amount of content laying around on CDs and other places that is done in Director. And we feel that we can move it to the Web fairly easily with Shockwave.

IRC: In helping all the different groups within Apple get Shockwave material up on the Web, what problems are you finding?

Carl: The typical problem I assume that everybody is having is size. When you designed at first, the actual size of the animation and sound, and so forth, had ceased to be a problem. The size criterion has been relaxed in multimedia design over the last couple of years because you were going to publish it on a CD. So what if the thing is 25 megs? If it runs fast, that's what you cared about. Run fast, look pretty. Those were the two criteria. Size was the variable that you just let go to heck. So one of the real challenges in repurposing existing content is learning how to trim down the source movies by a whole lot.

IRC: So do you train your groups in bandwidth techniques?

Carl: At this point, most of the people who are using Shockwave and are considering it a part of their website, already have a background in Macromedia Director. We don't have any kind of program right now to actively encourage people to do this. Most of the people who are using it are encouraged by Shockwave itself and already know how to use Director. Like I've said, we have done a ton of Director stuff in-house. It's been a major platform for content development. So the experience is there really.

IRC: Are there any good examples of Shockwave uses by Apple's internal groups?

Carl: Yes, there was a major project of our group in Austin. They prototyped an online interactive training for Apple's QuickTime Conferencing system. Shockwave was used with great success to demonstrate the exciting possibilities of online interactive training.

Online Training at Apple

We now leave the interview to take a look at the QuickTime Conferencing interactive training. Early on in the life of Shockwave, in December of 1995, Apple's Austin pod prototyped this Shockwave-based interactive training program for the Apple Training group.

This project focuses on the Apple QuickTime Conferencing Kit—a product designed for communicating with real-time audio and video over the Net. The online training was designed with the tech support audience in mind as a way to teach as much as possible about the features, specifications, and support issues related to each product in the kit. Having proven that the concept worked, similar Shockwave training materials could be developed to meet the needs of other audiences and products as well.

We include some of the prototype pages and their Shockwave movies in the Chapter 20 folder on the accompanying CD. The pages we include are demonstrations of the QuickTime Conferencing hardware and how to connect to the network.

Warning

> Do not click on the buttons in the prototype pages. If you do so, the page will try to pull in a page from the Net, and you will receive an error message. This is because the `goToNetPage` commands in the Shockwave movies are referencing absolute addresses for pages behind Apples' firewall.

The introductory page, shown in figure 20.4, describes the proof-of-concept of the Apple Interactive Training System. The page has a menu bar on top with an animation of the Apple logo and slick rollover buttons. Open the file called ABOUT.HTM (found in the Chapter 20 folder on the accompanying CD) in a Shockwave-enabled Netscape Browser to check it out.

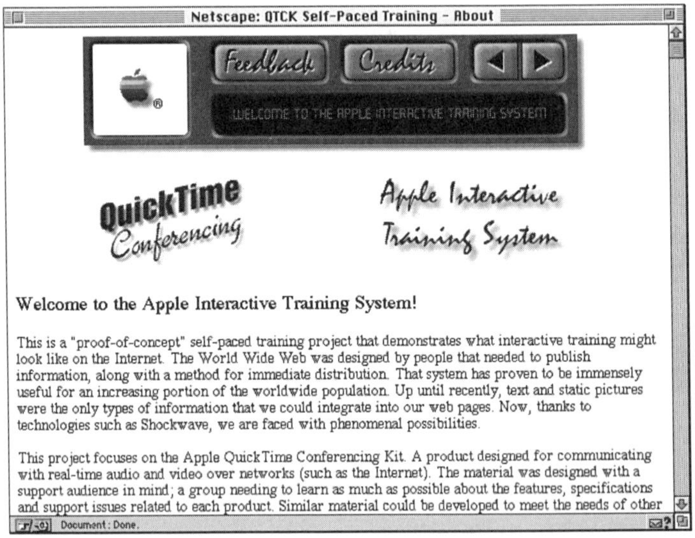

Figure 20.4

This is an introductory page of a "proof-of-concept" of Apple's Interactive Training on QuickTime Conferencing. This page utilizes an embedded Shockwave movie to demonstrate the various parts of the QuickTime Conferencing Camera.

The training program shows how to install the hardware and software for the system, as well as troubleshoot. Figure 20.5 shows the QuickTime Conferencing camera as demonstrated by the interactive tour. In the Chapter 20 folder on the accompanying CD, open the file called QTCCAM.HTM to see this Shockwave movie about the QuickTime Conferencing Camera. Click on the part of the camera you are interested in to get a pop-up of descriptive text and detail images.

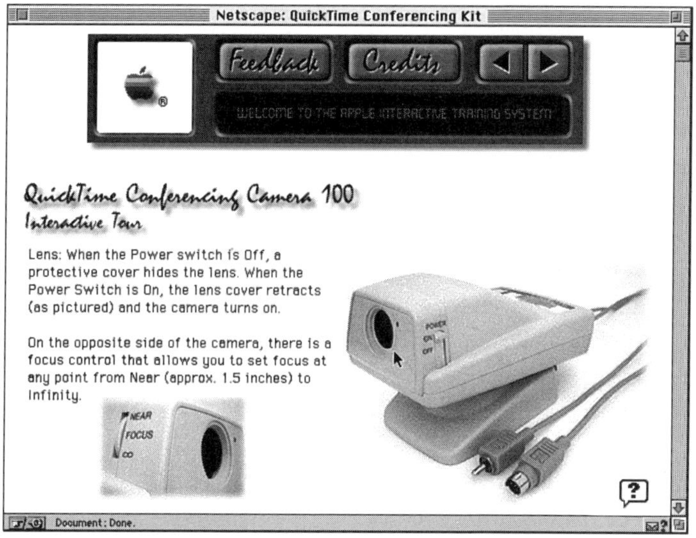

FIGURE 20.5

The Interactive Training shows the parts of the QuickTime Conferencing Camera. Here we see details about the lens.

The QuickTime Conferencing kit includes the Apple Media Conference software that works with the camera, manages communications and shared windows, and so on. Figure 20.6 shows the Shockwave movie describing how to use the software. Because the movie is a proof-of-concept, not all concepts are active. The "Setting Up" topic is implemented. The top-level menu of the prototype has the subject matter arranged in lists of topics and key phrases. You also can switch to an index or a searchable database—all in a fast-click experience. Open the file QTCGUIDE.HTM to see the Shockwave movie.

The prototype shows how selecting a section from the top-level menu brings up pages of detail text. Figure 20.7 shows the first page of the section called "About Networks and Bandwidth." This is key support information presented in a very structured searchable format with a full keyword index.

The proof-of-concept was a great success and there are plans to put several other training programs online using Shockwave. The Apple Training group has a lot of interactive training content previously created with Director. They can now, with relative ease, put it online for the use of the their technical support force.

FIGURE 20.6

This is the top menu level of the interactive tutorial for the QuickTime Conferencing software—called Apple Media Conference.

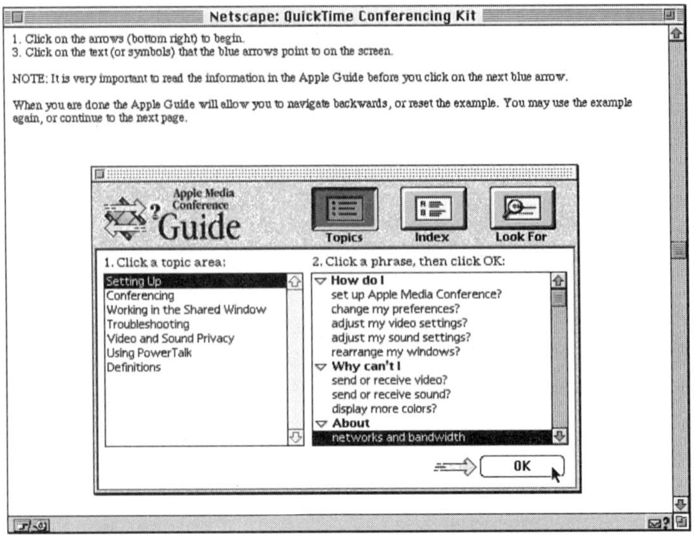

FIGURE 20.7

The second level into the interactive tutorial brings up detailed information. This is the first of several pages on the subject of networks and bandwidth.

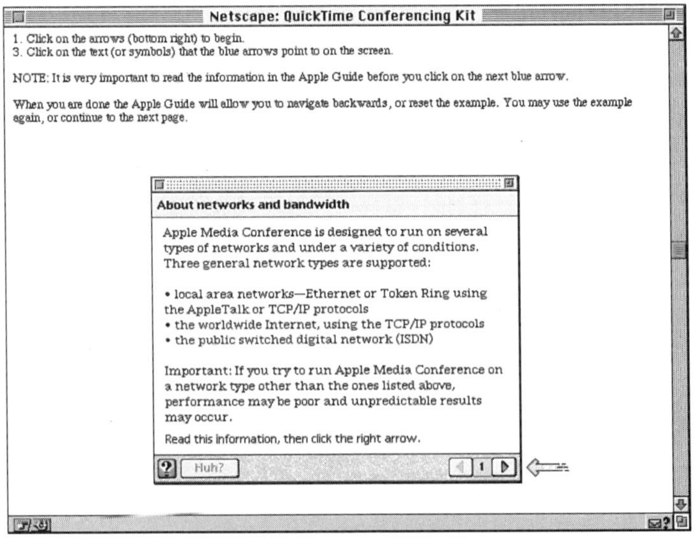

Compound Applications on the Web

IRC: Is your main criteria in choosing between the multimedia delivery technologies the ease of repurposing content that already exists? Do you use anything else besides Shockwave? Do you use Java?

Carl: Java stuff is just beginning right now. We have done a number of demonstration pieces. But we don't have anything publicly available right now, although we have some plans for moving that way. They really are tremendously different things. Shockwave is terrific in building window interface pieces. Things that have a specific look and feel and do a specific amount of interesting things like providing little widgets and selection tools and bright shiny baubles for the user.

Java can be forced into that, but it's a programming language. Its back end is going to be much better at doing programming tasks than providing sparkly little interfaces, whereas Director on the other hand, has a real problem with the Lingo language underneath. You are not going to want to create something really complex like a stand-alone program that does heavy calculation or provides communications pieces. That would be very hard to do in Shockwave. In Java, the programming pieces are there and the user interface multimedia prettiness is not.

If Shockwave is going to communicate with Java, you may be able to use Shockwave for the user interface and use Java as the medium to communicate with other applications and the Net.

They are two very different tool sets. I think the most exciting thing will be when these two tool sets bang into each other, because the things that Java isn't any good at should be very easy to do in Shockwave and vice versa. The thing that is going to make Shockwave and Java work well together is the hooks between them. If I need to throw a wad of goo at you that looked pretty, Shockwave is the way to do that. But if that wad of goo then needs to be communicated back to something on the server, Java may the best way to do that.

The Shockwave and Java Connection

IRC: Are there any specific projects you can think of that could use hooks between something like Java and Shockwave? What would the Shockwave part of it do and what would the whole thing look like?

Carl: We announced the licensing of the Natural Intelligence Java Virtual Engine, the virtual machine technology. We just licensed that from them to put into the operating system itself. So it should be relatively trivial for people who are making traditional applications as well as people who are using OpenDoc to create applications that talk down into Java applets that then communicate around through the Net.

Note

> In May 1996, Apple licensed the Java programming language and plans to integrate it into the operating systems of its platforms. Java requires an interpreter in order to execute on any operating system. The Java Virtual Machine (VM) translates the general Java commands into specific native commands for the given platform.
>
> As a result, Java code is typically slower than the compiled code. To combat this drawback, Apple is implementing a just-in-time (JIT) compiler that converts Java code into native code as it is read, significantly enhancing Java's performance. Apple has licensed Natural Intelligence Inc.'s Java Virtual Machine and JIT compiler to use as the basis for its implementation of Java in the Mac OS. They will form a hybrid version of Java by combining this with code licensed from Sun Microsystems.
>
> Like most major OS vendors, Apple sees the advantage of providing the guaranteed presence of a Java interpreter in its OS. Now that Java is a Cyberdog part and later when it is built in to the OS, Shockwave developers will be able to interact with Java in new and interesting ways.

One of the things you might want to build on top of that is a really pretty user interface or a really nice-looking control panel. And you could do that with the Java piece. But if Shockwave is going to communicate with Java, you may be able to use Shockwave for the user interface and use Java as the medium to communicate with other applications and the Net.

So if you have any connected applications, like say Claris FileMaker, they don't need to understand how to talk to Shockwave. You'd actually use something like Java as the intermediary so that you talk down into Java and Shockwave and whatever else will get it. Those interfaces are set as either an OpenDoc part or as a normal application. Then, you would be able to have a piece of Java code sit in the operating system receiving messages from both environments.

IRC: That's very intriguing. Just as a hypothetical solution, can you think of something that has already been envisioned or just something off the top of your head that would take advantage of a link between Shockwave and Java?

Carl: One of the quintessential examples is the shopping basket. You are going to make a nice store interface. Users are going to go shopping for CDs and you want to give them little multimedia clips. You want the store to have a real pretty look and feel that demos whatever you are trying to sell really well. In order to do that, you are going to need to send a Shockwave movie to the client off of the server. But to talk back to the server, you are going to need to do that with something else. There are some tools for doing that in Shockwave, but they aren't tremendous.

So what we need is a Java applet running at the same time as your Shockwave. The Java applet is maintaining state information and information about the things you are shopping for as well as information about how you purchase when you actually decide to buy. And it would talk to another Java applet on the server and exchange information—perhaps even out of band. So it is not even an http transaction; it is some kind of encrypted transaction between the two of them.

Then the Java application on the server could actually talk to a FileMaker database through the operating system's built-in Java virtual environment. They require no custom APIs up to that point. That's where it gets to be a little exciting. All this can be written custom by hand or on a special case basis. We are talking about using generalized off-the-shelf tools that will be available in the future to do relatively complex client-server kind of computing pieces with relative ease. Shockwave is really good at one thing and Java is really good at what it does, and the back-end applications of the Macintosh already exist. So linking them could be a very powerful combination—everybody doing what they're good at.

OpenDoc and Shockwave

IRC: Looking down the road to the future a bit, what features or capabilities or fixes would you like to see in future releases in Shockwave?

Carl: One thing that will happen in the future is that Shockwave will be able to run outside of the browser environment, for example, running under OpenDoc—Apple's container environment. [See figure 20.8.] We see Shockwave being a really nice cross-platform content delivery tool. There won't be any reason why you would have to use something like Netscape and be constrained by that Netscape window. You'll be able to create documents in OpenDoc and send those documents out. Those documents should be able to read Shockwave applications. The user may not even know really that he is using the Web.

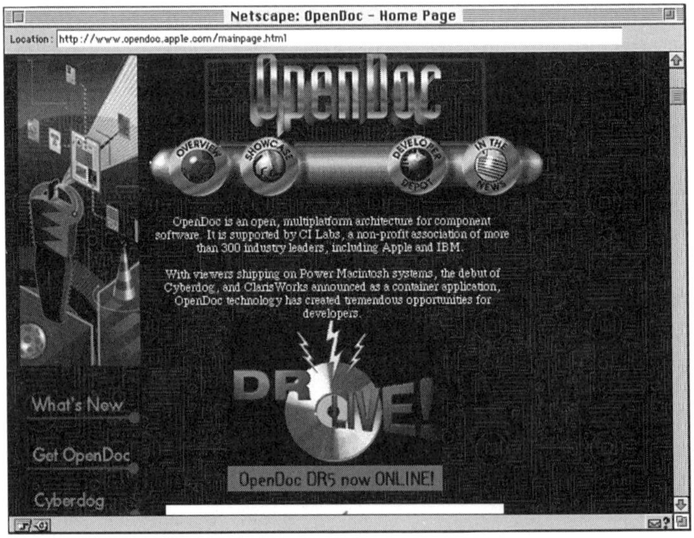

FIGURE 20.8
You can visit Apple's OpenDoc site at http://www.opendoc.apple.com/.

Let's say I'm the world expert on Golden Retriever dogs. I could put together a document that has all sorts of information about an upcoming dog show and distribute that to the world. That document itself will have windows inside of it that are OpenDoc containers. In one place I might put a scrolling list of all the dog show mailing lists that are available. In another place I might put a window into the Web page. Elsewhere I can put an actual

Shockwave movie. So this document is not going to look like a Netscape Web page.

It is going to have text in it where the text should be. But it also may have a window that pops in and runs the Shockwave document. This allows me to create a custom interface for the person at that point in the document. And because of the integration list, all sorts of different tools will be available in the OpenDoc environment. You could pull in all sorts of different media types—perhaps a form software, a database look, or even a spreadsheet piece that all plug in to this single OpenDoc environment. When it needs to go out to the Web, the OpenDoc container will know how to do that because of the Cyberdog technology that is built into it.

We should be able to play the Shockwave documents whenever we need to play a fairly complex animation. I think that is going to be really exciting, too. It kind of eliminates the boundaries of the actual browser technology, enabling us to get back to creating documents that are media-rich. So you can put the animated multimedia content wherever you need it to be instead of being constrained by the browser window.

AUTHORS' NOTE

What is OpenDoc? OpenDoc is a multi-platform, component software architecture that enables developers to evolve current applications into component software or to create new component software applications. OpenDoc software will run on Apple Macintosh, as well as Windows, Windows NT, OS/2, and AIX systems.

OpenDoc components, also known as parts, are the fundamental building blocks of an OpenDoc document. Replacing today's traditional monolithic applications, these components are smaller applications that perform specific functions. These components are dynamically bound together to make up an OpenDoc document, also known as a compound document. Macromedia has announced they will publish Shockwave as an OpenDoc Part, allowing integration of Shockwave into compound documents in OpenDoc.

Component software is a modular way to develop software as reusable building blocks that can be easily connected together. This enables developers and users to create customized solutions that are precisely tailored to their needs.

Implementations of OpenDoc for Windows, OS/2, and AIX are being handled by IBM—you can get info at OpenDoc@Austin.IBM.com. You can get the OpenDoc software for the Macintosh by filling out the form on Apple's OpenDoc home page: `http://www.opendoc.apple.com`. You will receive a copy of OpenDoc for the Mac OS and be placed on the mailing list to receive updates of the OpenDoc technology.

OpenDoc is interoperable with OLE 2.0, thus, OpenDoc components can be embedded in Microsoft applications that support OLE and vice versa. Unlike Microsoft's OLE, OpenDoc is not proprietary. OpenDoc is an open, vendor-neutral, cross-platform architecture that is interoperable with other major compound document architectures. The OpenDoc source code will be licensed to developers through the Component Integration Laboratories (CI Labs).

CI Labs is a non-profit industry association facilitating the transition to component software. CI Labs was founded in September 1993 by Apple, IBM, and WordPerfect/Novell and has many other members. Shockwave developers creating parts for compound documents may want to contact CI Labs (info@cilabs.org) for information on OpenDoc integration, interoperability validation, and so on.

IRC: It seems like the OpenDoc environment might be an interesting delivery wrapper around your Shockwave content or if you are already doing OpenDoc, Shockwave may be a great way to provide the multimedia parts.

Carl: OpenDoc is our container environment. OpenDoc is a completely different way of looking at a program. In the OpenDoc environment you run things called containers and a container can have any parts you choose to install in there. Whereas today, you use application tools to create a document. In OpenDoc we have a document and inside it are the tools that you want to use to do things inside that document. You can have new tool sets just by plugging in the tools.

Then relatively quickly, you can combine containers with many different media and document types to use them together in different ways. The nice thing about that is rather than trying to have multiple different applications that create documents that you have to stitch together, the tools are all available inside the OpenDoc container.

Shockwave is a way to plug in Director animation pieces, as well as the FreeHand and Authorware pieces, into the OpenDoc environment. I know that Macromedia is working on that so you will have the ability to play Director movies as an OpenDoc container.

Shockwave for Cyberdog

Carl: Another neat thing about where we are headed is our set of tools called Cyberdog. [See figure 20.9.] These are merely examples of how in OpenDoc, you can implement the various Net technologies like FTP, Web, e-mail, and so forth. They are a basic core set of tools, but we are releasing those in such a way that people can rewrite those tools and create better ones. There are people already out there creating and jazzing up what we are doing.

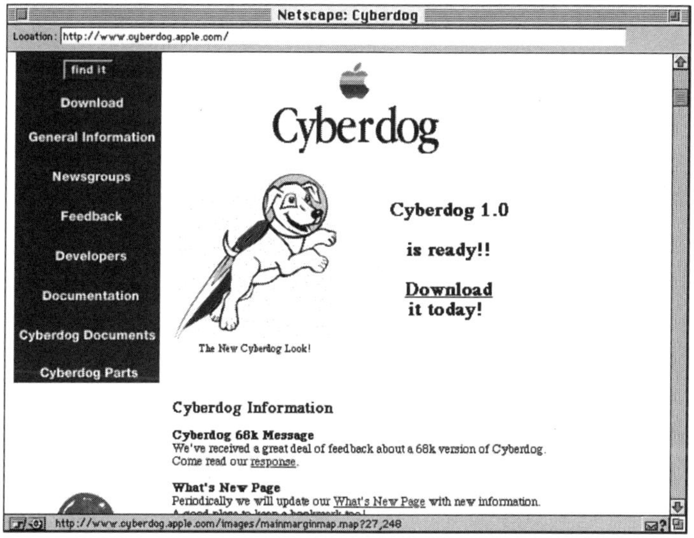

FIGURE 20.9

You can visit Apple's Cyberdog site at http://www.cyberdog.apple.com/.

AUTHORS' NOTE

Cyberdog brings live Internet connections to OpenDoc documents. In Cyberdog, Internet addresses are objects that can be drag-and-dropped in documents, the Finder, and so on. If you double-click on an Internet address, Cyberdog opens the object, whether it's a Web page, a picture, or a file. Using a document with embedded Cyberdog parts opens the viewer and its data is brought to life. With this capability, you can customize your access to all of the Internet and bring the Internet live to documents you create.

In May 1996, Apple and Macromedia announced an agreement to develop Shockwave for Cyberdog, providing enhanced interactive and multimedia viewing on the Web for Cyberdog users. Apple will bundle the Shockwave plug-in with the Apple Internet Connection Kit, which is included in many Macintosh computers. Macromedia's

Shockwave part is an important endorsement of the OpenDoc-based Cyberdog technology.

Cyberdog provides integrated access to all services on the Internet and a public set of APIs to replace, extend, or build new components. Shockwave developers interested in creating shocked OpenDoc documents with extended Internet functionality should visit the Cyberdog website at http://www.cyberdog.apple.com/. Cyberdog 1.0 is currently available free of charge from the Cyberdog site.

Shockwave and Personal Web Servers

IRC: Looking toward the broader future of the Web, what is Apple's plan? What are some of the existing things you can envision in general? What cool stuff on the Web do you see emerging? And if you have a lot of bandwidth on top of it, what will the Web let you do?

Carl: There are a couple of things we feel are going to happen very quickly. One is that websites will become fairly ubiquitous. Everyone will have a website. It will be built into operating systems to the point where every machine is going to respond to requests for Web documents. The number of websites is going to go through the roof because of this, if you count just regular websites.

But most of these are not heavy-duty websites. These are not the kind of sites where millions of people are going to come check your machine everyday. You are going to be sharing a certain amount of information with a fairly small audience of people who are interested in that kind of information.

One thing that will happen in the future is that Shockwave will be able to run outside of the browser environment.

If everybody has a website, if every machine serves websites, things change a little bit. One of the things that will change is the ability for agent technologies to actually have some place to go and to gather information about what is going on. Anything from current environmental variables to updates on projects to calendaring information to personal information to joint projects under groupware would work a whole lot better if everybody has a server.

As time goes on, servers are going to spread out and get very small. The way they are going to stay very small is to use some kind of reverse caching type environment. If everybody in my department has a Web server, I don't want everybody in the world coming up and getting on my machine to gain access to the documents on my personal Web server. What I want to be able to do is to have departmental servers that are gathering those documents up and then serving them out.

I can see at Apple actually, everybody having a Web server. The servers then would be gathered by departmental servers and those are gathered by an even higher hierarchy of Web servers that are outside the firewall. So if you come to a website and you try to get to my home page, you are actually getting it from a machine that has harvested it off my departmental server which has harvested it off of me.

The neat thing about this kind of environment is that it is not going to require very much of a hit on the part of the personal Web server. You are also going to be able to have agent technology out there gathering up all sorts of interesting information like doing report gathering, status reports on various projects, and building up all sorts of status type documents. This creates a little bit more of the living type Web. That's one place where we see the world really heading toward.

The thing that Shockwave gives to this vision is a rapid interface development environment to make things prettier and move faster for these personal Web servers. And that fits in with the way things are developing on the server side. With things like the Apple WebSTAR API, the Information Server API from Microsoft, and the Netscape API, you have the ability to quickly build a very small server that does fairly complex, powerful things.

Conclusion

With the development of Shockwave for OpenDoc, we can expect many exciting opportunities to create True Applications and Broadband Environments using Shockwave parts. This critical merging of technologies enables Shockwave development to be tied to software development in general and it allows rapid integration of multimedia interfaces into powerful custom-made applications.

As the Apple case demonstrates, businesses can leverage Shockwave technology to draw on multimedia talent and assets that already exist internally. While Shockwave allows for rapid prototyping of graphical interfaces, Java and OpenDoc allow for more robust programming and a common API to applications on and off the Web.

CHAPTER 21

Voice Recognition Interfaces: Digital Dreams

This chapter tackles an exciting use of Shockwave's open architecture—speech recognition. Taking advantage of Shockwave's extensibility and Apple's PlainTalk technology, Tim and Dana Morgan of Digital Dreams have made speech-aware Shockwave movies a reality. Here, we examine the uses of speech on the Web and the Xtras in Shockwave.

The majority of this chapter is taken from an exchange we had with Tim and Dana. The discussion covers their dreams for speech applications, speech on the Web, and tips for speech-aware Shockwave.

Authors' Note

Where does this fit into the Big Picture?

In this chapter we are talking about an Xtra that extends the functionality of Shockwave. Speech recognition can be applied at any level of the big picture. (See figure 2.1 in Chapter 2, "Power on the Web.") As we discuss, speech—when applied properly—can add another dimension to the interface.

Speech recognition can be used to navigate inside 3D or VR spaces found in broadband environments. It can be applied to any true application in the form of a command and control interface and some cases, data entry. Speech can form the user interface of a game or a quiz, as you will see later in this chapter.

Speech can even be used to control plain old HTML. Digital Dreams has used speech recognition in Shockwave to provide a generic engine for speakable linking in Web pages.

The Interview with Digital Dreams

Digital Dreams was founded in 1993 by Tim and Dana Morgan to promote the use of speech recognition and other emerging technologies. They have licensed their speech XObject for the Mac version of the Star Trek Omnipedia CD, published by Simon & Schuster. Currently, they are focusing on their speech recognition plug-ins for the Web. Figure 21.1 shows their home page.

Now, Tim and Dana have created ShockTalk, their speech recognition Xtra for Shockwave for Director 5. They have had copious experience with speech technology. Tim was one of the original inventors of the award-winning Voice Navigator when he was Vice President of Research and Development at Articulate Systems. Tim handles the software development side of Dreams.

Digital Dreams works very closely with Apple on speech technology. Dana consults with Apple's Speech Group as well as Apple's Multimedia Program. Dana handles the consulting side of Digital Dreams' business.

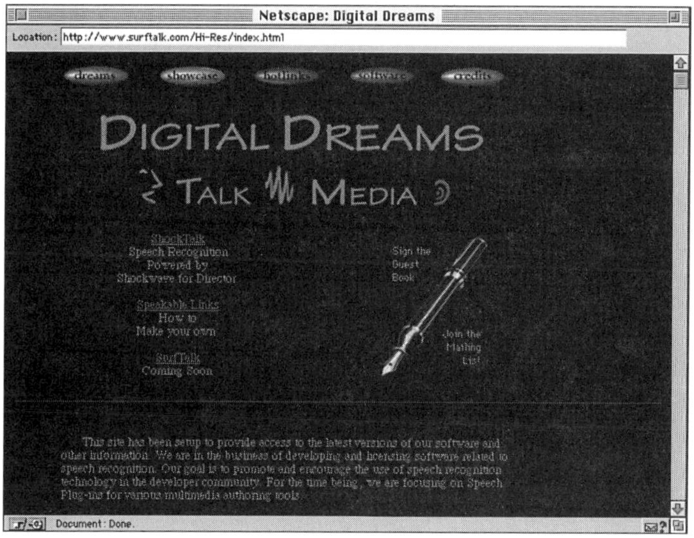

FIGURE 21.1

You can visit the Digital Dreams website at http://www.surftalk.com/ to get the latest in speech recognition for Shockwave.

Speech Recognition and Shockwave

Digital Dreams is trying to spread their excitement about speech recognition. With Shockwave, they were able to get speech to a fairly broad audience on the Web very quickly. Their speech Xtra is a valuable way for Shockwave developers to provide the element of dialogue in their movies. This opens profound possibilities for the user interface.

We found it very valuable to hear from those who have successfully used Shockwave as a vehicle for technology demonstration. Shockwave's open architecture is very powerful in that one can piggy-back new technology onto the Web and package it in a rich multimedia wrapper. ShockTalk is a great example of using Shockwave to repurpose Xtras for the Web. This experience also is instructive and worthy of discussion.

Dreams for Speech Applications

InfraRed Communications: What is Digital Dreams and what are you seeking to accomplish?

Tim: Our mission is really to evangelize speech technology. We want to get the developers and the end-user community to start using speech technologies at the level of the interface. The technology itself is at a very good point right now. If you design your application correctly, you can create a very successful end-user experience. You can actually do things that you either couldn't do or that would be cumbersome to do without speech.

From a business point of view, what we are doing is developing and licensing software. We started out essentially developing these plug-ins for different authoring environments. Shockwave happens to be one of them and HyperCard is another. We have a cross-platform strategy, although the Macintosh is clearly the favorable platform today. For one thing, the core speech recognition technology is free on the Mac. And it is really very good compared to other technologies out there. Superior performance. So that is really what we are about.

Dana: I think the important thing that we do is to bridge the gap between various different multimedia authoring tools and Apple's speech technology. We make it very easy for developers to integrate the technology. I think that is key. Because if I'm a developer, I don't want to add anything to my overhead. I don't want to add any additional burdens on my production staff, and I want to avoid adding to the price tag of the title.

Apple's Speech Technology Platform

Dana: The speech manager technology is free from Apple and that's key. [Figure 21.2 shows Apple's speech website at `http://www.speech.apple.com.`] But more than being free, the technology is superior and very usable in real-world environments. That is so critical in speech recognition.

Apple has implemented a new toolbox feature called push-to-talk. This means the speech manager will not listen until you push a particular key down. The end user can customize any key to trigger. And that puts it one step ahead of the competition. You need to have that kind of control, especially in the world of games where the gaming environment is very noisy.

FIGURE 21.2

Visit Apple's Speech Program website for updates on the latest in speech technology and download the latest version of PlainTalk™. Go to http://www.speech.apple.com/.

Good Applications for Speech Recognition

IRC: Can you give a sense of what applications are making the best uses of speech recognition right now?

Tim: I would say the areas that we have worked in have basically been enter/edutainment. The first title we worked on was the Star Trek Omnipedia title. There the speech recognition works very well. Interestingly, since it was a cross-platform title, they needed to have a speech-recognition engine for Windows and a speech-recognition engine for the Macintosh. The developer of the title, a company called Imagery, did a lot of testing and clearly came back and said that the Macintosh implementation was far better than the Windows implementation.

That was due to a combination of two things. First, it was the way we had built the XObject. The plug-in was very easy to use and had a lot of simple methods, whereas, we didn't build the Windows object. That was built by the recognition engine provider who really didn't have much understanding of multimedia. That makes a lot of difference depending on who actually designs the core plug-in.

Dana: Ideally, a developer should be developing a product with speech in mind from the get-go. A lot of times you see the developers say, "Oh, we've developed an application so now let's add speech recognition." So they slap speech recognition on as an afterthought and that shows. A well-executed, speech-savvy product has to be designed around speech from the very beginning.

In the educational market, there are currently more than 100 titles incorporating text-to-speech. But the number of speech recognition titles is very few. That's a problem. For one, Apple hasn't been able to evangelize the technology to the fullest because only just now, with the release of PlainTalk version 1.5 and the accompanying SDK [Software Developer's Kit], the technology has passed the boundary of real-world usability. With the addition of the push-to-talk feature and improvements in the digital sound processing, Apple now needs to evangelize their technology and educate consumers on the availability and the viability of the technology.

Speech Recognition and the UI Paradigm

IRC: What can speech recognition add to the user interface that should be part of early design planning?

Dana: Speech adds a great deal to the interface. Developers have tended to only mirror the existing functions already in a graphical user interface [GUI]. They'll make a one-to-one correspondence of a speech command for every menu, menu item, and dialog box. The beauty of speech is that it adds an extra dimension to the user experience and allows the user to circumvent the modality of the GUI. An example of this is a speech macro, such as "print four copies." Tim can add more to this idea.

Tim: There are some big wins with speech technology compared to graphical user interface. The biggest win is that you can convey more information in the spoken word. In one sentence you can convey more information than you can in point and click. The model for the GUI is essentially point and click, select a menu, select an object, do an action to it.

A very obvious comparison is if you want to print five copies of a document. What you have to do now with a GUI is select a document, then go to the Print menu, which then brings up a dialog box, and you type in the value five and hit OK. Whereas, you could just say "print five copies" and the information you would have to enter in a modal situation forced upon you by the graphical interface can be circumvented by using speech.

Dana: I'd like to insert an idea that's been put forward by Kim Silverman, the principal research scientist for text-to-speech at Apple. He is one of the people I work with at Apple's speech program. The first user interface [UI] paradigm we had on desktop computers was remember-and-type—with the Unix or DOS command-line interface. And then we moved from the remember-and-type to the point-and-click graphical user interface—on Mac and Windows. But now, the graphical user interface is becoming far too complicated. There is a lot of stuff going on in the environment. Now we are emerging into a new UI era—the ask-and-tell paradigm.

One thing that drives me nuts is that game developers are creating these beautiful, rich environments and we are using what is really a primitive method of input—the keyboard and mouse. As a user, you are totally consumed by whatever is in front of you on the screen. You are immersed in this world and you should just be able to say "Open that door," or "Walk up that staircase." Whereas now you have to return to pointing and clicking the mouse again. You are back to your computer instead of in the immersive world.

I just edited an article for *Apple Directions* on the new games SDK [Software Developer's Kit] that Apple is putting out. It has various different tools called game sprockets. There's an input sprocket and there is a speech sprocket, and so forth. In the section where they discuss the speech sprocket, it is said that the most important issue for developers is trying to get above the crowd. How are their titles going to get shelf space? They are going to have to differentiate themselves. And how do they do that? They do that by adding something no other title has. By adding speech to get away from point and click in your rich immersive environments, you can rise above the noise. To me that is critical.

One thing that drives me nuts is that game developers are creating these beautiful, rich environments and we are using what is really a primitive method of input—the keyboard and mouse.

Tim: It does draw the user more into the experience. If you can get them in a dialogue, literally talking as opposed to just point and clicking, they can be using a joystick to point at things and at the same time be engaging in some dialogue. It's just that extra level of interaction.

Speech on the Web

IRC: Switching gears a little to the Web. How has the Web facilitated your business strategy of evangelizing speech recognition?

Tim: First, we have announced a product that actually integrates speech recognition into the Web browser. It allows you to navigate the Web hyperlinks by voice. You say the words to go to whatever the text link is. This is kind of beyond Shockwave. It's a stand-alone add-on to Netscape Navigator.

Then we have our ShockTalk plug-in that is available right now, which allows speech recognition through Shockwave. This allows webmasters, for instance, to embed a small Shockwave movie on their Web pages by referencing a Shockwave movie that will automatically make their website speakable.

Speakable Links

IRC: Can you describe that speakable links application?

Tim: So using the ShockTalk Xtra for Shockwave, which basically enables speech recognition within any Shockwave movie, we created a speakable links application. Speakable links look at the HTML page on which the ShockTalk Xtra is embedded, read the HTML text, pick out the anchors in that text, and turn the anchors into speakable items. It is a preconfigured

Shockwave movie so you don't need to be a Macromedia Director or Shockwave developer to use it. It's a very simple application, 12 KB file size and very accurate. In fact, the ShockTalk plug-in itself is less than 20 KB.

IRC: How does it work? How would somebody go about getting ShockTalk and actually embedding the speakable links movie?

Tim: In order to do a speakable links page, that's already done for you so there is really no work to do. You just embed the movie.

AUTHORS' NOTE

When Tim says there really is no work to do, it's no joke. Figure 21.3 shows a sample speakable page made by Digital Dreams. This page was made speakable by embedding their movie SHOCKTALK.DCR and adding some simple HTML.

When the page loads, the movie does a `getNetText` **and parses the anchors directly out of the HTML itself and then listens for the voice commands. You command the navigation of links by saying "Link to," followed by the name of the link. It works really well and there is a nice vertical bar on the page giving visual feedback of the listening status. You can find the sample page SHOCTALK.HTM in the Chapter 21 folder on the accompanying CD-ROM.**

Webmasters can make any Web page speakable by adding the following lines of HTML to the page:

```
<TABLE border=0 width=620>        <!-- begin shocktalk table -->

<TR>

<TD width=20 vAlign=top><EMBED SRC="shocktalk.dcr" width=16
➥height=480></TD>

<TD width=580 vAlign=top>         <!-- total width must be less
                                  ➥than table width -->

<!-- place main contents here (including embedded tables) -->

</TD>

</TR>

</TABLE>                          <!-- end shocktalk table -->
```

You should note that the SHOCKTALK.DCR movie uses Shockwave's `getNetText` **command and so it will only work when you are online. Remember that Macromedia disabled** `getNetText` **when running locally, so the Shockwave movie can't read local drives at will.**

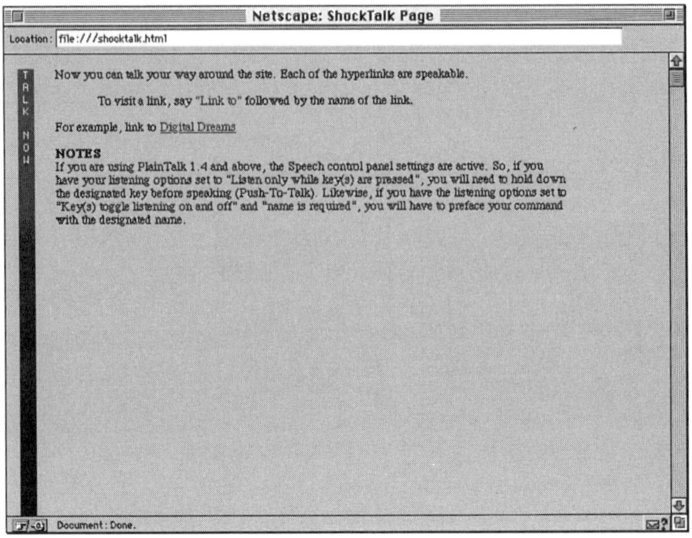

FIGURE 21.3

Making a page speakable is simple. This sample page was made speakable with the SHOCKTALK.DCR movie (12 KB) and a little bit of HTML.

IRC: How can someone get ShockTalk?

Tim: There is a free downloadable demo on the Digital Dreams website. And there is comprehensive documentation. The demo has a three month expiration date, or you can purchase an authoring version for $49.00. That's all you need to deliver speakable Shockwave movies. If you want to create a speakable title for CD-ROM delivery and you need to distribute the plug-in along with the CD, then we are asking a $449.00 license fee. But if you are focusing on Shockwave and delivering cool content on the Web, it is $49.00. You can point your viewers to us so they download the demo version of ShockTalk or purchase one.

Speakable Applets

Tim: I think the Web has a huge potential for speech applications. I think that one of the things we'll start to see on the Web is sites that are specifically geared to make use of speech—websites that are speech-centric so to speak. These sites would engage you in some kind of dialogue. It may ask you questions. You may be able to speak to fill out forms.

One of the things we've demonstrated is the concept of speakable applets, if you will—little applications that incorporate speech that can be delivered over the Web currently using Shockwave technology. I can see applications like Trivial Pursuit, games you can play with other people where you will respond verbally. It's basically the quiz show format. It asks you one of the multiple-choice questions and you answer. I think you will see a lot of what I call speakable applets.

One of the things we've demonstrated is the concept of speakable applets—little applications that incorporate speech that can be delivered over the Web currently using Shockwave technology.

A good example of that for developers to look at is our Capital Quiz speakable applet. Essentially, the way it works is you create a new instance of the XObject or Xtra. You create a language object which contains the words and phrases that you are expecting. So after you define that language, or lexicon of speakable items, you then start listening. When the plug-in gets notified that one of those phrases in your lexicon has been recognized, it sends your Lingo script a message saying it recognized a particular phrase. Then you have a handler that interprets what that means. It's as simple as that. That's the real basics of it.

Capital Quiz

We'll step away from the interview for a minute. The image shown in Figure 21.4 is from the Capital Quiz speakable applet. The quiz asks you to name the capital city of a state chosen at random. You can tell it that "you don't know," or ask to "repeat the question," and so on. The quiz is fun and functional.

You can author your own speakable Shockwave applet using Digital Dreams' speech XObject (for Director 4) or their speech Xtra (for Director 5). To get some idea how it works, look at the following example.

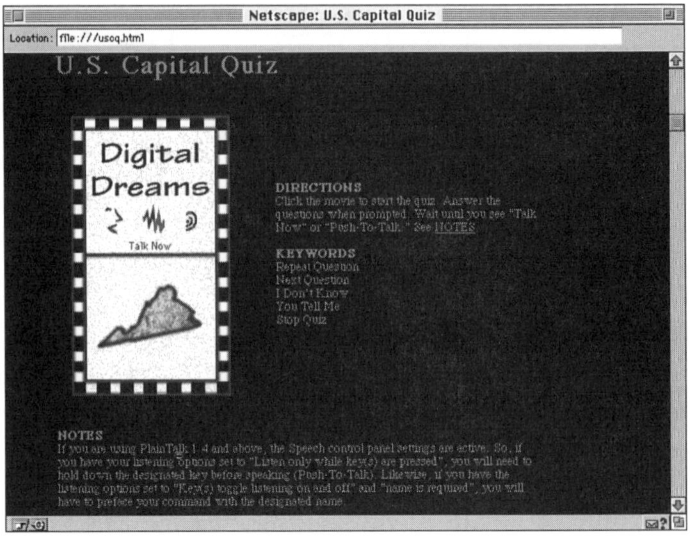

Figure 21.4

The Digital Dreams Capital Quiz asks questions and responds to spoken answers.

Let's say you wanted to make a speakable Blackjack game in Shockwave for Director 5. The game would need to recognize the phrases "hit me" and "I'll stick" at the very least. Here's a bare-bones set of scripts to make it work.

The first script is an `onStartMovie` script which initializes the Director movie for speech whenever the movie starts. It creates an instance of the speechXtra into the object `gSpeechObj`. Then it creates the language containing our two phrases.

```
on startMovie
  global gSpeechObj
  -- is the object already instantiated?
  if objectP( gSpeechObj ) then set gSpeechObj = 0
  -- load the Xtra
  openXLib "SpeechXtra"
  -- create new instance, pass callback script, use feedback window
  set gSpeechObj to new(xtra "SpeechXtra", birth (script "aCallBack"),
  ➥1)
  put value( gSpeechObj ) into result
  if (result < 0) then
    alert "Error" && result && "trying to create the Speech Xtra."
  else
    -- create the main language
```

```
      set MainLM = gSpeechObj(mNewLanguage, "<Main>")
      -- add a couple of speakable phrases
      gSpeechObj(mAddPhrase, MainLM, "Hit me", 1)
      gSpeechObj(mAddPhrase, MainLM, "I'll stick", 2)
      -- make it active
      gSpeechObj(mSetLanguage, MainLM)
      -- we can release our reference to it after making it active
      gSpeechObj(mRelease, MainLM)
      gSpeechObj(mStartListening)
    end if
  end
```

When `gSpeechObj` recognizes that a phrase in the active language has been spoken, it calls the `doRecognize` handler and passes the recognized phrase. As written now, the `doRecognize` handler just echoes the phrase into the message window. When you write your own speakable movies, the `doRecognize` handler is where you'll trigger responses to your phrases.

```
on doRecognize phrase, phraseID
  -- echo phrase
  put phrase
end doRecognize
```

Repurposing Xtras for the Web

IRC: What advantages does Shockwave offer in delivering speech recognition on the Web?

Tim: First off, Shockwave really enabled us to provide speech recognition on the Web. The day that I heard Shockwave supported Xtras was the day we had a version up on the Web demonstrating the technology. Before Shockwave, I was waiting to see exactly how we could deliver speech recognition on the Web.

Today you can find a Netscape plug-in that will let you do speech recognition to do speakable links. In fact, that's all it does. But it requires you to have a separate file with associated links and phrases. That is redundant information. Shockwave allows us to circumvent that whole redundancy and maintenance issue. Because now we can be embedded on the person's page and scan the HTML within the page and the links are automatically speakable. And, furthermore, what you cannot do with a dedicated speech recognition plug-in is deliver the kind of interactive animated experience that Shockwave gives you along with the speech recognition. There is nothing else that offers that. This is a breakthrough technology.

IRC: Can you comment on the types of experiences that Shockwave enables, especially when Shockwave is modified for speech recognition?

Tim: I think it can be used as an educational tool. You can provide essentially multiple-choice question-and-answer forums using ShockTalk. That's one area.

Dana: The first thing that I thought of was the Trivial Pursuit-type games. The thing that is so valuable about the Net, but is difficult to do with speech and it doesn't necessarily have to do with ShockTalk, is just searching and acquiring information on the Net. That doesn't have anything to do with Shockwave per se.

When all the Director developers who are building Shockwave apps start really working with speech recognition, it will be interesting. We've investigated and looked at hundreds and hundreds of Shockwave movies—I'd say 600 or 700 different sites. And we've seen really cool applications of Shockwave with very small footprints.

Being able to interact with these movies by voice would be great. And again it goes back to encouraging developers to adopt this new technology. So there is a lot of evangelism that has to go on.

What you can't do with a dedicated speech recognition plug-in is deliver the kind of interactive animated experience that Shockwave gives you along with the speech recognition. There is nothing else that offers that. This is a breakthrough technology.

Tim: Here's another use that ShockTalk enables. I've talked to the Simon & Schuster folks about online demos, given that they have three titles now that incorporate speech recognition for the Macintosh. With Shockwave they can essentially offer previews of those titles, including the speech-recognition component using ShockTalk which is very cool for them. If people are questioning whether this really works, they could go to the Simon & Schuster website and get a ShockTalk preview of the CD and see if the speech recognition stuff really works.

IRC: Sure, that might be a boon to their sales. And repurposing for that would be easy because those titles were probably created in Director.

Dana: Yeah. And it should be said that interesting speech-recognition applications will be enabled with the Shockwave plug-in for Authorware. Authorware is the premiere training environment, and now it can be online. San Francisco State University is offering multimedia courses on the Net. So with Authorware, you could have online quizzes and classes. [And if Digital Dreams makes a speech recognition Xtra for Authorware it could be speakable—auth.]

Or if you're in a corporate intranet environment and you are learning about policy. I'm a new manager and I need to find out about the Human Resources policies. A speech-enhanced online training and education will be more interactive and maintain the user's interest as well as his retention of the information.

Tim: One of the areas of commercial success in the speech recognition community has been voice activated banking. The transfer of funds from one account to the other can be done with speech recognition via the telephone, for instance. Well, now you have Internet banking, like Wells Fargo online. I just went to my Wells Fargo account yesterday and transferred money online from my accounts. I could do that using speech online.

Dana: You have to understand that Tim and I believe speech will be prevalent on all consumer appliances eventually. It is the most natural form of communicating.

Tips for Speech-Aware Shockwave

Tim: And it does require some design. You can do a bad implementation of speech that basically doesn't work and gives the impression to the end user that speech recognition technology doesn't work. Or you can do a well-designed implementation that has a very high accuracy rate and offers a very good experience.

Rules for Speech Implementation

Noel: Ok, we want to encourage the readers of our book to try out ShockTalk to create speakable Shockwave movies. So what tips can you offer them for successful implementation of speech?

Tim: Don't try to do too much. Keep the complexity of the language model—the number of words you can say at any particular time—to a minimum. Make sure you do testing to verify that the words in your lexicon don't conflict with each other. Avoid similar sounding words and "copy/paste" sort of phrases that might conflict with voice-controlled system functions.

As much as possible, try to provide visual feedback for the user. Provide feedback for what a user can say at any particular point in time and also for whether it is actually listening. The user needs some visual feedback as to what state the system is in.

Dana: Also, on feedback, you should give the user some verification when their words are recognized. And do something different. Don't do the one-to-one mapping of every link or every button to speech. Do something different with speech. This is a new technology that is going to add a whole new dimension to the user's experience. Don't limit yourself to the obvious. Experiment and have fun with it. We haven't thought of everything you can do with speech.

Tim: Also, you don't want to use single-syllable words. Interestingly enough, all speech recognition systems work better if you give them more information—longer words, more phrases. So, a two- or three-word command is going to get much better recognition accuracy versus a one-word command. The more information there is in the utterance, the more likely the recognizer is going to pick it up.

IRC: I'm curious about that rule. What is the nature of that?

Tim: It basically comes down to the amount of information that is in an utterance. It is easier to decipher meaning if you have more information, more context. If I shout to you across a room just one word out of nothing and you have no context, you will find it very difficult to figure out exactly what I said. The recognizer has exactly the same problem. That problem is not unique to the technology; it is just information theory really. It is much easier to recognize something in context than in isolation.

Don't do the one-to-one mapping of every link or every button to speech. Do something different with speech. This is a new technology that is going to add a whole new dimension to the user's experience. Don't limit yourself to the obvious. Experiment and have fun with it.

IRC: In terms of the software platform itself, what is it that users have to do? What hoops do you make your users jump through in order to get their platform up?

Tim: Today, you need a Power Macintosh computer with Apple's speech-recognition technology installed. Apple's speech technology is available free from the Web at `http://www.speech.apple.com`. And you need to install a ShockTalk plug-in. That assumes you have Shockwave installed already. And a compatible browser. I don't know yet if it works with Internet Explorer on the Mac. I've been told it should.

Frequently Encountered Glitches

IRC: What kind of technical difficulties are frequently encountered?

Tim: The most common problem that people run into is having the plug-in installed in the wrong place. In Shockwave for Director 4, ShockTalk goes in the Netscape plug-ins folder alongside of Shockwave. For Shockwave for Director 5, the ShockTalk plug-in has to go in the Shockwave folder inside Netscape plug-ins folder.

The other issue in speech recognition is do you have your sound input control panel setup correctly? In other words, is it listening to the microphone or the internal CD? It will only work if it is listening to the microphone. And I think those are the two major issues. Oh, and is the microphone plugged in? That's a real basic one, but a lot of people get caught on that.

Dana: And with push-to-talk, they need to assign a key. That is something that people might forget—to assign and then push the key.

There are also some tips for speech usage. When you are using the push-to-talk feature, don't press down the key really hard because all that does is throw a bunch of noise up. Don't shout, just speak naturally. And, when you push-to-talk, pause a little before you say the command.

User Feedback

IRC: Do you have any feedback so far from the Web users? Are there any interesting implementations from other developers?

Tim: I haven't seen any interesting implementations from other developers yet. We've had a lot of positive feedback from people checking out the Capital Quiz and the speakable links on our site. We've had, at this point, something in the order of 10,000 downloads of the ShockTalk plug-in since it was released in March 1996. There are a considerable number of people experimenting with it.

People are experimenting, and they are really trying to see how they can create a Shockwave movie that incorporates speech recognition.

Text-to-Speech

IRC: What we are finding is that people are still getting their bearings enough to use Shockwave in non-trivial ways like creating interfaces and immersive experiences. The speech-awareness challenge is a very exciting one, I think.

Tim: As far as I can tell, the big challenge is keeping the content small—small enough so that you can deliver it at 28.8k. One of the advantages, of course, of speech recognition and text-to-speech is that the content itself is extremely small. The content is basically text, ASCII text, because all the technology is on the client machine. So, for example, the Capital Quiz right now weighs in at 260 KB, of which about 100 KB is digitized audio, and if we replaced the audio with speech synthesis, text-to-speech, it would lose 100 KB. So there is another true advantage of using this technology.

IRC: And you can use the ShockTalk plug-in for text-to-speech?

Dana: Yes. And one of the beauties of voice synthesis is that it gives more than a 10 to 1 savings in the size of the audio in your files. And it saves production costs. Instead of hiring voice talent for voice-over, you use high-quality synthesized voices.

There are dozens of different voices you can choose from. There are funny ones like Bubbles and Whisper. Or the new children's voice like Princess used primarily for children's educational titles.

And flexibility is a huge plus. If you have to go back in to revise or edit the files, that costs a lot of money and time in voice-over. But with text-to-speech, you just change the text or change the voice assignment and that's it.

How About Windows?

Tim: The biggest challenge is the other platform. Because there is no free speech technology on Windows. There are plenty of speech technologies on that platform, but they all cost money. They all have fairly large licensing costs associated with them. I've worked with a number of them. We are essentially working to OEM some technology on that platform so we can provide a multiplatform solution.

Now Microsoft has their own speech recognition technology that is basically equivalent to PlainTalk. But they have not released it publicly. They have OEM'd it with a couple of products. My sense is that they will release it publicly and distribute it with the operating system in less then a year's time, probably more like six months, at which point it becomes a non-issue. Then our ShockTalk Xtra for Windows will support Microsoft's speech API and ShockTalk for the Mac will continue to support PlainTalk. And from the Shockwave point of view, you won't need to know the difference. Use the same Lingo, the same script.

IRC: That will be very cool. Now can you speculate on how speech recognition will fit into the immersive online environments of the future, when there is really good 3D and broadband and so forth?

Tim: I definitely see speech recognition applied in various kinds of 3D VR domains for doing basic stuff like command and control within those environments. I'm not really sure how the broadband streaming technology is going to affect speech recognition, given that the technology is implemented on the host machine anyway. It doesn't take much bandwidth or need to be streamed. It isn't server-dependent.

Dana: And the future of speech recognition on the Net relates to the future of Shockwave and other Internet technologies in general. The applications could be networked games, being able to play games over the Net by voice, chats, workgroups, learning applications, distance learning. Or there could even be interactive serials. You could become a character on *Melrose Place* online or God knows what. Speech again is just another interface. It's another way to provide command and control, or with speech out it has almost limitless opportunities for dialogues.

Conclusion

Once speech recognition becomes standard and free on the Windows platform, we expect speakable applications to really flourish. The mixture of Tim and Dana's exciting speech technology with the creativity of the thousands of Shockwave developers is sure to produce some explosively cool speakable applications.

So far, the killer app for speech on the Web seems to be the speakable links concept. Future immersive environments will be defined by how fun, easy, and human-like their interfaces can be. We expect speech will play an important role in the formation of immersive worlds as today's prototype speech applications become tomorrow's human language verbal interfaces.

Chapter 22

Education and Non-Profit: Rainforest Action Network

The theme of this chapter is how Shockwave can be used by educational and non-profit organizations on the Web. The suspense-filled plot is the story of how a non-profit organization, the Rainforest Action Network, came to have their website shocked and what it all meant.

Along the way, we meet characters from the Institute for Global Communications (IGC), the Electronic Publishing and Instructional Curriculum (EPIC) program at the University of California at Santa Cruz, and the Rainforest Action Network (RAN).

AUTHORS' NOTE

Where does this fit into the Big Picture?

In this chapter we have several varieties of Shockwave examples. The shocked RAN page is an interactive kiosk-type piece in the True Multimedia category of the Big Picture. (See figure 2.1 in Chapter 2, "Power on the Web.") The Wacky Microscope example is part of a True Application— online education. The implications of the discussion with Professor Marti Atkinson project possible True Applications and Broadband Environments.

A Shockwave Conspiracy

We have seen by now that Shockwave can be an excellent tool for training and education. The realities of the marketplace have meant that a vast majority of educational Shockwave pioneering has focused on training in the corporate setting. In writing this book, we wanted to explore how Shockwave is viewed by educators and students of new interactive Web technology.

Just a quick look at the various libraries of Shockwave content, such as the Macromedia Vanguard Gallery (`http://www.macromedia.com/shockwave/epicenter/vanguard/`), shows that current Shockwave content is generally developed for use in corporate sites. The reason is simple. Corporations are entities that have both the interest and the means to maintain a cutting-edge position vis a vis new Web technology. Many individuals and all types of organizations have begun to use the Web for many purposes, but in general, large companies have been most able to take advantage of new Web technologies such as Shockwave.

As we have discussed in several other chapters, Shockwave can facilitate several important corporate goals on the Net, such as furthering brand recognition and identity, creating rich interactions with the clients and customers, keeping the users in the site longer, delivering marketable content, front-ending software products, and so on. But these goals are not the exclusive province of corporate Web strategies. Many different types of organizations and institutions on the Web can use Shockwave to their advantage.

As supporters of various social change movements, we were curious to see how Shockwave could be used by non-profit organizations. In the process of addressing this question, we confirmed one of our assumptions—almost no non-profit organizations or community organizations were using Shockwave at all. Even the non-profits with a fairly developed presence on the Web seem to have entirely missed the boat to Shockland.

Because the Institute of Global Communications is the only non-profit Internet service provider (ISP) in the USA, it seemed a logical starting place to try to find what non-profits are thinking about Shockwave. The following section provides some background on IGC.

The Institute for Global Communications

IGC, through its IGC Networks—PeaceNet, EcoNet, ConflictNet, LaborNet and now, WomensNet—serve individuals and organizations working toward peace, environmental protection, human rights, social and economic justice, sustainable and equitable development, health, and nonviolent conflict resolution.

Since beginning operation in 1986, the IGC Networks have grown to more than 13,000 users in 133 countries. Through close working relationships with the Association for Progressive Communications (APC) and the APC member and partner systems in more than 20 countries, this community of environmental and peace activists includes another 20,000 Canadian, European, Asian, Latin American, South Pacific, and African members.

IGC achieves near self-sufficiency in the basic functions of the networks through the monthly subscriber fees of its members. For a non-profit organization, self-sufficiency is quite an accomplishment. Additional funding is provided to IGC by various foundations. Figure 22.1 shows the IGC home page.

FIGURE 22.1

You can visit the Institute for Global Communications website at http:// www.igc.apc.org/.

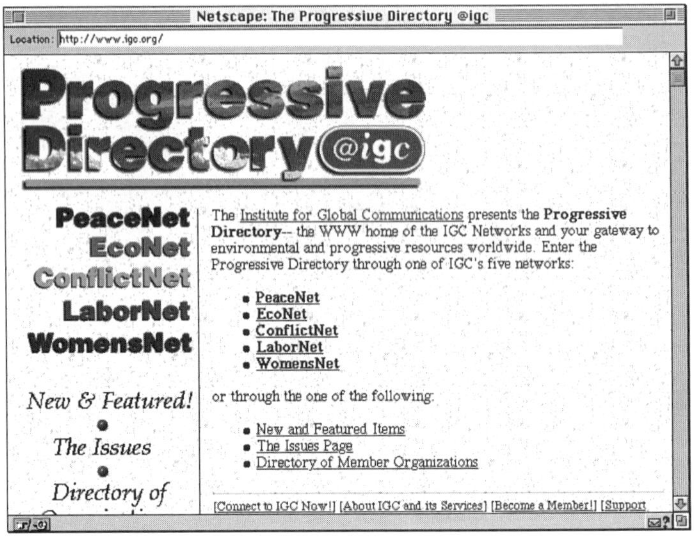

IGC has an extensive array of fascinating online resources. IGC is also one of the best news sources on the Web. Of course, the news you get is clearly from the perspective of individuals and organizations that share the goals of social justice in common. From our perspective, this is a refreshing reminder of the potential of the Internet to bring common people together for the uncommon purpose of improving the world we live in.

As luck would have it, a good friend of ours, Josue Guillen, had recently been hired by IGC to become part of their outreach staff. What we asked of Josue was to grant an interview. But what we got was a bit more than we bargained for.

The Interview with Josue from IGC

InfraRed Communications: What are non-profits doing on the Web today?

Josue Guillen: Mostly, non-profits are creating Web pages simply to have them—to create a presence. A lot of them are registering domain names, just to get them registered. They are not using them yet but reserving them for the future. I don't think many non-profit organizations have really thought through what you can really do on the Web.

Fund-raising is always a consideration for non-profits. The more content you have accessible, particularly to potential contributors, the better you can appeal to them. Trying to impress both foundations and the donor base is important. For the most part, what non-profits are thinking about the Web is "Let's tell the world what we are doing and just put it up there." That is as far as it has gotten really. Most non-profits are not even to the point where they offer a membership form online or an online donation form.

One particularly huge website on the IGC network is the Rainforest Action Network (RAN). IGC is a really cool environmental activism group that puts the public spotlight on destroyers of the rain forests. They are one of the few organizations on IGC's servers using things like credit card orders, online membership, and donations, and online protest actions such as automatic faxing. [See figure 22.2.] That's probably the most technologically advanced of the websites that we host at IGC.

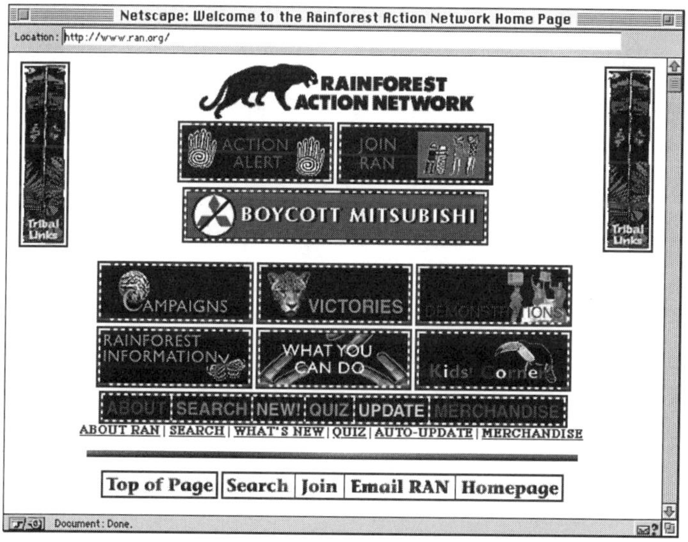

FIGURE 22.2

The Rainforest Action Network is hosted on IGC's Web server. Relative to many other non-profits, their site is very advanced. You can find RAN's site at http://www.ran.org/.

IRC: What other organizations' sites are served by IGC?

Josue: We have some unions on our servers—the Teamsters and AFSCME, for example. Grass-roots community organizations like the Center for Third World Organizing. A handful of different foundations are online, or planning to launch websites. There's a whole lot of organizations.

Developing Non-Profit Uses of the Web

IRC: What goals are your member organizations pursuing on the Web? Why are they committing resources to be on the Web?

Josue: At the moment, *they* are there because *it* is there—because they want to stay with the technology or they just want to be ready when someone suggests a purpose or a use. I'm fascinated by this because those of us on the IGC staff can recommend different directions to our member organizations. Our advisory role is going to grow as the IGC staff develops strategies and even more expertise.

We've developed a Content and Community Department. What we seek is useful content. And getting people and organizations learning and talking to each other is our goal. So whenever you mention the words 'training' and 'presentation' as a possible use for Shockwave, I immediately start thinking about how we can test it out and work on creating pilot projects and an organizing model.

How about it guys? Let's take a community group on IGC and figure out how to shock their site in a productive way. Let's try and get, at the very least, their members to look at that Shockwave Web page, and then take it from there.

Now that I think of it, the Rainforest Action Network would be perfect as a shocked site. They are set up for online membership and donations. They can process credit cards or First Virtual transactions. It is very big and developed. That would be a perfect organization to work with on a pilot shocking project.

IRC: Well, let's figure out a way to hook up RAN with some people willing to volunteer their Shockwave development work. We would do it ourselves [at InfraRed—auth.], but we have this book to write. It might turn out to be a really interesting experiment to see how Shockwave can be used to promote RAN's work.

Josue: Cool. You find the Shockwave developers. I'll talk to the folks at RAN to see if this fits in with their plans.

Willing Victims

Without a doubt, our cunning friend Josue was pleased at having roped us into shocking the Rainforest Action Network for free. He is a true organizer. But really, it was not a difficult pitch at all. We were willing victims—although when we told Josue we didn't have the time to do it ourselves, we weren't kidding. So we had to pass the baton to some other willing victims. Luckily, the perfect combination of talent and social awareness was soon to be found.

We had been invited to the University of California at Santa Cruz by Professor Marti Atkinson to give a talk on Shockwave to the students in her Advanced Web Topics class. The students had been slaving away for months learning PERL and CGI and now Shockwave. As we made the long drive down the coast, we wondered if perhaps some of the students would volunteer to help shock the Rainforest Action Network.

Santa Cruz Advanced Web Topics Class

Marti Atkinson's Advanced Web Topics class is—as they might say in Santa Cruz—way cool. The class absorbs major Web technologies very rapidly in order to produce instructional websites for the real Web. The class is part of the school's Electronic Publishing and Instructional Curriculum (EPIC) whose mission is to explore and harness emerging digital communications for educational purposes. Figure 22.3 shows the EPIC home page.

The whole class is engaged in a collaborative project to build online educational exhibits for San Jose's Tech Museum of Innovation. These various online exhibits produced by the class form the bulk of the HyperTech site. They create exhibits on topics such as DNA, earthquakes, robotics, and so on. Figure 22.4 shows the HyperTech main menu page.

FIGURE 22.3

You can visit the Electronic Publishing & Instructional Curriculum (EPIC) website at http://epic.cse.ucsc.edu/.

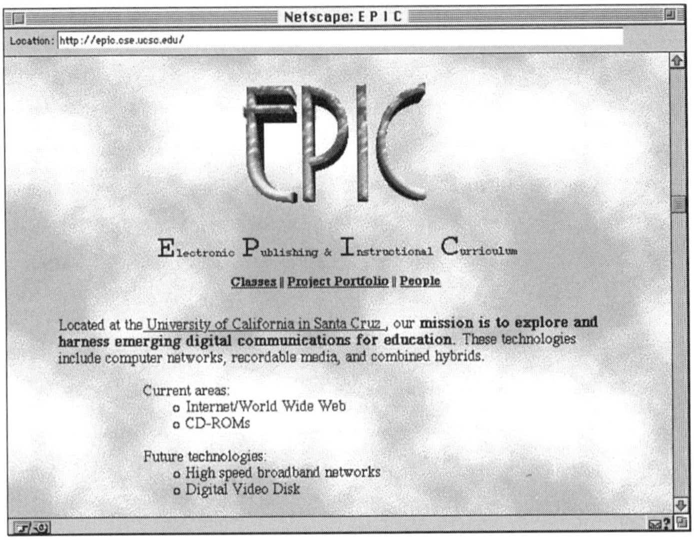

FIGURE 22.4

You can visit the HyperTech online educational website at http://www.thetech.org/hyper/.

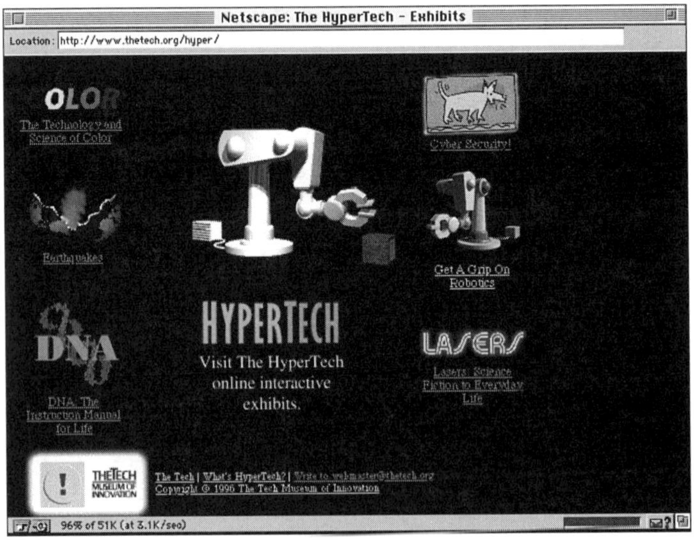

Willing Victims, Part II

In the course of our talk on basic Shockwave techniques, it became clear that many of the students were interested in the humanism of the Web—how Shockwave could be used for education, communication, collaboration, and so on. After the talk we showed them the IGC site and the Rainforest Action Network and asked for volunteers to help shock the RAN site.

To our pleasant surprise, and despite their stressful workload, five students came forward—Eddo Stern, Brandt Herrett, Cassie Ferguson, Mike Ziemba, and Dylan Thede. We wanted to know why they volunteered to help shock RAN, so we talked with Dylan Thede.

But the responsibility rests on those who understand the technology to bring it to the rest of the population so they, too, can learn how it can benefit them in their lives as opposed to keeping them down.

IRC: What interests you about shocking the Rainforest Action Network?

Dylan: It comes to this point. So far, those who do have the knowledge to manipulate this new medium of the Web have given very little toward betterment of people or betterment of the world. What we've seen is primarily commercial or entertainment uses. It's a very clubbish, exclusionary sort of thing. But the responsibility rests on those who understand the technology to bring it to the rest of the population so they, too, can learn how it can benefit them in their lives as opposed to keeping them down.

Dylan's comment and other comments like it from the other volunteers, gave us confidence that this team of students would do a great job on the shocking RAN project (of course you'll be the judge of that). Later on, Professor Marti Atkinson and several of her colleagues from her class took us out to dinner. Everyone present made some very interesting observations on the issue of Shockwave and education. In the following section, we present some of what Marti had to say.

Interviewing Professor Marti Atkinson

IRC: What do you do in the Advanced Web Topics class?

Marti: Advanced Web Topics is an attempt to keep up with the changing technology on the Web. It is an attempt to identify how we can harness it for educational purposes, which is my interest in multimedia. The Tech Museum project has illustrated how the Web can be used in collaborative education. Museums are starting to get interested in that.

The idea of a museum without walls has come into circulation in the last few years. The Exploratorium in San Francisco was on the forefront of that. It is an easy step for them to go from exhibits on the floor to exhibits online. What we've been pushing for is the expansion of what they think of as an exhibit. We want to offer more interactivity so there is more to an exhibit than pushing a button. Perhaps the user could work with some data or be able to build things—interacting in virtual environments.

The direction that I'd like to move, before there is broadband, is using CD-ROM and online hybrid technologies. We are looking into using Shockwave to bridge the two. That way we can get a jump on what broadband is going to be like and play with the possibilities and see where you can push it.

IRC: What have been some of the obstacles to taking that next step in interactivity?

Marti: Well, partially it's the tools, or lack of tools. Shockwave is a great step in the right direction. You can create much more interactive objects. Objects that do things. In the long-run, we will need to see a more object-oriented programming environment for the Web that you can program objects and interact with them, sort of like the direction that ScriptX was going but never quite managed to pull off.

So you could have a world that's electronic, but very similar to our world. For instance, you could pick up a chemical beaker—a virtual chemical beaker—full of some horrendous acid, and pour and mix and create an explosion. Or you could take a virtual trip into the interior of a volcano or walk on the face of the Moon or explore the bottom of the oceans.

Having content like that on the Web would be an ideal method of distribution—everybody could find it and it would always be up to date. Hybrid CD/Web titles are useful because you can put updates on the Web, but maintain the same user interface as on the CD and not scare people off by forcing them to learn two separate interfaces.

One great problem we grapple with in academia is how to move the research developed in the universities out into the schools much faster. In our case, the research is on teaching methods. Better ways of teaching are being developed, but it is not getting filtered down to all the teachers out there. If and when the teachers get wired—and that's a whole other issue in itself—they can get the latest methods and curricula. They can find out what's the best way to teach subject X or creative kinds of projects to involve their students in. A lot of teaching materials already exist out on the Web, and now we can create a collaborative working environment.

IRC: Have you seen any interesting uses of Shockwave for online interactive education?

Marti: Yes, I saw a Shockwave movie on the New York Hall of Science site that I really liked. [See figure 22.5.] It's in an exhibit on microbes with a Shockwave microscope that lets you zoom and pan the image of different cells.

FIGURE 22.5

You can see the "Wacky Microscope" Shockwave movie at http://www.nyhallsci.org/electron_frame.html. The image of the cells pan and zoom much like a real microscope.

IRC: What has been the effect of the Web on education in general?

Marti: There is an incredible potential for Web education. You can experience and see so much that was previously unreachable. You can take a trip to Nairobi or attend a lecture of a top professor across the continent or get the latest research results that relate to your studies or perform virtual experiments. It gives you the awesome power to get at this content, and all at will. As a repository of information, it allows us to accumulate the findings and learn from our experiences.

There is an incredible potential for Web education. You can experience and see so much that was previously unreachable.

In academia, a tremendous amount of research can go into a study whose result may become just one line in a textbook somewhere. But is that line in a textbook the best way to communicate the knowledge? The Web offers the possibility of a more experiential learning—an interactive learning with a rich media representation of knowledge, rather than plain text. And with broadband, you can have collaborative workspaces and real distance learning. The potential is enormous.

The Web has also changed the role of the teacher. The role has changed from that of the all-knowing figure at the head of the class to that of a collaborator or facilitator. As they say, we used to be "the sage on the stage." Now we are "the guide on the side." It's a lot harder and you need to work in smaller groups—more like a lab setting than a lecture.

It also means that the students have to adjust to the fact that the teacher does not have all the answers. Nobody can. There's too much to know. In the first quarter of the Advanced Web Topics class, my poor students would say "Tell us what to do," and I'd say "I don't know, we'll figure it out as we go." So it's also learning how to deal with change—how to constantly deal with new things we've never seen before.

IRC: So now, what happens in schools where there is no Web access? What happens to the students who are growing up without the Web?

Marti: It brings up a long-standing discussion we've had in education. Either people learn to control technology or they become controlled by it. More and more, the people who are lucky enough to have access and status move forward, and those who live in poorer neighborhoods or rural areas don't. As we become a society where the distribution of information is essential, these division will only be more extreme. The $64,000 question is how can we use this technology to better humankind, rather than to maintain the status quo or go backward?

The Rainforest Action Network

In many ways, the Rainforest Action Network, in its campaign to save the world's rain forests, demonstrates key ways in which the Web medium can be used to make our world better and sustainable. The RAN website, `http://www.ran.org`, has proven to be an effective tool for distributing information, communicating organizational objectives, providing activists with a means of action, and generating much-needed income. Because "Action" is RAN's middle name, the Action Alert button occupies a prominent place on the home page. Clicking to the Action Alert page gives news and analysis of the burning issues of the month (see fig. 22.6).

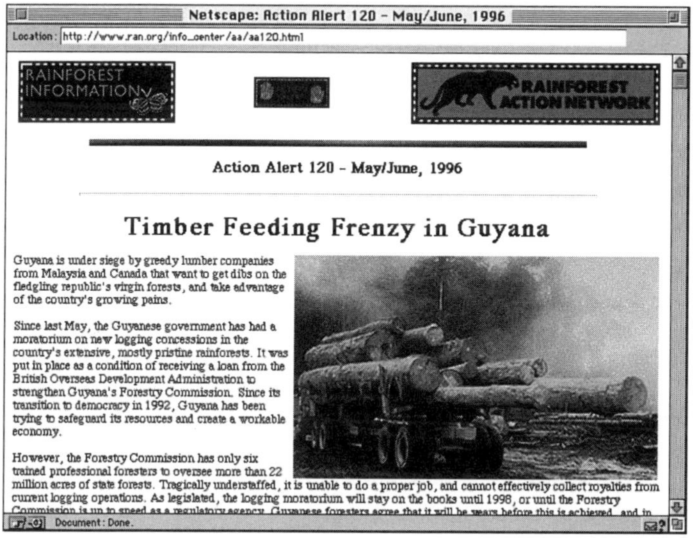

Figure 22.6

This is RAN's monthly Action Alert page, which has information on critical rain forest issues. Pictured here is the Action Alert of May/June 1996 warning of an impending deal to destroy 1.5 million acres of rain forest in Guyana.

The Action Alert page gives more than passive information. You can take action by sending a letter of protest targeted at rain forest destroyers. The Internet activist can send protests by way of e-mail, or RAN's fax-server. There is a letter template online. Just edit the letter and click the "Send" button.

RAN's statistics show that nearly one out of ten visitors use the Action Alert fax/e-mail feature. This is an extremely high rate of return, especially when compared to snail mail letter-writing campaigns that usually get only a one to three percent response. The RAN site also enables members to find and contact the local Rainforest Action Group near them or establish a new one where none exists.

Visitors can join RAN and make donations online. RAN has a secure server for credit card charges. Astonishingly, the memberships generated from RAN's "Join Online" page have covered the initial investment of machines and additional staffing in just five months of operations. What's more, RAN is getting an extremely high percentage of international members joining through the website, thus facilitating their campaigns that span the globe.

Interview with RAN's Media Director

After we assembled the student team at UC Santa Cruz, the next step was to coordinate with the staff of the Rainforest Action Network. Josue from IGC put us in touch with Mark Westlund, RAN's Media Director.

IRC: Mark, what organizational goals are driving RAN's Web strategy?

Mark: Our goal is to put the tools of activism into as many hands as possible. So the Net is a very effective way of doing this. Many of our target rain forest destroyers—such as Mitsubishi, Texaco, Shell Oil, and others—are transnational corporations, and with the Net we are able to get the information to people in affected areas, as well as the company's home turf. I'm willing to bet that by visiting our home page, more Japanese nationals have found out about Mitsubishi's significant role in destroying the environment than through any other available media outlets.

IRC: What is RAN's current strategy for maintaining leadership and presence on the Web?

Mark: You can go two ways in designing a website. You can go with simple text that's easy to download or you can use a lot of graphics to create a real environment. The text-heavy sites can be viewed anywhere, on any machine—and if the content is well-presented, you can get your point across. Earth Island's page is a good example of this type of design.

RAN, however, strives to marry content with visuals to create our own environment and imbue the page with RAN's organizational personality. This is much more exciting to visit, and Web surfers really feel like they have found something special. For instance, the Join Online section tries to illustrate the actions your money can initiate. [See figure 22.7.] There are GIFs of our activists climbing up office buildings and hanging up our banners. It's exciting.

FIGURE 22.7

The unshocked Join Online section starts with a page illustrating RAN's banner-hanging actions and describes what the different donation amounts can pay for.

Part of our strategy, too, is keeping up with current Web technology. We use Shockwave and real audio, and are working on a new section with frames and GIF animation. Because RAN is a membership organization, we are trying to keep current with ways to exchange money on the Net. We added a secure server for credit card membership sign-ons and for merchandise sales—and we recently added First Virtual as an option. I don't think a preferred method of exchange has been established yet on the Net, but we want to be there when it does.

IRC: In what ways has the Web facilitated RAN's goals?

Mark: We are able to send thousands of letters by way of our Web Action Alerts. What makes our Action Alerts particularly effective is that they conclude with a letter of protest to the targeted rain forest destroyer. In the case of the Saro-Wiwa alert, for instance, the virtual activist sends e-mail to President Clinton, urging an embargo on all Nigerian oil products. With the mahogany alert, the letter goes by way of fax-server directly to Brazil's Minister of the Environment. The letter template can be edited online, or transmitted as is. Just click the Send button and there you are—you've made an honest to goodness political statement.

IRC: Can you describe the key design and technical challenges that RAN has faced in implementing your Web strategy?

Mark: Because the site is so multi-leveled, with sections for each campaign—and within each campaign, numerous subsections for specific topics—it was imperative to develop an easy way of letting the viewers know where they are and how to get out. Our Web weaver, Jay Cheroske, designed a three-part navigation bar that can take you back to the section index, the subsection index, or back to the home page. The greatest technological challenge was developing the scripts for the fax server on the Action Alerts, but once the weaver was comfortable with Perl and CGI, the problem was fairly well solved.

IRC: How does the Shockwave movie that the UC Santa Cruz students made fit into the RAN website?

Mark: Shockwave is used to jazz up the Join Online section. It begins with an animation of a bulldozer destroying a healthy rain forest. [See figure 22.8.]

Rolling over the different donation amounts brings up text and an image describing RAN's activities, just like in the unshocked page, only more appealing. For instance, you see that a $35 donation allows RAN to give a slide show about the rain forest. [See figure 22.9.]

FIGURE 22.8

The shocked RAN page starts with an animation of rainforest destruction.

FIGURE 22.9

The shocked RAN page has rollover buttons for each dollar amount, creating a lively menu of action that the potential member's contribution can instigate.

To drive the point home, when the viewer clicks on a donation amount, RAN's panther logo shoots out of the button and lands on the bulldozer. As the bulldozer is pushed back, the forest is restored bit by bit. [See figure 22.10.] That's meant to represent to the potential member the end result of his or her contribution—restoring the rain forest. All in all, it's rather upbeat and compelling.

Figure 22.10

Clicking on the donation amounts shoots out a growling panther, forcing the bulldozer to retreat from the advancing forest.

Note

To see the shocked RAN page, use a Shockwave-enabled browser to open the file SHKJOIN.HTM from the Chapter 22 folder on the accompanying CD.

Credits for the production team:

Marti Atkinson	consultant
Cassie Ferguson	graphic design
Brandt Herrett	Director production
Noel Rabinowitz	Director production
Eddo Stern	Director production
Dylan Thede	team coordination
Mike Ziemba	sound design

IRC: Who are the supporters of RAN and why might Shockwave help build support?

Mark: RAN supporters fall into all age and economic brackets—but with upwards of 17,000 people a week visiting our website, we need to talk to these people in a way that makes sense to them and that they will remember. Once someone has visited our page, I want to leave them with a strong impression of RAN and a strong sense of urgency about world rain forest issues. Shockwave will certainly help me grab people's attention. We can't afford to let RAN sink into the background on the Web. We have to stand out.

Anything we can do to make RAN's page more active, and more interactive, will get people more involved in rain forest issues and in RAN causes. Shockwave is still in its baby stages, and we plan to grow with it. We already have plans to do a movie with a counter showing how many acres of rain forest are being destroyed. We want to have an animated panther logo and animated section headings. And, of course, as new software develops, we plan to stay on the leading edge.

Conclusion

Ultimately it is our hope that the great communication potential of the Web can be developed for the greater social good and not merely made servant to the profit motive. It appears that Shockwave for educational uses and for the development of non-profit organizations holds much promise in this regard. The RAN Shockwave story shows what can be done when the hopeful idealism of young developers is put together with the purposeful efforts of non-profit social change organizations. We were pleased to have played our part in this effort and we see it as just the beginning of building interactivism on the Web with Shockwave.

Part VI

Wrapping It Up

CHAPTER 23

Future of Shockwave

This book would not be complete without some speculation, prediction, and general comments about the future of Shockwave and the network in general. Although we can only begin to cover these issues in the space of one chapter, we will discuss some of the more exciting developments relating to Shockwave as well as some of the potential opportunities and pitfalls brought about by the growing importance of the Internet and related technologies.

Shockwave Everywhere

The biggest complaint about Shockwave has been that users have had to download the plug-in to be able to see Shockwave movies. This is changing. In 1996 alone, Macromedia has announced that Shockwave for Director will be included in Microsoft's Internet Explorer 3.0 as well as future versions of Windows 95; Apple's Cyberdog and Internet Connection Kit; future versions of America Online; and even Oracle's Network computer. Netscape is also introducing a technology called LiveConnect, which may have profound effects on Shockwave.

By including Shockwave with the operating system or networking software, Macromedia is pushing to make Shockwave for Director a fundamental data type on the World Wide Web, much like GIF or MPEG files. This obviously creates a tremendous opportunity for Shockwave developers—the potential audience for Shockwave movies will approach the total size of the potential audience for the entire Web.

At press time, Macromedia had announced agreements for the inclusion of only Shockwave for Director on these platforms. It is probable, however, that eventually these agreements will also include the other flavors of Shockwave.

Microsoft, Macromedia, and You

In many ways, this is the most exciting announcement of all. The inclusion of Shockwave with Windows 95, the most popular operating system around, means that many millions of PC users will have the Shockwave plug-in. It also opens up new possible uses for Shockwave. Because Shockwave will be implemented as an ActiveX control, it will be available not only in Internet Explorer, but any other application that can handle ActiveX controls. This means that future versions of Visual Basic and Visual C++ will probably be able to create applications that include Shockwave movies. Again, this opens up tremendous new fields of opportunity for Shockwave developers.

Microsoft's commitment to include Shockwave in the next version of Windows 95 is important for another reason: it adds a major amount of respectability to Shockwave. It means that Shockwave will be perceived as not just a neato toy that only people who spend far too much time surfing the Web have, but as a basic part of the Windows system. This will make Shockwave far easier to sell to potential clients.

Microsoft has indicated that in the next version of Windows 95 the Internet will be integrated much more tightly into the desktop. So the importance of Internet-related technologies in general will be much higher. Because Shockwave will be the first ActiveX control that Microsoft packages with Microsoft Internet Explorer, the Windows 95 operating system, and the Windows 95 original equipment manufacturer's kit, it will have clear leadership in this category.

Note

ActiveX is Microsoft's container technology, which, in theory, is the future of software. Conceptually, any product that is ActiveX-compatible can use any ActiveX control. ActiveX is an evolution of OLE (Object Linking and Embedding); Apple's equivalent container technology is OpenDoc.

Unleashing the Cyberdog

In May 1996 Apple Computer and Macromedia announced the development of Shockwave for Director for the Apple Cyberdog Internet software suite. This provides enhanced interactive and multimedia viewing on the Web for Cyberdog users. Apple also intends to bundle the Shockwave plug-in in the Apple Internet Connection Kit, which is included in many Apple Macintosh computers.

Macromedia's Shockwave part is an important endorsement of the OpenDoc-based Cyberdog technology, which enables developers and users to build compound documents and applications for Internet access and information management.

Cyberdog, described in greater detail in Chapter 20 "Creating Complex Applications: Apple Computer," is Apple's new integrated software suite that provides easy and intuitive access to Internet resources. The advantage to Cyberdog is that it offers the first Internet suite of products with a common look and feel, offering easy drag-and-drop control across different Internet services, as well as tight integration with the Mac OS and Macintosh OpenDoc-compliant applications.

We anticipate that when future versions of Shockwave are contained within component integration systems such as OpenDoc, whole new classes of applications can be created using Shockwave. It represents the explosive combination of Shockwave's rich metaphors and user interfaces with the power of any OpenDoc-compliant software product or custom-made application.

America Online, Shockwave, and You (and 5,999,999 of Your Closest Friends)

Macromedia's announcement that Shockwave will be available for the America Online service is important for two reasons. The first is that America Online represents six million potential Shockwave viewers, which is a sizable audience for any technology. The second reason is that AOL is the first proprietary network to endorse Shockwave.

Although many people with America Online accounts also have other accounts with regular Internet service providers, AOL still constitutes a large portion of the consumer audience on the Internet. Because AOL provides subscribers with a suite of software, those developers creating Shockwave movies for AOL will be able to depend on every user having Shockwave.

Although the spectacular rise of the World Wide Web has meant a decline in the relative importance of the proprietary services such as AOL, CompuServe, and Prodigy, these services are still important because of the size of their user base and the size of their pocketbooks. AOL's adoption of Shockwave will very probably force a similar action by the other online services.

Look Ma, No Disk! Shockwave on the Network Computer

The concept of the *network computer*—a machine without a disk, designed to be connected to a network—has generated a large amount of controversy. To many, it is a return to the much-hated dumb terminals of the far-away mainframe days. To others, it is the magic key to finally getting computers into a vast number of homes. Whatever the case may be, Macromedia and Oracle—one of the largest proponents of the network computer (or NC) concept—have announced that Oracle's Reference Design for the NC will include Shockwave. This means that if the NC concept does take off, Shockwave developers will be well-positioned in this area to take advantage of the market that will result.

Overall, it appears that Macromedia is finally beginning to have some success at positioning Shockwave as a fundamental data type for computing in the second half of the '90s.

LiveConnect

Netscape has launched its own form of component architecture, called LiveConnect. Netscape's inline plug-in APIs provide a means of incorporating dynamically loadable modules into the client process itself. Together with Java and JavaScript facilities, plug-ins such as Shockwave enable high-performance applications on the Web to deliver rich content, such as sound, graphics, and video. Netscape LiveConnect enables you to integrate the functioning of Java, JavaScript, and plug-ins like Shockwave (see fig. 23.1)

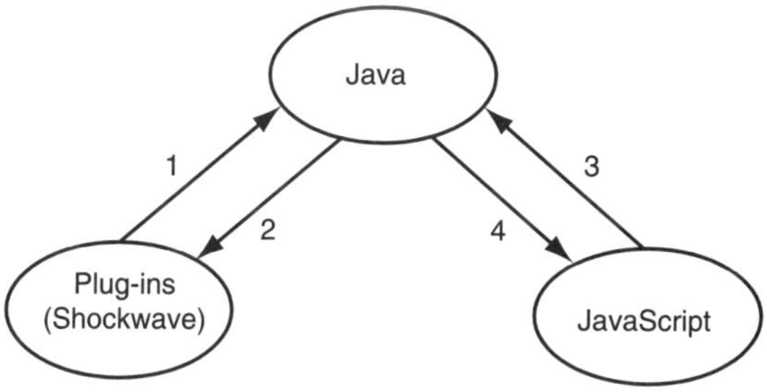

FIGURE 23.1

Netscape's LiveConnect lets plug-ins communicate with Java applets. Shockwave will likely implement hooks to LiveConnect in future releases.

Fundamentally, Netscape LiveConnect enables you to:

- Call Java methods from plug-ins
- Call native plug-in methods from Java
- Call Java methods from JavaScript
- Call JavaScript from Java methods

Although there is no direct connection from plug-ins to JavaScript, the combination of (1) and (4) allows plug-ins to call JavaScript code, and (2) and (3) allows JavaScript to manipulate plug-ins.

Should Macromedia release future versions of Shockwave with hooks to the Netscape LiveConnect API (and they would be crazy not to), you will be able to create Shockwave movies that can be controlled by Java and JavaScript, or use your Shockwave movie to control Java and JavaScript components.

Broadband Technology

The principle factors in the evolution of broadband digital communications are economic and not technological factors. The profit motive and the flow of capital are the primary determinants of broadband evolution. For example, comparing between T-l connections at 1.544 Mbps and ISDN at 64 kbps, there is virtually no technology difference in the cabling and central switching hardware, yet there is a large price difference for the connection.

The technology has existed for a long time to provide Internet access at ISDN and T-1 speeds very inexpensively, but the telco monopolies priced the high-speed data lines astronomically out of proportion to the cost of providing them. Thus, only large corporations with both the economic means and the compelling business need have had access to high-speed connections.

The only universally accessible network connection is via modems on voice-grade lines. Modems were developed as an end-run around the artificially inflated prices of fast digital lines. The modem's capability to deliver data over voice-grade lines at 28.8 kbps is a technological marvel, yet in principle, modems are a technologically unnecessary and almost comical way to move data. In this sense, the 28.8 kbps modem is a technologic absurdity of the free market.

Recall that in the '80s, the telcos actively sought to ban data transmission on their voice-grade lines, arguing that they were somehow being cheated by modem users who had evaded purchasing their high-speed data lines. Today, bandwidth is no longer being held hostage by the telcos—it is being held hostage by the telcos and the cable monopolies.

The so-called Information Superhighway—the establishment of a unified integrated services network offering high-speed voice, data, and video into every U.S. home and office—today looks more like an Information Super-Bar-Room-Brawl. The vision of a coherent full-service network with universal access that began with the High Performance Computing Act of 1991 has ended with the infamous Telecommunications Act of 1996.

The promise of the full-service network has deteriorated into a dogfight between incompatible technologies for less-standardized networks. The economic risk of bringing fiber to the curb gave the telcos cold feet, and they quietly sounded a retreat from the full-service network.

Since the telco and cable industry lobbies have convinced the government not to undertake a project to construct a public information infrastructure, the Telecommunications Act of 1996 was devised to unleash and manage the private competition slaughterhouse. The pathway toward the golden age of a universally accessible full-service digital network is now split into a tangle of private delivery networks.

Wireless cable (our favorite oxymoron) broadcast from local grids or satellites are being developed for one-way video services (such as DirecTV), with billions of dollars recently wagered in "public" FCC auctions of frequencies. Wireless cable is not ideal for broadband Internet access.

The telco monopolies are modifying copper-line networks (similar to T-1) into Asymmetric Digital Subscriber Line (ADSL), which can carry 1–6 Mbps downstream and 128 kbps–1.5 Mbps upstream. This will offer voice and data and enables the telcos to compete with the cable companies for delivering video.

The cable monopolies are creating hybrid fiber/coax networks for interactive television and Internet service. This is based on the cable modem technology. Test networks offering up to 10 Mbps speeds into the home are already in operation by @Home, Continental Cable, and others. Don't bet the farm just yet, but it appears that cable modems are setting the pace for widespread implementation of broadband Internet access.

Mature technologies such as ISDN are rapidly falling in price, anticipating the stiff competition from ADSL and cable modems. Broadband ISDN is also being implemented. The speeds on local area networks will see a marked increase with the infusion of cheap 100BaseT networks. Multimedia and digital video facilities already utilize reliable networks that carry multiple streams of uncompressed serial digital video (240 Mbps each). These high-performance video networks offer a glimpse into the capabilities of multimedia LANs of the future.

Backbone bandwidth has been steadily rising and will accelerate, facilitated by the implementation Asynchronous Transfer Mode (ATM) networks. The theoretical limits of switching speeds are astronomically fast, even those based on today's electronic devices. By the end of the century, 5 GB backbones should be common. Further into the future, all-optical technologies are likely to go into cables, routers, repeaters, and multiplexers that operate at terabit speeds.

Shockwave technology is eminently scaleable to whatever bandwidths can be imagined. No matter how much bandwidth there is, it still won't be enough. The Machiavellian and anarchic progression toward broadband means that the lowest common denominator of bandwidth will be fairly low for some time to come. Designing multiple bandwidth alternatives will be a solution in some cases until such time as some form of dynamic bandwidth allocation is devised for Shockwave. In any event, whether the fabric of the broadband network will be made of fiber or of cable, we are confident that Shockwave is a robust technology that will assume an important place in the networked multimedia of the next century.

Recent developments support this projection. For instance, Macromedia is working with @Home, creators of a 10 Mbps cable modem system being tested in Sunnyvale, California. Shockwave was used to demonstrate @Home's innovative multimedia user interface and links to numerous websites with live multimedia content. Macromedia and @Home also announced plans to work together on Shockwave for Director development and on new Java-based tools to support the authoring of rich multimedia content and applications for the World Wide Web.

More recently, Macromedia and Interaxx Television Network, a leader in interactive television technology and applications, became strategic partners. Interaxx will become a licensee of Macromedia's Director Portable

Player. Macromedia's portable playback technology enables Director applications, authored on a Macintosh or PC, to be played back on a variety of devices, including many using a standard television display.

Interaxx has selected Macromedia's Director as the main authoring tool to develop its interactive content, which will be delivered via participating cable TV and digital satellite systems to the Interaxx Television Network's Home Station running Director's playback engine. The Interaxx Home Station brings a breadth of multimedia content to the home, and combines multimedia PC architecture, analog/digital settop box capabilities, and advanced telephony services.

The Interaxx platform, which supports entertainment, shopping, video games, educational applications, travel, video-on-demand, telephony, and Internet access, is a glimpse at what the future of broadband environments will look like, and where multimedia content fits in.

Pitfalls and Challenges on the Super-Duper Info Highway

With Shockwave, Macromedia has provided Web developers with a tremendously powerful tool. It can make your message, whether it be artistic, political, or commercial, much more powerful. As a pioneer in the field of Internet multimedia, however, you have both the privilege and responsibility of using this power wisely. The Internet is potentially the most powerful and democratic method of communication to arise since Gutenberg came up with movable type. Unlike television or magazine publishing, there is little difference between the tools needed to make a Web page and the tools needed to view it. There is also effectively no limit to the different points of view that can be transmitted over the Web. With Shockwave, you have the power to increase the effectiveness of your message, while providing a more exciting experience for the visitors to your website. Alternatively, you also have the power to waste bandwidth at an unprecedented rate, by adding flash without substance.

Although the economic potential of the Internet is easy to see, its potential for enabling positive changes in our society is almost as tremendous. By providing citizens with the ability to speak directly to their representatives, almost instantaneously, it can mean the difference between a government that many citizens see as an enemy, and one that the vast majority sees as an advocate, or even friend. It can also mean the difference between a lesbian teenager in a small town finding like-minded young people to share her experiences with, and her contemplating suicide.

As someone who provides content for the Internet, you are undoubtedly aware of its tremendous potential. You should be aware, however, that this potential is at serious risk. There are three main factors that threaten any positive effect the Internet can have: deregulation, lack of privacy, and privatization.

Deregulation and Overregulation

Currently, almost all personal access to the Internet is through the phone system. The Telecommunications Act of 1996 (TCA) recently passed in Congress would allow cable companies, long-distance companies, and even utility companies (collectively referred to as "telecommunications companies") to compete for the right to provide higher-speed access to homes and businesses. This could mean cheaper, higher-speed access to the Internet for many people. However, it will almost certainly mean that large segments of the population will be left out of any new standards. The thing that made the telephone a nearly ubiquitous instrument of communication was a policy called *universal access,* which required telephone companies to provide lifeline, or very low-charge rates to low-income people. This is why the telephone is so powerful. Under new regulations, however, companies setting up new networks are not only without obligation to provide lifeline service, but are free to wire only areas that they deem desirable. This will mean many areas, particularly low-income and rural areas, will be without high-speed access to the Internet.

The Telecommunications Act has also made it harder for cities and counties to require telecommunications companies to provide access to public buildings and schools in exchange for the use of the public right-of-way. This means that many schools, libraries, and community centers—the primary points of access for those who cannot afford a computer in their home—will be stuck with outdated connections.

The most well-known problem with the Telecommunications Act is the section known as the Communications Decency Act. This section, which occasioned a burst of protest among many people who spend a lot of time online, makes it a crime to provide "indecent" information to minors over the Internet. This act is blatantly unconstitutional (in the United States, anyway) and has a potentially chilling effect on freedom of speech on the Internet. In fact, the Act specifically forbids the discussion of anything related to abortion. Simply by sending the previous sentence to our publisher over e-mail, we are technically in violation of the Hyde Amendment to the TCA (not that we did, of course).

Privacy: A Concept of the Past?

The question of privacy is one that has also received some notice. Many readers may remember the fracas over the Clipper chip. This was an attempt by the National Security Agency (NSA) of the United States to require any hardware performing encryption to use a special chip-based algorithm, to which the government would have a universal decryption key.

As this book goes to press, in Germany a bill is up in the parliament that would require all online and telecommunication service providers to make their users' data available to a new government watchdog office. This new office is to have complete access to all user data at will. Although the providers are to foot the bill for the government's access into their systems, they're to do it in such a way that not even they themselves are to be aware of what or when the government is taking advantage of that access.

A final word on privacy: You don't have it. There are very few legal protections for any information you may have stored physically outside your house. This includes any mail stored on a server, as well as a voice-mail box you may rent. This is clearly one area in which the law has not caught up to the technology, but be clear that your e-mail is by no means private.

Privatization: A Concept of the Future

Much of the physical infrastructure of the Internet was funded by tax money. In the United States, the backbone of the Internet is still the NSFnet, funded by the National Science Foundation to allow researchers to communicate, and the remnants of ARPAnet, built by the defense department. Recently, driven by pressure from the telecommunications industry, there has been a rush to privatize the network, selling it piecemeal to the largest bidders.

Judging from the experience of privatization in other industries, this will mean an abandonment of any goals of universal service, and a concentration on high-profit areas. This concentration, in tandem with the deregulation discussed earlier, will likely result in extremely selective provision of service, as well as higher rates for access to advanced services.

Resources

For more information on the issues we have raised in this chapter, we suggest you visit the following sites:

- **Institute for Global Communications**
  `http://www.igc.org`
- **Center for Democracy and Technology**
  `http://www.cdt.org`
- **EPIC**
  `http://www.epic.org`
- **Benton Foundation**
  `http://www.cdinet.com/Benton/`
- **Rewired**
  `http://www.rewired.com`
- **Voters Telecommunications Watch**
  `http://www.vtw.org`
- **Electronic Frontier Foundation**
  `http://www.eff.org`

Final Words

This volume should be your start on the road to providing powerful, Shockwave-based solutions on your website. We hope we have inspired you to expand the horizons of your work, as well as given you the tools and techniques to solve any problems you might come across.

The Web is your playground, and we look forward to seeing what you do with Shockwave.

APPENDIX

A

HTML Quick Reference

This appendix contains a reference to the <embed> command as it is used for each Shockwave application. All three applications share three parameters: source filename, height, and width. Any Shockwave file can be embedded with just these three parameters.

The syntax for the source filename parameter is src="filename.ext".

The height and width parameters are expressed in pixels. The syntax for these variables is height=yDimension and width=xDimension. The following are valid <embed> tags for FreeHand, Authorware, and Director:

```
<embed src="map.fhc" width=300 height=300>

<embed src="trainer.aam" width=640 height=480>

<embed src="Movies/flashy.dcr" width=480 height=360>
```

Note

In the following examples, square brackets, [ ], indicate optional parameters. Several values separated by a vertical bar are a group from which one value should be chosen. Italics indicate a placeholder describing the value.

Shockwave for FreeHand

The full possibilities of the <embed> tag with Shockwave for FreeHand are

```
<embed src="filename.fhc" height=yDimention width=xDimension
➥[toolbar=top|bottom]>
```

Height, Width, and Shockwave for FreeHand

Because Shockwave for FreeHand files are zoomable, it is possible to display the files in a zoomed state by default. Simply embed the file with height and width at a percentage of the original file size. For example, if a file's size is 200×150, setting the width and height parameters to 400 and 300 respectively will cause the file to display originally at 200 percent size:

```
<embed src="filename.fhc" height=300 width=400>
```

The Toolbar Parameter

This optional parameter enables Shockwave for FreeHand files to have a toolbar associated with the image, which gives the user the capability to zoom without remembering key/mouse-click combinations. The toolbar can appear at the top or the bottom of an image, but the image must be at least

85 pixels wide in order to display the graphic toolbar. The toolbar expands to fit the width of your image. The graphic toolbar is 20 pixels in height. You must add 20 pixels to the height portion of your HTML code in order to display the toolbar. If this parameter is omitted, the toolbar does not display. The possible values for this parameter follow:

Value	*Result*
top	Toolbar displays at the top of the image
bottom	Toolbar displays at the bottom of the image
(omitted)	Toolbar does not display at all

For example, to display the toolbar at the top of a 200×200 image, the `<embed>` tag would read:

```
<embed src="map.fhc" width=200 height=220 toolbar=top>
```

Shockwave for Authorware

Shockwave for Authorware adds two parameters to the standard ones detailed in the preceding section: palette and window. The full possibilities of the `<embed>` tag for Shockwave for Authorware follow:

```
<embed src="filename.aam" width=xDimension height=yDimension
➥[palette=foreground¦background] [window=inPlace¦onTop¦onTopMinimize]>
```

The Palette Parameter

This optional parameter provides the Shockwave for Authorware developer with the capability to have Shockwave for Authorware take over the palette or enable the browser to maintain control. Allowing Shockwave for Authorware to take over the foreground means that delicate images display exactly as desired, but may cause ugly results with the Netscape interface or other images on the page by displaying them in a different palette than expected (which can cause pink buttons with bright green shadows, for example). The possible values for this parameter follow:

Value	*Result*
foreground	Shockwave for Authorware has full control over the palette. Default for window=onTop and onTopMinimize.
background	Browser maintains control over the palette. Default for window=inPlace.

The following is an example of embedding an Authorware file with full control over the palette:

```
<embed src="trainme.aam" height=342 width=512 palette=foreground>
```

The Window Parameter

This optional parameter enables the developer to control the appearance of the Shockwave for Authorware window in relation to the browser window. The possible values for this parameter follow:

Value	*Result*
inPlace	Displays the piece embedded within the HTML page in the browser window. You can use inPlace only in Windows.
onTop	Displays the piece in a separate window on top of the browser window. This makes your piece look more like a separate application. This is the default.
onTopMinimize	Displays the piece in a separate window and minimizes the browser. This setting makes your piece look the most like a separate, stand-alone application.

If you are using the `inPlace` setting, there are two additional factors to bear in mind:

- Don't try to use a title bar on your presentation window. (The Title Bar setting is in the File Setup dialog box.) Embedding `inPlace` doesn't allow the display of a title bar. Instead, the height of your presentation window will be reduced by the height of the title bar. This clearly makes for a less-than-ideal user experience.

- Avoid using the `ResizeWindow` and `MoveWindow` functions, which, according to Macromedia, "can produce unpredictable results with inPlace." Be aware that "can produce unpredictable results" is software-manual-speak for "will probably crash and will probably do so in a spectacularly ugly manner and at the least convenient time."

The following is an example of embedding a file so that it appears as part of the page on Windows and in a separate window on the Macintosh:

```
<embedsrc="trainme.aam" height=342 width=512 window=inPlace>
```

Shockwave for Director

Shockwave for Director adds not only two new parameters to the three basic ones, but also enables the user to specify arbitrary parameters. The additional fixed parameters are `palette` and `bgcolor`. The full possibilities of the `<embed>` tag for Shockwave for Director are:

```
<embed src="filename.dcr" width=xDimension height=yDimension
➥[palette=foreground¦background] [bgcolor=backgroundColor]
➥[name1=value1...nameN=valueN]>
```

The Palette Parameter

This optional parameter provides the Shockwave for Director developer with the capability to have Shockwave for Director take over the palette or allow the browser to maintain control. Allowing Shockwave for Director to take over the foreground means that delicate images will display exactly as desired, but may cause ugly results with the Netscape interface or other images on the page by displaying them in a different color than expected. The possible values for this parameter follow:

Value	*Result*
foreground	Shockwave for Director has full control over palette.
background	Browser maintains control over the palette; this is the default

The following is an example of embedding a Director file with full control over the palette:

```
<embed src="movie.dcr" height=342 width=512 palette=foreground>
```

The Bgcolor Parameter

The optional `bgcolor` parameter enables you to set the background color of the plug-in area while it is loading. The normal value range for this parameter is in the form #RRGGBB, where RR, GG, and BB are two-digit hexadecimal numbers representing red, green, and blue values respectively. For example, BGCOLOR=#FFFFFF is white, BGCOLOR=#000000 is black, and BGCOLOR=#FF0000 is red. See the Netscape documentation on the BGCOLOR body tag for more information on these values. The following is a file embedded with a 50 percent gray background:

```
<embed src="Movies/movie.dcr" width=400 height=300 bgcolor=#777777>
```

User Parameters

Shockwave for Director 5 has added the capability to specify arbitrary parameters. For more information on this capability, see Chapter 12, "Talking with the Outside World: Parameters and JavaScript." The following demonstrates a file embedded with a parameter named userName and a value of "Rosa Luxembourg":

```
<embed src="Movies/movie.dcr" width=300 height=300 userName="Rosa
➥Luxembourg">
```

APPENDIX

B

Lingo for Shockwave Quick Reference

This appendix is a quick reference for the network-specific additions to Shockwave for Director.

External Parameter Access

When a Shockwave title is invoked from within HTML, it is specified with either an `<embed>` or `<object>` tag, enabling optional parameters for the Shockwave title. The following functions enable access to those parameters.

External parameters have the general form of "name=value," where the "=value" portion is optional. For the purposes of the following examples, assume that the Shockwave movie was embedded with the following tag:

```
<embed src="example.dcr" height=240 width=320 userName="walter">
```

The ExternalParamCount

The function `the externalParamCount` returns the number of external parameters in the `<embed>` tag, including every parameter. The following handler would go to frame 4:

```
go frame (the externalParamCount)
```

ExternalParamName(n)

If *n* is an integer, the function `externalParamName(n)` returns the *n*th parameter name from the external parameter list. If *n* is a string, this function returns *n* if any of the external parameter names matches *n* (case-insensitive). If there is no such parameter name, `externalParamName` returns void. The following function would put "userName" into the field named "result":

```
put externalParamName(4) into field "result"
```

ExternalParamValue(n)

If *n* is an integer, this function `externalParamValue(n)` returns the *n*th parameter value from the external parameter list. If *n* is a string, this function returns the value associated with the first name that matches *n* (case-insensitive). If there is no such parameter value, `externalParamValue` returns void. The following handler would put "walter" into field "result":

```
put externalParamValue("userName") into field "result"
```

Lingo Network Extensions

Several new commands are available for accessing the network from Director Lingo scripts. This section lists each of these new commands and functions and explains their usage.

Because the network is essentially an asynchronous place—that is, it takes time to get things from the Net, and in the meantime, Director can continue to interact with the user—most of the network commands involve starting an operation, and then checking to see whether it has completed, and then getting the results. This is different from most Lingo commands, which immediately return the result.

Four commands are available to start asynchronous operations:

- `GotoNetMovie uri`
- `GotoNetPage uri, target`
- `GetLatestNetID()`
- `GetNetText uri`

GotoNetMovie uri

This command retrieves and goes to a new Director movie from the network. The new movie occupies the same display area as the calling movie. The `uri` parameter is a universal resource identifier that specifies the HTTP item containing the movie. At present, only HTTP URLs are supported as valid `uri` parameters. The following code plays the movie CLOSER.DCR, located in the same directory as the current movie:

```
GoToNetMovie "closer.dcr
```

GotoNetPage uri, target

This command opens an arbitrary URI, whether or not it is a Director movie. This command opens a new page within the net browser. The target parameter is optional. If present, it specifies the target frame or window by name, or is one of the special values allowed by browsers for frame targeting (see the Netscape release notes on targeting windows for details).

The following example opens the HTML document CONTACT.HTM in the current window:

```
GoToNetPage("contact.htm")
```

`GoToNetPage` causes the Netscape browser to go to another Web page. An optional second argument enables the Director movie to use "FRAME" and "TARGET" commands on frame-capable Internet clients such as Netscape 2.0. Lingo does not distinguish between "FRAME" and "TARGET" commands. It first looks for a frame with the name specified in the second parameter. If it doesn't find one, it looks for a window with that name. If it doesn't find one of those either, it opens a new window with that name.

This example displays the document FRED.HTML in a frame called "top" in the current browser window:

```
GoToNetPage("fred.html", "top")
```

To be valid, the window or frame name specified by the second parameter must begin with an alpha-numeric character. All other window names are ignored. Frame and window names are case-sensitive. The preceding command would not work if your frame was named "Top."

This optional second argument also can use magic TARGET names to perform special window functions. These begin with the underscore character. Any targeted window name beginning with an underscore that is not one of these reserved names is ignored.

The `_blank` argument, for example, displays the new page in a blank browser window and keeps the original window displaying the Director movie open, enabling users to return to the movie after viewing the new page.

This example displays the Macromedia home page in a blank window while keeping the window that displays the Director movie open:

```
GoToNetPage("http://www.macromedia.com/", "_blank")
```

By using this TARGET argument, you allow the Director movie to remain in the original browser window even after it has called a new HTML document. If you omit the second parameter, the Director movie quits as soon as the new page is displayed. If you later return to the URL where the Director movie is embedded, the movie starts over from the beginning.

These reserved magic target names follow:

```
TARGET="_blank" -- opens a new browser window
TARGET="_self" -- the target will load in the same window it was
➥called from
TARGET="_parent" -- the target will load in the FRAMESET parent of the
➥document
TARGET="_top" -- the target will load in the full body of the window -
➥eliminating frames in the window
```

For more information on the TARGET and FRAME tags, see Netscape's documentation at `http://www.netscape.com/assist/net_sites/frames.html`.

GetLatestNetID()

This function returns a unique identifier for the last asynchronous operation that was started.

Each of the functions (`NetDone`, `NetError`, `NetTextResult`, `NetMIME`, `NetLastModDate`, and `NetAbort`) take as an optional parameter the unique identifier returned by `GetLatestNetID`.

The following code starts a `GetNetText` operation and then puts the ID for that operation into the global variable `gID`:

```
global gID
GetNetText "Data/settings.txt"
put GetLatestNetID() into gID
```

GetNetText uri

This command starts the retrieval of an HTTP item, to be read by Lingo as text. The `uri` parameter is a universal resource identifier specifying the HTTP item to be retrieved. At present, only HTTP URLs are supported as valid `uri` parameters.

The following example starts the loading of the text file MSG.TXT:

```
GetNetText "msg.txt"
```

The `GetNetText` command also can be used to pass values to CGI scripts. This enables Shockwave applications to use CGI scripts currently used by HTML forms with little or no modification to the existing CGI script.

To call a cgi script called "process.cgi" at the URL "http://www.company.com/cgi/," use the following lingo:

```
GetNetText "http://www.company.com/cgi/process.cgi"
```

Variables from the Shockwave application can be passed as values to the CGI script in this manner as well. Suppose we have a variable called `IDNumber` in the Shockwave application. We want to submit this variable to the CGI script called "process.cgi". Furthermore, we want to submit this variable as the value of the CGI variable "thingie." If we were to use traditional HTML forms instead of Shockwave, this would be submitted to the CGI script by using the `<SELECT NAME="thingie">` tag and the actual value of `IDNumber` with some type of VALUE command. For example, assuming the value of `IDNumber` is 8, the line we want to pass to the CGI script is `http://www.company.com/cgi/process.cgi?thingie=8`.

With Shockwave for Director, however, we would use the following two lines of Lingo code:

```
put "http://www.company.com/cgi/process.cgi?thingie" & "=" &
➥string(IDNumber) into tempText
GetNetText tempText
```

Two functions enable a Lingo script to determine the state of the asynchronous operation:

- `NetDone()`
- `NetError()`

NetDone()

This function returns true when the asynchronous network operation is finished. Until that point, it returns false. The following code goes to the frame named `parseText` if the latest network operation is done:

```
if NetDone() then go frame "parseText"
```

NetError()

This function returns the empty string until the asynchronous network operation is finished. It returns OK if the operation completed successfully, or a string describing the error if it failed to complete successfully. The following code repeats until either an OK or error comes from the latest network operation, then goes to a frame called "error" or "success," depending on the result of the network operation:

```
on exitFrame
   case netError() of
      "" : go the frame
      "OK" : go frame "success"
      otherwise go frame "error"
   end case
end exitFrame
```

Once an asynchronous operation has finished, three functions are available to retrieve the results:

- `NetTextResult()`
- `NetMIME()`
- `NetLastModDate()`

NetTextResult()

This function returns the text result of the operation. For a `GetNetText` operation, this is the text of the HTTP item. The following puts the result of the latest `GetNetText` operation into field `"result"`:

```
put NetTextResult() into field "result"
```

NetMIME()

This function returns the MIME type of the HTTP item.

```
put netMime() into field "Mime Type"
```

NetLastModDate()

This function returns the last modified date string from the HTTP header for the item. The following puts the date into a field called `"date"`:

```
put netLastModified into field "date"
```

NetAbort

This command aborts a network operation without waiting for a result. The following handler cancels the latest network operation and alerts the user to that fact:

```
on cancelOp
   NetAbort
   Alert("Network Operation cancelled")
end cancelOp
```

Note, however, that the `NetTextResult`, `NetMIME`, `NetLastModDate`, and `NetAbort` functions can only be called from the time `NetDone` or `NetError` report that the operation is complete until the next operation begins. Once the next operation is started, we discard the results of the previous operation in order to preserve memory space.

It is possible to have more than one operation active at a time. When two operations are started, the Lingo script needs a way to identify them. After an operation is started, and until the next operation is begun, the `GetLatestNetID()` function can be called to retrieve a unique identifier for that operation.

NetStatus msg

The `netStatus msg` command sets the status area of the browser window to `msg`. To badger the user when she doesn't do anything for a period of time you can use the following:

```
on timeOut
   netStatus "press a button to go to a page"
end timeOut
```

Two functions enable Shockwave titles to have persistent state:

- `setPref prefName,prefValue`
- `getPref(prefName)`

SetPref prefName,prefValue

The `setPref prefName,prefValue` command remembers the `prefName/prefValue` pair in persistent storage (in other words, on disk). The `prefName` must be a string representing a valid filename, minus an extension, for the system the title will run on. To be safe, this requires limiting the name to eight alphanumeric characters. The following function stores the `userName` as `"Elizabeth Gurley Flynn"`:

```
on storeName
   setPref "userName", "Elizabeth Gurley Flynn"
end storeName
```

GetPref(prefName)

The `getPref(prefName)` function returns the `prefValue` that was associated with `prefName` in a previous `setPref` call. If there is no such value, `getPref` returns void. The `prefName` must be a valid filename, minus extension, for the system the title will run on. To be safe, this requires limiting the name to eight alphanumeric characters. The following handler puts the user name stored in the last example into field `"User Name"`:

```
on getName
   put getPref("userName") into field "User Name"
end getName
```

INDEX

A

B

E

F

M

N

Q

R

T

U

V

W

X

Z

Fold Here

NO POSTAGE
NECESSARY
IF MAILED
IN THE
UNITED STATES

BUSINESS REPLY MAIL

FIRST-CLASS MAIL PERMIT NO. 9918 INDIANAPOLIS IN

POSTAGE WILL BE PAID BY THE ADDRESSEE

NEW RIDERS PUBLISHING
201 W 103RD ST
INDIANAPOLIS IN 46290-9058

REGISTRATION CARD

Shockwave Power Solutions

Name ______________________________ Title ____________

Company ______________________________ Type of business ____________

Address ______________________________

City/State/ZIP ______________________________

E-mail/Internet ______________________________ Phone ____________

Would you like to be placed on our preferred mailing list? ❑ yes ❑ no

Have you used/purchased New Riders books before? ❑ yes ❑ no

Where did you purchase this book? Check one.

❑ Bookstore chain ❑ Independent bookstore ❑ Computer store
❑ Wholesale club ❑ College bookstore ❑ Other ____________

What influenced your decision to purchase this title? ______________________________

____

Which of the following operating systems do you use? Check all that apply.

❑ Windows 3.x ❑ Windows 95 ❑ Windows NT
❑ Macintosh ❑ SGI ❑ Other ____________

What are the names of the software programs you use currently? ____________

____

____

Which of the following best describes your work environment? Check one.

❑ Self-employed ❑ Small business ❑ Large business

Which of the following do you create/develop for? Check all that apply.

❑ Games ❑ Motion pictures ❑ Web sites
❑ Print ❑ Other

What online services and Web sites do you visit on a regular basis? ____________

____

____

What trade shows do you attend? ______________________________

What computer book titles do you consider your most valuable sources of information?

____

What applications/technologies would you like to see us publish in the future?

____

A Note from the Publisher and Authors

Macromedia's Shockwave for Director is bringing animation and true interactivity to the World Wide Web. We're pleased to bring you our second Shockwave book, *Shockwave Power Solutions,* a guide to realizing your Web goals using Shockwave for Director, FreeHand, and Authorware.

The *Shockwave Power Solutions* CD-ROM includes demonstration versions of Macromedia's Director, FreeHand, and Authorware products. Please note that these demonstration versions are *save-disabled,* meaning that you cannot save or distribute any content you create with these demonstration products.

Shockwave Power Solutions includes tutorials and examples of content created with Authorware, FreeHand, and versions 4 and 5 of Director. The *Shockwave Power Solutions* CD-ROM contains the various Shockwave plug-ins, which enable you to view shocked pages, and the book's examples, with your Web browser.

As this book went to press, Shockwave for Director 5 was still in beta testing; therefore, the version of Shockwave for Director included in the *Shockwave Power Solutions* CD-ROM is compatible only with shocked files created in Director 4. To properly view the Shockwave for Director 5 examples in this book, you will need the Shockwave for Director 5 plug-in from the Macromedia website.

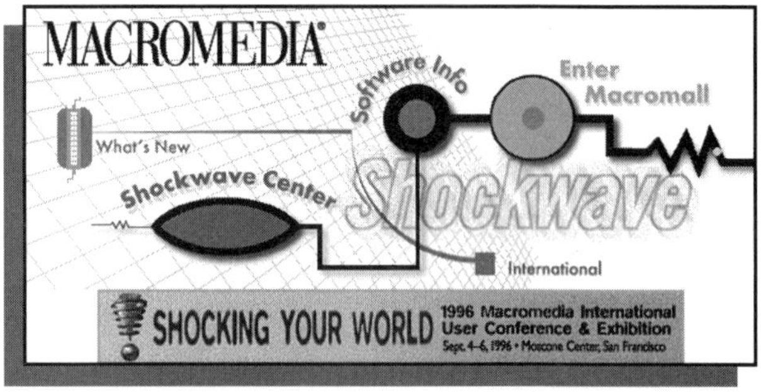

The second generation of Shockwave is upon us, and that is why we are bringing you *Shockwave Power Solutions*. To stay on top of this groundbreaking Web technology, please check out the following two websites on a regular basis:

- **Macromedia: http://www.macromedia.com.** By visiting the Macromedia site often, you'll be kept up-to-date with the most current Shockwave news, plug-ins, and developments.
- **New Riders Publishing: http://www.mcp.com/newriders.** This is where you'll find any updated information on *Shockwave Power Solutions,* as well as updates to and information about our first Shockwave book, *Macromedia Shockwave for Director User's Guide*.

New Riders

Thank you for selecting *Shockwave Power Solutions*! Look for these other Macromedia titles from New Riders:

- *Inside Macromedia Director 5 with Lingo for Macintosh (available now)*
- *Inside Macromedia Director 5 with Lingo for Windows (available now)*
- *Lingo! (available now)*
- *Macromedia Authorware 3 Internal System Functions (available now)*
- *Inside Extreme 3D (available Fall '96)*
- *Extending Director (available Winter '96)*

New Riders